T0369951

DUMBARTON OAKS
MEDIEVAL LIBRARY

Daniel Donoghue, General Editor

THE LIFE AND DEATH OF THEODORE OF STOUDIOS

DOML 70

The Life and Death of Theodore of Stoudios

Edited and Translated by

ROBERT H. JORDAN

and

ROSEMARY MORRIS

DUMBARTON OAKS
MEDIEVAL LIBRARY

HARVARD UNIVERSITY PRESS

CAMBRIDGE, MASSACHUSETTS

LONDON, ENGLAND

2021

Printed in the United States of America

First Printing

Library of Congress Cataloging-in-Publication Data

Names: Jordan, R. H., editor, translator. | Morris, Rosemary (Historian), editor, translator.

Title: The life and death of Theodore of Stoudios / edited and translated by Robert H. Jordan and Rosemary Morris.

Other titles: Dumbarton Oaks medieval library ; 70.

Description: Cambridge, Massachusetts : Harvard University Press, 2021. | Series: Dumbarton Oaks medieval library ; DOML 70 | Includes bibliographical references and index. | Greek with English translation following; introduction and notes in English.

Identifiers: LCCN 2021007533 | ISBN 9780674261198 (cloth)

Subjects: LCSH: Theodore, Studites, Saint, 759–826—Early works to 1800. | Christian saints—Byzantine Empire—Biography—Early works to 1800.

Classification: LCC BR1720.T38 L54 2021 | DDC 270.3092 [B]—dc23

LC record available at https://lccn.loc.gov/2021007533

Contents

Introduction

The three texts contained in this volume, translated into English for the first time, commemorate the life of one of the most celebrated of Byzantine churchmen. Theodore of Stoudios (759–826) played a leading role in both monastic and political life in Byzantium. He is celebrated as a saint in the Orthodox Church, particularly for his stalwart defense of icon veneration during the period of Second Iconoclasm. He was also responsible for lasting reforms in monastic organization, widely imitated by later founders throughout the empire. The survival of much of his vast literary output—homilies, letters, verses, and hagiography—testifies to his lasting influence.[1]

Theodore lived in turbulent times. Byzantium faced both external threats—from Arab, Slav, and Bulgar attacks over its eastern and northern borders—and consistent internal political instability. During his lifetime, four rulers were deposed, and one was killed in battle. Faced with these misfortunes and attempting to understand the reasons for the divine wrath that had caused them, Byzantines questioned one of their hitherto most profoundly held beliefs: that religious images could legitimately act as a means of intercession with God, could ensure divine protection, and thus should be venerated. Those who supported this view—the iconodules (lovers of images)—clashed with the so-called

iconoclasts (breakers of images), who, in opposition, particularly cited the prohibition of idolatry in the Ten Commandments. The two periods when Byzantine emperors supported iconoclastic views and thus attempted to impose them on both church and laity are usually referred to by historians as First (ca. 730–787) and Second Iconoclasm (815–843).[2]

The Monastery of Stoudios

The monastery known as "of Stoudios" or "of the Stoudites" and dedicated to Saint John the Baptist was founded in approximately 454 in the Psamathia quarter of Constantinople by the consul Stoudios. Turned into a mosque (İmrahor İlyas Bey Camii) by the Ottomans, its church still survives.[3] There is little information about the monastery between the mid-fifth and the late eighth centuries, but it increased its influence under the leadership of Theodore of Stoudios and, in the eleventh century, provided a patriarch of Constantinople (Alexios Stoudites, 1025–1043).[4] Its abbots were also used as imperial emissaries: Euthymios of Stoudios played an important role in establishing regulations for Mount Athos in 972.[5] After 1204 the monastery entered a period of decline but was restored in 1293 and was one of the most important houses of the later Byzantine period.[6]

The "Life of Theodore of Stoudios" by Michael the Monk

The *Life of Theodore of Stoudios* by Michael the Monk, known as the *Vita B* (*BHG* 1754) from the order in which it occurs in the *Patrologia Graeca,* is the earliest of three long hagiogra-

phies devoted to the saint that were composed in the century after his death.[7] The other two, known as the *Vita A* (*BHG* 1755) and the *Vita C* (*BHG* 1755d), are dependent on this first *Life,* though their precise relationship is still debated.[8] The *Vita B* was written in the second half of the ninth century, certainly after 868, as it implies that the abbot Nicholas of Stoudios was dead; he died in February of that year.[9] Its author, Michael, was a Stoudite monk; he refers to Theodore as "the chief shepherd of our flock" (*Life* 1.1). His position in the monastery is unclear, as is his later career, though it has been suggested that he later became abbot of the Constantinopolitan monastery of Dalmatos and a patriarchal official.[10] He has been identified as the author of a number of *enkomia* on saints; he may also have written other hagiography.[11]

Michael was not the first to write a *Life* of Theodore; an "extensive record in narrative form and in the style of a panegyric" (*Life* 1.2) already existed, but its elevated style meant that the Stoudite monks had found it difficult to follow, and he was instructed to write a more accessible version. This earlier work is also mentioned in the *Life of Saint Nicholas of Stoudios* and may have been written by the future patriarch Methodios I (843–847), known to have composed other hagiographies.[12] Michael also had access to other materials on Theodore's life. Various commemorations had been composed by Stoudites in the years following his death, including the necrological note found on fol. 344v of the *Uspenskij Gospel Book* (835), shorter biographical treatments, and celebratory verses.[13] Five books of Theodore's *Letters* had already been collected by Michael's own time (*Life* 16.4); he makes frequent mention of them and, in at least one case, quotes directly from one.[14] He cites the beginning of the last

of Theodore's homilies (*Life* 31.5) and was undoubtedly familiar with many others.[15] His exposition of icon theory (*Life* 21.2–3) indicates knowledge of Theodore's own treatises on the subject.[16] Michael specifically mentions two of Theodore's own biographical works: the *Funerary Catechism for his Mother* (*Life* 3.2) and the "splendid encomium" (*Life* 4.3) written to commemorate his uncle, Plato of Sakkoudion.[17] He clearly used our second text, the *Encyclical Letter of Naukratios,* a section of which (*Letter* 14–23) is followed virtually word for word in the *Life* (35.1–5). He may also have known of our third text, the *Translation and Burial of the Remains of Theodore of Stoudios and Joseph of Thessalonike.*[18] His work influenced later hagiographies both of Theodore and, probably, of Nicholas of Stoudios, but did not prove as popular as the *Vita A,* written in a more elevated style.[19] It has also been suggested that a miniature in the Theodore Psalter of 1066 (London, British Library Add. 19352, fol. 27v) was inspired by the account in the *Vita B* of the discussions between Leo V and the clergy of December 814 (*Life* 22).[20]

Michael's work is an interesting combination of historical narrative and hagiography. His writing has a number of noticeable stylistic characteristics: the use of long words and strong verbs (often compounds), pairs of nouns and adjectives, verbs with adverbs, and accompanying pairs of participles. This often leads to long but well-crafted sentences. He quotes a wide range of scripture; other quotations generally came from the fathers of the Church. But he knew of at least two works by Josephus and, in one instance, quotes Aristotle; he also includes a Homeric tag.[21] He had an interest in the etymology of names and a certain antiquarian bent: the classical "Macedonian" names for the months are used

on the rare occasions when he gives a precise date (*Life* 23.4 and 26.3), and he alludes to the contests of the Olympic Games (*Life* 11.4 and 27.4).[22]

After a short introduction explaining how his work came to be written, Michael describes Theodore's birth (759) into a family of high administrative officials in Constantinople, his education, and his entry into the monastic life at the monastery of Sakkoudion, where his uncle Plato was abbot and which he subsequently headed (781).[23] Following a clear break in the narrative, Theodore's part in the "Moechian Controversy" is related.[24] The patriarch Tarasios (784–806) refused to marry the emperor Constantine VI and his mistress, Theodote, a kinswoman of Theodore, but the priest Joseph, steward of Hagia Sophia and abbot of the monastery of Kathara, agreed to do so, a move that provoked protests from Theodore and his uncle, eventually leading to their banishment by the emperor.[25] Following a passage of moral teaching, in which Theodore's stand is compared to that of John the Baptist against Herod, Michael then describes the downfall of Constantine VI. The emperor was overthrown and blinded (797), probably at the instigation of his mother, the empress Irene (a matter that Michael omits to mention), who then ruled alone. Theodore, Plato, and their monks were set free and returned to Sakkoudion; Joseph of Kathara was deposed from the priesthood by Tarasios.

A new phase in Theodore's life began in 798 when he and his uncle were invited by the patriarch and the empress to take over the monastery of Stoudios. Michael's description of life there at this period (798–806) portrays a monastic "golden age," brought abruptly to a halt by controversies surrounding the election of the patriarch Nikephoros (806)

and the decision of the emperor Nikephoros I (802–811) to order him to reinstate Joseph of Kathara. Michael mentions nothing of the first issue—still less the fact that Theodore was probably himself a candidate for the patriarchal position—preferring to portray mutual admiration between Theodore and both patriarchs, Tarasios and Nikephoros.[26] He focuses on the second matter and, in a lengthy apologia, both defends the decisions originally taken by Tarasios and supports Theodore's later vehement opposition to the patriarch Nikephoros's action (*Life* 17.2–18.1).[27]

Theodore's continued disobedience to imperial orders led to a further period of exile on the Princes' Islands off Constantinople, which was only ended by Nikephoros I's death in battle in 811. On the accession of Michael I Rangabe (811–813), Theodore and his monks were allowed to return to Stoudios. Michael then describes their educational activities and alludes to other monasteries founded by Stoudites (*Life* 20). This peaceful period was interrupted by the revolt and subsequent accession of the emperor Leo V (813–820) and the beginning of a further period of iconoclasm. The three chapters that follow (*Life* 21–23) form the most dramatic part of Michael's narrative. Drawing on Theodore's own writings, he expounds icon theory in a simplified manner for his monastic audience and then turns to an account of the confrontations between the iconoclast and iconodule parties that took place in 814 and early 815. In a scene that may have been based on an already-existing narrative, Theodore is made the main spokesman for the iconodule churchmen.[28]

After the deposition of the patriarch Nikephoros in March 815, Theodore continued his opposition to imperial

religious policies, moves that led to a third period of exile (815–820). The physical hardships endured by Theodore and his disciple, Nicholas, are emphasized in the next group of chapters (*Life* 24–28). Michael identifies their chief persecutors, names those Stoudite monks who stood firm against them, and praises the laymen who disobeyed their orders to punish the two monks.[29]

The murder of Leo V and the accession of Michael II in 820 led to Theodore's release. Michael recounts miracles that occurred as he made his way toward Constantinople, adding to them the later recollections of the monks Theodore and Sophronios. This collection of edifying tales ends with another obvious "joining passage."[30] After a short period in Constantinople, Theodore and his monks left the city again in around 821 and eventually settled on the promontory of Saint Tryphon near Cape Akritas on the west coast of Asia Minor. Michael clearly had very little information about the following five years, and the final section of the work, describing Theodore's last illness and death, is greatly dependent on the *Encyclical Letter of Naukratios.* In contrast to the author of the *Translation and Burial,* Michael maintains that Theodore died at Saint Tryphon, whence his body was subsequently moved to the island of Prinkipo (*Translation and Burial* 6.2).[31] After eighteen years there, it was ceremonially reburied at Stoudios in 844 alongside that of his brother Joseph and his uncle Plato.

The "Encyclical Letter of Naukratios"

The *Encyclical Letter of Naukratios* (*BHG* 1756), the earliest of our texts, was written a short time after the death of Theo-

dore on November 11, 826. It was intended for the internal use of the scattered Stoudite communities. Naukratios does not say *where* he was writing, something that has contributed to the difficulty of establishing the location of Theodore's death. He was now clearly the *de facto* leader of the Stoudite monks, but he was not consecrated by the patriarch, the iconoclast Anthony Kassimatas (821–827), or by the exiled ex-patriarch Nikephoros.[32]

Naukratios (b. 760–765) was one of Theodore's disciples at the monastery of Sakkoudion in 780/81 (*Life* 8.3). He accompanied his master into exile in Thessalonike in 797 and entered the monastery of Stoudios with him in 798, where he became steward. When the Stoudites were scattered in 815, Naukratios, together with Theodore's brother Joseph, was first held under house arrest at Sakkoudion and then banished elsewhere.[33] After Theodore's release in 820, Naukratios rejoined him and remained with him until Theodore's death in 826. If the writer of the *Translation and Burial* is to be believed, Naukratios then lived with other Stoudites on the island of Prinkipo, until they were allowed to return to Constantinople in 843. At that point, he and Athanasios, the abbot of Sakkoudion, conceived a plan to translate the remains of Theodore and his brother back to Stoudios for reburial, a ceremony that took place on January 26, 844 (*Translation and Burial* 7–9).[34] Little is known of Naukratios's period as abbot of Stoudios, but he received the young Saint Evaristos into the monastery during this time.[35] At some point after 846 both Naukratios and Athanasios were censured by the patriarch Methodios, deprived of their positions, and confined to their respective monasteries.[36] Follow-

ing the patriarch's death in 847, they regained their posts. Naukratios died on April 18, 848, and was buried in the main church at Stoudios.[37]

Naukratios's *Encyclical Letter,* a highly rhetorical document, generally follows the form of the *paramythetikos logos,* or "consolatory letter," as laid down by Menander Rhetor (late third century CE).[38] It has a bipartite structure: the lamentation for the deceased is followed by passages of consolation for those who remain. After a short introduction in which Naukratios confirms the rumors of Theodore's death (*Letter* 1), he extols Theodore's virtues and his outstanding qualities as a teacher, a monastic leader, and a stalwart defender of orthodoxy (*Letter* 3–10). He then offers consolation to the Stoudites: they should see Theodore as a member of the company of the righteous, extending from the biblical patriarchs to the saints and martyrs of more recent times (*Letter* 11–12). The lengthy description of Theodore's illness and death that follows (*Letter* 13–25) contains the full text of Theodore's last *katechesis* (15–19), his final words, and precise information about the day and time of his death.[39] The early part of his work is greatly dependent on Basil of Caesarea's *Letters* 28 and 29, and the account of Theodore's burial (*Letter* 24–25) on the latter's own letter describing that of Metropolitan Michael of Synnada,[40] but Naukratios adds the detail that Theodore "was consigned and buried in his own cell" (*Letter* 25), though where this was is not clear. Naukratios's *Letter* was the subject of a widely circulated epigram; no other writings by him have survived.[41] The *Letter* was clearly a highly popular text; over thirty manuscripts predating the fifteenth century are known.[42]

The "Translation and Burial of the Remains of Theodore of Stoudios and Joseph of Thessalonike"

The *Translation and Burial* (*BHG* 1756t) was the second of our three texts to be written. Its author was a Stoudite monk and an eyewitness of the events he describes. It was written after April 848, as the abbot Naukratios is described as θεῖος (holy), an indication that he was dead (*Translation and Burial* 8.1), and was probably first delivered on an anniversary of the event it describes to an audience in Stoudios that included both monks and laypeople.[43] It alternates a simple narrative style with highly rhetorical passages of description, speech, and invocation. After a brief introduction, the author gives a short account of Theodore's life, which led Charles van de Vorst to suggest that this work might have been one of the preexisting accounts of Theodore's life used by Michael the Monk (*Translation and Burial* 2–6).[44] In contrast to Michael, however, the author clearly states that Theodore died on the island of Prinkipo.[45] Michael indeed knew of the ceremony marking Theodore and Joseph's reburial at Stoudios, but gives little detail of it, and what there is may have come from Stoudite oral tradition rather than from this work.

Following the biography of Theodore, the author narrates the circumstances leading up to the reburial of his remains and those of his brother Joseph, though he does not give the precise date of this event (*Translation and Burial* 8.1–10.1).[46] The next section describes in highly rhetorical terms the ceremonies that accompanied the transportation of Theodore's coffin from Prinkipo to Stoudios and thence to its burial place in the main church. This took place in the

presence of the patriarch Methodios, and the writer emphasizes the reverence he showed to Theodore's remains (*Translation and Burial* 10.2–12.1).[47]

The author breaks off his description of Theodore's burial to relate the story of the rediscovery of his brother's remains. His account of Joseph's life is brief, and he knew neither the date of his death nor precisely where he had died in exile.[48] After March 843, Joseph's remains were brought to Constantinople and were buried in Stoudios at the same time as were his brother's (*Translation and Burial* 13).[49]

Following this excursus, the author returns to his description of the joint burial ceremony, during which the remains of the brothers were placed in the tomb that already held those of their uncle Plato. By the writer's own time, this had become a shrine and had been decorated with images of the three saints.[50] The work ends with an extended prayer for Theodore's intercession with God (*Translation and Burial* 15) containing some phrases borrowed from the *Orations* of Gregory of Nazianzos. It does not seem to have been a popular text, probably because of its specific relevance to Stoudios.[51] Only three manuscripts are known, but the account possibly influenced the portrayal of the translation of Theodore's remains from Prinkipo in the *Menologion of Basil*.[52]

Though we have worked in close collaboration, the establishment and translation of the Greek texts is primarily the work of Robert Jordan, and the Introduction and Notes to the Translations that of Rosemary Morris. Alexander Alexakis most generously provided considerable assistance with

the collation of manuscripts, particularly those of the *Letter of Naukratios,* and with the Notes on and to the Texts. The chapter divisions in the *Life of Theodore* by Michael the Monk and in the *Encyclical Letter of Naukratios* are the work of Jordan; those in the *Translation and Burial* follow the sections of the edition published by Charles van de Vorst.[53] Citations from the Old Testament are given from the Rahlfs edition of the Septuagint; for the New Testament, citations are from the Nestle-Aland Greek text. In both cases, the English translations come from the *Revised Standard Version.*[54] References to the Psalms show the Septuagint numbering first, with the usual Western numbering afterward in parentheses. The spelling of Greek names and places follows that of the *Oxford Dictionary of Byzantium.*

We would like to acknowledge with thanks the help and guidance received from members of the Dumbarton Oaks Medieval Library editorial board in reviewing the volume and making numerous excellent suggestions for improvements to the translation and notes. Alice-Mary Talbot and Claudia Rapp reviewed early drafts; Richard Greenfield and Alexander Alexakis provided great support and assistance in the later stages and saw the final versions through to the press. We must particularly thank Olivier Delouis, who generously shared his great expertise in all things Stoudite, read our work, and made many valuable suggestions for its improvement. John Kee, Summer Intern at Dumbarton Oaks (2020), drafted the Index; Louis-Patrick St-Pierre, a research fellow at Queen's University, helped with the proofreading. We are extremely grateful to the many friends and

colleagues who have assisted our work by providing advance copies of articles and rare publications of texts, by assisting with translation, and by patiently answering endless queries. Thanks are due to Jeffrey Anderson, Roman Cholij, Fr. Maximos Constas, Barbara Crostini, Ken Dark, Christian Gastgeber, Michel Kaplan, Dirk Krausmüller, Nicholas de Lange, Paul Magdalino, Athanasios Markopoulos, and Ken Parry. Ilaria Ciolli of the Vatican Library and Julia A. Schneider of the Medieval Institute of the University of Notre Dame provided assistance with the acquisition of manuscript microfilms. As ever, we are deeply appreciative of the kindness and professionalism of the staff of the John Rylands University Library, Manchester, and the J. B. Morrell Library, University of York (with special thanks to the interlibrary loans department). Last, but certainly not least, our profound thanks go to Margaret Jordan and Alan Forrest for their encouragement and support during our journey through the life and death of Theodore of Stoudios.

Notes

1 For Theodore's life and times, see *ODB,* vol. 3, pp. 2044–45; Thomas Pratsch, *Theodoros Studites (759–826): Zwischen Dogma und Pragma* (Frankfurt-am-Main, 1998). See Georgios Fatouros, *Theodori Studitae Epistulae* (Berlin, 1992), vol. 1, pp. 21*–38*, for a list of Theodore's works.

2 For the general history of the period, see Warren T. Treadgold, *The Byzantine Revival: 780–842* (Stanford, CA, 1988), and Leslie Brubaker and John Haldon, *Byzantium in the Iconoclast Era c. 680–850: A History* (Cambridge, 2011). For a shorter view of the theological and artistic debates, see Leslie Brubaker, *Inventing Byzantine Iconoclasm* (London, 2012).

3 Olivier Delouis, *Saint-Jean-Baptiste de Stoudios à Constantinople: La contribution d'un monastère à l'histoire de l'Empire byzantin (v. 454–1204),* 2 vols. (unpublished doctoral thesis, Université Paris 1 Panthéon-Sorbonne, 2005),

chapter 1 for the foundation of the monastery. For its architecture, Thomas F. Mathews, *The Early Churches of Constantinople: Architecture and Liturgy* (University Park, PA, 1971), 19–27. For archaeological material, see Delouis, *Saint-Jean-Baptiste,* 27–34, and for recent bibliography, Ken Dark and Feredun Özgümüş, *Constantinople: Archaeology of a Byzantine Megapolis* (Oxford, 2013), 33–34.

4 Delouis, *Saint-Jean-Baptiste,* 67–76.

5 "*Typikon* of Emperor John Tzimiskes," trans. George Dennis, *BMFD,* vol. 1, no. 12.

6 *ODB,* vol. 3, pp. 1960–61.

7 A Greek edition, French translation, and Commentary on the *Vita B* were being undertaken by Tatiana Matantseva in Paris in the 1990s as part of her doctoral studies but have remained unpublished.

8 See Olivier Delouis, "Écriture et réécriture au monastère de Stoudios à Constantinople (IX–X s.): Quelques remarques," in *Remanier, métaphraser,* ed. Smilja Marjanović-Dušanović and Bernard Flusin (Belgrade, 2011), 101–10, at 107, and Dirk Krausmüller, "The *Vitae B, C* and *A* of Theodore the Stoudite: Their Interrelation, Dates, Authors and Significance for the History of the Stoudios Monastery in the Tenth Century," *AB* 131 (2013): 280–98.

9 Charles van de Vorst, "La translation de S. Théodore Studite et de S. Joseph de Thessalonique," *AB* 32 (1913): 27–49, at 29.

10 Dirk Krausmüller, "Reconstructing the Hagiographical Oeuvre of Michael, Monk of Stoudios, Archimandrite of Dalmatos and Patriarchal Synkellos (9th–10th Centuries)," *Parekbolai: An Electronic Journal for Byzantine Literature* 10 (2020): 1–42, ejournals.lib.auth.gr/parekbolai.

11 Three *enkomia* contained in Biblioteca Apostolica Vaticana Ms. Vaticanus graecus 1669, which also includes the *Vita B* (see Note on the Texts, *Life of Theodore*), are also by Michael: Peter Hatlie, "The Encomium of Ss. Isakos [*sic*] and Dalmatos by Michael the Monk (BHG[3] 956d): Text, Translation and Notes," in *Eukosmia; Studi miscellanei per il 75º di Vincenzo Poggi SJ,* ed. Vincenzo Ruggieri and Luca Pieralli (Catanzaro, 2003): 177–311; Dirk Krausmüller, "The *Encomium* of the Apostle Philip by Michael the Monk (BHG 1530a): Edition and English Translation," *Jahrbuch der Österreichischen Byzantinistik* 69 (2019): 233–55; Tatiana Matantseva, "Eloge des archanges Michel et Gabriel par Michel le Moine (BHG 1249a)," *Jahrbuch*

der Österreichischen Byzantinistik 46 (1996): 97–155. See also Dirk Krausmüller, "The *Encomium* of the Five Martyrs Eustratius, Auxentius, Eugenius, Mardarius and Orestes (*BHG* 646b) by Michael the Monk: Edition and Translation," *AB* 138, no. 2 (forthcoming). Passages in the *Life of Saint Nicholas of Stoudios* show similarities with the *Vita B,* but opinion is divided on whether this work can also be attributed to Michael or simply made use of his text; see Van de Vorst, "La translation," 32; Delouis, *Saint-Jean-Baptiste,* 329; and Krausmüller, "Reconstructing the Hagiographical Oeuvre."

12 Dirk Krausmüller, "Patriarch Methodios, the Author of the Lost First Life of Theodore of Stoudios," *Symbolae Osloenses: Norwegian Journal of Greek and Latin Studies* 81, no. 1 (2006): 144–50, http://dx.doi.org/10.1080/00397670701495161.

13 Olivier Delouis, "La vie métrique de Théodore Stoudite par Stéphane Mélès (*BHG* 1755m)," *AB* 131, no. 1 (2014): 21–54, at 23–25 for the main *dossier* of material on Theodore; and Olivier Delouis, "Paratextes et épitomés: Deux notices hagiographiques sur Théodore Stoudite (*BHG* 1758)," in *Mélanges Bernard Flusin,* ed. André Binggeli and Vincent Déroche, Travaux et mémoires du Centre de recherche d'histoire et civilisation de Byzance 23, no. 1 (Paris, 2019), 213–26, at 218 for shorter works about him.

14 *Ep.* 71 is quoted in the *Life* 23.5, and mention is made in the *Life* 26.2 of a "catechetical letter," probably *Ep.* 381.

15 *Lesser Katecheseis* 31. The names of the Stoudite monks praised in the *Life* 8.3 and 28.1 were probably culled from the letters and homilies.

16 *Theodori praepositi Studitarum Antirrhetici adversus Iconomachos,* PG 99:327–436. English translations: Catherine P. Roth, *St. Theodore the Studite: On the Holy Icons* (Crestwood, NY, 1981), and Thomas Cattoi, *Theodore the Studite: Writings on Iconoclasm* (New York, 2015), 45–119.

17 Stephanos Efthymiadis and J. Michael Featherstone, "Establishing a Holy Lineage: Theodore the Stoudite's Funerary Catechism for his Mother (*BHG* 2422)," in *Theatron. Rhetorische Kultur in Spätantike und Mittelalter/Rhetorical Culture in Late Antiquity and the Middle Ages,* ed. Michael Grünbart (Berlin, 2007), 13–51. *Laudatio sancti Platonis hegumeni* (or *Oratio funebris in Platonem*), PG 99:803–50.

18 Van de Vorst, "La translation," 35.

19 *Pinakes* cites eleven known manuscripts of the *Vita B* dated to before the eighteenth century; three of the *Vita C;* but twenty-four of the *Vita A*

(https://pinakes.irht.cnrs.fr/). For the use of the *Vita B* in a *Life of Nicholas of Stoudios,* see Dimitry Y. Afinogenov, "Rewriting a Saint's *Life* in the Monastery of Stoudiou: Two *Lives* of St. Nicholas the Studite," in *The Heroes of the Orthodox Church: The New Saints, 8th–16th c.,* ed. Eleonora Kountoura-Galake (Athens, 2004), 313–22, at 317–18.

20 For the Theodore Psalter, see the British Library's online facsimile (http://www.bl.uk/manuscripts/FullDisplay.aspx?ref=Add_MS_19352), and Tatiana Matantseva, "La conférence sur la vénération des images en décembre 814," *REB* 56 (1998): 249–60, at 358.

21 Josephus, *Against Apion,* ed. and trans. Henry St. J. Thackeray, in *The Life; Against Apion,* Loeb Classical Library 186 (Cambridge, MA, 1926), 162–412 (*Life* 15.2, 22.1, 28.1); Josephus, *The Life of Josephus,* in Thackeray, *The Life; Against Apion,* 1–159 (*Life* 22.1); Aristotle (*Life* 22.5); Homer (*Life* 26.5).

22 The name of the patriarch Tarasios is derived, for example, from the Greek verb ταράσσω, "I confound, agitate, stir up" (*Life* 4.4).

23 See Pratsch, *Theodoros Studites,* 45–67, for a prosopographical study of Theodore's family. For the possible location of Sakkoudion, see Marie-France Auzépy, Olivier Delouis, Jean-Pierre Grélois, and Michel Kaplan, "À propos des monastères de Médikion et de Sakkoudion," *REB* 63 (2005): 183–94, and Klaus Belke, *Bithynien und Hellespont* (Vienna, 2020), vol. 2, 979–80.

24 "But now, as time is calling, we must move on . . ." (*Life* 11.4). The Greek word μοιχεία means "adultery." For a summary of the controversy, see *ODB,* vol. 2, pp. 1388–89.

25 Jean-Claude Cheynet and Bernard Flusin, "Du monastère Ta Kathara à Thessalonique: Théodore Stoudite sur la route de l'exil," *REB* 48 (1990): 193–211.

26 Pratsch, *Theodoros Studites,* 135–46.

27 Writings by Theodore against Tarasios (for being too lenient toward iconoclasts at the Second Council of Nicaea and maintaining communion with Constantine VI after his "adulterous" marriage) and against Nikephoros (for allowing the restoration of priestly orders to Joseph of Kathara) were cited by patriarch Methodios I (843–847) when criticizing the Stoudites of his own day. See Jean Darrouzès, "Le Patriarche Méthode contre les iconoclastes et les Stoudites," *REB* 45 (1987): 15–57, and Delouis, *Saint-Jean-Baptiste,* 286–304.

28 See Pratsch, *Theodoros Studites,* 215–31, for a detailed survey of events in 814 and 815. For the roles played by other iconodule churchmen (none named by Michael) and a reconstruction of the confrontation with the emperor in December 814, see Michel Kaplan, "L'évêque à l'époque du second iconoclasme," in *Monastères, images, pouvoirs et société à Byzance,* ed. Michel Kaplan (Paris, 2006), 183–205, and Matantseva, "La conférence sur la vénération des images," at 255–56.

29 The list of steadfast monks in *Life* 28.1 gives each of them a complimentary epithet. The Stoudite martyr, Thaddaios, is mentioned in *Life* 27.6.

30 *Life* 32.3: "So, I will leave my discourse on this topic and make a start on the rest of his life."

31 Pratsch, *Theodoros Studites,* 290, believes Theodore died at Saint Tryphon; Fatouros, *Epistulae,* vol. 1, p. 19*, considers that he died on Prinkipo.

32 See Delouis, *Saint-Jean-Baptiste,* 293, for the difficulties that later arose concerning the appointment of Naukratios as abbot of Stoudios and Athanasios as abbot of Sakkoudion. Michael relates that Naukratios was "the steward *(oikonomos)* . . . who also became [Theodore's] successor" (*Life* 35.2).

33 *Ep.* 130.

34 Naukratios and Athanasios may have made inquiries about the location of Joseph's remains before they returned to Stoudios; see notes to *Translation and Burial* 13.2.

35 Charles van de Vorst, "La vie de s. Évariste, higoumène à Constantinople," *AB* 41 (1923): 288–325.

36 See note 27, above. The *Life of Saint Ioannikios* by Peter, written in approximately 847, censures the habit of "the followers of Athanasios and Naukratios" of stirring up trouble against the patriarch Methodios; see Denis F. Sullivan, trans., *Life of St. Ioannikios,* in *Byzantine Defenders of Images: Eight Saints' Lives in English Translation,* ed. Alice-Mary Talbot (Washington, DC, 1998), 323–24, 338–39.

37 The date is given in the *Life of Saint Nicholas of Stoudios,* PG 105:904C.

38 Menander Rhetor, "The Consolation Speech," *Treatise* 2.8, in Menander Rhetor and [Dionysius of Halicarnassus], *Ars Rhetorica,* ed. and trans. William H. Race, Loeb Classical Library 539 (Cambridge, MA, 2019), 262–67. For Menander Rhetor, see *ODB,* vol. 2, pp. 1338–39, and Martha Vinson, "Rhetoric and Writing Strategies in the Ninth Century," in *Rhetoric in Byzantium,* ed. Elizabeth Jeffreys (Aldershot, 2003), 9–22.

39 Theodore of Stoudios, *Lesser Katecheseis* 31; see notes to *Life* 16.1.
40 *Ep.* 533 to the metropolitan Peter of Nicaea, written after May 826.
41 *Database of Byzantine Book Epigrams* (https://www.dbbe.ugent.be/persons/29547).
42 *Pinakes* (https://pinakes.irht.cnrs.fr/).
43 Van de Vorst, "La translation," 27.
44 Van de Vorst, "La translation," 27, and see note 12, above.
45 See note 31, above.
46 The writer states that "eighteen years had now passed" since Theodore's death (9.1). The precise date—January 26, [844]—is given in the *Life of Saint Nicholas of Stoudios,* PG 105:904B.
47 There is no hint of the subsequent breach between Methodios and the Stoudites; see notes 27 and 36, above.
48 Joseph died on July 15, 832; see notes to *Translation and Burial* 13.1.
49 Van de Vorst, "La translation," 47, for the dating.
50 Doula Mouriki, "The Portraits of Theodore Studites in Byzantine Art," *Jahrbuch der Österreichischen Byzantinistik* 20 (1971): 249–80, discusses the form and location of these portraits.
51 Considerable passages from it were, however, later borrowed by Theoktistos the Stoudite for his *Life of the Patriarch Athanasios I of Constantinople* (*BHG* 194).
52 *Pinakes* (https://pinakes.irht.cnrs.fr/). For the *Menologion of Basil,* see notes to *Translation and Burial*, 11.1, and Mouriki, "Portraits of Theodore Studites," 251.
53 See Van de Vorst, "La translation."
54 Alfred Rahlfs, ed., *Septuaginta,* revised by Robert Hanhart, 2 vols. (Stuttgart, 2006); Barbara Aland, Kurt Aland, et al., eds., *Novum Testamentum Graece: Nestle-Aland,* 28th ed., 4th corrected revised printing (Stuttgart, 2015).

LIFE OF THEODORE OF STOUDIOS

Βίος καὶ πολιτεία τοῦ ὁσίου πατρὸς ἡμῶν καὶ ὁμολογητοῦ Θεοδώρου ἡγουμένου μονῆς τῶν Στουδίου συγγραφεὶς παρὰ Μιχαὴλ Μοναχοῦ. Εὐλόγησον πάτερ.

I

Πολλοὶ μὲν τῶν ἁγίων κατὰ διαφόρους χώρας τε καὶ πατριὰς ἐν τοῖς ἀνόπιν διαλάμψαντες χρόνοις, δίκην ἡλίου ταῖς τῶν οἰκείων ἀρετῶν ἀκτῖσι τοὺς παρατυγχάνοντας κατεφώτισαν, καὶ πρὸς ζῆλον ἐνθέου πολιτείας τοὺς ἐραστὰς τῶν καλῶν, ἢ καὶ τοὺς ἄλλως ἐξ ἀπροσεξίας ἔχοντας, συνήλασάν τε καὶ πρὸς τὸ κρεῖττον ἠρέθισαν. Οὐδὲν δὲ ἧττον καὶ ὁ τοῦ καθ' ἡμᾶς συλλόγου πεφηνὼς ποιμνιάρχης καὶ τῆς Χριστοῦ ὁμολογίας πυρσολαμπὴς στῦλος Θεόδωρος, ἐν τοῖς ἡμετέροις ἀνατεταλκὼς οἷά τις πολύφωτος ἀστὴρ τόποις καὶ χρόνοις, τὴν οἰκουμένην πᾶσαν μικροῦ δεῖν ταῖς ἀσκητικαῖς λάμψεσι καὶ τοῖς τῆς ἀθλητικῆς ὁμολογίας περιέβαλεν ἀγωνίσμασι. Καὶ τοσοῦτός γε ὤφθη τῶν ἐν ἀμφοτέροις διαπρεψάντων καρτερίᾳ τε βίου καὶ ἀρετῆς ἀνδρείᾳ ἐκθυμότατος ζηλωτής, καὶ εἰς ἑαυτὸν τὰ τούτων συλλελεχὼς ἀριστεύματα, ὡς μέχρις ἑῴας καὶ νότου, ἑσπέρας τε καὶ τῶν ἀρκτικῶν διαδραμεῖν τοὺς τῆς

The life and conduct of our saintly father and confessor Theodore, abbot of the monastery of Stoudios, composed by Michael the Monk. Bless us, father.

I

Many of the holy ones, who in earlier times shone in different lands and families, enlightened like the sun those whom they encountered with the rays of their own virtues, drawing those who loved things that are good to an emulation of the godly way of life and spurring on to a better course those who were indifferent as a result of carelessness. No less too did Theodore, who came to be the chief shepherd of our flock and a blazing pillar of confession in Christ, rising like some splendid star in our place and time, suffuse almost all the world with the brilliance of his ascetic feats and the brave deeds of his confessional trials. As a very ardent emulator of those who had been conspicuous both for the steadfastness of their lives and the bravery of their virtue, he was seen to have gathered in himself that which caused them to excel, with the result that reports of his teaching spread as far as the regions of the east and south, and those of the west and north. So too, offshoots from the

διδασκαλίας αὐτοῦ φθόγγους μερῶν· οὐ μὴν ἀλλὰ καὶ τῆς ὑπὸ Θεοῦ κατευλογηθείσης αὐτοῦ πνευματικῆς τῶν μαθητῶν φυτουργίας περὶ αὐτοὺς ἐκταθῆναι τὰ κλήματα καὶ παραδείσους ψυχῶν τῷ ὄντι ἀμφιλαφεῖς καὶ ἀρετῆς ἐντεῦθεν συγκροτηθῆναι παιδευτήρια, καὶ οὐκ ἔστι τὸ παράπαν χῶρος, οὗ τὸ ὄνομα τῆς πολιτείας αὐτοῦ καὶ τὸ ἐπώνυμον οὐκ ἀφίκετο.

2 Ἀλλ' ὅπως μὲν ὁ ἀοίδιμος ἐκεῖνος καθηγητὴς καὶ πατὴρ τῆς καθ' ἡμᾶς ἐβίω ζωῆς, κατὰ πόδας τῆς αὐτοῦ κοιμήσεως ἔνιοι τῶν αὐτοῦ φοιτητῶν ᾠδικῶς ὑπηνίξαντο, κεφαλαιώσαντες τὰ πολυμερῆ τῆς κατὰ πλάτος ὑψηλοτάτης αὐτοῦ πολιτείας ἀνδραγαθήματα ἐν ὀλίγαις ἐπέων λέξεσιν· μεθ' οὓς καὶ ἕτεροι τῶν τῆς Ἐκκλησίας ἱερομυστῶν ἐν συγγραφῆς εἴδει καὶ ἐγκωμίων σχηματισμῷ γλαφυρῶς ἄγαν κατεπεκτάδην συνέταξαν ὑπόμνημα, εἰς γῆρας θησαυρίσαντες λήθης φάρμακον.

3 Καὶ ἦν μὲν ἀκόλουθον τοῖς φιλοπόνοις καὶ μὴ λίαν ἀναπεπτωκόσιν ἐξ ἀμαθίας τὸν νοῦν τοῖς ἤδη πονηθεῖσι κατεντυγχάνειν, κἀκεῖθεν ἐκδιδάσκεσθαι τὴν ἅπασαν τοῦ πανιέρου πατρὸς ὑπερανεστηκυῖαν τῶν πολλῶν βιοτήν, καὶ τὸ ὠφέλιμον δρέπεσθαι, εἴπερ ἐθέλοιεν, θαυμάζειν τε τῆς σοφίας αὐτοῦ τὸ βάθος καὶ τὸν τρόπον τῆς κοινοβιακῆς ἀναστροφῆς, τάς τε ἀκριβεῖς αὐτοῦ παραδόσεις καὶ θεοτερπεῖς νομοθεσίας, ἃς ἐκεῖνος τοῖς αὐτοῦ νομοθετήσας καὶ παραδεδωκὼς μαθηταῖς, "ἄλλος τις Βασίλειος" ἐν τοῖς κατ' αὐτὸν ἐφημίζετο χρόνοις.

4 Ἀλλ' ἐπεὶ τὸ κοινὸν τῆς ἀδελφότητος, καὶ ἡ τῶν πολλῶν διάνοια μικρὰ βλέπουσα ὡς τὰ πολλὰ τὸ πεζὸν καὶ

spiritual plantation of his disciples that had been blessed by God spread out around them, and really luxuriant gardens of souls were established and from them schools of virtue; and there is nowhere at all which the fame of his conduct and his name did not reach.

Immediately after his death, some of his disciples made 2
reference in verse to how that famous teacher and father of our life used to live, summarizing in a few poetic phrases the numerous courageous deeds of his far-reaching and most sublime way of life. After them others of the holy initiates of the Church also compiled very elegantly an extensive record in narrative form and in the style of a panegyric, treasuring up for their old age a remedy for forgetfulness.

Subsequently, those who were industrious and whose 3
minds had not flagged too much through ignorance were able to consult what had already been established and from that could learn all about the all-holy father's mode of life, which surpassed that of most men, culling what was beneficial, if they wished to, and admiring the depth of his wisdom and the manner of his cenobitic life, as well as his strict traditions and precepts that brought delight to God; those which he decreed and handed on to his disciples, gaining the name "second Basil" among his contemporaries.

But since the community of the brethren and most 4
people's understanding (which expects brevity) is known to

ἁπλοϊκώτερον τῆς φράσεως προτιμᾶν ἐπίσταται (ὡς ἀνύστακτον συντηροῦν τὸν ἐπόπτην τῶν λεγομένων νοῦν, καὶ ὄνησιν ἐμποιοῦν ταῖς σφῶν αὐτῶν ὑπὲρ τὸ σκληρὸν καὶ βαθύγλωσσον τῶν νοημάτων ψυχαῖς), φέρε, ταῖς ὑμετέραις πειθαρχήσαντες ἐντολαῖς, πατέρων αἰδεσιμώτατοι, τοὺς περὶ τοῦ θείου τούτου προπάτορος ἡμῶν καὶ πανσόφου διδασκάλου τῆς οἰκουμένης λόγους καὶ ἡμεῖς οἱ ταπεινοὶ καὶ οὐδενὸς λόγου ἄξιοι, ὡς οἷόν τε, καταθώμεθα, πολὺ μὲν κατόπιν τοῦ πρὸς ἀξίαν ἰόντας, ὡς ἐνὸν δὲ τῇ ἀσθενείᾳ ἡμῶν πρὸς τὸ εὔληπτόν τε καὶ καταφανὲς μεταποιουμένους.

2

Ἡ τὸν μέγαν τοῦτον καὶ ἀκαταγώνιστον τῆς ὀρθοδόξου πίστεως ἀριστέα καὶ τοῦ μοναδικοῦ τάγματος διαβόητον κυβερνήτην ἐνεγκαμένη τε καὶ ἐκθρέψασα Θεόδωρον, ἡ τῶν πανταχοῦ γῆς πόλεων προκαθημένη πέφυκε πόλις, καθ᾽ ἣν ἐκράτει τῆς ἀρχῆς τηνικάδε ὁ ἐξ ἀσεβοῦς ἀσεβέστερος ἐκραγεὶς γόνος, Κωνσταντῖνος ὁ Κοπρώνυμος, καὶ τῆς Χριστομανικῆς αἱρέσεως δευτερωτὴς ἀναφανεὶς γενικώτατος, ἐκθλίβων τὸν νέον Χριστοῦ Ἰσραήλ, καθάπερ ποτὲ ὁ Αἰγύπτιος νοῦς Φαραώ, τῷ πηλῷ καὶ τῇ πλινθείᾳ τῆς εἰκονομαχικῆς πυργοποιίας διὰ τῶν πικρῶν τῆς τοιαύτης οἰκοδομίας ἐργοδιωκτῶν, καθ᾽ ὅτι ἔβλεπεν

prefer prose and a simpler mode of expression for the most part (as it keeps the mind vigilant in contemplation of what is being said and creates enjoyment in their souls more than does the difficult and verbose expression of ideas), come now, obeying your commands, most reverend fathers, let me too, being humble and of no account, set down to the best of my ability a narrative about this godly forefather of ours and this all-wise teacher of the world, a narrative that falls far short of his due but, as far as my weakness permits, strives after ease of understanding and clarity.

2

The city which produced and reared Theodore, this great and invincible champion of the orthodox faith and famous guide of the monastic order, is the one that presides over cities everywhere on earth. At that time Constantine Kopronymos, the even more impious offspring that burst forth from an impious father, held power there, and had proved to be a most prominent exponent of the heresy raging against Christ. He was oppressing the new Israel of Christ, as once the Egyptian mind of Pharaoh did with clay and brickmaking, building the tower of his war against icons with the assistance of the harsh taskmasters of this construction,

αὐτὸν πρὸς τὴν γῆν ἐπειγόμενον τῆς Εὐαγγελικῆς πολιτείας, καὶ ἀνυπερθέτως τοῖς Δεσποτικοῖς ἐξακολουθοῦντα θεσμοθετήμασιν.

2 Γονεῖς δὲ αὐτῷ, εὐσεβεῖς τε καὶ εὐπατρίδαι, καὶ τῆς ἀποκληρωθείσης αὐτοῖς πρὸς τῶν φυσάντων προσηγορίας διὰ πραγμάτων τὰς σημασίας ἐπιδήλους ἔχοντες, ὧν ὁ μὲν πατήρ, φῶς ἀληθῶς—κατὰ τὴν λάλον τῶν Ἀθηναίων γλῶτταν—παρὰ Θεοῦ γεννηθείς, φωτεινὸς τοῖς τρόποις καὶ τῇ κλήσει γεγένηται, καλοκαγαθίας μεταποιούμενος καὶ σωφροσύνης αἴγλῃ ἀξίως κατακοσμούμενος, καθὼς καὶ ὁ μετὰ ταῦτά γε πρὸς τὸν Θεὸν καὶ τὰ θεῖα τῆς θεόφρονος αὐτοῦ ψυχῆς ἔδειξεν ἔρως. Τὴν γὰρ οὐ πολλοστὴν ἀπὸ βασιλέως διέπων ἀρχήν, καθ' ὅτι ταμίας ἐχρημάτιζε τῶν βασιλικῶν φόρων, ταύτην τε καὶ τὴν ἄλλην ἅπασαν τοῦ βίου παρ' οὐδὲν λογισάμενος τέρψιν, πανοικεὶ τῷ Θεῷ καὶ παμβασιλεῖ προστρέχει καὶ τὸν ἄζυγα τῆς ἐν βασιλείοις αὐλαῖς <διατριβῆς> ἀνταλλάττεται βίον. Μᾶλλον δὲ τὰ καπνοῦ τρόπον καὶ ὀνείρου διαλυόμενα παριδών, τῶν ἑστώτων καὶ εἰς ἀεὶ τὸ μόνιμον ἐχόντων ἀγαθῶν τὴν μετουσίαν πορίζεται καὶ γίνεται τοῦ καταλόγου τῶν τῷ Θεῷ καθωσιωμένων, ὁ καὶ πρὸ πέντε ἐτῶν τὴν τῆς συνεύνου γνῶσιν δι' εὐλαβείας περιουσίαν ἀνδρείως ἠθετηκώς.

3 Καὶ αὐτὴ δὲ ἡ μήτηρ, ὡς περιφανὴς καὶ ἐπίδοξος, πυκνότητι φρενῶν πυκαζομένη καὶ καλῶς εἰδυῖα τῶν τε ἰδίων τέκνων καὶ τοῦ οἴκου προΐστασθαι, ἅτε "ὑπὸ Θεοῦ κτισθεῖσα," καὶ τὴν ὁμοίαν προσηγορίαν τοῖς ἔργοις σφραγισθεῖσα· τὸ γὰρ κοινὸν τῆς θεοκτισίας ὄνομα ἰδιάζον αὐτῇ παρυπάρξαν διὰ τῆς κατ' ἀρετὴν εὐζωίας, Θεοκτί-

because he saw the new Israel moving toward the promised land of the Gospel's way of life and following without hesitation the Master's ordinances.

Theodore's parents were pious and came from a noble family, showing in their actions clear indications of the names assigned to them by their parents. His father, truly created—in the eloquent language of the Athenians—by God as a light, became one who was luminous in his character and name, striving after goodness and worthily adorned by the radiance of his abstinence, as later, at least, the love of his godly-minded soul for God and divine things also showed. For although the position he held was not far from that of the emperor in that he was administrator of the imperial accounts, he counted this and every other pleasure in life as nothing and with his whole household sought out God the King of all instead, exchanging the imperial court for this unfettered life. Rather, disregarding things which dissipate like smoke and dreams, he secured his participation in the good things which are stable and eternal and came to be enrolled among those who have dedicated themselves to God, since five years earlier, in an abundance of piety, he had also nobly renounced carnal knowledge of his wife. 2

Theodore's mother was herself of very distinguished and famous stock and, since she was endowed with a shrewd mind and good sense, she took charge of her own children and household, seeing that she had been "created by God" and was confirmed in the same name by her deeds. Since the common name of God's creation suited her because of her good and virtuous way of life, she both was and had been 3

στη καὶ ἦν καὶ ὠνόμαστο, τὸν ἐξ ἀμφοῖν ἔπαινον διὰ τῆς σεμνῆς κερδαίνουσα πολιτείας. Ἀλλ' ὁποῖον δὴ τὸν τοῦ βίου δρόμον ἡ ἀεισέβαστος αὕτη πεποίηται, αὐτὸς ἐκεῖνος ὁ θεοδώρητος αὐτῆς καρπὸς τοῖς ὑπ' αὐτὸν ἀδελφοῖς ἐν κατηχήσεως εἴδει τηνικαῦτα ὑπηγόρευσεν εὐηγορίας γλῶτταν θεόθεν πεπλουτηκώς· ὅθεν τοὺς βουλομένους τὰ κατ' αὐτὴν εἰδέναι ἐκεῖσε παραπέμποντες, ἡμεῖς τῶν περὶ τοῦ πατρὸς ἡμῶν λόγων ὀφειλομένως ἐχόμεθα.

3

Τὴν μὲν οὖν πρώτην τῆς ἡλικίας ἑπταετηρίδα ἁρμοζόντως τῆς φύσεως διηνυκώς, ταῖς εἰσαγωγικαῖς καὶ στοιχειώδεσι τῶν μαθημάτων ἐνασχολεῖσθαι προάγεται τέχναις· *αἱ γὰρ ἐκ παίδων μαθήσεις συναύξουσαι τῇ ψυχῇ, ἑνοῦνται αὐτῇ* καὶ παράμονοι τῷ κεκτημένῳ γίνονται. Ἐπεὶ δὲ προβὰς καθ' ἡλικίαν καὶ γραμματικῆς ἔμπειρος ἐγεγόνει τέχνης, εἶτα καὶ διαλεκτικῆς, ἣν δὴ φιλοσοφίαν καλεῖν οἱ ταῦτα δεινοὶ γινώσκουσιν· πρὸς δὲ τοῖς εἰρημένοις καὶ τῆς ἐν ῥήτορσι φράσεως τὸ κάλλος, ὡς οἷός τε ἦν, ἀπηνθίσατο φύσεως τάχει, καὶ γνώμης φιλοπονίᾳ τοῖς πᾶσι περίπυστος ὢν ἐγνωρίζετο.

2 Οὐ μόνον δὲ διὰ ταῦτα αἰδέσιμος ἦν τοῖς ἥλιξι καὶ τοῖς ἤδη προβεβηκόσιν, ἀλλὰ γὰρ καὶ ἐκ τοῦ τρόπου τῆς ἀγωγῆς μᾶλλον οὐκ ἀθαύμαστος αὐτοῖς ἐνομίζετο, ἀρετῆς

named Theoktiste, gaining praise in both respects through her chaste way of life. Her God-given offspring himself, whose tongue was enriched by God with noble language, compiled at that time, in the form of a catechesis for the brethren under him, an account of the life this ever-revered lady had adopted; so I refer those who want to know about her to that discourse, and focus, as I ought, on an account of our father.

3

So then, after spending the first seven years of his life in a way appropriate to his nature, he advanced to occupy himself in the preliminary and elementary skills of learning; *for the lessons of childhood, developing along with the soul, are united with it* and become ingrained in the one who acquires them. As he advanced in age, he also became practiced in the skill of grammar, then of dialectic as well, which those who are adept at these things like to call philosophy. In addition to the things already mentioned, he also plucked for himself, as far as he was able, the beauty of rhetorical expression by means of his natural quickness, and as the industriousness of his intellect became widely known, he was recognized by each and every one.

He was respected by his peers and those who were older 2
than him not only for these qualities, but they were also full of admiration for the way he behaved, seeing that he had a

ἅτε ἐρῶν καὶ τὴν ἁγνείαν σύνοικον ἐπαγόμενος, τῶν τε φαύλων τὰς συνουσίας ἀποδιδράσκων, καὶ τοῖς σώφροσιν ἀεὶ συναρτώμενος, ὡς δὲ καὶ τοῖς οἴκοις τῶν εὐχῶν οὐχ ἥκιστά γε ἐν ταῖς συνάξεσι μολών, καὶ τοῖς *Βίοις* τῶν πρὶν διαλαμψάντων ἁγίων ὡς ἔν τισιν εὐωδεστάτοις λειμῶσι, καθάπερ τις φιλόπονος μέλιττα τῷ λογισμῷ ἐφιζάνων καὶ περιϊπτάμενος, καὶ τοῦτό τε κἀκεῖνο, πάντα δὲ μᾶλλον συλλήβδην ἐρανιζόμενος πρὸς ἑνὸς χρήματος κατασκευήν, λέγω δή, τῆς ἀειμνήστου καὶ σεβασμίας ἀρετῆς, *ὑπὲρ μέλι καὶ κηρίον* τὰ τῆς ψυχῆς γλυκαινούσης αἰσθητήρια.

3 Ἦν γὰρ ἐκ παιδὸς ἀρτίφρων καὶ Χριστομαθὴς ὁ θαυμάσιος, πρὸς τῆς ἐνυποστάτου τοῦ Θεοῦ καὶ Πατρὸς σοφίας τῆς πᾶσαν ἔννοιαν καὶ βουλὴν ἐπικαλεσαμένης, ἤγουν ἐκ τοῦ μὴ ὄντος ὑποστησάσης, καθάπερ ἐξαίρετόν τι δῶρον τὴν κυριωτάτην τῶν γενικῶν ἀπειληφὼς ἀρετῶν, ᾗ παρέπεσθαι καὶ τὰς λοιπὰς οἶδεν ὁ λόγος, τοῖς γε μὴ ψιλὴν ἔχουσιν αὐτῆς τὴν ὀνομασίαν, ἀλλ᾽ ἐμπεδοῦσι διὰ τῶν ἔργων αὐτῶν ὅπερ ὀνομάζονται παρωνύμως.

4 Ὑφ᾽ ἧς ἐντελῶς ὁ θεῖος οὗτος ἰθυνόμενος Θεόδωρος, τὴν εὐθεῖαν καὶ βασιλικὴν διώδευσε τρίβον, καὶ μακρὰν ἐγεγόνει τῶν τῆς ἀφροσύνης ποδῶν, ἣ τοὺς χρωμένους αὐτῇ ὑποσκελίζειν πέφυκεν καὶ εἰς Ἅιδην ἀπωλείας καταβιβάζειν· ἀλλὰ γὰρ οὕτω τὰ πρῶτα διαπλάσας ἑαυτὸν ἄριστα καὶ πανσόφως, μᾶλλον δὲ διαπλασθεὶς ὑπὸ τῆς θείας χάριτος, ἣ χεῖρα βοηθείας ὀρέγει τοῖς ἀγαθὸν αἱρουμένοις, καὶ συνεργεῖ καὶ σθένος δίδωσι πρὸς τὴν τῶν κρειττόνων ἐπιτυχίαν.

passion for virtue and made purity his partner in life, avoiding the company of bad people and always attaching himself to those who were abstemious. He went to the houses of prayer, especially for religious services, and was drawn to the *Lives* of holy men who had been illustrious in earlier times, like an industrious bee alighting in some very fragrant meadows and flitting about, gathering now this and now that or rather, in short, everything for the formation of one thing, namely that virtue, ever to be remembered and revered, which sweetens the senses of the soul *more than honey and honeycomb.*

From his youth this wonderful man held sound views and 3
was a disciple of Christ through the wisdom of the enhypostatic God and Father which called up every thought and counsel, that is to say, brought them into existence out of what was not, since he had received as a special gift this most supreme of the cardinal virtues. Reason knows that the other virtues follow wisdom, at least in those who do not merely bear its name but confirm through their deeds the appellation that they have received.

Guided entirely by wisdom, then, the godly Theodore 4
traveled the straight and royal path, keeping far away from the track of foolishness, which tends to trip up those who follow it and take them down to perdition in Hades. He had thus fashioned himself from the beginning in the best and most wise way, or rather, had been fashioned by divine grace, which extends a helping hand to those who choose what is good, assisting and giving them strength to attain what is better.

4

Ὁπηνίκα τοῦ πονηροῦ τυράννου καὶ Φαραωγνώμονος ἄνακτος καταποθέντος οὐ τῷ Ἐρυθραίῳ πόντῳ, τῷ δὲ πυρὶ τῆς Γεέννης, ἧς καὶ τὰ ὑπεκκαύματα, *ξύλα* δηλαδὴ καὶ *χόρτον* καὶ *καλάμην*, τὰ τῆς μοχθηρᾶς ἐκφόρια ζωῆς παρὰ πάντα τὸν ἑαυτοῦ βίον, ὥσπερ τις γῆ κεχερσωμένη καὶ ὑλομανοῦσα ἐξήνεγκεν, εἶτα μετ' ἐκεῖνον ἀμέσως τοῦ νεωτέρου Λέοντος καὶ υἱοῦ αὐτοῦ ἐκ προγόνων διαδοχῆς εἰς ὀλίγον τοῦ καιροῦ τῇ βασιλείᾳ διαρκέσαντος καὶ θανατωθέντος, ἐπεὶ μηδ' ἐβούλετο συνιέναι τὸ διὰ τοῦ Δαυῒδ προφητευόμενον, ἐκ Δαυῒδ ἀνατεταλκέναι ἰφθιμότατον κέρας, ὃ *συνέθλασε τὰ κέρατα τῶν ἁμαρτωλῶν* δαιμόνων τε καὶ ἀνθρώπων ἐναγῶν, ὁ ἄρχων τῆς εἰρήνης Χριστός, ὁ μέγας καὶ μόνος ἀΐδιος βασιλεύς, *ἐξήγειρε κέρας σωτηρίας* ὁμοῦ καὶ εἰρήνης τῇ αὐτοῦ Ἐκκλησίᾳ, τὴν φερώνυμον δὴ λέγω καὶ τοῖς ἔργοις μᾶλλον Εἰρήνην ἢ τὴν προσηγορίαν.

2 Τότε δὴ τότε καὶ ὁ θεῖος Θεόδωρος πάντη διέδρα τὴν κοσμικὴν ματαιοπονίαν, καὶ οἷόν τις αὐτογύμναστος πῶλος πρὸς τὸν τῆς ἀρετῆς ηὐτομόλησε χαλινόν, ἀπὸ γενέσεως ἄγων εἰκοστὸν καὶ δεύτερον ἔτος. Τῆς γὰρ θεοφιλεστάτης Εἰρήνης ὑπὸ Θεοῦ προαχθείσης εἰς τὸ τῆς μονοκρατορίας κῦρος, καὶ τοὺς ὑπολελειμμένους σπινθῆρας τῆς εὐσεβείας τε καὶ μονήρους διαβιώσεως ἐκ τῶν ἐσχατιῶν καὶ ὑπεροριῶν ἢ καὶ καθείρξεων ἀνακαλεσαμένης, οὕς, καὶ ὡς *ἅλας τῆς γῆς* καὶ ὡς *φωστῆρας κόσμου λόγον ζωῆς ἐπέχοντας*, περιεῖπε καὶ ἀπεσέμνυνεν, ὡς ἁλίζειν

4

At that time the evil tyrant, the one who ruled in the same manner as Pharaoh, was utterly engulfed, not in the Red Sea but by the fire of Gehenna, the fuel for which, that is *wood, hay,* and *straw,* the product of a wicked way of living throughout his life, he had produced like some dried-out land overgrown with brush. Then the younger Leo, his son, who immediately succeeded him, lasted only a short time in the imperial office and died, since he was not willing to understand David's prophecy, that from David there had risen a most mighty horn which *had crushed the horns of sinful* demons and accursed men: for Christ, the prince of peace, the great and only eternal king, *raised up* for his Church *a horn of salvation* and of peace, I mean Irene, who bore her name more for her actions than as a simple appellation.

It was also at that very time that the godly Theodore fled 2
completely from the vain labor of the world, and at the age of twenty-two, like a self-trained colt, voluntarily submitted himself to the bridle of virtue. For when God promoted his most beloved Irene to the supreme power of sole rule, she recalled from remote retreats and places of banishment or even prisons the sparks of piety and monastic life that still remained. Since they, as the *salt of the earth* and as *lights of the world, were maintaining the word of life,* Irene honored them and highly extolled them as people who knew how to

εἰδότας τὰ τῆς Ἐκκλησίας διεφθορότα τῇ πικρᾷ νόσῳ τῆς αἱρέσεως μέλη, πρὸς δὲ καὶ τῆς ὀρθοδόξου πίστεως τῷ φωτὶ ἐναυγάζειν αὐτῶν τοὺς τῆς διανοίας ὀφθαλμούς.

3 Εἰσελήλυθε τηνικαῦτα ἐν τῷ ἄστει, τῆς κατὰ τὸν Ὄλυμπον ἀφορμηθεὶς λόχμης, καὶ ὁ τῆς προκατονομασθείσης ἀοιδίμου Θεοκτίστης ὁμαίμων, Πλάτων ὁ σεβασμιώτατος (περὶ οὗ καὶ λαμπρῶς ἐσπουδάσθη τῷ μεγάλῳ Θεοδώρῳ ἔπαινος τὴν αὐτοῦ ἐκτιθεμένῳ ἀξιοπρεπῶς πολιτείαν), συναγωνισόμενος—τό γε εἰς αὐτὸν ἧκον—καὶ συμπονήσων τοῖς ἄλλοις πατράσιν, εἴς τε τὴν κατὰ τῆς αἱρέσεως ἀνατροπὴν καὶ καθαίρεσιν καὶ εἰς τὴν τῶν θείων εἰκόνων προσκύνησιν, τοῖς συνελθοῦσι τῇ Νικαέων τριακοσίοις καὶ ν´, ὧν ἡ ἄθροισις πρεπόντως ἑβδόμη σύνοδος ὠνόμασται, κατάπαυσις τῶν πρὸ αὐτῆς γενομένη καὶ σφραγὶς καὶ τέλος τῆς ὀρθοδόξου ἡμῶν πίστεως.

4 Καὶ δὴ Ταρασίῳ τῷ προμάχῳ τῆς εὐσεβείας καὶ οἰκουμενικῷ πεφηνότι φωστῆρι, τῷ φερωνύμως ἐκταράξαντι πᾶσαν τῆς ἀσεβείας τὴν ἅλμην, καὶ γαλήνην τῇ Ἐκκλησίᾳ σὺν Θεῷ πρυτανεύσαντι ἑνωθείς, σύμβουλος αὐτῷ τὰ πάντα καὶ συλλήπτωρ δεξιὸς καθίσταται, ἐκείνου δι᾽ αἰδοῦς πάσης καὶ τιμῆς ἔχοντος τὸν πανόσιον διά τε τὸ βεβηκὸς τῆς ἀσκήσεως καὶ τὸ τοῦ γένους ὑπερτενές. Ταύτης οὖν εἵνεκα τῆς προφάσεως τὰς διατριβὰς ὁ θαυμάσιος Πλάτων ἐν Κωνσταντινουπόλει ποιούμενος, καὶ ἄλλους μὲν πολλοὺς τῶν συνήθων πρὸς καταφρόνησιν ἀνεπτέρωσε τῶν παρόντων καὶ φθειρομένων· μάλιστά γε μὴν τὴν ἰδίαν ἀδελφὴν καὶ τὸν ὁσιόφρονα ἀδελφιδοῦν Θεόδωρον,

season with salt the limbs of a Church which had been corrupted by the bitter disease of heresy and, furthermore, how to enlighten the eyes of their minds with the light of the orthodox faith.

At that point, setting out from his wooded retreat on Olympos, the brother of the aforementioned celebrated Theoktiste, the most revered Plato (about whom great Theodore also composed a splendid encomium, describing his way of life in a worthy fashion) came into the city. Plato's purpose was to join in the struggle—at least as far as he was able—and labor together with the other three hundred and fifty fathers who had assembled in the city of Nicaea for the overthrow and destruction of the heresy and to restore veneration of the holy icons. Their gathering has fittingly been named the seventh council, as it became a conclusion for those before it and a seal and completion of our orthodox faith. 3

Plato joined Tarasios, the champion of piety revealed as a light for the whole world, who, as befits his name, had greatly confounded all the bitterness of impiety and with God's help had bestowed tranquility on the Church. He was appointed his counselor and right-hand man in everything, while Tarasios held the all-saintly one in complete respect and honor because of his established ascetic practice and the high status of his family. Staying on in Constantinople for this reason, the admirable Plato also prompted many others of his acquaintance to disdain this present ephemeral life; in particular, he roused his own sister and his saintly-minded nephew Theodore, both of whom had long before 4

πολλῷ πρότερον τῷ πόθῳ τῆς οὐρανίου ζωῆς τὰ ἐντὸς ἔχοντας πυρπολούμενα, πρὸς πλείονα ζῆλον τῆς ἀμείνονος διήγειρε τῶν μοναστῶν πολιτείας.

5

Ὅστις Θεόδωρος θάρσους ἐπίμεστος ταῖς ὑποθήκαις τοῦ ὁσίου γεγονώς, συμβούλῳ τῇ μητρὶ χρησάμενος, δι' αὐτῆς τὰ σωτήρια καὶ ἀνήκοντα τῷ πατρὶ ἀναφέρει· καὶ ταύτῃ θηρεύει τοῦτον σὺν τρισὶν ἀδελφοῖς πρὸς τὸν ἴσον τῆς ἀρετῆς συνθέσθαι πόθον, ἐφυστερίζοντα τοῖς ἐξ αὐτοῦ, τοὺς γὰρ ἑαυτοῦ δύο συναίμονας μετὰ τῆς μιᾶς ἀδελφῆς αὐτῶν προεζωγρήκει ταῖς χρησταῖς τῆς μητρὸς παρακλήσεσι. Καὶ οὕτω συμφωνησάντων πάντων εἰς τὸ ἀποτάξασθαι τοῖς τοῦ κόσμου καὶ Θεῷ προσοικειωθῆναι διὰ τοῦ ἀποστολικοῦ σχήματος, ἀπεμπολοῦσι σπουδῇ πάντα τὰ τῆς κοσμικῆς ζωῆς καὶ ἐν βασιλικοῖς ἀξιώμασιν ἐπιτήδεια, ἔτι δὲ καὶ αὐτὴν τὴν οἰκίαν· καὶ τὸ ἐξ αὐτῶν συγκομισθὲν χρυσίον πένησι διανείμαντες, ἀξιοῦσι τοῖς κατ' οἶκον ἐξυπηρετουμένοις οἰκέταις τῆς ἐλευθερίου ζωῆς, μετὰ τῶν ἐπιβαλλόντων αὐτοῖς λεγάτων.

2 Καὶ δὴ τῶν αὐτόθι ὁμοθυμαδὸν ἀναστάντες, ἀπαίρουσιν εἰς τὸν προωρισμένον αὐτοῖς τοῦ Σακκουδίωνος χῶρον, οἰκεῖον ὄντα αὐτῶν καὶ πάνυ ἐπιτήδειον εἰς μοναστῶν περιοχὴν καὶ ἀνάπαυλαν. Κάταλσον γάρ ἐστι τὸ κτῆμα

been inwardly burning with a desire for the heavenly life, to greater imitation of the better way of life lived by monks.

5

Theodore was greatly encouraged by the advice of the saintly Plato and, with his mother as a counselor, presented to his father through her an appropriate proposal for salvation. In this way he sought that his father would develop a yearning for virtue equal to that of his three siblings, as the former lagged behind his children, for Theodore had already captured his own two brothers along with their one sister thanks to the kindly entreaties of their mother. Thus, after they had all agreed to renounce the world and devote themselves to God by means of the apostolic habit, they hastily sold off all their worldly possessions and whatever imperial officials have to have, and even their house itself. And after they had distributed to the poor the money realized by these sales, they decided to grant freedom to their household servants, along with the legacies that were due to them.

There and then, setting out with one accord, they de- 2
parted to the estate of Sakkoudion which they had decided on in advance since it belonged to them and was very suitable as a secluded abode for monastics. The property is

μηνοειδῶς τε περικυκλούμενον καὶ δι' ἑνὸς ἀμφόδου τὴν εἴσοδον ἔχον· τὸ δὲ μεσαίτατον αὐτοῦ πεδιάσιμον, ἐν ᾧ πεφύκασι δένδρα διάφορα, κάρπιμά τε καὶ ἄκαρπα, καὶ ὁ περικαλλὴς τοῦ Θεολόγου ναός, ὕδωρ τε πρὸς αὐτάρκειαν, μηδὲν ἄλλο πρὸς ὡραϊσμὸν τοῦ βλέπειν τοῖς οἰκήτορσιν ἐμπαρέχον, ἢ τὸν οὐρανὸν καὶ τὴν ἀρκτικὴν θάλασσαν. Ὅστις ἐξ ἐκείνου καὶ μέχρι σήμερον ἀνθεῖ καὶ βρίθει τῷ πλήθει τῶν εἰς αὐτὸν στρεφομένων ἀδελφῶν, καὶ περιβόητός γε καθέστηκεν διὰ τὴν χάριν τῶν βαλόντων εἰς αὐτὸν ἀρχὴν καὶ θεμέλιον ἀγγελομιμήτου ζωῆς θεοφόρων καὶ ὁμολογητῶν πατέρων ἡμῶν.

6

Καθ' ὃν δὴ ἐναυλιζόμενος κατ' ἀρχὰς ὁ μέγας Θεόδωρος σὺν τοῖς μετ' αὐτοῦ, καὶ ταῖς τοῦ πανοσίου Πλάτωνος χερσὶν ἑαυτὸν ὅλον ἐκδεδωκώς, καὶ ὑπ' αὐτοῦ τὴν τοῦ ἁγίου σχήματος ἀναλαβὼν παντευχίαν, οὐκ ἦν τὸ παράπαν ὃ μὴ ταῖς ἐκείνου βουλαῖς ἑπόμενος ἤθελέν τε καὶ ἔπραττεν. Τῆς γὰρ αὐταρεσκείας τὸν κίνδυνον ὑφορώμενος, μακρὰν τῶν ἰδίων θελημάτων εἶναι ᾤετο δεῖν, τὴν ἀποστολικὴν ῥῆσιν εἰς μαρτύριον ἔχων τὴν λέγουσαν· "*Ζῶ δὲ οὐκέτι ἐγώ, ζῇ δὲ ἐν ἐμοὶ ὁ Χριστός.*"

2 Διὸ οὕτως ὑπετάσσετο τῷ ἀοιδίμῳ Πλάτωνι, συστολὴν ἤθους καὶ φρονήματος, οὐ μόνον εἰς αὐτόν, ἀλλὰ καὶ πρὸς

wooded, curving round in the shape of a crescent moon with a single track leading to it; the middle part consists of level ground on which different trees grow, both fruit-bearing and nonfruit-bearing, and there is a very beautiful shrine of John the Theologian there and an adequate water supply; it provides its occupants with nothing beautiful to look at except the sky and the sea to the north. From then until now this estate has flourished and abounded in the large number of brothers moving into it, and it has become very well-known through the grace of our fathers, those inspired confessors, who began there and laid a foundation for the life that imitates the angels.

6

To begin with, great Theodore lived there with his companions, surrendering himself totally into the hands of the all-saintly Plato and receiving from him the full armor of the holy habit; there was nothing at all that he wished or did without following Plato's advice. For he was wary of the danger of self-indulgence, and thought it necessary to disregard his own wishes, having the testimony of the apostolic verse which says, "*It is no longer I who live, but Christ who lives in me.*"

In this way he subjected himself to the celebrated Plato, 2
displaying reverence both in his conduct and thought not

τοὺς ἐφεξῆς μείζονάς τε καὶ ἐλάττονας ἐπιδεικνύμενος, ὡς ἀθέλητός τις ὢν καὶ ἀβούλητος ἄνθρωπος ἢ ἀνδριὰς ἄψυχος, τῷ φόβῳ τοῦ Κυρίου τὰς σάρκας ἔχων καθηλωμένας, καὶ ἄπρακτος διαμένων πρὸς πᾶν ὃ περπερεία καὶ ζῆλος καὶ φθόνος καὶ θυμὸς καὶ ὀργὴ καὶ ἐριθεία διὰ τῆς τοῦ νοὸς ἀπροσεξίας οἶδεν ἀπογεννᾶν. Τὴν δέ γε μεγαλοψυχίαν καὶ σπουδὴν καὶ ἄοκνον ταχυτῆτα μετὰ τῆς ἐθίμου εὐσχημοσύνης ἐπὶ ταῖς ἐν χερσὶ διακονίαις οὕτω δι' ἐπιμελείας κατώρθου, ὡς εὐθέως μὲν τὸ προκείμενον αὐτῷ ἔργον εἰς πέρας ἄγειν, διαθέειν δὲ ὧδε κἀκεῖσε πρὸς ἕκαστον τῶν ἀδελφῶν καὶ τοῖς ἢ δι' ἀσθένειαν ἢ καὶ ῥᾳθυμίαν ἠσθενηκόσιν ἐπαμύνειν, καὶ τὰ τούτων ἐλλείμματα τῇ παρ' ἑαυτοῦ ἀναπληροῦν βοηθείᾳ· ὃς οὐδὲ ξυλοφορεῖν ἢ σκαπάνῃ κεχρῆσθαι καὶ κηπεύειν τὴν κατάλληλον τῇ ἀσθενείᾳ τροφὴν ἀπηυδόκησέν πω· ἀλλ' αὐθαίρετος ταῦτά τε καὶ τὰ παρόμοια δρῶν καὶ κόπρον ἐκκομίζων τῶν βοσκημάτων κρύβδην, καθευδόντων τῶν ἀδελφῶν, ἐν νυκτεριναῖς τε καὶ μεσημβριναῖς ὥραις ἐφωράθη πολλάκις.

3 Ἐφ' ᾧ λέγεται καὶ τοὺς συνασκουμένους ἐκπλήττειν, ἐναργῆ καὶ μεγάλην διδοὺς τὴν ἀπόδειξιν δι' ὧν ἔδρα τῆς προσούσης αὐτῷ κατὰ τὸν ἔνδον ἄνθρωπον διαπύρου καὶ τελείας πρὸς Χριστὸν ἀγάπης, *ὃς ἐν μορφῇ Θεοῦ ὑπάρχων, οὐχ ἁρπαγμὸν ἡγήσατο τὸ εἶναι ἴσα Θεῷ, ἀλλ' ἑαυτὸν ἐκένωσεν μορφὴν δούλου λαβών, γενόμενος ὑπήκοος μέχρι θανάτου, θανάτου δὲ σταυροῦ.*

only toward him, but also in turn toward those of greater or lesser importance, as though he were a man without volition or without will, or a lifeless statue, keeping his flesh nailed down in the fear of the Lord and remaining unaffected by anything that boastfulness and jealousy, envy and anger, wrath and selfish ambition can engender through mental inattentiveness. But he perfected magnanimity, zeal, and unhesitating speed, along with his customary gracefulness, in manual duties, acting with such diligence that he would immediately complete any task set before him, and he would run hither and thither to each of the brethren to assist those who were weakened either by illness or even laziness and make up for their deficiencies with his own help. Nor did he refuse to carry wood, or use a mattock and cultivate the food appropriate for sickness, but was often found, during both the night and midday hours while the brethren were sleeping, doing these and similar tasks of his own accord, even secretly clearing out the manure from the livestock.

In this he is said to have astounded even his fellow ascet- 3
ics, providing great and obvious proof by his actions of his characteristically innate ardent and perfect love for Christ, *who, though he was in the form of God, did not regard equality with God a thing to be grasped, but emptied himself, taking the form of a servant, and became obedient unto death, even death on a cross.*

7

Ταῦτα γὰρ καὶ τὰ ἄλλα πάντα τὰ περὶ αὐτοῦ γεγραμμένα θεῖά τε καὶ ἀνθρώπινα νήφοντι ἀναθεωρῶν λογισμῷ, ἐφωτίζετο τὴν ψυχήν, κατενύσσετο τὴν καρδίαν, ἐπυρπολεῖτο τὸν νοῦν διὰ παντὸς τῇ ἐφέσει τῆς πρὸς αὐτὸν εὐαρεστήσεως καὶ κατὰ τὸ ἐγχωροῦν ἐκμιμήσεως.

2 Ἐξεδωμάτωσε μέντοι καὶ εὐκτήριον ἐπ' ὀνόματι τοῦ Θεολόγου Ἰωάννου καὶ *υἱοῦ τῆς βροντῆς* ταῖς τοῦ μεγάλου Πλάτωνος πειθαρχῶν ἐντολαῖς, οὐρανότυπον σχῆμα προβεβλημένον, εὐανθῆ ποικιλοεργίαν οὐ μόνον κατὰ τὸ μετέωρον αὐτοῦ τεχνησάμενος καὶ τοῖς οἰκοῦσιν ἐνδιαίτημα ξένον καὶ καλλιπρεπὲς περιποιησάμενος, ἀλλὰ καὶ αὐτὸ τοὔδαφος ταῖς ποικίλαις καὶ διαχρύσοις ἐγκαταστράψας ψηφῖσιν, ὡς ἂν καὶ οἱ πόδες αὐτῶν ταῖς αὐγαῖς τῶν λίθων κατατρυφῷεν. Ἐν ᾧπερ τὰς ἐντεύξεις τῷ Κυρίῳ μετὰ τῶν συνόντων ἀποδιδούς, μᾶλλον φιλοθεΐας καὶ κατανύξεως ἤστραπτεν ἀμαρύγμασιν, πρὸ πάντων εἰσιὼν ἐν τῷ οἴκῳ τοῦ Θεοῦ καὶ ὕστατος ἐκεῖθεν ἀπογινόμενος, καίτοι σπουδαιοτάτων ὄντων ἐνίων τῶν Θεοῦ χάριτι αὐτόθι λοιπὸν ἀποταξαμένων.

7

By carefully examining with a vigilant mind these words and everything else written about Christ, both human and divine, Theodore's soul became enlightened, his heart was stricken with contrition, and his mind became fired with a continual yearning to be well pleasing to him and imitate him as far as possible.

He also built a chapel dedicated to John the Theologian, 2
the son of thunder, obeying the commands of great Plato. He created it in a way that represented heaven, contriving not only to make its upper part brightly colored and skillfully crafted, and producing an extraordinary dwelling place of fitting beauty for those living there, but also making the floor itself gleam with mosaics of various colors and tinged with gold, so that even their feet might take delight in the sheen of the stones. In this place, as he was offering up entreaties to the Lord along with his companions, his sparkling love for God and his compunction would make him shine even more brilliantly; he would enter the house of God before them all and be the last to depart from it, even though some of those who, by the grace of God, had renounced the world here were extremely zealous.

8

Πρὸς δὲ τοῖς εἰρημένοις καί τινας ἰδικωτέρας ἐποιεῖτο δεήσεις, ἑαυτὸν ἀποδιαστέλλων τῶν ἄλλων κατὰ τὸ λεληθός, καὶ μάλιστά γε καθ' ἃς ἡμέρας ἦγον ἀργίαν, ἐν αἷς καὶ λιβάσι δακρύων τὰς παρειὰς κατέκλυζεν καὶ τοὔδαφος ἐν ᾧπερ ἐτύγχανεν ὤν· τὸ γὰρ τῆς κατανύξεως χάρισμα πλουσίως εἰλήφει παρὰ Θεοῦ, παρ' οὗ *πᾶν δώρημα τέλειον* δίδοται τοῖς ἀξίοις καὶ πρὸς τοῦτο ηὐτρεπισμένοις.

2 Ἐγκράτειαν δὲ τοσοῦτο μᾶλλον ἐξήσκησεν, ὅσῳ καὶ πλέον αὐτὴν συμβαλλομένην εὗρεν τοῖς τῷ Χριστῷ καθαρῶς τε καὶ ἀρυπάρως λατρεύειν ἐθέλουσιν· τὸν γὰρ λογισμὸν ἐπιστήσας ὥσπερ δικαστὴν ἀδέκαστον πνεύματι καὶ σαρκί, οὕτω δι' αὐτοῦ ἐποιεῖτο ἑκατέρου τὸ δέον, ὡς μήτε διὰ τῆς ἄγαν ἀσιτίας τὸ ὁρατὸν αὐτοῦ ἐκλύεσθαι καὶ πρὸς τὰς ἐν Χριστῷ διακονίας ἄπρακτον παρὰ τὸ εἰκὸς καθίστασθαι, μήτ' αὖ διὰ τὸν κόρον τῶν εἰσκριθέντων τὰς ψυχικὰς ἕξεις *ἀκηδίας* ἐνέχεσθαι πάθεσιν, ἐξ ἧς ὁ *περιεκτικὸς τῷ μοναχῷ* συνάγεται *θάνατος*. Ἀμέλει ἐν τούτοις ἐγχρονίσας ὁ μακαρίτης ἀρχετύπου τάξιν ἐπεῖχεν τοῖς πράγμασιν, (εἰ καὶ μηδέπω σαφῶς τοῖς ὀνόμασιν) πάσης ἁπλῶς ἀρετῆς τοὺς ἀκριβεῖς ἐμποιῶν τοῖς μεταλαμβάνουσι χαρακτῆρας.

3 Πρὸς ὃν δὴ βλέποντες οἱ συνασκηταί, καὶ μάλιστα ὁ θαυμάσιος Ἰωσήφ, ὁ καὶ τὴν φύσιν αὐτῷ καὶ τὴν προαίρεσιν προσφυῶς οἰκειούμενος, ἐμορφοῦτο τὴν ψυχὴν τῷ ἐκείνου κάλλει, τοιουτοσθενῆ προθυμίαν τῇ τῶν πρακτέων

8

In addition to what has been related, Theodore would also make some more personal supplications, separating himself from the others without being noticed, especially on the days when they were having a rest from their duties. At those times he would flood his cheeks and the floor where he happened to be standing with streams of tears, for he had received the gift of compunction in abundance from God, from whom *every perfect gift* is given to those who are worthy and ready for it.

The more he practiced abstinence, the more he found it 2
was helpful to those who wish to serve Christ in a pure way and without defilement. Setting up his mind as an impartial judge over his spirit and his flesh, he gave both their due in this way so that his visible body did not fail through excessive fasting and become inappropriately incapable of performing his ministries in Christ, nor again, on account of eating too much, did his spiritual habits become subject to bouts of *accidie* by which *all-embracing death* is brought *upon a monk.* Of course, after spending time on these things, the blessed one began to assume the position of a role model through his actions (though clearly not yet in his words), reproducing the exact characteristics of simply every virtue in what he undertook.

His fellow ascetics looked up to him, especially the admi- 3
rable Joseph who, being naturally connected to him both by kinship and by deliberate choice, began to model his soul on the beauty of Theodore's, so strong was the eagerness he

ἐνδεικνύμενος ἐξομοιώσει· διὸ καὶ ἄλλος τις εἶναι Θεόδωρος παρ' αὐτοῖς εἰκάζετο, πολὺς ἐν ἀρετῇ καὶ γνώσει γεγονώς. Ὃς καὶ θείᾳ ψήφῳ τῆς ἐν Θεσσαλονίκῃ ἁγίας τοῦ Θεοῦ ἐκκλησίας ἐν καιρῷ ἰδίῳ τοὺς οἴακας ἐγχειρισθείς, πλείστας ὑπερορίας καὶ φρουρὰς ὑπὲρ τῆς ὀρθοδόξου ἐκαρτέρησε πίστεως· μεθ' οὗ καὶ Ἀντώνιος καὶ Τιμόθεος, Ἀθανάσιός τε καὶ Ναυκράτιος, καὶ πλεῖστος ἄλλος ὅμιλος ἐφεξῆς, οἳ διὰ τῆς ἀσκητικῆς τηνικάδε ζωῆς καὶ τῆς ἀθλητικῆς ὕστερον ἐνστάσεως *ἐνέκρωσαν τὰ μέλη τὰ ἐπὶ τῆς γῆς*, καὶ τοῦ Ἀντιπάλου πᾶσαν τὴν δύναμιν κατεπάτησαν.

9

Ὁ γοῦν πατὴρ ἡμῶν Θεόδωρος πάντων μὲν τῶν θεοφόρων Πατέρων μετῄει τοὺς βίους καὶ τοὺς λόγους ἐν συντετριμμένῃ καρδίᾳ καὶ πνεύματι ταπεινώσεως, μίαν ἐπιζητῶν εἰς τὸν προκείμενον αὐτῷ σκοπὸν λυσιτέλειαν, τὸ πῶς δεῖ εὐαρεστῆσαι Θεῷ τοὺς τὴν ἐπὶ τὸ αὐτὸ ζωὴν ἑλομένους, διαφερόντως δὲ ἐραστὴς καὶ μιμητὴς λέγεται γεγονέναι τοῦ οὐρανοφάντορος Βασιλείου. Τούτου γὰρ ταῖς ἀσκητικαῖς νομοθεσίαις καὶ ταῖς ἄλλαις μάλιστα τῶν θεοσόφων βίβλων ἐμφιλοσοφῶν δογματοθεσίαις, καὶ τὸ πλάτος τῆς σοφίας τε καὶ φρονήσεως αὐτοῦ μεγάλως ἀποθαυμάζων, ὅλον ἑαυτὸν ἐμπαρεῖχεν εἰς ἀφομοίωσιν τοῦ μεγάλου, τῆς ἐπ' ἀγαθοῖς ῥᾳθυμίας ἐν αὐτῷ λοιπὸν χώραν οὐκ ἐχούσης.

displayed in imitating his deeds; for that reason, he was considered among them as a second Theodore, being great in virtue and knowledge. In due course, by a sacred vote, Joseph was entrusted with the helm of the holy church of God in Thessalonike and endured very many periods of exile and imprisonment on behalf of the orthodox faith. His fellow monks were Anthony and Timothy, Athanasios and Naukratios, and very many others after them, who by their ascetic life at that time and their later combative determination *mortified their limbs on earth* and trampled underfoot all the power of the Adversary.

9

Our father Theodore followed the lives and words of all the divinely inspired Fathers with a contrite heart and in a spirit of humility, seeking an advantage for the aim that was set before him, namely, how those who choose the communal life must be well pleasing to God. In particular he is said to have become a follower and imitator of Basil, the revealer of heaven. For, meditating on Basil's ascetic rules and especially on the other precepts of his books of divine wisdom and greatly admiring the breadth of his wisdom and understanding, he surrendered himself entirely to imitation of the great man. From then on there was no place in him for laziness regarding good deeds.

2 Παρεωραμένην γὰρ εὑρὼν κατ᾽ ἐκείνου καιροῦ τὴν τῶν ἀσκητικῶν αὐτοῦ διατύπωσιν ὑπὸ τῶν ἐν κοινοβίοις διαιτᾶσθαι ἀνεχομένων—τῷ δούλους, φημί, καὶ βοσκημάτων νομάδας καὶ θήλεα περιποιεῖσθαι κτήνη—πλήττεται μὲν ἱκανῶς τὴν καρδίαν ἐπὶ ταῖς τοιαύταις τῶν νόμων ὑπεροψίαις. Ἀνδρειοῦται δὲ αὖθις καὶ πρόσεισι συνετῶς τῷ πρεσβύτῃ Πλάτωνι, μὴ δεῖν φάσκων παρεᾶσαι τὴν τοιαύτην τῶν πολλῶν ἀθεράπευτον νόσον, ἀλλὰ τῷ καθ᾽ ἑαυτοὺς ὑποδείγματι τὴν ἐξ ἀπιστίας ἢ καὶ φιλοκοσμίας συμβαίνουσαν τοῖς πολλοῖς ἀναστεῖλαι καινοτομίαν· καὶ γὰρ ἀκαλλὲς ἁγίοις τὸ παρακερδαίνειν ζητεῖν, ἃ τοῖς ἐν κόσμῳ πρέπει καὶ πολιτείαν ἐπιτηδεύουσιν τὴν οὐκ εἰς ἅπαν ἡγιασμένην.

3 Ὃ δὴ καὶ θᾶττον ἢ λόγος ἐπεραίνετο, Χριστοῦ συνεργοῦντος καὶ τοῦ πανοσίου Πλάτωνος ἐπικυροῦντος τὸ τῆς ἀξιώσεως σωτηριῶδες· τὸν μὲν γὰρ ἑσμὸν τῶν οἰκετῶν, ἐλευθερίαις ἐγγράφοις ἐφοδιάσαντες, αὐτεξουσίῳ ποδὶ πολιτεύεσθαι εἴασαν, τὰ δ᾽ ἄλλως ἔχοντα τῶν πραγμάτων τοῖς ἐνδεέσιν ἐσκόρπισαν, καὶ τούτῳ τῷ τρόπῳ καθιστᾶσι σφᾶς αὐτοὺς ἐπιδηλοτέρους ἀκουστὰς τῶν πατρικῶν παραδόσεων καὶ τῆς μοναχικῆς εὐκοσμίας ἀκαπηλεύτους ζωγράφους.

4 Περιηχηθείσης πανταχοῦ τῆς ἀγαθῆς ταύτης τῶν ἀειμνήστων πράξεως, ἣ τοὺς μὲν τῶν καλῶν ἐραστὰς πρὸς τὸν ὅμοιον τῆς ἀρετῆς διήγειρε ζῆλον, τοὺς δὲ τὴν ἀληθῆ τῆς ἀσκήσεως παραχαράττειν συνεθισθέντας τρίβον πρὸς φθόνον ἐρρίπισε τὸν μισόθεον, ἀλλ᾽ οὔτε τοῖς ἐκείνων ἡδόμενοι λόγοις, ὡς μέγα τι κατωρθωκότες, πρὸς κενοδοξίας

After discovering that the rules of Basil's ascetic treatises were disregarded at that time by those still living in cenobitic monasteries—I mean by the acquisition of slaves, pastured livestock and female animals—he was heartbroken by such contempt for the rules. But plucking up courage again, he sensibly approached his elder, Plato, stating that they must not leave such a disease on the part of the majority untreated but, by their own example, remove the innovation adopted by the majority out of a lack of faith or even love of the world; for it was unseemly for holy men to seek to make the improper gains which are fitting for those in the world who pursue a way of life that is not totally sanctified. 2

No sooner was this said than it began to be done with the assistance of Christ and the confirmation of all-saintly Plato for the salvific request. By providing the multitude of their household slaves with documents of emancipation, they allowed them to live and move about freely, and they donated the rest of their possessions to the needy. In this way they established themselves as people who listened carefully to the teachings of the Fathers and correctly displayed monastic good order. 3

This beneficent action by those who are held in everlasting remembrance became widely known, and began to rouse those who love what is good to a similar zeal for virtue, but it also incited those who had become accustomed to falsify the true path of asceticism to the envy that is hated by God. Nevertheless, Plato and his fellow monks were neither flattered by the words of the former group, which suggested that they had achieved something great, and thus were pre- 4

ἐξεκυλίσθησαν ὄλισθον, οὔτε τούτων τῷ φαυλισμῷ ἡττηθέντες τῆς θεοφιλοῦς ἔχεσθαι κατωλιγώρησαν ἐντολῆς, ἀλλ' εἴσω τῶν τῆς ὀρθῆς κρίσεως ἑαυτοὺς περιφυλάσσοντες κλείθρων, τὴν ἐξ ἑκατέρων βλάβην φρονίμως ἐξέκλιναν.

10

Ἀμέλει τούτων οὕτω προβάντων καὶ τῆς κατ' αὐτοὺς ἀδελφότητος αὐξηθείσης, καὶ δίκην λιπαρᾶς καὶ εὐγείου χώρας τῇ ἐμπειρίᾳ τῶν εὐφυῶν καλλιεργηθείσης φυτοκόμων καὶ καρπὸν ἀποδιδούσης τῷ δεσπότῃ πολυπλασίονα, χρῆναι καλῶς ὑπειληφὼς Πλάτων, ὁ σοφὸς ποιμνιάρχης, τὸν πολλῷ πρώην ἑαυτὸν τῇ Τριάδι διὰ τῆς παντελοῦς τῶν μελῶν νεκρώσεως ἀξίως ἱερουργήσαντα καὶ τῆς ἁγνείας καθαρώτατον ὄντα τέμενος ἀποφῆναι καὶ θυηπόλον τῆς ἀναιμάκτου καὶ παμφαοῦς θυσίας, εἰσελαύνει σὺν αὐτῷ πρὸς τὸν θεόληπτον πατριάρχην Ταράσιον, ἀχθομένῳ μὲν ὅτι μάλιστα διὰ τὴν εἰς αὐτὸν γνώμην τοῦ ὁσίου, εἴκοντι δ' ὅμως δι' εὐπείθειαν καὶ τοῦ μὴ δόξαι φρονεῖν τοῦ πατρὸς βελτίονα. Οὓς ὁ θεῖος ἱεροθέτης καθάπερ τινὰς *θησαυροὺς ἐπιθυμητοὺς* μετὰ πολλῆς προσηκάμενος τῆς θυμηδίας, ἐπιτίθησι τῷ Θεοδώρῳ τὴν χεῖρα καὶ τελεσιουργεῖ ἐπ' αὐτῷ τὴν τῆς ἱερωσύνης τελείωσιν, ἀπὸ τῆς ἐλάττονος τῶν ὑποδιακόνων ἀρξάμενος καὶ μέχρι τῆς τοῦ πρεσβυτέρου τάξεως ἐληλυθώς.

vented from falling into vainglory; nor, overcome by disparagement from the latter, did they neglect to follow the commandment which is pleasing to God but, protecting themselves behind the bars of right judgment, they prudently repelled the harm from each group.

10

After they had proceeded in such a fashion and their brotherhood had increased like a rich and fertile land cultivated by the experience of skillful gardeners, rewarding its owner with fruit in abundance, Plato, the wise shepherd, rightly realized that Theodore, who much earlier had worthily sacrificed himself to the Trinity by the complete mortification of his limbs and was a most pure temple of purity, ought also to be declared a priest of the bloodless and radiant sacrifice. Plato went with him to the God-inspired patriarch Tarasios, and although Theodore was extremely vexed at the saintly man's decision concerning himself, he nevertheless gave way because of his ready obedience and so that he would not seem to have better ideas than his spiritual father. The godly prelate received them with great delight like *desirable treasures,* laid his hand on Theodore, and bestowed on him the consecration of the priesthood, beginning from the lesser order of subdeacons and going right up to that of priest.

2 Ἐπεὶ δὲ ταχέως πρὸς τὸ οἰκεῖον ἐξέπλευσαν μοναστήριον, οὐκ ᾤετο δεῖν ὁ θεῖος Θεόδωρος τοῖς προτέροις ἐμπεριέχεσθαι ἀγωνίσμασι, τὸ τῆς ἀρετῆς ἀεικίνητον εὖ εἰδώς. Ἀλλ᾽ ὃν τρόπον στρατιώτης μαχιμώτατος πρώην πολλῷ τοὺς ἀνταγωνιζομένους αὐτῷ τροπωσάμενος καὶ τῆς κατ᾽ αὐτῶν νίκης τὸ κλέος ἀράμενος, πλείονα ῥώμην καὶ προθυμίαν εἰς τὸ ἑξῆς ἐπιδείκνυται, οὕτω δὴ καὶ Θεόδωρος, ὁ τῆς ἀρετῆς ἀθλητής, τὸν τῆς χειροτονίας βαθμὸν βραβεῖον νίκης τῆς κατὰ τῶν πολεμίων παθῶν ἄρασθαι λογισάμενος, καὶ μειζοτέρων ἀγώνων ὑπόθεσιν τὴν προτίμησιν κρίνας, *οὐκ ἐδίδου ὕπνον τοῖς ὀφθαλμοῖς, οὐδὲ τοῖς βλεφάροις αὐτοῦ νυσταγμὸν ἢ ἀνάπαυσιν τοῖς κροτάφοις* ψαλμικῶς εἰπεῖν· ἀλλ᾽ ἐκτήκων ἑαυτοῦ τὰς σάρκας ταῖς παννύχοις μελέταις τῶν ἱερῶν γραφῶν, ἐκράτει μικροῦ καὶ τοῦ κατὰ τὴν φύσιν ὀφλήματος καὶ τὴν ἀναγκαιοτάτην ἔκτισιν τῆς οὐσίας ὑπερφυῶς ἐδείκνυεν δεχομένην, ὡς οὐδ᾽ αὐτῆς ὅλης ὥρας διὰ τοῦ ἡμερονυκτίου μεταλαγχάνων τοῦ ὕπνου, τὰς δὲ λοιπὰς ταῖς ἀγαθοεργίαις καταναλίσκων.

3 Οὕτω τοίνυν μεγεθυνόμενον ταῖς ἀρεταῖς ὁσημέραι τὸν Θεόδωρον βλέπων ὁ τρισόσιος Πλάτων, ἠβουλήθη πολλάκις, ὡς ἤδη τὴν εὐφυῆ καὶ ἀπόλεκτον ἐξησκηκότα ζωήν, καθηγούμενον αὐτὸν ἀναδεῖξαι τῆς πρὸς οὐρανὸν τρεχούσης ὑπ᾽ αὐτὸν ἀδελφότητος, εἰς ἁπλῆν ἑκατοντάδα τῇ τοῦ Χριστοῦ ἐπεκταθείσης προνοίᾳ. Ἀλλ᾽ οὐκ ἔπεισε τὸν ἐπὶ πᾶσιν ἄλλοις κηροῦ μαλακώτερον πειθαρχοῦντα, συνεγνωκὼς εἰδότα σαφῶς τὸ ἐπηρτημένον κρῖμα τοῖς τῇ τοιαύτῃ

After they had quickly sailed away to their own monastery, godly Theodore decided that he should no longer engage in his former contests, as he was well aware of the ever-changing nature of virtue. But like a very belligerent soldier who long ago put his adversaries to flight and gained the fame of victory over them displays greater strength and eagerness for what comes next, so also Theodore, the champion of virtue, reckoned that he had gained the step of ordination as a prize of victory over the hostile passions and decided that the preferment was grounds for greater contests. He thus *did not grant his eyes sleep or his eyelids drowsiness or his temples rest,* to speak like the Psalmist; rather, by mortifying his own flesh in all-night study of the holy scriptures, he would almost surpass his natural obligation and would superhumanly discharge the most necessary payment possible for his existence, as he did not partake of sleep even for one whole hour during day and night and spent the remaining hours in good works. 2

When the thrice-saintly Plato saw Theodore being exalted every day by his virtues in this way, and as he was already practicing a well-ordered and chosen way of life, he often wished to proclaim him *kathegoumenos* of the brotherhood, which under his own leadership was hastening toward heaven and had by Christ's providential care increased to one hundred in number. But Plato did not persuade Theodore, who in all other respects obeyed more compliantly than wax, being conscious that he clearly knew the judgment hanging over those who recklessly advance to such a 3

ἀρχῇ ῥιψοκινδύνως προσβαίνουσιν· ἧς καὶ τὸ δυσκατόρθωτον ὁ πολὺς ἐν θεολογίᾳ ὑπέγραψε φάσκων· "*Χαλεποῦ ὄντος τοῦ εἰδέναι ἄρχεσθαι, κινδυνεύει πολλῷ χαλεπώτερον εἶναι τὸ εἰδέναι ἄρχειν ἀνθρώπων.*"

4 Πλὴν οὐκ ἔδει μέχρι παντὸς κρύπτεσθαι τὸν νοητὸν *λύχνον ὑπὸ τὸν* τῆς ὑφεδρίας *μόδιον, ἀλλ' ἐπὶ τὴν λυχνίαν τεθῆναι* τῆς ποιμαντικῆς ἀναβάσεως πρὸς τὸ φαίνειν *πᾶσι τοῖς ἐν τῇ οἰκίᾳ* τῇ τῶν φωτοποιῶν αὐτοῦ πράξεων ἐκπρεπεῖ λαμπαδουχίᾳ. Νόσῳ γὰρ ληφθεὶς ἐν μιᾷ ὁ ὅσιος Πλάτων, καὶ λάβρῳ πυρετῷ τὰ ἔνδον περικαιόμενος ἐφ' ἱκανὰς ἡμέρας ὡς καὶ δόξαι πολλοῖς τῶν προσκαίρων ἀφίπτασθαι, ἐπείπερ εἰκὸς ἦν τὸν μετ' ἐκεῖνον προστησόμενον τῆς ποίμνης ψήφῳ τῆς ἀδελφότητος εἰς τοῦτο τάξεως ἐλθεῖν, σύνοδον ποιεῖται πάντων τῶν ἐν πνεύματι υἱῶν αὐτοῦ, καὶ τούτοις βραχέα ἄττα περὶ τῆς ὁρωμένης αὐτοῦ διεξελθὼν νόσου, ἀξιοῖ διενθυμηθῆναι καὶ εἰπεῖν τίνα αἱροῦνται καταστῆναι αὐτοῖς εἰς ποιμένα.

5 Τῶν δὲ ὥσπερ μιᾷ φωνῇ τὸν μέγαν Θεόδωρον ὀνομαστὶ προχειρισαμένων, μετακαλεῖται αὐτὸν εἰς τὸ μέσον ἐλθεῖν καὶ δὴ λόγοις τε καὶ σχήμασιν ὡς θανατηφόρος πέλει ἡ νόσος πρὸς αὐτὸν βεβαιωσάμενος, εἶτα καὶ τοῦ πνευματικοῦ συλλόγου τῶν ἐν Χριστῷ ἀδελφῶν τὴν εἰς αὐτὸν ἐξενεχθεῖσαν προσειπὼν ψῆφον, καὶ ὡς θέλημά ἐστι προηγούμενον τὴν αὐτῶν ἀναδέξασθαι φροντίδα, πείθει μόλις ποτὲ εἰς τοῦτο ἐλθεῖν, τρισκαιδέκατον ἄγοντα ἔτος τῆς ἀνοθεύτου αὐτοῦ ἐν Κυρίῳ ὑποταγῆς, τῆς δέ γε πάσης ἡλικίας πέμπτον καὶ τριακοστόν. Οὕτω τοιγαροῦν ἔρχεται εἰς τὴν τῶν ἀδελφῶν προστασίαν, φόβῳ μὲν καὶ τρόμῳ

position of authority. Indeed, the great theologian has acknowledged the difficulty of succeeding in this, stating, "*Though it is difficult to know how to be under authority, to know how to exercise authority over men is likely to be much more difficult.*"

However, the spiritual *light* was not destined to be hidden 4
forever *under the bushel* of his subordinate ministry, *but* had *to be placed on the lamp stand* of pastoral ascent to give light *to all those in the house* by the extraordinary illumination of his enlightening actions. For, one day, saintly Plato was stricken by an illness and was consumed internally by a violent fever for several days with the result that many thought he was flying away from this transitory world. Since it was appropriate that his successor as leader of the flock should attain this rank by a vote of the brotherhood, Plato convened a council of all his spiritual sons and, after briefly describing to them his obvious illness, demanded that they consider the matter and say whom they chose to appoint as their shepherd.

As if with one voice they put forward the great Theodore 5
by name, so Plato summoned him to come into their midst and, confirming to him by words and gestures that his illness was fatal, then added that the vote of the spiritual assembly of the brethren in Christ had been declared in his favor and that it was their wish that he should take their care upon himself as leader. With difficulty Plato eventually persuaded Theodore, who was then in the thirteenth year of his sincere submission to the Lord and the thirty-fifth of his lifespan, to agree. In this way, then, Theodore came to the leadership of the brethren, gripped by trembling and fear

συνεχόμενος διὰ τὸν παρεπόμενον ἐξ ἀβουλίας ταῖς τῶν ποιμαινομένων ψυχαῖς ὄλεθρον.

II

Ὅμως οὖν διανίσταται καί, τῆς φίλης ἀπραγμοσύνης τὸ περιὸν ἀφειδήσας, ἐναγώνιος γίγνεται καὶ παρασκευάζεται πρὸς τὸν καταρτισμὸν τῆς ποίμνης. Καὶ δὴ τῷ μόνῳ πανσόφῳ καὶ δυνατῷ Θεῷ τῷ τοὺς ἀσθενεῖς περιζωννύοντι δύναμιν καὶ αὐτοὺς σοφοῦντι τοὺς τυφλοὺς τεθαρρηκώς, ἀναλαμβάνει *τὰ ὅπλα τοῦ φωτός*, τὰς γραφικάς, φημί, εἰσηγήσεις, καὶ καθίσταται ἐν μέσῳ τῆς ἱερᾶς ἐκείνης συγκλήτου οἷά τις ἐμπειροπόλεμος καὶ κραταιὸς ὑπερτίναξ· καὶ τῆς διδασκαλίας διαχειρισάμενος τὴν διαπρύσιον σάλπιγγα, ὑποφωνεῖ τοῖς συνασπισταῖς τὴν πρὸς τοὺς νοητοὺς δυσμενεῖς ἐπιστημονικὴν παράταξιν, "τόξα" τούτοις καὶ "δόρατα," "θυρεούς" τε καὶ "κράνη," καὶ "φωνὰς τροπαιοφόρων ἀλαλαγμῶν" διεσμιλευμένως ἐναρμοσάμενος.

2 Καὶ στερεοῖ οὕτω γε τὰς τούτων ψυχὰς κατὰ τῶν ἀφανῶν Μαδιηνέων καὶ δείκνυσιν αὐτοῖς τὸ ποῖα ποίοις, καὶ τίνα τίσι, καὶ πῶς καὶ πότε κεχρῆσθαι προσήκει τῶν ἐνθυμημάτων καὶ λογισμῶν, καὶ λόγων τε καὶ πράξεων, δι' ὧν σὺν Θεῷ δυνήσονται τῶν νοητῶν Ἀλλοφύλων τοὺς λόχους ὑπεκδραμεῖν καὶ τὰ κατ' αὐτῶν τῆς νίκης σύμβολα περιφανῶς ἀναστήσασθαι.

because of the destruction that comes upon the souls of a flock as a consequence of any ill-advised action.

II

Despite this, Theodore roused himself and, neglecting his beloved freedom from worldly occupations for a while, readied himself for combat and prepared to put the flock in order. Trusting in the only all-wise and mighty God who girds the weak with strength and makes the blind wise, he took up *the weapons of light,* namely scriptural admonitions, and stood in the midst of that holy gathering like a mighty and battle-hardened defender. Taking in hand the ringing trumpet of instruction, he outlined to his comrades-in-arms a skillful plan of battle to face their spiritual enemies, cleverly equipping them with "bows" and "spears," "shields" and "helmets," and "triumphant battle cries."

In this way he fortified their souls against the invisible 2
Midianites and showed them which arguments, reasoning, words, and actions it was fitting to use on what people; which on whom; and how and when, by which means, with God's help, they would be able to escape the ambushes of the spiritual Philistines and publicly raise the standards of victory over them.

3 Εἶχεν μὲν οὖν ὁ ἱερὸς πατὴρ ἡμῶν καὶ τὸν οἰκεῖον βίον ἀληθῶς σιωπῶσαν παραίνεσιν καὶ τὸ κατ' ἀμφοῖν δὲ κατάστημα τῶν ἠθῶν ἀξιόπιστον προὐβάλλετο πρέσβυν δυσωπῆσαι αὐτοὺς δυνάμενον πρὸς ἀνάληψιν τῶν ὑπὲρ ἀρετῆς πόνων. Ἀλλ' ἐπειδὴ πρὸς τῷ ἄγαν ἐξασκῆσαι σοφίαν θείαν τε καὶ ἀνθρωπίνην καὶ τὸ διδασκαλικὸν ἀπειλήφει παρὰ *τοῦ τῶν φώτων Πατρὸς* χάρισμα, πλήρης ἦν τῶν ἀεννάων ὑδάτων τοῦ Πνεύματος, ὅθεν συνεχῶς τὴν λογικὴν ἀνεστόμου τῆς διανοίας κρήνην, καὶ τὰ ῥεῖθρα τῆς ζωηφόρου ἐξέβλυζε διδασκαλίας· καὶ τὸν μὲν καταπιμπρᾶσθαι μέλλοντα τῇ πυριφλέκτῳ τῶν παθῶν καμίνῳ κατεδρόσιζέ τε καὶ ἀπετέφρου τοὺς τῆς ἡδονῆς ψυχοβλαβεῖς ἄνθρακας· τὸν δὲ νοσοῦντα κατὰ τὸν ἔνδον ἐκ πονηρῶν λογισμῶν ἄνθρωπον καὶ πρὸς τὸν τῆς ἁμαρτίας ὑπὸ τούτων ἐπειγόμενον θάνατον, ὥσπερ τις οὐράνιος ἀκέστωρ, ἐπισκεπτόμενος καὶ τὴν ἀλεξίκακον τῶν σωτηρίων λόγων ἐπιδιδοὺς τῷ κάμνοντι κύλικα, τῆς κατεχούσης λώβης παραδόξως ἀπήλαττεν.

4 Καὶ οὕτως ἀμφοτέρωθεν, πράξεως δὴ λέγω καὶ θεωρίας, ὠφέλιμος ἦν ὅτι <μάλιστα> τοῖς φοιτῶσι Θεόδωρος, πῇ μὲν ἰδίᾳ ἑκάστῳ πρὸς τὴν ἐξαγγελτικὴν ποιότητα καὶ τὰς ἀντιδόσεις ποιούμενος τοῖς κακοσίτοις, πῇ δὲ κατὰ κοινοῦ ἐπ' ἐκκλησίας μετὰ τὴν συμπλήρωσιν τῶν ἑωθινῶν ὕμνων πᾶσιν ὁμοῦ διαλεγόμενος τὰ συμφέροντα, καὶ τοῦτο τρὶς τῆς ἑβδομάδος τὸ πνευματικὸν τοῦ λόγου σιτηρέσιον ὡς εὐγνώμων ἐπίτροπος τοῖς συνδούλοις οἰκονομούμενος φόβῳ τε καὶ πόθῳ τῷ πρὸς τὸν κοινὸν Δεσπότην καὶ Σωτῆρα τῶν ὅλων Χριστόν. Ἀλλ' ἰτέον λοιπὸν τοῦ

Our holy father also truly maintained his own life as a silent exhortation, and he proffered his established behavior in both spheres as a trustworthy ambassador able to win them over to undertake hardships for the sake of virtue. But since, in addition to his mighty practice of asceticism, he had received divine and human wisdom and the gift of teaching from *the Father of lights,* he was filled with the everflowing waters of the Spirit, from which he would continually voice the spiritual serenity of his thinking and pour forth streams of life-bringing teaching. He would drench someone who was about to be burned up in the blazing furnace of the passions and reduce to ashes the smoldering coals of pleasure that destroy the soul. As for someone who was inwardly sick from evil thoughts and was consequently hastening to a sinful death, like a heavenly healer visiting the one who was troubled and administering the apotropaic cup of salvific words, he would miraculously rid him of the corruption that held him fast. 3

Theodore was thus helpful in both ways to those who resorted to him, I mean in action and in contemplation. He would concoct for each one individually, according to the nature of his confession, remedies for their deficiencies, whereas communally in church after the completion of the early-morning hymns he would preach what was profitable to all of them together. Three times a week he would dispense this spiritual nourishment of the word to his fellow servants, as a considerate guardian, in fear and in longing for Christ the common Master and Savior of all. But now, as 4

καιροῦ καλοῦντος ἡμᾶς ἐπὶ τὰ τῆς ἀθλήσεως σκάμματα τοῦ μεγάλου τούτου τῆς εὐσεβείας παγκρατιαστοῦ.

12

Κατ᾽ ἐκεῖνον τὸν καιρὸν ἐβασίλευσεν μονοκρατορήσας Κωνσταντῖνος ὁ τῆς φιλοχρίστου Εἰρήνης υἱός, ὅστις τὸ τῆς νεότητος ἀνειμένον τε καὶ ἀπαιδαγώγητον ἔχων καὶ *τοῖς τῆς* σαρκὸς *διαπύροις* ἡττηθεὶς *σκιρτήμασιν,* ἀθετήσας τὴν πρότερον αὐτῷ κατὰ νόμους γεγαμημένην καὶ ταύτην ἀποκαρθῆναι βεβιασμένως ποιήσας, ἑτέραν μοιχικῷ τρόπῳ κατὰ τὸν πάλαι Ἡρῴδην ἀνυποστόλως ἠγάγετο, ἧς τὸ ὄνομα Θεοδότη, σκάνδαλον παρεισάξας ὁ δείλαιος μέγιστον, οὐ μόνον τῇ τοῦ Θεοῦ Ἐκκλησίᾳ, ἀλλὰ καὶ πᾶσι τοῖς τῶν ἐθνῶν ἀρχηγοῖς καὶ τοπάρχαις. Ὁ μὲν γὰρ θεῖος πατριάρχης Ταράσιος, τὸ τοιοῦτον ἀπευδοκῶν συνοικέσιον, τὴν εἰς αὐτοὺς στεφανικὴν ἀποστρέφεται χειροθεσίαν, τῷ παρανόμῳ τῆς μείξεως οὐ συναινῶν ἐνεργήματι· *ψυχαῖς* γὰρ *βεβήλοις ἀσυναφὴς ὁ Χριστός,* ὥς πού τις ἔφη τῶν πρὸ ἡμῶν ἁγίων.

2 Ἰωσὴφ δέ τις πρεσβύτερος καὶ οἰκονόμος τυγχάνων τῆς αὐτῆς ἁγιωτάτης Μεγάλης Ἐκκλησίας, τῶν μοιχωμένων τε συνήθης ὤν, ἀναδέχεται τολμηρῶς τὸ ἐγχείρημα καὶ στεφανοῖ τοὺς ἀθέσμους, ἔξω θεσμῶν ἀποσκιρτήσας θείων καὶ ἀνθρωπίνων. Καὶ γίνεται προβολὴ τοῦ τοιούτου

time is calling, we must move on to the wrestling grounds of this great pancratiast's contest for right belief.

12

At that time Constantine, the son of the Christ-loving Irene, was emperor and sole ruler. As a result of his easygoing and undisciplined youth he had been overcome by *the fiery surges* of the flesh and had repudiated his previous lawfully married wife. He forced her to be tonsured and, like Herod in the past, openly took up with another woman, named Theodote, in an adulterous manner. The wretched man thus introduced a very great scandal, not only into the Church of God, but also among all the leaders and chieftains of the nations. For the godly patriarch Tarasios, who disapproved of such cohabitation, refused to marry them, not consenting to their unlawful sexual intercourse, for *Christ is not united to profane souls,* as one of the holy men before our time declared somewhere.

But a certain Joseph, who was a priest and steward of the 2
same most holy Great Church and well acquainted with the adulterers, boldly assented to the undertaking and, transgressing divine and human laws, married the unlawful couple. And it became a pretext for this sort of evil, not only in

κακοῦ, οὐ μόνον ἐπὶ τῆς βασιλευούσης, ἀλλὰ καὶ ἐπὶ ταῖς ἐξωτάτω χώραις· οὕτω γὰρ ὁ τῆς Λογγιβαρδίας ῥήξ, οὕτως ὁ τῆς Γοτθίας, οὕτως ὁ τῆς Βοσπόρου τοπάρχης, τῇ λύσει ταύτης τῆς ἐντολῆς ἐπερειδόμενοι, μοιχικαῖς ὀρέξεσι καὶ ἀκράτοις ἐπιθυμίαις ἑαυτοὺς περιέπειραν, τὴν τοῦ βασιλέως Ῥωμαίων πρᾶξιν εὐπροφάσιστον ἔχοντες ἀπολογίαν, ὡς ἐκείνου μὲν τῷ αὐτῷ περιπεσόντος, ἀποδεδεγμένου δὲ παρά τε τοῦ πατριάρχου καὶ τῶν σὺν αὐτῷ ἀρχιερέων.

3 Ταῦτα οὖν τὰ παράνομα διαγνοὺς ὁ κατὰ Χριστὸν Ἰησοῦν χαρακτηριζόμενος ἄνθρωπος, καὶ *πᾶσαν* ὡς δυνατὸν ἑκάστοτε *δικαιοσύνην* προφανῶς *ἀποπληρῶν*, τοῦ τε ὁμοφύλου γένους πατρικοῖς προμηθούμενος σπλάγχνοις, ἠνιᾶτο, ἐδυσφόρει καθ' ἑαυτόν, τὴν ἁπάντων ὁμοῦ ἀπωδύρετο ἀπώλειαν, τῶν τε νῦν καὶ τῶν μετὰ ταῦτα· ἐδεδίει γὰρ εἰκότως μήπως εἰς νόμον τοῖς ἀνοήτοις ἡ τοῦ κρατοῦντος ἀλογιστία παραδεχθεῖσα, ἀνίατον παραπέμψῃ ταῖς ὕστερον γενεαῖς τὸ πρακτέον. Διά τοι τοῦτο οὐ παρασιωπᾷ τοῦ μὴ ἐλέγξαι τὸ πῆμα, ἀλλ' ἀπορρήγνυσιν ἑαυτὸν σὺν τῷ ἰδίῳ πατρὶ τῆς ἐκείνων εὐθὺς κοινωνίας· ἀκουστὴ δὲ γίνεται ἡ κατὰ Θεὸν αὐτῶν τῆς μοιχείας ἀποστροφὴ εἰς τὰ τοῦ βασιλέως ὦτα.

4 Ὁ δὲ πρῶτα μὲν ἐπιεικεύεται οὐκ ἀγανακτῶν πρὸς τὸ κακόφημον, καὶ δι' ἑτέρων τοῦτο μαθὼν καὶ ὑπ' αὐτῆς τῆς μοιχαλίδος, τρόπον τινὰ κατεπτηχὼς τὴν τῶν μακαρίων διάζευξιν, ὡς τὸ ἀσύγκριτον ἐχόντων καὶ περίβλεπτον ἐν τῇ τῶν μοναχῶν πολιτείᾳ. Ἔπειτα δὲ κινεῖται παντοίως

the capital, but also in countries very far away. So the king of Longibardia, so the king of the Goths, so the governor of Bosporos, relying on the relaxation of this commandment, entangled themselves in adulterous appetites and intemperate desires, considering the conduct of the Roman emperor a plausible excuse, since he had been caught in the same situation but had been accepted both by the patriarch and his bishops.

When Theodore, a man who used to model himself on 3
Christ Jesus, clearly *fulfilling all righteousness* to the best of his ability on every occasion and caring for his own family with fatherly compassion, became aware of those illegalities, he was distressed. He was privately angry and at the same time bitterly lamented the perdition of everyone, both at that time and in the future, for he feared (with good reason) that the ruler's lack of judgment, if it were accepted as legal by the unintelligent, would pass on to later generations an action that was irremediable. For this reason, he would not stop criticizing the calamitous event, but, along with his own spiritual father, at once cut himself off from communion with that group; and their godly rejection of the adultery reached the emperor's ears.

At first Constantine showed forbearance, not becoming 4
annoyed by the criticism when he learned of it through others and from the adulteress herself, and stopping some way short of a rift with the blessed men, since they were incomparable and distinguished in the monastic way of life. But

μηχανώμενος τοὺς ἀχειρώτους χειρώσασθαι εἰς τὸ συνθέσθαι τῷ κατ' αὐτὸν μύσει, μάλιστα τοῦτ' ἐλπίσας, διὰ τὸ συγγενίδα αὐτῶν εἶναι τὴν εἰς τὰ βασίλεια προσειλημμένην. Ὅθεν καὶ προετρέψατο αὐτὴν χρυσίον αὐτοῖς ἀποστεῖλαι, μετὰ τῆς ἑπομένης ἐξ αὐτῶν προσκυνήσεως. Ὡς δὲ ἐψεύσθη τῆς ἐλπίδος, ἀνωτέρους αἰσθηθεὶς τῆς ἑαυτοῦ κολακείας τοὺς θεοφόρους, ἑτεροίως τὴν πρὸς αὐτοὺς ἐπιτηδεύει πάλην. Προσποιησάμενος γὰρ τὴν τῶν αὐτομάτως γῆθεν ἀναδιδομένων θερμῶν ἀπόλαυσιν, τὴν εἰς Προῦσαν ποιεῖται ἄφιξιν ἀνακτορικήν, οἰηθεὶς ὡς πάντως ἐλεύσονται πρὸς αὐτὸν οἱ ἀοίδιμοι, τὴν ἐξ ἔθους μετὰ τῶν ἄλλων ἀπονεμοῦντες προσκύνησιν. Ἐπεὶ δὲ τῶν δοκηθέντων αὐτῷ οὐδὲν εἰς πέρας ἀπέβη, θυμαίνεται μὲν κατὰ φρένα, παλινοστεῖ δὲ ὡς τάχιστα εἰς τὰ βασίλεια, μεγάλα φυσῶν κατὰ τῶν ἀθώων.

5 Καὶ δὴ μεταπεμψάμενος τὸν ἐπὶ τῶν Σχολῶν Δομέστικον, ἀποστέλλει σὺν αὐτῷ καὶ τὸν στρατηγὸν τοῦ Ὀψικίου πρὸς τοὺς ὁσίους, τὰ τῆς κακώσεως ἐνεργήσοντας. Οἵτινες καταλαβόντες τὸ μοναστήριον, μαστίζουσι μὲν βουνεύροις εἰς κόρον τὸν ἀεὶ τοῦτο διὰ Χριστὸν διψῶντα Θεόδωρον, καὶ ἑτέρους τρεῖς τῶν τὰ πρῶτα φερόντων ἀδελφῶν. Ἐξορίζουσι δ' αὐτὸν σὺν ἄλλοις δέκα τῶν ἐπισημοτάτων τῆς ἀδελφότητος ἐν Θεσσαλονίκῃ, προστάξαντες τοῖς ἀπάγουσιν αὐτοὺς ἐγκεκλεισμένους παραφυλάττειν ἀσφαλῶς, οὐχ ἅμα πάντας καὶ κατὰ τὸ αὐτό, ἀλλ' ἀνὰ μέρος ἕκαστον καὶ ἀποστάδην ἀλλήλων ἐν διαφόροις οἰκίσκοις, πρὸς τὸ μὴ ἐξεῖναι τὸν τυχόντα πρὸς τὸν ἕτερον ἀπελθεῖν. Τὸν μέντοι μακάριον Πλάτωνα ἐν τῇ τοῦ ἁγίου

then he made a move, contriving in every way to force the uncompromising pair (Plato and Theodore) to assent to his personal defilement. He hoped especially for this, since the woman who had been admitted to the palace was their kinswoman. For this reason, Constantine persuaded her to send them some gold, in the expectation that obeisance from them would follow. But when he was disappointed in his hope, he realized that the divinely inspired men were above this flattery and pursued the battle against them in another way. On the pretext of seeking relaxation in the geothermal baths, he organized an imperial visit to Prousa, thinking that the famous Plato and Theodore would certainly come to him to render the customary obeisance along with others. But when none of his expectations were fulfilled, he became enraged and returned as quickly as possible to the palace, engorged with anger against the innocent men.

Constantine sent for the Domestic of the Schools and 5
dispatched him, along with the military governor of Opsikion, to the saintly men to mistreat them. When they reached the monastery, they flogged Theodore, who for the sake of Christ had always been thirsting for this treatment, with ox tendon whips until they were satisfied; they also flogged three others of the leading brethren. Then they banished him, along with ten others from among the most notable of the brotherhood, to Thessalonike. They ordered their escorts to keep them securely confined, not all together in the same place but each separately and apart from each other in different dwellings so that there was no opportunity for them to visit one another. The blessed Plato,

Σεργίου μονῇ ἐκπέμπουσιν, ἀπρόϊτον καὶ αὐτὸν ἐκεῖσε μένειν ἐγκελευσάμενοι.

13

Ἀλλ' οἷον καὶ ὅσον κατόρθωμα τῇ οἰκουμένῃ πάσῃ ὁ τοῦ θεοφόρου πατρὸς ἡμῶν ἐκτετέλεκεν ἄεθλος ἔξεστιν εὐθὺς συνιδεῖν. Οἱ γὰρ ἐν τοῖς κλίμασι τῆς κατὰ Χερσῶνα καὶ Βόσπορον παροικίας ἐπίσκοποι καὶ πρεσβύτεροι, πρὸς δὲ καὶ τῶν μοναστῶν οἱ θεοειδέστεροι, τὴν τοῦ θείου πατρὸς ἡμῶν ἐπακούσαντες πρᾶξιν, καὶ συνηγοροῦσαν εὑρηκότες τοῖς θείοις Εὐαγγελίοις, ζηλοῦσιν ἐν καλῷ τὴν αὐτοῦ παρρησίαν, ὡς πληροῦσθαι κἀνθάδε τὸ *ὁ ζῆλος ὑμῶν ἠρέθισε τοὺς πλείονας* εἰς τὸ ἀγαθόν. Καὶ πάραυτα μὲν ἀπρόσδεκτα τίθενται τὰ προσφερόμενα δῶρα τῶν τὰ αὐτὰ τῷ νεωτέρῳ Κωνσταντίνῳ πραξαμένων ταῖς τοῦ Θεοῦ Ἐκκλησίαις· ἀφορίζουσι δ' αὐτοὺς καὶ τῶν σεπτῶν καὶ ἀχράντων τοῦ Χριστοῦ μυστηρίων. Λέγουσι καὶ αὐτοὶ συνῳδὰ τῷ ἱερόφρονι Θεοδώρῳ πρὸς τοὺς φαυλίσαντας τὴν Χριστιανικωτάτην παράδοσιν· "Οὐκ ἔξεστιν ὑμῖν ἔχειν γυναῖκας παρὰ τοὺς τεθέντας Χριστόθεν νόμους·" τέλος, ἀπελαύνονται καὶ αὐτοὶ τῶν ἰδίων ἐκκλησιῶν καὶ κατασκηνώσεων, καὶ τἄλλα δὲ πάσχουσιν, ὅσα τοῖς δρῶσίν ἐστιν καταθύμια, *θυμοῦ* στρατηγοῦντος μάλιστα, *τοῦ δεινοῦ ὁπλίτου,* καὶ χειρὸς βιαίας ἐπιτιθεμένης.

however, they sent away to the monastery of holy Sergios, with orders to keep him confined there.

13

But one can immediately see the nature and magnitude of the achievement that the opposition of our divinely inspired father Theodore accomplished for the whole world. For when the bishops and priests in the regions of the diocese of Cherson and Cimmerian Bosporos, as well as the most godlike of the monks, heard of our godly father's action and found that it corresponded to the divine Gospels, they rightly and zealously imitated his freedom of speech so that there too the statement, *your zeal roused most of them* to what is good, was fulfilled. They immediately declared that the donations offered to the churches of God by those who had behaved like the young Constantine were unacceptable; moreover, they excommunicated them from the sacred and undefiled mysteries of Christ. They also issued a statement in agreement with holy-minded Theodore to those who had debased the most Christian tradition: "You cannot have wives contrary to the laws laid down by Christ." In the end, they too were expelled from their own churches and dwellings and suffered whatever else those who did this had in mind, especially since *anger, the fearsome hoplite,* took the lead and a violent hand was laid upon them.

2 Ἐκ δὴ τούτου φόβος ἐπιπίπτει καθ' ὅλην μικροῦ τὴν ὑπὸ τῶν Ῥωμαίων ἀρχὴν ἐπὶ τοὺς τὰ τοιαῦτα πράσσοντας, καὶ γίνεται τοῖς ἀκολασταίνουσι κημὸς ὁ τῶν εὐσεβῶν διωγμός· καὶ ἀναστέλλεται ταύτῃ τοι ἡ τοῦ κακοῦ τοῦδε φορὰ τοῦ μὴ πρόσω προβαίνειν. *Τὰ γὰρ ἀνεπίπληκτα τῶν παθῶν ἕρπει μὲν ἀεὶ πρὸς τὸ αἴσχιον, ὡς ἔχις, καταδράττεται δὲ καρδίας καὶ νοῦ καὶ εἰς ὄλισθον ἄγει παντελῆ τὸν ἁλόντα.* Ὅπερ ἵνα μὴ γένηται, ἐν τοῖς προειρημένοις ἀθληταῖς ἡ χάρις τοῦ παναγίου ἐκλάμψασα Πνεύματος, ἤλεγξεν ἀναφανδὸν τῆς παρανομίας τὸ ἔργον, καὶ οὕτω μᾶλλον ὁ μέγας Θεόδωρος διαβοητότερος καθίσταται, μιμητὴς τοῦ Προδρόμου δεικνύμενος καὶ Ἠλιοῦ τοῦ Θεσβίτου, οὐ μόνον ἐν τοῖς περιοίκοις, ἀλλὰ καὶ πανταχοῦ τῆς οἰκουμένης. Ἐν γὰρ τῇ Θεσσαλονικέων τὸν ἅπαντα χρόνον τῆς Κωνσταντίνου βασιλείας περιφρουρούμενος πόλει, εἰς τὰς ἐξωτάτω χώρας τὰ τῶν ἰδίων κατορθωμάτων ἀπέπεμπε προσρήματα.

3 Γεγράφηκε δὲ καὶ τῷ πάπᾳ τῆς πρεσβυτέρας Ῥώμης, δι' οἰκείων αὐτοῦ μαθητῶν δῆλα ταῦτα καταστησάμενος, καὶ ἀπεδέχθη παρ' αὐτοῦ μεγάλως ὡς μὴ ὑποστειλάμενος ἀναγγεῖλαι τὰ φίλα Θεῷ· παρ' οὗ καὶ ἀντίγραφα ἐδέξατο καταγεραίροντα αὐτοῦ τὴν ὑπὲρ τοῦ καλοῦ ἔνστασίν τε καὶ ἄθλησιν, ὡς ἐξισουμένην τῇ τοῦ θείου Προδρόμου ἀξιοπρεπῶς παρρησίᾳ. Ἀλλ' ἐπειδή, φησὶν ἡ Γραφή, "*Βασιλεὺς θρασὺς ἐμπεσεῖται εἰς κακὰ*" καὶ "*αἱ ὁδοὶ τῶν ἀνόμων σκοτειναί, οὐκ οἴδασι πῶς προσκόπτουσιν,*" οὐ μετὰ πολὺν χρόνον ἐπανάστασιν πρὸς τοῦ ἰδίου ὑποστὰς στρατεύματος ὁ Κωνσταντῖνος, ἀπορφανίζεται μὲν ἀμφοτέρων τῶν

Consequently, across almost the whole Roman empire, 2
fear assailed those who were acting in this way and persecution by the devout became a restraint on the licentious; in that way the headlong rush of this evil was checked from going any further. *For passionate behavior that goes unpunished always slithers on* like a viper *to greater disgrace and, laying hold of heart and mind, leads the person who is caught to total perdition.* So that this would not happen, the grace of the all-holy Spirit shone out in the previously mentioned combatants and openly reproved the lawless deed. Thus, the great Theodore became even more renowned, proving himself an imitator of John the Forerunner and of Elijah the Tishbite not only among neighboring people but everywhere in the world. For, although he was closely guarded in Thessalonike during Constantine's entire reign, he continued dispatching news of his own achievements to the most distant regions.

Theodore also wrote to the pope of old Rome, clearly set- 3
ting down these matters through his own disciples, and was firmly approved of by him as someone who did not shrink from proclaiming what was dear to God. From him he also received a reply, honoring his constancy and struggle on behalf of the good as a worthy rival to the bold speech of the divine Forerunner. But since, as Scripture says, "*An arrogant king falls into evil deeds*" and "*the ways of the* lawless *are dark, they do not know how it is they stumble,*" a short time later Constantine succumbed to an insurrection by his own army, was

ὀφθαλμῶν, ἐκρίπτεται δὲ καὶ αὐτῆς τῆς βασιλείας, ὥσπερ τι φορτίον εἰδεχθὲς καὶ δυσβάστακτον· καὶ ἀνίσταται πάλιν ἡ τούτου μήτηρ καὶ Χριστοφιλὴς Εἰρήνη, ἣν ἐκεῖνος πρώην ἀσωτότατα διαπραττόμενος, τῶν βασιλικῶν ἀλλοτρίαν ἀπέφηνεν ἐνδιαιτημάτων.

14

Αὕτη οὖν ἡ θεοφιλεστάτη ἄνθρωπος ἅμα τῷ ἐπειλῆφθαι τὰ τῆς βασιλείας πηδάλια ἀνακαλεῖται μὲν τῆς ἐξορίας τὸν μέγαν Θεόδωρον, ποιεῖ δὲ αὐτὸν ἑνωθῆναι τῷ ἁγιωτάτῳ πατριάρχῃ Ταρασίῳ, τοῦ Ἰωσὴφ μετὰ τὴν ἐκβολὴν Κωνσταντίνου τῆς ἱερατικῆς ἀπογυμνωθέντος ἀξίας, καλῶς πεπραχέναι λέγουσα καὶ θεαρέστως τοὺς ἀμφοτέρους, τὸν μὲν ὡς τῶν Εὐαγγελικῶν δογμάτων μέχρις αἵματος καὶ ποινῶν ἀναφανέντα συνίστορα, καὶ διὰ τούτου τοῖς μεταγενεστέροις τὴν καθαρὰν πραγματευσάμενον τῶν ψυχῶν σωτηρίαν, τὸν δὲ ὡς οἰκονομήσαντα συμφερόντως καὶ τοῦ οἰστροῦντος ἄνακτος τὴν κακότροπον ἐκμοχλεύσαντα γνώμην τὰ χείρω τῶν πρὸ αὐτοῦ βεβασιλευκότων ἐπαπειλοῦντος ποιήσειν εἰς τὴν τοῦ Χριστοῦ Ἐκκλησίαν, εἰ τῶν κατὰ νοῦν ἀποπέσοιεν.

2 Ταῦτα δὲ καὶ ὁ θεῖος Ταράσιος ἐβεβαίωσε, συναφθεὶς τῷ καθ’ ἡμᾶς πατρί, ὡς ἀνεγράψατο αὐτὸς οὗτος ὁ ἀθλητὴς τοῦ Σωτῆρος Θεόδωρος· οἷς καὶ ἡμεῖς στοιχήσωμεν

deprived of both eyes, and was ejected from the imperial rule itself, like a repulsive burden that is hard to bear. Once again, his mother, the Christ-loving Irene, was restored, whom he, in an outrageous action, had previously excluded from her imperial living quarters.

14

As soon as this woman, the most beloved of God, took the helm of imperial power, she recalled the great Theodore from exile and brought about his communion with the most holy patriarch Tarasios, since Joseph had been stripped of his priestly rank after the expulsion of Constantine. She said that both of them had acted nobly and in a manner pleasing to God: Theodore because he had proved himself as an advocate of the Gospel ordinances to the point of enduring bloodshed and punishments and because of this had secured for posterity the pure salvation of souls; Tarasios because he had made an expedient dispensation and had thwarted the malicious aims of the enraged ruler when the latter was threatening to inflict more harm on the Church of Christ than had his imperial predecessors, if they failed to implement his wishes.

These things the godly Tarasios also confirmed when he 2
joined forces with our father, as Theodore himself, this combatant of the Savior, recorded. Let us too conform to them

καὶ μηδέτερον μέρος κακίσωμεν, ἀλλ' ἑκατέρους ἀποδεχόμενοι ταῖς Εὐαγγελικαῖς φωναῖς πειθαρχεῖν εἰσέτι μὴ παραιτησώμεθα. Τὰ γὰρ οἰκονομικῶς γινόμενα, οὐ νόμος, ἀλλ' οὐδὲ πάντη τὸ ἄψεκτον κέκτηνται, ἐπεὶ καὶ Παῦλος ᾠκονόμησε περιτεμὼν τὸν Τιμόθεον, καὶ οὐκ εἰς νόμου τάξιν τοῦτό γε κεκράτηκεν· αὐτὸς γὰρ καὶ ταύτην ἀνέτρεψεν, διωλύγιον ἐκβοῶν, "*Εἰ περιτομὴν κηρύσσω, τί ἔτι διώκομαι;*" Τοίνυν πνευματικῆς εὐφροσύνης συναπολαύσας τῷ πανιέρῳ Ταρασίῳ ὁ πατὴρ ἡμῶν Θεόδωρος, ἔξεισιν εἰς τὸ κατ' αὐτὸν φροντιστήριον, καὶ συντρέχουσιν ἐπὶ τὸ αὐτὸ ἔνθεν κἀκεῖθεν τὰ διασκορπισθέντα τῇ αὐτοῦ ἀπουσίᾳ πρόβατα.

3 Ἀνεῖται δὲ τῆς φρουρᾶς καὶ ὁ τῶν πατέρων πατὴρ Πλάτων, ὁ ὁσιώτατος καὶ ἀρχιτέκτων πεφηνὼς ταύτης τῆς θεοσυστάτου τῶν ἀδελφῶν ἱερᾶς σκηνοπηγίας, καὶ συναγείρεται πλεῖστος ὅμιλος ὡς αὐτοὺς ἔκ τε τῶν πέλας καὶ τῶν πόρρωθεν, οἷά τινας προμάχους γενναιοτάτους ἀπὸ τῆς ὑπὲρ εὐσεβείας πολεμικῆς ἐπανελθόντας θεάσασθαι παρατάξεως. Διαφημίζεται δὲ κατὰ τὸ μᾶλλον ἔτι ἡ τοῦ Σακκουδίωνος προσηγορία, καὶ Θεόδωρος ἐν τοῖς ἁπάντων ἐμεγαλύνετο στόμασιν, καὶ τὸ ἔργον αὐτοῦ τῆς διὰ Θεὸν ὑπερορίας εἰς πᾶσαν διατρέχει τὴν ὑπ' οὐρανόν, καὶ διδάσκει πάντας ὁμοῦ τοῖς Εὐαγγελικοῖς ἕπεσθαι παραγγέλμασιν· τὸν μὲν ἄνδρα μιᾶς εἶναι γυναικὸς κύριον, τοῦ θείου λόγου θεσπίσαντος, ὡσαύτως δὲ καὶ τὴν γυναῖκα ἑνὸς ἀνδρὸς σύνοικον, καὶ ταῦτα ἐννόμως, ἀλλ' οὐ νόθῳ τινὶ καὶ μοιχικῷ συνοικεσίῳ· *πορνεία γὰρ καὶ τὰ σαρκὸς*

and not reproach either side but, accepting both, never refrain from obeying the Gospel precepts. For things that come to pass by way of dispensation are not law, nor are they completely free from blame either, since even Paul made an accommodation by circumcising Timothy, and that, at any rate, has not been raised to the status of a law, for he himself also overturned this, saying loud and clear, "*If I preach circumcision, why am I still persecuted?*" So then, after our father Theodore had happily joined all-holy Tarasios in spiritual gladness, he went off to his monastery and the sheep that had been scattered in his absence came running together from all directions.

Plato, the father of fathers, the most saintly master 3
builder of this holy tabernacle of brethren established by God, was also released from prison and a very numerous company joined them from far and wide, in order to see the return of the most noble champions from the battle for piety. The name of Sakkoudion was spread abroad even more and Theodore was extolled on everyone's lips. News of what he had done by being banished for the sake of God traveled everywhere under the heavens and taught all alike to follow the Gospel precepts: that a man should be the husband of one wife as the word of God had decreed, and in just the same way a woman should be the wife of one man, and that lawfully, and not in some illegitimate and adulterous cohabi-

πάθη κατακιβδηλεύει μὲν τὸν ἄνθρωπον, τῆς πρὸς Θεὸν δὲ συναφείας προδήλως ἐξίστησιν.

4 Ἐκ δὴ τούτου πολλοὶ τῆς μεγαλωνύμου πόλεως οἰκήτορες, καὶ μέντοι καὶ τῶν ἐξωτέρων πολιχνῶν καὶ ἀστυγειτόνων ἄνδρες, οὐ μόνον τῶν ἡμετέρων ἀλλὰ καὶ τῆς ἀπὸ τῶν ἔξωθεν ὁρμωμένων παιδείας ἐπισημότατοι, πρὸς τὸν μέγαν τοῦτον συνερρύησαν παιδοτρίβην, μοναχικῆς πολιτείας τε καὶ φιλοσοφίας ἐν πείρᾳ γενέσθαι προθέμενοι. Οὓς ὁ θεῖος τῆς εὐσεβείας διδάσκαλος ἀσμένως ὑποδεχόμενος, τοῖς τῆς ἐμπράκτου σοφίας αὐτοῦ κατήρδευε νάμασι, τὸν ἐντετηγμένον ταῖς ψυχαῖς αὐτῶν ἐξ ἁμαρτίας ἀποκαθαίρων μολυσμόν, καὶ πρὸς ὁσιότητος καὶ δικαιοσύνης ὁδὸν τὰ κατὰ Θεὸν αὐτῶν καταρτίζων διαβήματα.

15

Ἀλλὰ τῶν ἀθέων Ἀγαρηνῶν κατὰ τοῦτο τοῦ καιροῦ τὴν καθύπερθεν παροικίαν ληϊσαμένων καὶ φόβον θανάτου ταῖς τῶν πλησιοχώρων ἐντεκόντων ψυχαῖς, ἀναγκαῖον ἐφάνη τοῖς πατράσιν τὰ τοῦ καιροῦ δρᾶσαι συμφερόντως καὶ τὴν βασιλεύουσαν πόλιν μὴ κατοκνῆσαι καταλαβεῖν. Ὃ καὶ διὰ τάχους ποιήσαντες, ὑπεδέχθησαν φιλοφρόνως παρά τε τῷ θεσπεσίῳ ἀρχιερεῖ Ταρασίῳ καὶ τῇ εὐσεβεστάτῃ Αὐγούστῃ· ὑφ᾽ ὧν καὶ προτραπέντες λιπαρῶς, τὴν εὐαγεστάτην μονὴν τοῦ Στουδίου, πάλαι πρὸς αὐτοῦ

tation; for *fornication and the passions of the flesh debase people and* manifestly separate them *from union with God.*

As a consequence, many inhabitants of the renowned city, as well as men from the outlying towns and suburbs, men who were most notable not only for their spiritual but also their secular education, flocked to this great instructor, eager to have an experience of the monastic way and approach to life. The godly teacher of piety gladly received them and watered them with the streams of his efficacious wisdom, cleansing the defilement deeply ingrained in their souls by sin and equipping them to walk in a godly manner on the road of sanctity and righteousness. 4

15

But since at that time the godless Agarenes had plundered the northern parts of the province and engendered fear of death in the souls of those in the neighboring regions, the fathers thought they should act with expediency in the circumstances and move to the imperial city without delay. They quickly did so and were received in a kindly way both by the holy patriarch Tarasios and by the most pious Augusta. At their earnest entreaty they took over the most sacred monastery of Stoudios, which had been built long

οἰκοδομηθεῖσαν καὶ ἐνδιαίτημα ὁσίων ἀνδρῶν γεγονυῖαν, ὁ Κοπρώνυμος Κωνσταντῖνος οὐδ' εἰς δέκα τὸν ἀριθμὸν ἐάσας τούτους ἔσεσθαι, παραλαμβάνουσιν, ἱκανὴν οὖσαν πρὸς ὑποδοχὴν τῆς πολυανθρώπου ἐκείνης τῶν Ναζιραίων πληθύος.

2 Ἔδει γὰρ ἔδει τὸν τοῦ μεγάλου Προδρόμου μιμητὴν ἀναφανέντα καὶ τὴν νόσον τῆς μοιχείας ἐκφάνδην ἀποκηρύξαντα τῷ ἐπωνύμῳ αὐτοῦ κατοικισθῆναι ναῷ, καὶ τοῦτον οὐρανὸν ἐπίγειον ταῖς ἀπαύστοις ἀποφῆναι πρὸς τὴν Τριάδα δοξολογίαις. Καὶ τίς γὰρ τὰς ἐνταῦθα τοῦ πατρὸς ἀγγελομιμήτους καταστάσεις καὶ κοινωφελεῖς διατυπώσεις κατὰ λόγον εἰπεῖν ἐξισχύσειεν; Ἃς ἐκεῖνος τοῖς πανταχόθεν ὡς αὐτὸν ἀφικνουμένοις παρεδίδου τε καὶ ἐδίδασκεν, πρὸς μίαν ἐνάγων τὴν τῶν πολλῶν φρονημάτων τοῦ Εὐαγγελίου σύμπνοιαν *καθ' ὅτι φίλον ἀεὶ παντὶ τὸ ὅμοιον.* Οὐ γὰρ μόνον τοὺς ἄρτι τῆς κοσμικῆς ἀποφοιτῶντας παρελάμβανεν χλιδῆς, ἀλλὰ καὶ τοὺς ἤδη γεγυμνασμένους τοῖς τῆς ἀσκήσεως πόνοις τῇ ὑπ' αὐτὸν προσιόντας κατέταττεν ὁμηγύρει, τὸ τοῦ Κυρίου πληρῶν λόγιον τὸ φάσκον, "*Τὸν ἐρχόμενον πρός με οὐ μὴ ἐκβάλω ἔξω·*" μὴ προτιμῶν τὸν ὑπ' αὐτοῦ κεκαρμένον ποτὲ τοῦ ὑφ' ἑτέρου τοῦτο παθόντος, καθάπερ οἱ πολλοὶ τῶν ἀνθρώπων ἀφιλοσόφως ποιοῦσιν ἰδίοις πάθεσι ψυχῆς δουλούμενοι, ἀλλὰ τοὺς πάντας ἐπ' ἴσης ἀγαπῶν καὶ προμηθούμενος, καὶ πρὸς τὴν ἀρετὴν ἑκάστου τὴν τιμὴν καὶ τὸ γέρας ἀποδιδούς, ὡς ἐκ τούτου πληθυνθῆναι τὸν ἀριθμὸν τῶν μαθητῶν ἐν ταύτῃ τῇ νέᾳ Ἱερουσαλὴμ σφόδρα καὶ μικροῦ τὸν χιλιοστὸν ἐπιφθάσαι ψῆφον. Οὓς δὴ καὶ καθορῶν

before by him and had become a dwelling place of saintly men. It was large enough to receive that numerous throng of Nazirites, even though Constantine Kopronymos had limited its numbers to less than ten.

It was destined that he who had proved to be an imitator 2
of the great Forerunner and had publicly denounced the sickness of adultery should dwell in the shrine named after him and that it would prove to be a heaven on earth with unceasing praise to the Trinity. For who could describe in detail Father Theodore's institutions that imitate the angels and his rules for the common benefit? These he would impart and teach there to those who came to him from all directions, bringing together as one the consensus of the Gospel's many tenets, *because similarity is always dear to everyone.* For not only would he take in those who had recently left behind worldly luxury, but would also integrate into his company those who came already trained in ascetic hardships, fulfilling the Lord's words, "*He who comes to me I will not cast out.*" He never preferred those he had tonsured himself over those who had been tonsured by someone else, as most people unwisely do, being slaves of their soul's passions; but loving them all equally and providing for them, he gave honor and reward to each man's virtue. Consequently, the number of disciples increased greatly in this new Jerusalem and almost reached the tally of a thousand. Observing

προθυμίᾳ ψυχῆς τὸν ζυγὸν τοῦ Χριστοῦ πειθηνίως ὑπερχομένους, διατίθεται καὶ αὐτὸς κατὰ τὸν ὑψηλὸν Μωϋσέα καὶ δημαγωγεῖ τὸν λαὸν τοῦ Θεοῦ σοφίας λόγοις καὶ ἠθῶν καθαρότητι, πρὸς τὴν νοητὴν ὡς ἄριστα χειραγωγῶν τῆς ἐπαγγελίας κατάπαυσιν. Καὶ γὰρ *ἀρετὴν μέν*, φασί, *νομοθέτου, τὸ τὰ βέλτιστα συνιδεῖν καὶ πεῖσαι τοὺς χρησομένους περὶ τῶν ὑπ' αὐτῶν συντεθειμένων, πλήθους δέ, τὸ πᾶσι τοῖς δόξασιν ἐμμεῖναι καὶ μήτ' ἐν εὐτυχίαις μήτ' ἐν συμφοραῖς αὐτῶν μηδὲν μεταβάλλειν·* ὅπερ ἐστὶ Θεοῦ θεραπείας τρόπος ὁσιώτατος.

3 Τοιγαροῦν καθίσταται νομοθέτης ἐπ' αὐτοὺς ἐξαπλῶν τὰ θεοπαράδοτα κρίματα, ἅπερ αὐτός, πρὸς τὸ ὄρος ἀναβὰς τῆς ὑψηλῆς πολιτείας καὶ τῷ γνόφῳ ὑπεισδὺς τῆς θείας καὶ μακαρίας γνώσεως, πρὸς Θεοῦ ἀπειλήφει ὡς ἔν τισι *πλαξὶ λιθίναις*, τοῖς τῆς ἑαυτοῦ στερροτάτης καρδίας πυξίοις, τῷ τοῦ Πνεύματος ἐνσημανθέντα *δακτύλῳ*. Καὶ ὥσπερ ὁ θεόπτης ἐκεῖνος τῷ κηδεστῇ συμβουλεύσαντι πειθαρχήσας, προὐβάλλετο *χιλιάρχους καὶ ἑκατοντάρχους καὶ πεντηκοντάρχους καὶ δεκάρχους*, οἷς τὰ τυχόντα τῶν πραγμάτων ἀναφερόμενα δεξιόν τε ἐλάμβανεν τέλος, καὶ αὐτὸς τῆς ἐντεῦθεν ἀπηλλάσσετο φροντίδος, οὕτω δὴ καὶ ὁ καθ' ἡμᾶς Μωσῆς ποιεῖ, λαβὼν ἐκεῖθεν τὰς ἀφορμάς, εἰ καὶ μικρόν τι περὶ τὴν κλῆσιν διαφέρεται. Προχειρίζεται μὲν γὰρ διακονιῶν κεφαλάς, τίθησι δὲ τὰς ὀνομασίας οἰκείας τῷ ἐπιτηδεύματι, ἐπιστημονάρχας καὶ παιδευτὰς καὶ ἐπιτηρητὰς τούτους ἀποκαλέσας· καθίστησι δὲ καὶ ἐν ἄλλαις προσηγορίαις τοὺς ἁπάσης τῆς ἀδελφότητος

them obediently submitting to Christ's yoke with spiritual eagerness, he himself enacted rules like the lofty-minded Moses and guided the people of God with words of wisdom and purity of character, leading them in the best way possible to their promised resting place. For they say that *the virtue of a lawgiver is to determine what is best and persuade those who will be subject to it about what was agreed to by them, whereas the virtue of the multitude is to abide by all that was decided and not change any of it in times either of good fortune or of disaster;* this is *the most saintly form of God's service.*

So Theodore became a lawgiver for them, explaining the 3
judgments handed down by God, which he himself, who had ascended the mountain of his lofty way of life and entered into the darkness of divine and blessed knowledge, had received from God, imprinted *by the finger* of the Spirit on the tablets of his own most steadfast heart as though on some *stone slabs.* The one who saw God followed the advice of his father-in-law and appointed *commanders of a thousand, a hundred, fifty, and ten,* and everyday matters were referred to them and were correctly managed so that he himself was freed from concern about them. So our Moses acted in the same way, taking this as a basis, even though he made a small change concerning titles. For he appointed supervisors of monastic tasks and assigned his own designations to each function, calling them *epistemonarchai, paideutai* and *epiteretai;* he also established other titles for the most preeminent

μᾶλλον ὑπερεξέχοντας, οἷον τὸν τὰ δεύτερα φέροντα, τὸν οἰκονόμον, τὸν παροικονόμον καὶ τοὺς ὡς ἄλλως ὠνομασμένους.

4 Ἐκανόνισε μέντοι καὶ πᾶσι τοῖς πεπιστευμένοις τὰς διαφόρους διακονίας ἀνὰ μέρος διὰ στίχων ἐκ μέτρων ἰαμβικῶν, μᾶλλον δὲ σαφέστερον εἰπεῖν, ἀπὸ τῆς κυριωτάτης καὶ πρώτης, φημὶ δὴ τῆς τοῦ ἡγουμένου, ἀρξάμενος καὶ μέχρι τῆς τελευταίας τοῦ ὀψοποιοῦ καταπαύσας, ποιήσας ἐν ἑκάστῳ τῶν τε ἐπιβαλλόντων καὶ τῶν μηδαμῶς προσηκόντων τὴν καθ' ὑπόθεσιν εἴδησιν. Διωρίσατο δὲ συνεκδοχικῶς καὶ τοῖς διαμαρτάνουσι τῆς ὀφειλομένης σπουδῆς καὶ καθυστεροῦσι κατά τινα γοῦν ἀπειρημένην αἰτίαν ἐπὶ ταῖς τῶν θείων ὕμνων συνάξεσιν, ἔτι γε μὴν καὶ <τοῖς> τῆς ἐπὶ πάσῃ τῶν ἀδελφῶν ὑπηρεσίᾳ συντεταγμένης ὥρας ἀποτυγχάνουσιν, ἤτοι σκεῦος συντρίβουσιν, ἢ παροινίαν τινὰ καὶ φαυλισμὸν πρὸς τὸν πέλας ποιουμένοις, ἀνάλογον ἐπιτίμησιν τεθεικώς. Τὴν δέ γε τῶν ἐσθημάτων χρῆσιν οὐκ ἀποτεταγμένην οὐδὲ κατὰ τὸ βουλητὸν ἑκάστῳ προκεῖσθαι συντέταχεν, ἀλλὰ κἂν τούτῳ ἀποστολικὸν αὐτοὺς φέρειν πεποίηκε χαρακτῆρα, καθὼς ἡ τῶν Πράξεων ὑποτίθεται βίβλος ὡς· "*Πάντες οἱ πιστεύσαντες ἦσαν ἐπὶ τὸ αὐτό, καὶ εἶχον ἅπαντα κοινά,*" καὶ πάλιν· "*Τοῦ δὲ πλήθους τῶν πιστευσάντων ἦν ἡ καρδία καὶ ἡ ψυχὴ μία· καὶ οὐδὲ εἷς τι τῶν ὑπαρχόντων αὐτῷ ἔλεγεν ἴδιον εἶναι, ἀλλ' ἦν αὐτοῖς ἅπαντα κοινά.*" Διά τοι τοῦτο ἠφόρισεν αὐτοῖς οἰκίαν, ἐφ' ᾗ συλλήβδην ἀποτιθέμενοι τὰ δεδουλευκότα καθ' ἓν σάββατον πέπλη, ἀντελάμβανον ἕτερα διὰ χειρὸς τῶν εἰς τοῦτο καθυπουργεῖν τεταγμένων ἀδελφῶν. Τοῦτο δὲ τάξας αὐτοῖς,

members of the whole brotherhood, such as the *deutereuon,* the steward, the assistant steward, and other officials.

Theodore also gave detailed regulations in verses of iambic meter for all those entrusted with the different monastic tasks. To be more precise, beginning with the first and most important ministry, that of the abbot, I mean, and ending at the final one of the cook, he described in each case by topic what was proper and what was not at all appropriate. He also gave detailed rules for those who failed to demonstrate the necessary enthusiasm and those who for some forbidden reason arrived late at the gatherings for divine hymns. What is more, he imposed proportional punishment on all the brothers who failed to demonstrate the diligence demanded by each task, or who broke a pot, or gravely offended and disparaged a fellow monk. He prescribed that the use of clothing was not to be specifically assigned or up to each individual according to his wish, but in this too he made them bear the apostolic imprint as the book of Acts presents it: "*All who believed were together and had all things in common,*" and again, "*Now the company of those who believed were of one heart and one soul, and no one said that any of the things which he possessed was his own, but they had everything in common.*" For this very reason he set a building aside for them in which they collectively put away their used garments each Saturday and received in exchange others from the hands of the brethren appointed to render this service. After setting this rule for them, the father did not exempt 4

οὐκ ἀπέκρινεν τὰ ἑαυτοῦ ὁ πατὴρ τῆς κοινῆς ἱματιοδόχου ἑστίας, ἀλλ᾽ ὡς πανταχοῦ καὶ ἐν τούτῳ τύπος ἐγεγόνει τοῦ ποιμνίου, δύο σαφῶς εἰδὼς πάσης εἶναι παιδείας τρόπους καὶ τῆς περὶ τὰ ἤθη κατασκευῆς, ὧν ὁ μὲν λόγῳ διδασκαλικῷ, ὁ ἕτερος δὲ διὰ τῆς ἀσκήσεως τῶν ἠθῶν κατορθοῦται. Διὰ τοῦτο διδοὺς καὶ αὐτὸς κατὰ τὴν ἑβδόμην τὸν ὑποδύτην, ἀντεδέχετο ἕτερον οὐ διοίσοντα τῶν πολλῶν, ἀλλὰ τῆς αὐτῆς ὄντα ἐκείνοις ἁδρότητος, ἢ τάχα γε καὶ τῆς χείρονος. Μνημονεύων δὲ ἀεὶ τοῦ ἀποστόλου λέγοντος, ὅτι "*δωρεὰν ἄρτον οὐκ ἔφαγον,*" ἀλλ᾽ "*αἱ χεῖρες αὗται* διηκόνησαν καὶ ἐμοὶ *καὶ τοῖς* σὺν ἐμοί," ἀργίας ὑπομεῖναι τάξιν ἀκίνητον οὐκ ἠνέσχετο, ἀλλ᾽ ἐκοπία καὶ αὐτὸς ταῖς ἰδίαις χερσὶ γράφων δέλτους καὶ ταύτας τοῖς τῶν ἀδελφῶν συνεισφέρων ἔργοις· ἐξ ὧν καί τινες μέχρι τοῦ δεῦρο σῴζονται παρ᾽ ἡμῖν, σεβασταὶ τυγχάνουσαι καὶ πάσης ἀποδοχῆς ἄξιαι.

16

Συνέταξε μέντοι καὶ πλείστας ὅσας βίβλους οἴκοθεν καὶ ἐξ αὐτοῦ τὸ τάλαντον τῆς σοφίας διὰ καθαρότητος ὑπερβολὴν καὶ αὐτὸς ἄνωθεν εἰληχώς· καὶ πρώτην μὲν τὴν καὶ μέχρις ἡμῶν τρὶς τῆς ἑβδομάδος ἐκκλησιαζομένην τῶν *Μικρῶν* λεγομένων *Κατηχήσεων,* ἑκατὸν οὐσῶν πρὸς τριάκοντα καὶ τεττάρων, σχεδιασθεισῶν αὐτῷ κατὰ τὸ

himself from the communal distribution of clothing, but in this also, as in every other respect, became a model for the flock, knowing clearly that there are two methods of all training and formation of conduct: one is accomplished through instruction, the other through the practice of the conduct. For that reason, he himself would hand in his undergarment every week and receive another that would be no different from those of the majority, but of the same quality as theirs or perhaps even worse. Always mindful of the apostle who said, "*I did not eat bread without paying*" and "*these hands* ministered both to me *and those* with me," he could not bear to stay still in a state of idleness, but would toil away himself, writing books with his own hands and contributing these to the works of the brethren. Some of these are preserved with us up to now, and are revered and worthy of all honor.

16

In fact Theodore wrote very many books on his own initiative, after he had received his talent of wisdom from on high on account of his extreme purity. The first book is that of the so-called *Lesser Katecheseis,* delivered three times a week in church until our own times; there are one hundred and thirty-four of these catecheses, improvised by him in

σύνηθες τῆς πρὸς τοὺς ἀδελφοὺς ὁμιλίας, δευτέραν δὲ καὶ τρίτην καὶ τετάρτην, τῶν *Μεγάλων Κατηχήσεων*· ἃς οὐ σχεδιαστικῶς ἀλλὰ νουνεχέστερον καθ' ἑαυτὸν συντάξας ἐκδέδωκεν, πλὴν ἐν ἑκατέραις δείκνυται σαφῶς ἡ ἐν τοῖς χείλεσιν αὐτοῦ ἐκχυθεῖσα θεία καὶ οὐράνιος χάρις τοῦ λόγου. Οὐδὲ γὰρ <οἷόν> ἐστιν οὕτως ἀπώνασθαί τινος ἑτέρας βίβλου τῶν θεοσόφων Πατέρων τὸν συνετῶς μετιόντα, ὡς οἶμαι, τῆς ἐν κοινοβιακαῖς τάξεσι θεωρουμένης ὠφελείας, ὡς ἐκ τῶν μνημονευθεισῶν ἡμῖν τοῦ πατρὸς *Κατηχήσεων*· πᾶσαν γὰρ περιέχουσιν ἀρετῆς εἰδέαν, καὶ πᾶν ἄκος τῶν κατὰ κακίαν ποικίλων καὶ διαφόρων νοσημάτων ἐπιστημονικώτατα διδάσκουσιν, καὶ φωτισμὸν καὶ κατάνυξιν ταῖς τῶν ἀναγινωσκόντων ἐμποιοῦσι ψυχαῖς.

2 Ἔστι δ' αὐτῷ πεπονημένη καὶ πανηγυρική, δι' ἧσπερ ἐνίας τῶν Χριστωνύμων ἑορτῶν καὶ τῆς Θεομήτορος καὶ πάσας δὲ τοῦ μεγάλου Βαπτιστοῦ καὶ Προδρόμου καί τινων ἄλλων ἐπιφανεστέρων ἁγίων, οὐδὲν ἧττον λαμπροτάτας τῶν ἀρχικωτέρων ἀπέφηνεν πανηγυριαρχῶν.

3 Συντέταχεν δὲ καὶ ἑτέραν ἔμμετρον ἰδιαζόντως ἰαμβικὴν χρησιμωτάτην πάνυ, καθ' ἣν τήν τε διάπλασιν καὶ τὴν ἔκπτωσιν ὑπηγόρευσε τοῦ γενάρχου, πρὸς δὲ καὶ τὴν ἁμαρτίαν καὶ τὴν φθορὰν ὡς θέμις ἐξετραγῴδησεν· εἶτα διῃρημένως τοῦ Κάϊν τὸν κατὰ τοῦ Ἄβελ φθόνον καὶ φόνον κατεκωμῴδησεν· καὶ μέντοι καὶ τὸν Ἐνὼχ καὶ τὸν Νῶε καὶ τοὺς ἐξ αὐτοῦ φύντας θεοφιλεστάτους τρεῖς πατριάρχας διεζευγμένως καὶ ἀκολούθως ἑκάστῳ καὶ τὰς σφῶν ἀοιδίμους συνεύνους κατὰ τὸ εἰκὸς ἀπεσέμνυνεν. Ἔτι γε μὴν καὶ πᾶσαν αἵρεσιν ἀπηριθμήσατο καὶ τῷ

the customary form of a homily to the brethren. The second, third and fourth books are the *Great Katecheseis* which he did not produce by improvisation but in private with more deliberation; yet the divine and heavenly grace of the language that poured from his lips is apparent in each collection. Thus, in my opinion, someone who is consciously searching for contemplative benefit while living under the cenobitic rule cannot acquire it from any other book of the Fathers, full of divine wisdom as they were, as much as from the father's *Katecheseis* that I have mentioned. For they encompass every form of virtue, teach most knowledgably every remedy for the various different diseases that arise from wickedness, and produce illumination and compunction in the souls of their readers.

Panegyric was also something he labored over. In this way 2
he described most splendidly some of the feasts of Christ and of the Mother of God, all those of the great Baptist and Forerunner, and those of some other more notable saints, with no less a degree of brilliance than previous presidents of festal assemblies.

He also wrote in his distinctive style another metrical 3
work in iambics that is very useful. In this he described the creation and fall of the ancestor of our race, in addition relating in tragic language his sin and his rightful ruin; then separately he attacked in the manner of comedy Cain's envy and murder of Abel. And then, indeed, separately and fittingly for each, he also extolled as was appropriate Enoch, Noah, and the three patriarchs born from him who were most beloved of God and their famous wives. Furthermore,

ἀναθέματι καθυπέβαλεν στίχοις, ὡς ἔφην, τριμέτροις καὶ καθαροῖς· τινὰς δὲ αὐτῶν καὶ παντελῶς ἀνέτρεψεν.

4 Αἱ δέ τοι τῶν *Ἐπιστολῶν* αὐτοῦ βίβλοι πέντε μὲν ἕως τοῦ παρόντος σῴζονται παρ' ἡμῖν· τοσούτῳ γε μὴν τῇ τε τῶν ἐννοιῶν σεμνότητι καὶ τῇ καθαρότητι τῶν λέξεων ὑπερηρμένον ἔχουσι τὸ κάλλος καὶ τὸν ἐπιστολιμαῖον χαρακτῆρα δι' ἀκριβείας ἠκονισμένον, ὡς μηδεμίαν ἀδακρυτὶ μετιέναι τόν γε μὴ λιθίνην πάντη τὴν καρδίαν ἔχοντα. Ἔστι δὲ πρὸς ταύταις καὶ ἑτέρα δογματικὴ διὰ πεζῆς λέξεως αὐτῷ πραγματευθεῖσα, καθ' ἣν ἐν τρισὶν ἀντιρρητικοῖς λόγοις, ὥσπερ τις ἄλλος Δαυῒδ τὸν Ἀλλόφυλον Γολιάθ, ἤτοι τὴν ἔκφυλον τῆς ἀληθείας τῶν εἰκονομάχων ἐκσφενδονήσας κατέβαλεν αἵρεσιν, καὶ τὸν δεινότατον ὀνειδισμὸν τῆς Ἐκκλησίας ἐξῆρεν. Ἀλλὰ γὰρ καὶ τοὺς ἄμφω βασιλεῖς ὡς τῆς εἰρημένης βλασφήμου αἱρέσεως κεφαλάς, φημὶ δὴ τὸν Κοπρώνυμον Κωνσταντῖνον καὶ τὸν θηριόγνωμον, μᾶλλον δὲ θηριώνυμον Λέοντα, οἷόν τισι δόρασι, τοῖς στηλιτευτικοῖς ὕψου μετεωρίσας λόγοις, ἐθριάμβευσέν τε καὶ παρεδειγμάτισεν, καὶ τὰς αὐτῶν ἀνοσιουργίας τοῖς μετὰ ταῦτα διῃρημένως προφανεῖς κατεστήσατο.

5 Τοιγαροῦν πᾶσαν τοῦ νοὸς ἔμφυτον τοῖς θείοις ἐνασχολήσας δύναμιν, καὶ διὰ πάσης *ἡμέρας καὶ νυκτὸς τὸν νόμον τοῦ Κυρίου ἐκμελετήσας,* καὶ τὴν βασιλείαν τῶν οὐρανῶν ἐντὸς ἑαυτοῦ τε καὶ τῶν ἑπομένων ὡς οἷόν τε καταστησάμενος, μᾶλλον δὲ βασιλείαν οὐρανῶν τῇ ταυτότητι τῆς πολιτείας τὴν περιώνυμον τοῦ Προδρόμου ἐκτετελεκὼς μονήν, ἣν αὐτὸς οἷά τις ἥλιος ἐν μέσῳ τοῦ πλήθους τῶν

in verses of clear trimeters, as I said, he enumerated every heresy and subjected it to an anathema; some of them he totally refuted.

His five books of *Letters* are still preserved with us up to the present day. They have a beauty elevated to such an extent by nobility of thought and clarity of language as well as an epistolary character sharpened with such precision, that no one who does not have a heart of stone can read a single one of them without tears. In addition to those books, there is also another doctrinal treatise by him in prose where, in three discourses of refutation, like a second David attacking the Philistine Goliath with a slingshot, that is to say, the heresy of the iconoclasts which is contrary to the truth, he brought this down and removed from the Church a source of most terrible reproach. For after unsettling both emperors, the leaders of the aforementioned blasphemous heresy, I mean Constantine Kopronymos and the bestially minded, or rather, bestially named Leo, with denunciatory speeches like spears from on high, he exposed and made a spectacle of them, making their profane actions quite plain in separate treatises for the next generations. 4

In this way then, after devoting all the innate power of his mind to divine things and *studying the law of the Lord* all *day and night,* he established the kingdom of heaven within himself and his followers as far as he was able; or rather, by the identical nature of its way of life he made the very celebrated monastery of the Forerunner a kingdom of heaven, and he himself radiated beams of his own virtue and wisdom, giving 5

νοητῶν ἀστέρων, τὰς τῆς ἰδίας ἀρετῆς καὶ σοφίας ἀκτινοβολῶν ἀστραπάς, καὶ τοὺς περὶ αὐτὸν καταφωτίζων καὶ πρὸς τὸ κρεῖττον ἐξαλλοιῶν καὶ μεταποιούμενος.

17

Ἀλλ' οὐκ ἤνεγκεν ὁ ἀεὶ χαιρέκακος καὶ πατὴρ τοῦ φθόνου, ὁ μελάντατος ὄντως καὶ βαθὺς κόραξ διάβολος, τὴν τοσαύτην τοῦ πατρὸς ἀρετὴν κατὰ τὴν εὐδαίμονα διαφημίζεσθαι, οὐδὲ τὴν τῶν ὑπ' αὐτὸν σῳζομένων καλῶς καὶ διϊθυνομένων πληθὺν ἀνεπηρέαστον παρεᾶσαι καὶ τηλικοῦτον ἀσκητικῆς εἶδος βιώσεως ἐν μέσῃ πολυανδρούσῃ ἐπιδείκνυσθαι πόλει, καίτοι πολλάκις καὶ διαφόρως ταῖς τοῦ μεγάλου καταβληθεὶς στρατηγίαις, ἀλλ' οἷα κατ' αὐτοῦ μεμελέτηκεν καὶ νῦν ἐπιτηδεύειν οὐκ ἀναβάλλεται. Τὸν γὰρ κατ' ἐκείνῳ καιροῦ τὰ τῆς βασιλείας ἐπειλημμένον σκῆπτρα, Νικηφόρος δ' ἦν οὗτος, ὃς τῷ μὲν δοκεῖν οὐ πόρρω τῶν εὐσεβῶς βεβασιλευκότων ὑπῆρχεν, τῇ δὲ ἀληθείᾳ μακρῷ τῶν τοιούτων ἀποδιώριστο, εἴπερ *ἡ πίστις χωρὶς τῶν ἔργων νεκρὰ* εἶναι καθωμολόγηται· τοῦτον τοιγαροῦν εὑρηκὼς σκεῦός τι σοβαρόγνωμον καὶ πονηρίας μεμεστωμένον, ὁ τοῖς ἀγαθοῖς ἔργοις τῶν δικαίων ἀεὶ ἐπιμαινόμενος ὑποβάλλει αὐτοῦ τῇ καρδίᾳ τοῦ ἀθῷον ἀποφῆναι τὸν τὴν μοιχοζευξίαν πρώην αὐτουργηκότα καὶ τῷ ἱερατικῷ βαθμῷ ἐγκαταλέξαι, ὡς παραίτιον γεγονότα

light to those around him, and changing and transforming them for the better, like a sun in the midst of a multitude of spiritual stars.

17

But the father of envy who always rejoices at the misfortune of others, the devil, that most black and crafty raven, could not bear that our father Theodore's great virtue should be celebrated throughout the fortunate city; nor could he allow the throng of those who were being so well saved and guided by him to go unmolested and such a great model of the ascetic life to be on display in the middle of a populous city. Although he had often been struck down in different ways by the strategies of the great man, yet the devil did not now delay in putting into practice what he had devised against Theodore. For at that point in time the man who held the scepter of imperial power, this was Nikephoros, did not seem very different from those who had ruled piously, but in truth was far removed from such people, if indeed *faith without works* has been acknowledged to be *dead*. Accordingly then, the devil, who is always enraged by the good deeds of the righteous, finding Nikephoros to be a vessel full of arrogance and evil, put it into his heart to declare innocent the man who had recently performed the adulterous marriage and admit him to the priestly rank, because, he said, he had been partly responsible for peace

εἰρήνης, φησί, καὶ τοῦ λυσιτελοῦντος φροντίσαντα. Καὶ δὴ τῷ ἱερόφρονι συντυχὼν πατριάρχῃ ὁ τὴν ὑποθήκην τοῦ ὄφεως παραδεξάμενος ἄναξ, ἀντιβολεῖ καὶ βιάζεται λυθῆναι τὸν Ἰωσὴφ τοῦ χωρισμοῦ, τοῦ δήσαντος αὐτὸν ἁγιωτάτου Ταρασίου οὕτως ἐάσαντος καὶ πρὸς τὸν Θεὸν ἐκδημήσαντος, ὑποσχόμενος αὐτῷ ὡς βασιλικαῖς ἐπικουρίαις συνελάσειεν ἅπαντας εἰς τὴν τοιαύτην καθυφεῖναι οἰκονομίαν. Οὕτως οὖν πείθει ἄκοντα πάντῃ καὶ μὴ βουλόμενον κατὰ νοῦν τὸν τῆς νίκης ἐπώνυμον πατριάρχην πρὸς τὸ δέξασθαι συλλειτουργὸν τὸν ἀνίερον.

2 Καὶ γίνεται πάλιν διαφωνία καὶ γνωμῶν σύγχυσις καὶ προσώπων διαίρεσις ἔν τε τοῖς ἱεράρχαις καὶ τοῖς μονάζουσιν, τῶν μὲν μὴ προσκροῦσαι τῷ ἄνακτι ἕνεκα τούτου καλῶς ἔχειν ὑπονοούντων, τῶν δὲ περὶ τὸν μέγαν Θεόδωρον ἀντιφασκόντων ὡς οὐ δίκαιόν ἐστι τὴν ἐξενεχθεῖσαν πρὸς τοῦ θεσπεσίου Ταρασίου ἐπὶ τῷ Ἰωσὴφ κρίσιν ἀνατραπῆναι ἐπὶ λυσιτελείᾳ τοῦ παντὸς τηνικάδε γεγενημένην· "Ἡ γὰρ ἐπὶ τῶν τοιούτων οἰκονομία," φησίν, "τὴν μοιχοζευξίαν προφανῶς συνίστησιν· πρὸς δὲ καὶ τὴν δικαίαν κρίσιν τοῦ Θεοῦ τὴν κατὰ τοῦ νεωτέρου Κωνσταντίνου ἤδη προελθοῦσαν ἄξιον συνιδεῖν καὶ μὴ λήθῃ ταύτην παραπέμψαι, κἀντεῦθεν στοχάσασθαι τὸ βούλημα τῆς θείας νομοθεσίας ὡς ἂν μὴ ἀποικίλῳ γνώμῃ καὶ ἀχαλινώτοις διανοίας ὁρμαῖς οἰκονομίας λόγους ἀναπλάττοιμεν τοὺς οὔτε γεγονότας πω, οὔτε μὴν ὄνησιν ἁπλῶς τῇ ὑφηλίῳ ἐκποιήσοντας πρὸς ὄλεθρον τῶν ἡμετέρων ψυχῶν."

3 Ἐκ δὴ τούτου ἀσύμβατοι μείναντες πρὸς τὰς κρίσεις ἀλλήλων διέστησαν, καθά ποτε Παῦλός τε καὶ Βαρνάβας

and had considered what was advantageous. And when the ruler, who had accepted the serpent's suggestion, met with the holy-minded patriarch, he entreated and bullied him into releasing Joseph from his deprivation of the priesthood, since the most holy Tarasios who had punished him had since left and departed to God; he also promised him that he would oblige everyone to give in to such a dispensation by means of his imperial assistance. In this way, then, he persuaded the patriarch Nikephoros, who was named after victory, to accept that unholy man as a colleague in the sacred ministry, although he was totally forced into this and it was against his will.

Again discord, confused opinions, and personal division 2
arose both within the ecclesiastical hierarchy and among the monks, with some considering that it was not good to offend the ruler concerning this matter, but those around great Theodore responding that it was not right that the judgment on Joseph pronounced by the inspired Tarasios should be overturned, as it had been to everyone's advantage at that time. "The dispensation regarding such matters," Theodore said, "clearly supported the adulterous marriage. In addition, it is right to be mindful of God's righteous judgment that has already befallen the young Constantine and not consign that to oblivion and henceforth to follow the intent of divine legislation so that, by a simplistic decision and reckless reactions we should not, to the destruction of our souls, fabricate grounds for a dispensation, grounds which do not exist at all and which would simply not yield any benefit for the world."

As a result of this, the two groups, which remained ir- 3
reconcilable over the judgments, were at odds with one

ἐν τῇ περὶ τὸν Ἰωάννην τὸν καλούμενον Μάρκον διαφωνίᾳ, καθὼς γέγραπται, *Ἐγένετο δὲ παροξυσμός, ὥστε ἀποχωρισθῆναι αὐτοὺς ἀπ᾽ ἀλλήλων, τόν τε Βαρνάβαν παραλαβόντα τὸν Μάρκον ἐκπλεῦσαι εἰς Κύπρον· Παῦλος δὲ ἐπιλεξάμενος Σίλαν ἐξῆλθεν, παραδοθεὶς τῇ χάριτι τοῦ* Θεοῦ *ὑπὸ τῶν ἀδελφῶν.* Ὅπερ ἐφθακὼς ὁ θεῖος Χρυσόστομος ἐν τῇ τῶν Πράξεων θεοφεγγεῖ ἑρμηνείᾳ τάδε φησίν· *τίς μὲν οὖν αὐτῶν ἐβουλεύσατο βέλτιον, οὐχ ἡμῶν ἀποφήνασθαι,* ἡμεῖς δὲ περὶ τῶν προκειμένων φαμὲν ὡς ἀμφότεροι καλῶς πεποιήκασιν, καθὰ δὴ καὶ Ταράσιος ὁ ἀοίδιμος ἐν τῇ κατ᾽ αὐτὸν ἀπεφήνατο οἰκονομίᾳ. Καὶ γὰρ δὴ καὶ αὐτὸς τότε τὸ θυμικὸν καὶ ζέον τοῦ ἄνακτος ὑφορώμενος καὶ εἰδὼς ὡς λίαν ἐστὶν εὐπάροιστος ἐπὶ τὸ πεφυκὸς ἀδικεῖν, καὶ νοσεῖ τὸ εἰς ἁμαρτίαν εὔκολον, ἵνα μή τι δριμύτερον ἐν τῇ τοῦ Θεοῦ κατεργάσηται Ἐκκλησίᾳ, ὑπενδίδωσι τὰς τῆς ἀκριβείας ἡνίας, καὶ παρασχὼν τὸ ἧττον καὶ μερικὸν τὸ καθολικώτερον φιλοσόφως ἐνεπορεύσατο, πληρῶν τὸ *ἐξαγοραζόμενοι τὸν καιρὸν ὅτι αἱ ἡμέραι πονηραί εἰσιν.*

4 Οὕτως οὖν κἀνταῦθα ἔστιν λογίσασθαι ὅτι ᾠκονόμησεν ὁ μακάριος Νικηφόρος, μὴ βουλόμενος, ἀλλὰ βιασθεὶς ὑπὸ τοῦ ἄνακτος. Ὁ δέ γε πατὴρ ἡμῶν Θεόδωρος τὴν ἀκριβῆ τῶν θείων νόμων φυλάττει κατάστασιν, θεόθεν κινηθεὶς καὶ οὐ πάθει κακίας κρατούμενος, ὡς ἂν καὶ τὸ ἄθεσμον τῆς κοίτης χώραν μὴ λάβοι νόμου ἐν τοῖς ἔχουσι τὸ ἐν ἀθραύστοις ὁρμαῖς ὀρεκτιᾶν βοσκηματώδεσιν ἀνθρώποις, καὶ τὸ ἀπροσωπόληπτον δειχθῇ τῶν εἰς Θεὸν ὁλικῶς πεποιθότων καὶ μὴ λαμβανόντων πρόσωπα κατὰ

another, just as Paul and Barnabas once were in their disagreement concerning John who was called Mark, as it is written: *And there rose a sharp contention, so that they separated from each other; Barnabas took Mark with him and sailed away to Cyprus, but Paul chose Silas and departed, being commended to the grace of* God *by the brethren.* In his divinely illuminating commentary on Acts, holy Chrysostomos referred to this, commenting that *which of them deliberated better is not ours to declare.* But I do say about the present instance that both parties acted well, as indeed the renowned Tarasios also declared in his dispensation. For at that time, the patriarch, distrusting the ruler's irascibility and quick temper, and knowing that the latter was very easily carried away by his nature into wrongdoing and suffered from a tendency to sin, relaxed the reins of strictness so that the emperor would not contrive something even harsher for the Church of God. By allowing something that was lesser and partial, he wisely procured what was more generally beneficial, fulfilling the saying, *buying up the time because the days are evil.*

So in this case then, it is possible to conclude that the 4
blessed Nikephoros compromised, not of his own free will but because he was forced to by the emperor. But our father Theodore, moved by God and not controlled by wicked passion, maintained the strict observance of divine laws. He did so in order that illicit intercourse should not become lawful among bestial people whose desires lie in incontrollable impulses, and so that no respect should be shown for it by those who have completely obeyed God and have not adopted attitudes contrary to their own souls, so as to

τῆς ἑαυτῶν ψυχῆς, ὥστε τὴν ἐντολὴν τοῦ Κυρίου προδιδόναι χάριν κράτους βασιλέως ἀδικώτατα δυναστεύοντος, κατὰ τὸ τοῦ Δαυῒδ μελῴδημα, *καὶ ἐλάλουν ἐν τοῖς μαρτυρίοις σου ἐναντίον βασιλέων, καὶ οὐκ ᾐσχυνόμην.*

18

Ἐπεὶ ὅτι γε μὴ καλῶς εἰς τοῦτο τάξεως ἦλθε τὰ τῆς ἐκκλησιαστικῆς διοικήσεως ἐπὶ τῶν ἡμερῶν τουτοινὶ τοῖν δυοῖν βασιλέοιν καὶ αὐτοὶ σαφῶς ᾔδεσαν οἱ θεόληπτοι πατριάρχαι· οὐδὲ γὰρ ἂν καλῶς δεδρακέναι τὸν μέγαν ἔλεγεν Θεόδωρον ἐκ Θεσσαλονίκης ἐπανελθόντα ὁ τῆς ὀρθοδοξίας πρόμος Ταράσιος, εἰ μὴ αὐτὸν ᾔδει τὴν ἀληθῆ τρίβον τοῦ Εὐαγγελίου ἀπλανῶς ὁδεύοντα· οὐδ' ἂν πάλιν ἀπεδέχετο αὐτὸν ὁ τῆς νίκης ἐπώνυμος ἱεροθέτης καὶ ὡς ἀθλητὴν ἀληθείας τοῖς ἐπαίνοις κατέστεφεν, εἰ μὴ *ὀρθοτομοῦντα* διεγνώκει *τὸν λόγον* τῆς πίστεως. Πρὸς δὲ τοῖς εἰρημένοις καὶ τοῦτο θετέον· ὅτι εἰ οὐκ εἶχεν ἕκαστος αὐτῶν μὴ εὖ πεποιηκέναι τὸ δέξασθαι εἰς ἱερωσύνης τιμὴν τὸν μοιχοζεύκτην διὰ βασιλικὸν φόβον, οὐκ ἂν μετὰ θάνατον τῶν ἀνάκτων καὶ τὴν παρὰ Θεοῦ εἰς αὐτοὺς γεγονυῖαν τοῦ ἱεροῦ Θεοδώρου παρὰ πόδας ἐκδίκησιν τοῦ χοροῦ τῶν ἱερέων τὸν τολμητίαν ἐχώριζον. Ἐντεῦθεν οὖν σκοπεῖν ἔστι τοῖς φιλοθέοις τὰς τῶν πραγμάτων φύσεις, καὶ μηδ' ἕτερον μέρος ἐκτρέπεσθαι τῶν θεσπεσίων τούτων ἡμῶν καθηγεμόνων.

betray the Lord's commandment because of the power of an emperor who ruled most unjustly, as suggested in the Psalm of David, *I spoke in your testimonies before kings and was not put to shame.*

18

The divinely inspired patriarchs themselves clearly knew that in the time of those two emperors matters of ecclesiastical administration had not gone well on this question of discipline. For Tarasios, the foremost leader of the orthodox faith, would not have declared that the great Theodore had acted well on his return from Thessalonike, if he had not known that he was proceeding unerringly on the true path of the Gospel, nor again would Nikephoros, the prelate named after victory, have welcomed him and crowned him with praise as a champion of truth, if he had not discerned that he was *rightly expounding the word* of faith. In addition to what has been related, this too must be set down: if either of them had considered that they had done well in accepting the performer of the adulterous marriage into the office of the priesthood out of fear of the emperor, they would not have removed the reckless fellow from the band of priests after the deaths of those rulers and the vengeance brought on them by God hard on the heels of holy Theodore. On this basis it is possible for devout people to examine the nature of their actions and not turn away from these, our inspired leaders, to any other party.

2 Πλὴν ὡς εἶδεν ὁ ὑψηλόφρων μέδων τὴν ἰδίαν ψῆφον ὑπὸ τῶν ἡμετέρων βδελυχθεῖσαν πατέρων καὶ οὐδενὸς λόγου ἀξιωθεῖσαν, κελεύει μετ' ὀργῆς τόν τε μέγαν Θεόδωρον καὶ τὸν τούτου σύμφρονα καὶ Χριστοῦ ἱεράρχην Ἰωσὴφ ἅμα τῷ θείῳ αὐτῶν καὶ καθηγεμόνι Πλάτωνι τὰς πρὸ τοῦ ἄστεως οἰκεῖν νήσους, οὐχ ἅμα καὶ κατὰ τὸ αὐτό, ἀλλὰ διεζευγμένως τούτων ἕκαστον εἰς ἄλλην καὶ ἄλλην παραφυλάττεσθαι, τὸ δὲ τῆς ἀδελφότητος πλῆθος ὑπὸ στρατιωτικῆς ἐν τῷ ἰδίῳ μοναστηρίῳ τηρεῖσθαι φάλαγγος. Αὐτὸς δὲ μετά τινας ἡμέρας παραγενάμενος ἐν τοῖς τοῦ Ἐλευθερίου βασιλικοῖς μελάθροις, προσκαλεῖται ἅπαντας ἱστορίας ἕνεκα· εἶτα διαστήσας τούτων τοὺς μειζοτέρους, πειρᾶται λόγοις τισὶ πιθανότητος τῆς πατρικῆς τούτους μεταστῆσαι βουλῆς. Ὡς δὲ τὴν προβολὴν εἶδεν τῶν ἑαυτοῦ ῥημάτων καθάπερ τι βέλος ἀκιδνὸν τῇ ἀντιτυπίᾳ τῆς στερεμνίας αὐτῶν ἀποκρουσθεῖσαν ἀντιφράσεως, πρὸς τὸ πλῆθος γίνεται τῶν ἀδελφῶν καί φησι πρὸς αὐτούς· "Ὅσοι ταῖς ἡμετέραις βούλεσθε πειθαρχεῖν παραινέσεσιν καὶ κοινωνικοὶ εἶναι τοῦ τε πατριάρχου καὶ τῆς καθολικῆς Ἐκκλησίας ἐν τοῖς δεξιοῖς μου ἀφορίσθητε, ὅσοι δ' αὖ τῇ προκατεχούσῃ ὑμᾶς γνώμῃ ἐμμένειν κεκρίκατε τὴν ἐξ εὐωνύμων στάσιν ἐκλέξασθε," σοφιζόμενος ἐν τούτῳ, ὡς ᾤετο, τοὺς ἀσοφίστους μὲν λόγων παρασκευαῖς τινας αὐτῶν ὄντας, βίου δὲ καὶ γένους καὶ τοῦ ζῆν αὐτοῦ καταφρονοῦντας ἅπαντας ὑπὲρ τῆς καθ' ὑπακοὴν θείαν ἀνεπιλήπτου ζωῆς. Τότε δὴ πάντες ὁμοθυμαδὸν τὴν εὐώνυμον κατειληφότες χώραν, λέγουσι πρὸς αὐτὸν μετὰ παρρησίας, "Ἡμεῖς ἀκριβῶς ἐπιστάμεθα, ὦ βασιλεῦ, ὅτι οἱ

But when the haughty ruler Nikephoros saw that our fathers despised his decree and considered it of no account, in a rage he ordered great Theodore and Joseph of Thessalonike, that hierarch of Christ who agreed with him, along with Plato, their uncle and leader, to live on the islands that lie in front of the city, not together in the same place, but each of them under guard separately on a different island. The majority of the brotherhood was to be held by a military unit in their own monastery. Some days later Nikephoros arrived in the imperial palace of Eleutheriou and summoned all of them for an interrogation. After separating the more important ones, he tried with some tempting words to detach them from their spiritual father's counsel. But when he saw that the thrust of his own words had been repelled like some feeble missile by the resistance of their firm counter argument, he turned to the main group of the brothers and said to them, "All those of you who are willing to obey our exhortations and to be in communion both with the patriarch and the universal Church, place yourselves apart on my right; but all those of you who have decided to abide by the opinion that you held previously choose the position on my left." In this, as he thought, he was cleverly outwitting those of them who were verbally unsophisticated but who had all despised life, family, and living itself for the sake of a blameless life in holy obedience. At that moment, however, all with one accord took up the space on his left and boldly said to him, "We know perfectly well, Emperor, that our 2

πατέρες ἡμῶν ἐκ τῆς θεοπνεύστου Γραφῆς ἅπαντα μυηθέντες καὶ Πνεύματι Ἁγίῳ φερόμενοι, τὰ κρείττω καὶ σωτηρίας ἐγγὺς καὶ πεφρονήκασι καὶ ἐδίδαξαν· διὸ καὶ αὐτοὶ ἀνενδοιάστως τοῖς αὐτῶν ἐξακολουθοῦντες ἴχνεσιν, τὴν παρ' ὑμῶν καινοτομηθεῖσαν οὐ προσιέμεθα δόξαν."

3 Ὁ δὲ καταπλαγεὶς ἐπὶ τῇ τοιαύτῃ τῶν ὁσίων ἀνδρῶν πεπαρρησιασμένῃ ἀπολογίᾳ, προστάσσει κατανεμηθῆναι αὐτοὺς εἰς τὰ αὐτόθι καὶ πρὸς σύνεγγυς τοῦ ἄστεως μοναστήρια φυλαχθησομένους, δηλαδὴ ὑπὸ ἀσφαλεστάτην φρουρὰν ὡς κριτοὺς καὶ ἀνηκόους βασιλικῶν τε καὶ ἱεραρχικῶν διατάξεων. Ἀλλ' οὐκ εἰς μακρὰν αὐτῷ τὰ τῆς ἀπονοίας ἀπέβη, συντόμως γὰρ ἡ θεία δίκη καὶ τοῦτον μετελθοῦσα πανστρατὶ ἐπὶ τῆς ξένης παρέλυσεν. Πρὸς Σκύθας γοῦν ὁ μάταιος στρατοπεδεύσας Νικηφόρος πολεμικῆς αὐτόθι ἔργον γίνεται χειρός, ὅπως, οἶμαι, κἂν τούτῳ προφανῶς ἀποδειχθῇ ὡς ἡ τοῦ θεοφόρου πατρὸς ἡμῶν ὑπὲρ ἀληθείας ἔνστασις οὐκ εἰκαία οὐδ' ἀπρονόητος, ἀλλ' ὑπὸ Θεοῦ μαρτυρουμένη καὶ πάλαι καὶ νῦν καὶ τὸ βέβαιον αὐτόθεν ἔχουσα.

19

Οὕτως οὖν πεπτωκὼς ὁ δείλαιος ἄναξ, μεγάλης μὲν τραγῳδίας ὑπόθεσις, μείζονος δὲ κωμῳδίας ἡ Ῥωμαϊκὴ γέγονεν ἀρχή, καὶ πεπλήρωται ἐπ' αὐτῷ ἡ τοῦ προφήτου Ὠσηὲ πρόρρησις, *Καὶ ὁ οἶκος τοῦ βασιλέως, ἐνωτίσασθε,*

fathers, who are initiated in everything by divinely inspired Scripture and are borne along by the Holy Spirit, understand what is better and bring us near to salvation, and that is what they have taught. For that reason, we too without hesitation follow in their footsteps and do not accept the novel doctrine promulgated by you."

Nikephoros, who was astounded at such a bold defense 3
by the saintly men, immediately ordered that they be assigned to monasteries close to the city to be kept under guard, that is, under the most secure imprisonment as men identified as dissidents from imperial and hierarchical decisions. But these senseless acts were not long in having consequences for him, for divine justice quickly followed and put an end to him, with all his army, in a foreign land. The foolish Nikephoros made war on the Scythians and at once fell victim at the hands of the enemy, in order, I think, that in this too it might be clearly demonstrated that our inspired father's opposition on behalf of the truth was not aimless or without providence, but was attested by God both in the past and in the present, and was validated in this way.

19

After the wretched ruler had perished in this way, the Roman empire became the subject of a great tragedy, or more of a comedy, and the prediction of the prophet Hosea was fulfilled in him: *Hearken, O house of the king, because the*

διότι πρὸς ὑμᾶς ἐστι τὸ κρῖμα· ὅτι παγὶς ἐγενήθητε τῇ σκοπιᾷ· καὶ ὡς δίκτυον ἐκτεταμένον ἐπὶ τὸ Ἰταβύριον, ὃ οἱ ἀγρεύοντες τὴν θήραν κατέπηξαν. Καὶ πεσοῦνται οἱ ἄρχοντες αὐτῶν διὰ ἀπαιδευσίαν γλώσσης αὐτῶν· οὗτος ὁ φαυλισμὸς αὐτῶν ἐν γῇ Αἰγύπτῳ εἰς κόλπον αὐτῶν, ἀνθ' ὧν παρέβησαν τὴν διαθήκην μου καὶ κατὰ τοῦ νόμου μου ἠσέβησαν. Ὅπερ δὲ εἰς αὐτὸν προεφήτευσεν καὶ ὁ μέγας οὗτος Θεόδωρος, τοῖς εἰρημένοις ἄξιον ἐπισυνάψαι· ἐπειδὴ γὰρ ἐπῆρτο μέγα φρονεῖν καὶ ὑπὸ τῶν ἰδίων ὑπασπιστῶν καὶ ὑπὸ τοῦ φυσικοῦ φρονήματος ὁ Καῖσαρ Νικηφόρος καὶ τὴν ὁρμὴν εἶχεν κατὰ τῶν Σκυθῶν ἀνεπίσχετον, μεταστειλάμενος τὸν ἱερὸν πατέρα ἡμῶν Θεόδωρον ἐν τοῖς πρὸ τῆς πόλεως τόποις, ἠξίου καὶ κατεβιάζετο αὐτὸν διὰ μέσου τινῶν μεγιστάνων ἐπιδοῦναι ἑαυτὸν τῇ ὑπ' αὐτοῦ ἐφευρεθείσῃ δῆθεν οἰκονομίᾳ. Ὁ δὲ ὅσιος ἔνθους ὥσπερ τῷ Πνεύματι γενόμενος, δηλοῖ αὐτῷ τάδε· "Σὲ μὲν χρεὼν ἐφ' οἷς πεποίηκας μεταμελεῖσθαι καὶ μὴ προστιθεῖν ἔτι τοῦ καὶ ἡμᾶς πρὸς τὸν ὅμοιον ἐφέλκειν ὄλισθον, ἐπεὶ δὲ μηδὲν τοιοῦτον βεβουλημένος τῶν ὧδε ἀποτρέχεις, τάδε λέγει Κύριος Παντοκράτωρ ὡς, 'Ἐπιστρέφων οὐκ ἐπιστρέψεις τῇ ὁδῷ ᾗ σὺ πορεύῃ σήμερον ἐκεῖ.'" Ἀμέλει τοῦ ἀπειθοῦς τούτου μέδοντος κατὰ τὴν προφητείαν τοῦ θεοφόρου ποιμένος ἡμῶν ἐν τῇ τῶν Βουλγάρων χώρᾳ τὸ ζῆν καταστρέψαντος, καὶ Σταυρακίου τοῦ υἱοῦ αὐτοῦ μόλις ἐκεῖθεν τραυματίου πρὸς τὴν βασιλεύουσαν ἀνακάμψαντος καὶ ἐν ὅλοις δυσὶ μησὶ τῆς ἀρχῆς κρατήσαντος καὶ παρελθόντος, ὁ τούτου ἐπ' ἀδελφῇ γαμβρὸς ἀρχαγγελώνυμος τὴν τοῦ κουροπαλάτου ἀμφέπων ἀξίαν, τὸ βασίλειον διεδέξατο.

judgment pertains to you; for you became a snare at the watchtower and like a net stretched out on Tabor which those who hunt for game pegged down. And their rulers shall fall on account of the boorishness of their tongues; this contempt of them in the land of Egypt shall be in their bosom, in recompense for the ways they transgressed my covenant and acted impiously against my law. Great Theodore's prophecy about him is also worth adding to what has been related. For when the Emperor Nikephoros, inflated with self-importance due to his supporters and his natural arrogance, had an unstoppable urge to attack the Scythians, he summoned our holy father Theodore to meet him just outside the city and, surrounded by some grandees, tried to put pressure on him to accept the dispensation he had supposedly devised. But the saintly man, as though inspired by the Spirit, revealed the following to him: "You need to repent of what you have done and add nothing else to draw me into a similar downfall as well. But since you have accepted no such advice and are ready to depart from here, thus says the Lord Almighty, 'When you return, it will not be on the same road as that on which you are setting out for there today.'" Indeed, that disobedient ruler ended his life in the land of the Bulgarians in accordance with the prophecy of our inspired shepherd, and Staurakios, his wounded son, barely made it back from there to the capital. After holding power for two months in all, he in turn passed away and his brother-in-law Michael, who was named after an archangel and held the rank of *kouropalates,* succeeded to the imperial power.

2 Ὅστις Μιχαὴλ χριστιανικώτατος ὑπάρχων καὶ πιστὸς ἐν Κυρίῳ, ἀνακαλεῖται τῆς ἐξορίας εὐθὺς τοὺς περὶ τὸν μέγαν Θεόδωρον, ἀνεῖσθαι δὲ κελεύει καὶ τοὺς κατὰ τὰ μοναστήρια ὑπὸ φρουρὰν ὄντας αὐτοῦ μαθητάς· καὶ γίνεται πρέσβυς Χριστομίμητος καὶ μεσίτης τῶν διεστώτων σὺν τῷ πάπᾳ τῆς πρεσβυτέρας Ῥώμης. Καὶ συνελαύνουσιν ἄμφω, ὁ μὲν δι' ἐπιστολῶν παραινετικῶν, ὁ δὲ δι' αὐτοπροσώπου συνομιλίας καὶ παρακλήσεως, τόν τε ἁγιώτατον πατριάρχην καὶ τὸν θεσπέσιον πατέρα ἡμῶν εἰς ὁμονοίας πρεπωδεστάτην συνάφειαν, τὸν τὴν μοιχοζευξίαν τετολμηκότα τῆς λειτουργίας ἀπείρξαντες κατὰ τὴν ἔμπροσθεν ἐπ' αὐτῷ γεγονυῖαν κρίσιν τοῦ ἀοιδίμου καὶ μεγάλου Ταρασίου. Καὶ οὕτω πάλιν Χριστοῦ τοῦ ἀγαθοῦ Θεοῦ ἡμῶν χάριτι καὶ φιλανθρωπίᾳ γίνεται σταθηρὰ γαλήνη ἐν τῇ αὐτοῦ ἁγιωτάτῃ καὶ καθολικῇ Ἐκκλησίᾳ, ἐκ μέσου τῶν σκανδάλων ἀφανισθέντων.

20

Ὁ τοίνυν πατὴρ ἡμῶν Θεόδωρος αὖθις τὴν οἰκείαν μονὴν τοῦ Στουδίου παραλαβών, καὶ τῶν διασπαρέντων αὐτοῦ φοιτητῶν αὐτόθι συνδεδραμηκότων, εἴχετο τῆς τε πρὸς τὸν πανίερον πατριάρχην φιλαιτάτης ὁμοφροσύνης τε καὶ συνδιαθέσεως καὶ τῆς πρὸς τοὺς ἑαυτοῦ μαθητὰς ἐξ ἔθους διδασκαλίας, τὰ τούτων ἤθη τῷ διδακτικῷ λόγῳ

This Michael, who was most Christian and faithful in the 2
Lord, at once recalled great Theodore's followers from their banishment and ordered that his disciples who were under guard in the monasteries were to be released. Michael also became an ambassador in imitation of Christ and a mediator, together with the pope of old Rome, for those who were in disagreement. Both of them, the one by means of hortatory letters, the other by means of face-to-face conversation and entreaty, brought together the most holy patriarch and our inspired father in an appropriately harmonious relationship, after they had removed from the priesthood the man who had dared to perform the adulterous marriage in accordance with the judgment that the renowned and great Tarasios had previously made against him. Thus, by the grace and benevolence of Christ our good God, a settled calm came about once more in his most holy and universal Church since the scandals had been removed from its midst.

20

Our father Theodore once again took over his own monastery of Stoudios, and, after his scattered disciples had assembled there, maintained most friendly agreement and conciliatory attitude toward the all-holy patriarch. He also kept up his customary teaching of his own disciples, ordering their behavior toward perfect obedience by an instruc-

πρὸς ὑπακοῆς τελείας ῥυθμίζων διάθεσιν, καὶ τὸν παρεισπεσόντα αὐτοῖς ἐκ τοῦ χρόνου τῆς αὐταρεσκείας ῥύπον τῇ τῆς νουθεσίας ἐμμελῶς ἀπαλείφων σπογγίᾳ. Καὶ οὕτω πάλιν ὁ λόγος τοῦ Θεοῦ ηὔξανεν καὶ τὸ στῖφος τῶν μαθητῶν ἐβελτιοῦτο αὐξανόμενον σφόδρα· καὶ ἦν ἀληθῶς ὁ εὐπρεπέστατος οὗτος χῶρος, οἷά τις ποικίλος καὶ εὐθαλὴς παράδεισος, ἐκ παντὸς γένους φυτῶν λογικῶν ἐν ἑαυτῷ περιέχων, ἐν οἷς πᾶν εἶδος ἐπιστήμης ὥσπερ τις καρπὸς πέπειρος χρησίμως ἐθεωρεῖτο. Μετὰ γὰρ τῆς εἰς ἄκρον κοινοβιακῆς εὐταξίας καὶ τῆς πρακτικῆς ὡς ἔνι φιλοσοφίας, οὐδὲ τῶν λογικῶν ἀμέτοχοι καθεστήκεσαν τεχνῶν· ἀλλὰ καὶ γραμματικῆς παρ' αὐτοῖς ἐφιλοπονεῖτο κατόρθωσις, δι' ἧς ἥ τε πρὸς τὸ γράφειν ὀρθῶς ἐγγίνεται τοῖς πεπονηκόσιν εἴδησις, καὶ ἡ πρὸς τὴν ἀνάγνωσιν ἐντυποῦται αὐτοῖς ἠθικότης. Καὶ φιλοσοφίας δὲ τεχνολογία καὶ δογμάτων πατερικῶν ἀποστήθησις, δι' ὧν πάσης αἱρέσεως φληνάφους ἀνατρέπειν εἶχον ἰσχνομυθίας, συλλογισμοῖς ἀληθείας καὶ συμπεράσμασι χρώμενοι· ἐξ ὧν σοφώτατοί τε καλλιγράφοι καὶ ἱεροψάλται, κονδακάριοί τε καὶ ᾀσματογράφοι, ποιηταί τε καὶ ἀναγνῶσται πρώτιστοι, μελισταί τε καὶ ἀοιδοπόλοι ἐν Χριστῷ ἐξεφάνθησαν.

2 Ὁμοίως δὲ καὶ αἱ τῶν βαναύσων τεχνῶν ἐπιτηδεύσεις καθ' ὅλου ὡς εἰπεῖν παρ' αὐτοῖς ηὑρίσκοντο· ὅθεν ὑφάνται τε καὶ ῥαφεῖς, σκυτοτόμοι τε καὶ σκηνοποιοί, λεπτουργοί τε καὶ οἰκοδόμοι, κανοποιοί τε καὶ μαλακουργοί, καὶ οἱ διὰ πυρὸς καὶ σιδήρου τὰ λειτουργικὰ κατασκευάζοντες σκεύη παρὰ τῷ ἐπιγείῳ τούτῳ ἐθεωροῦντο οὐρανῷ, πάντων μετὰ εὐταξίας καὶ ῥυθμοῦ ἐν τοῖς τόποις καθεζομένων

tive word and, with the sponge of admonition, diligently wiping away any stain that had occurred during the time they were able to do as they pleased. In this way, the word of God was again magnified, and the band of disciples began to improve and was greatly increased. That most worthy place was truly like a varied and flourishing garden containing within it spiritual plants of every kind, among which every form of knowledge was deemed as useful as a ripened fruit. For with the community's administration and its active functioning reaching the highest degree possible, they also did not neglect to participate in the intellectual skills. Even the correction of grammar was painstakingly practiced among them, as a consequence of which knowledge of how to write correctly was acquired by those who worked hard at it and reading with expression was impressed upon them. Systematic teaching about the religious life and memorization of the precepts of the Fathers enabled them to overturn the excessive subtleties of every nonsensical heresy, using truthful arguments and conclusions. As a result, they excelled as most skilled copyists and singers of psalms, composers of *kontakia* and writers of hymns, the best poets and readers, musicians and singers in Christ.

Similarly the cultivation of handicraft skills was to be 2
found everywhere among them, so to speak. As a result, weavers and tailors, cobblers and tentmakers, carpenters and builders, basketmakers and weavers of wickerwork, and those who by means of fire and iron tools produce liturgical vessels could be observed in this heaven on earth, with them all sitting in an orderly arrangement at the places of their

τῶν διακονιῶν αὐτῶν καὶ τὰ θεῖα τοῦ Δαυῒδ τῷ τῶν χειρῶν ἔργῳ ἀναμιγνύντων τερετίσματα. Καὶ ἦν ἰδεῖν *τὸν ἀμπελῶνα Κυρίου Σαβαὼθ* εὐκληματοῦντα καὶ ὄρη κοσμικῆς δυναστείας ὑπὸ τὴν σκιὰν αὐτοῦ καλύπτοντα, ἀλλὰ καὶ τὰς νοητὰς αὐτοῦ ἀναδενδράδας ὑπερηρμένας τῶν κέδρων τοῦ Θεοῦ, καὶ ἕως θαλάσσης τὰ κλήματα αὐτοῦ ἐκτεταμένα, καὶ ποταμῶν ἄχρι τὰς παραφυάδας αὐτοῦ. Ἔνιοι γὰρ τῶν προβεβηκότων πόνῳ τε ἀρετῆς καὶ ἡλικίᾳ γήρως τῆς αὐτοῦ μεγίστης μαθητείας ἀφορμὴν ξενιτείας τὴν ὑπόθεσιν τῆς προειρημμένης ἐπιδραξάμενοι διαστάσεως, μετὰ τὸ ἀφεθῆναι αὐτοὺς τῶν καθείρξεων, ἢ καὶ πρὸ τούτων, διεσπάρησαν κατὰ διάφορα τῆς ὑπ' οὐρανὸν κλίματα· ἐν οἷς καὶ σκηνώσαντες, κάλλιστα τῇ συνεργείᾳ τοῦ Ἁγίου Πνεύματος συνεστήσαντο μοναστήρια τὴν ἐπωνυμίαν "τοῦ Στουδιώτου" μέχρι τοῦ νῦν ἐπιφερόμενα.

21

Οὕτω τοιγαροῦν εὐδρομούσης τῆς τοῦ Χριστοῦ ποίμνης καὶ τῶν Ἐκκλησιῶν τοῦ Θεοῦ τοῖς ὀρθοδόξοις τῆς πίστεως δόγμασι καλῶς ἰθυνομένων καὶ αὐξουμένων, *ὗς* τις κάκιστος *ἐκ δρυμοῦ* τῆς Ἀρμενίων φύτλης ἀπορραγείς, ἐκώμασε καὶ ἀθρόον ταύτην ὡς οἷα *μονιὸς κατενεμήσατο ἄγριος*. Λέων γάρ, ὁ τῆς Ἀνατολῆς στρατηγός, ἐκτετιμηκὼς *μᾶλλον τὸ ἔξω φέρεσθαι τοῦ* καθήκοντος, τὸν ὑπὸ χεῖρα

duties, mingling the holy Psalms of David with the work of their hands. And it was possible to see the *vineyard of the Lord of Hosts* growing luxuriantly and covering the mountains of worldly power under its shadow, its spiritual vines rising above the cedars of God, its branches extending as far as the sea, and its side shoots to rivers. For some of those who had advanced under Theodore's excellent tutoring through the hardships of virtue and old age seized the opportunity of the previously mentioned banishment as a chance for travel in a foreign land and, after their release from imprisonment or even before this, scattered across various regions under heaven. After settling down in these regions, with the assistance of the Holy Spirit they established very beautiful monasteries that bear to the present time the additional name "of the Stoudite."

21

As Christ's flock was thus flourishing and the churches of God, well guided by the orthodox doctrines of the faith, were developing, a very evil *boar* of the Armenian race burst out from *a wood,* crashed in and immediately *devoured* them like *a solitary wild beast.* For Leo, the military governor of the Anatolikon theme, *valued too highly that which went beyond what was* appropriate, bribed the force under his command,

αὐτοῦ δωροδοκήσας στρατόν, καὶ τοὺς τούτων ἀρχηγοὺς ταῖς ὑποσχέσεσι τῶν μειζόνων σύμφρονας ἑαυτοῦ καταστησάμενος ἀξιωμάτων, ἀνταρσίαν ὠδίνει κατὰ τοῦ φιλοχρίστου ἄνακτος Μιχαήλ. Ἐλθὼν δὲ ἐπὶ τὰ Θρᾳκῷα μέρη οὐ πόρρω τῆς βασιλευούσης, ἀνακηρύττεται ὑπὸ τῶν δῆθεν Μακεδονικὴν εὐστάθειαν ἐπιδεικνυμένων αὔγουστος. Ἐκεῖθεν τε ἀπάρας, μηδενὸς ἀντιπράττοντος εἰσελαύνει εἰς τὰ βασίλεια, βασιλεὺς εἰκονοκλάστης πρὸς τῶν ἰδίων δορυφόρων ἀναφανδὸν φημιζόμενος. Οὕτω τοίνυν ἐπιδραξάμενος τῆς βασιλικῆς ἀρχῆς ὁ βίαιος οὗτος Θρᾷξ, ἅτε δὴ ὅλος τῷ τῆς ὑποκρίσεως τεθωρακισμένος προβλήματι (ἀψευδὴς γὰρ ὁ εἰρηκώς, "*Οὐχ ἁπλοῦν γένος εὑρίσκω τοὺς Ἀρμενίους, ἀλλὰ καὶ λίαν κρυπτὸν καὶ ὕπουλον*"), ἐν ἀρχῇ τῆς ἑαυτοῦ τυραννίδος, οὐ γὰρ ἂν εἴποιμι βασιλείας, εὐσέβειαν ὑποκρίνεται.

2 Ἔπειτα μετὰ τὸ περιγενέσθαι τῶν πολιτικῶν ὡς ἐβούλετο πραγμάτων, τὸ τῆς ὑποκρίσεως ἀπορριψάμενος προσωπεῖον, ἀνέδην ἀπογυμνοῖ τῆς πονηρᾶς αὐτοῦ καρδίας τὴν ἀπόθετον νόσον. Ὃς τῆς τοῦ ἀλητηρίου ἐμπληξίας—τῆς Κωνσταντίνου τοῦ Κοπρωνύμου θεοεχθείας καὶ Χριστομανίας—διάδοχον ἑαυτὸν ἀποδεικνύς, καὶ φάσκων μὴ δεῖν προσίεσθαι τὴν εἰκόνα τοῦ Χριστοῦ, μήτε τῆς ἀχράντως αὐτὸν τεκούσης ἁγίας ἀειπαρθένου, καὶ τῶν λοιπῶν δικαίων καὶ ὁσίων, ὡς τῶν τοιούτων ἀφομοιωμάτων εἰδώλοις προσεοικότων, οὐκ εἰδὼς ὁ παράφρων ὡς ὧν τὰ πρωτότυπα ἀντικειμένην ὑπόληψιν ἔχουσιν, τούτων προδήλως καὶ τὰ παράγωγα προσηγορίας ἀποίσεται τὰς ἐναντίας. Καὶ ὧνπερ ἀγαθῶν τὰ ὀνόματα λαμβάνομεν

made their officers his supporters by promises of more important ranks, and instigated a rebellion against the pious ruler Michael. After he had advanced on the areas of Thrace not far from the capital, he was proclaimed emperor by those who displayed a pretense of Macedonian steadiness; moving on from there, he entered the palace with no opposition, despite being openly spoken of as an iconoclast emperor by his own bodyguards. This, then, was the way this violent Thracian seized the imperial office, in that he had completely covered himself with the defensive armor of hypocrisy (for he was no liar who declared, "*I do not find the Armenians a straightforward race but very secretive and deceitful*") by pretending to be pious at the beginning of his tyranny, for I would not call it imperial rule.

Then, after he had gained control of the political situation in the way he wanted, he threw off the mask of hypocrisy, and without more ado laid bare the hidden disease of his evil heart. He showed that he was a successor to the wicked one's stupidity—Constantine Kopronymos's hatred of God and his fury against Christ—and claimed that there must be no acceptance of Christ's icon, or that of the holy and ever-virgin one who bore him without defilement, or those of the other righteous saints, because such representations resembled idols. The crazy fellow did not realize that things derived from prototypes which have a negative reputation will also take on their bad appellation; but, on the other hand, the names we acquire that are based on 2

πρωτοτύπως, ἀναιρετικὰ πάντως πεφύκασιν τῶν ἀρχετύπως λαμβανομένων πονηρῶν ὀνομασιῶν· τοιγάρτοι καὶ τὰ τούτων παράγωγα τῷ λόγῳ τῆς ὁμωνυμίας τοῖς πρωτοτύποις παρεοικότα, τὴν ἐκείνων ἕξουσιν ὀνομασίαν δήπουθεν, ἀγαθὴν ἀγαθοῦ καὶ πονηροῦ πονηράν.

3 Οὐκοῦν ἐπειδὴ ὁ Κύριος ἡμῶν καὶ Θεὸς Ἰησοῦς ὁ Χριστὸς ἀναιρετικὸς πέφυκεν τῆς πολυθέου τῶν εἰδώλων πλάνης, ἀλλότριον ἔσται δῆλον ὅτι καὶ τὸ τούτου εὐκλεὲς ἐκμαγεῖον τῆς εἰδωλικῆς ὑπολήψεως, καὶ οὐκ ἄν ποτε ἀγαθοῦ πρωτοτύπου παράγωγον γένοιτ' ἂν κακίας συνήγορον, ὥσπερ οὖν καὶ ἔμπαλιν· ἡ γὰρ κατ' ἐναντίωσιν φυσικῆς ποιότητος τῶν ἀρχετύπων γραφὴ τὴν κατάλληλον ἕλξει καὶ προσαρμόσει τῷ ἰδίῳ παραγώγῳ κλῆσίν τε καὶ ἐργασίαν. Οὐδὲ γὰρ ἂν ποιότης πυρὸς ψύχειν ποτὲ καταδέξοιτο, οὐδὲ πάλιν μέλιτος ἐνέργεια πικρότητα ἐμποιήσει τῷ κεχρημένῳ, καὶ τούτου χάριν οὐδείς πω τῶν ἐχόντων σύνεσιν καὶ λογισμὸν ἐπιδεχομένων τἀναντία τοῖς ἐναντίοις κατηγορήσειεν καὶ ἀλληλαίτια ταῦτα προσείποι τὸ σύνολον, ἐνὸν δὲ καὶ ἐξ αὐτῆς τῆς ἐτυμολογίας τὴν διαίρεσίν τε καὶ ἑτερότητα τῶν τοιούτων συνιδεῖν πάλιν. "Εἴδωλον" μὲν γὰρ εἴρηται ὡς εἶδος δόλου τυγχάνον, δόλος γὰρ ἀληθῶς καὶ ἀπάτη ψευδώνυμος τῆς εἰδωλολατρείας πολυθεΐα, πόρρω βάλλουσα τοῦ κατὰ φύσιν ὄντος Θεοῦ, καὶ τὴν κτίσιν ἐπανιστᾶσα κατὰ τοῦ δημιουργήσαντος αὐτὴν Δεσπότου· ὅθεν οὐκ ἂν τὸ τοιοῦτον εἰκὼν πρὸς τῶν ὑγιῶς ἐχόντων τὸ φρονεῖν ὀνομασθήσεται, καὶ πῶς ἔσται ταὐτὸν εἴδωλον καὶ εἰκὼν συνιδεῖν οὐκ ἔχω. "Εἰκὼν" δὲ λέγεται παρὰ τὸ ἐοικέναι τῷ ἀρχετύπῳ, εἴτε "ὁσίου,"

those of good people naturally counteract those who have received names modeled on those of evil people. Therefore, as subsequent copies resemble the things on which they are modeled by reason of having the same name, so the thing named will presumably possess good from a good model and evil from an evil one.

So, since our Lord and God, Jesus Christ, by nature coun- 3
teracts the polytheistic error of idols, it is clear that an impression taken from this glorious one will also be antithetical to something with a reputation for idolatry, and that something derived from a good prototype may never become an advocate of something evil, as is also the case with the opposite. For an image that is in disagreement with the natural quality of its archetypes will attract and attach the appropriate term and function to what it has mistakenly derived from it. For the quality of fire would never allow cooling, nor again will the characteristic action of honey produce bitterness for someone who uses it; because of this no one with any intelligence or mental capacity would ascribe opposite qualities to opposites and ever name these as causes of the other, when it is also possible at once from their etymology to understand their distinction and difference. An idol is called an "idol" as it is a form of deceit; for the falsely named polytheism of idolatry is truly a deceit and a fraud, because it falls far short of the one who is God in his nature and causes creation to rise up against the Master who fashioned it. Therefore, an icon would not be named as that kind of object by those whose thinking is sound, and how an idol and an icon could be considered the same thing, I cannot comprehend. For an icon is called an "icon" on account of its likeness to its archetype, as "saintly" from "saint" or

"ὁσία," εἴτε "ἁγίου" "ἁγία," καὶ τοσοῦτόν γε ἔχουσα τὸ ἐοικός, ὡς καὶ τῇ τοῦ παραδείγματος ταυτίζεσθαι προσηγορίᾳ. Πολλάκις γὰρ ἐπὶ τοίχου γραφῆς δένδρων ἢ ὀρνέων εἰκόνας ἰδόντες, οὔ φαμεν ὅτι "φοίνικος εἰκὼν τόδε," ἢ ὅτι "γεράνου τυχὸν ἐκτύπωμα" τὸ ὁρώμενον, καίπερ τοῦτο ταῦτα, ἀλλὰ "φοῖνιξ" καὶ "γέρανος·" οὕτω γ' οὖν καὶ σταυροῦ τύπον ἰδόντες, "σταυρὸν" ὀνομάζομεν, ὡσαύτως δὲ καὶ ἐπὶ τῶν ἁγίων εἰκόνων ἢ καὶ τῶν ἑτέρως ἐχόντων. Ἡ γὰρ εἰκὼν τοῦ Χριστοῦ "Χριστὸς" ὀνομάζεται κατὰ τὸ ἀνάλογον, καὶ ἡ τοῦ ἁγίου Γεωργίου, φέρε εἰπεῖν, "ὁ ἅγιος Γεώργιος" κεκλήσεται, ὥσπερ οὖν καὶ ἡ τοῦ βασίλεως εἰκὼν "βασιλεὺς" ὀνομάζεται, κατ' οὐδὲν διενηνοχυῖα οὗ ἐστιν εἰκὼν ἢ κατὰ τὸ τῆς οὐσίας οὐχ ὁμογενές.

22

Ὧν οὐδὲν ὁ θυμολέων ἐκεῖνος καὶ τὴν φρένα παχὺς ἐπιστάμενος, εὑρὼν *σκεύη ὀργῆς κατηρτισμένα εἰς ἀπώλειαν,* ἥλικάς τινας *ἀπερρωγότας ἀργοὺς καὶ ἐθάδας κακῶν, μειρακίων* τε ὡς ἀληθῶς *ἀπατεῶνας,* καὶ τὰ *σώματα πρὸς κάλλος ἀσκοῦντας,* συμβαίνοντας τοῖς αὐτοῦ θελήμασιν, προσφθείρεται αὐτοῖς καὶ δι' αὐτῶν τὸ ἀθέμιτον καὶ θεοστυγὲς διαγγέλλει τοῖς πᾶσι κήρυγμα. Ἐν οἷς ἐξῆρχεν ἄλλος τις Ἰαννῆς, (ἀλλ' οὐκ Ἰωάννης καλεῖσθαι ἄξιος), ὡς *ἐν τῷ Λαβυρίνθῳ* φέρεται πρῶτος κατὰ Ἀσσυρίους ἀναφυεὶς ἐκ γῆς ἄνθρωπος, μύθῳ οὐκ ἀληθείᾳ πρωτοπαγὴς

"holy" from "holy one," having so great a likeness as to be identical in its appellation with that on which it is modeled. For often when we see images of trees or birds in a wall painting, we do not say, "This is an image of a palm tree" or "what we see is a representation of a crane," although that is what they are, but simply say it is "a palm tree" and "a crane." So then, when we see the form of a cross, we call it "a cross," and we do just the same with reference to holy icons or even other things. For the icon of Christ is called "Christ" by analogy, and that of Saint George, say, will be called "Saint George." In the same way too, the image of the emperor is called "the emperor," for the image differs from him in no respect other than not being of the same kind of essence.

22

In his ignorance of all this, that raging and slow-witted lion, Leo, found some *fellows* who followed his wishes, *instruments of his wrath fashioned for perdition, dissolute idlers accustomed to wicked actions,* men who were truly *deceivers of young men* and *who trained their bodies for beauty;* they went along with his wishes and he, working with them for his evil ends, issued to everyone his proclamation which was unlawful and hateful to God. Their leader was another Jannes (but not worthy to be called John), who (as is recorded in *The Labyrinth*), was, according to Assyrians, the first man produced from the earth, and foolishly said in their myth, but

αὐτοῖς ληρῳδούμενος, ὁ δικαίως ἐπικληθεὶς Λεκανόμαντις, ἅτε γραμματικῆς ἐμπειρότατος ὢν ὑπὲρ τοὺς λοιποὺς καὶ τῆς πάντων ἀφυεστάτου ψευδολογίας δαιμονιώτερον ὄργανον, *πονηρότατός τε πεφυκὼς ἄνθρωπος καὶ ταράξαι μεγάλα πράγματα φύσιν ἔχων.* Καὶ πρῶτα μὲν προσβάλλει ἀμέσως τῷ ὀχυρωτάτῳ καὶ τροπαιωνύμῳ πύργῳ τῆς ὀρθοδόξου πίστεως, ἀπόπειραν ποιούμενος τῆς αὐτοῦ γνώμης, δειλὸν αὐτὸν καὶ ἄστομον πρὸς τῶν ἰδίων <εἰ>σηγηθεὶς συμφατριαστῶν, πῇ μὲν ὑποσχέσεις κοσμικοῖς ἀλλ' οὐ κατὰ Θεὸν ζῶσιν αὐτῷ προτεινόμενος, πῇ δὲ καὶ *πειρασμῶν νιφάδας* καὶ τὰς τοῦ βίου τοῦδε πολυπόνους ἐπιφοράς.

2 Ὡς δὲ τὸ ἀκράδαντον ᾔσθετο τοῦ γενναίου ἱεροφάντορος, καὶ πολὺ τῶν ἐλπισθέντων ὑπερανεστηκότα τοῦτον τῇ πείρᾳ κατέμαθεν, καθίσας ἐπὶ θρόνου καὶ τοὺς ἀμφὶ τὸν ἅγιον πατριάρχην μεταπέμπτους ποιησάμενος, ἠρεύξατο λεοντηδὸν ἐπηρμένῃ ὀφρύι τὰ περιττὰ καὶ ἀπόρρητα τῆς ἐναγοῦς ψυχῆς αὐτοῦ, ἐσφάλθαι λέγων τοὺς τῆς ἀληθείας μύστας καὶ τῶν θείων εἰσηγητὰς κατὰ τὴν πίστιν, καὶ διὰ τοῦτο χρῆναι τοὺς περὶ δογμάτων ἐπὶ τοῦ παρόντος ἀνακινεῖσθαι λόγους ὅπως, τῇ ἐποπτείᾳ τῶν διαφόρων δοξῶν, τὸ κρεῖττον ἀπὸ τοῦ χείρονος τῇ τῶν πολλῶν ἐγκρινόμενον ψήφῳ τὸ κῦρος λάβοι. Πρὸς δὴ ταῦτα, ὡς ἕκαστος ἦν παρεσκευασμένος τῶν εἰσκληθέντων, ἀπελογεῖτο τῷ βασιλεῖ, τὰς αὐτοῦ ἐκτόπους ἀνασκευάζοντες μυθολογίας, γραφικαῖς μαρτυρίαις καὶ πατρικαῖς δογματοθεσίαις τὴν τῶν σεπτῶν εἰκόνων παριστῶντες προσκύνησιν.

not in the truth, to be spontaneously generated. He was, however, rightly called Lekanomantis, seeing that he was unusually adept in the study of letters and a more demonic agent of most stupid falsehood than any of them; and *being a very evil person* by nature, *he naturally stirred up great trouble.* To begin with, Leo immediately attacked that most strong and triumphantly named tower of the orthodox faith, Nikephoros, after those in his cabal had suggested that the latter was a coward and toothless, now testing his will with worldly but ungodly promises, now threatening *showers of tribulations* and painful afflictions in this life.

But when Leo realized that the noble teacher of the holy 2
mysteries was unshakable and discovered by this test that he had greatly surpassed his expectations, seated on his throne, he summoned the associates of the holy patriarch. Then, with a raised eyebrow, he roared out like a lion the extraordinary and unspeakable contents of his polluted soul, saying that the experts in the truth and the teachers of divine matters were baffled regarding the faith and for that reason dogmatic pronouncements should be discussed at the present time, so that by the contemplation of differing beliefs what was better instead of what was worse might be selected by a majority vote and receive its validity. In response, each of those who had been summoned made such defense to the emperor as he had prepared, discrediting his outlandish tales and arguing for the veneration of holy icons with evidence from scripture and edicts of the fathers.

3 Ἐπεὶ δὲ μετὰ τὸ ἀκοῦσαι ταῦτα τοὺς *ἐφευρετὰς τῶν κακῶν* καὶ τῷ ψεύδει χαίροντας εἰς μέσον προὐβάλλετο, παρεγγυῶν διάλεξιν ἀμφοτέρων ἐπὶ αὐτοῦ περὶ τῶν προκειμένων γενέσθαι, οἱ καθ' ἡμᾶς πατέρες τὸ ἀνίατον αὐτοῦ τῆς γνώμης προγινώσκοντες, μὴ δεῖν εἰς λόγους ἐλθεῖν μετὰ τῶν ἐρεσχελεῖν ἡδέως συνηθισμένων ἔκριναν, μάλιστα κριτοῦ μὴ μεσάζοντος ἀδεκάστως.

4 Πρὸς οὓς ἀγανακτικῶς φερόμενον τὸν ὠμότατον ὁ πυρίπνους θεωρῶν στῦλος τῆς εὐσεβείας Θεόδωρος τάδε φησὶ πρὸς αὐτὸν ἀποτόμως, "Τί δήποτε καὶ ὅτου χάριν, ὦ βασιλεῦ, τῆς Ἐκκλησίας τοῦ Θεοῦ εἰρηνευούσης, κλύδωνα καὶ ζάλην ἐν αὐτῇ ἀναρριπίζειν προήχθης; Τί τὰ καλῶς ἐκριζωθέντα τῆς ἀσεβείας ζιζάνια καταφυτεύειν καὶ αὐτὸς ἐν μέσῳ τοῦ περιουσίου καὶ ἐκλεκτοῦ τοῦ Κυρίου λαοῦ ἀδιακρίτως ἐπείγῃ; Οὐκ ἤκουσας τοῦ μακαρίου Παύλου τοῦ ἀποστόλου Τιμοθέῳ γράφοντος· 'Παράγγελλε αὐτοῖς *μὴ ἑτεροδιδασκαλεῖν μηδὲ προσέχειν μύθοις καὶ γενεαλογίαις ἀπεράντοις, αἵτινες ζητήσεις ματαίας παρέχουσι μᾶλλον ἢ οἰκονομίαν Θεοῦ τὴν ἐν πίστει*'· καὶ πάλιν, '*Εἴ τις ἑτεροδιδασκαλεῖ καὶ μὴ προσέρχεται ὑγιαίνουσι λόγοις καὶ τῇ κατ' εὐσέβειαν διδασκαλίᾳ, τετύφωται μηδὲν ἐπιστάμενος, ἀλλὰ νοσῶν περὶ ζητήσεις καὶ λογομαχίας ἐξ ὧν γίνονται φθόνοι, ἔρεις, βλασφημίαι, ὑπόνοιαι πονηραί, διαπαρατριβαὶ κατεφθαρμένων ἀνθρώπων τὸν νοῦν καὶ ἀπεστερημένων τῆς ἀληθείας, νομιζόντων πορισμὸν εἶναι τὴν εὐσέβειαν. Ἀφί*στασο ἀπὸ τῶν τοιούτων'· καὶ αὖθις· '*Ταῦτα ὑπομίμνησκε διαμαρτυρόμενος ἐνώπιον τοῦ Θεοῦ μὴ λογομαχεῖν εἰς οὐδὲν*

But when, even after he had heard this, Leo began to introduce *inventors of evils* who rejoiced in falsehood, recommending that a discussion by both sides should take place in his presence about the matter in hand, our fathers, already knowing the incorrigible nature of his mind, decided that they must not engage in debate with people cheerfully accustomed to engage in frivolous talk, especially with a judge who was not officiating impartially. 3

When Theodore, that fire-breathing pillar of piety, saw 4
this most savage ruler react angrily toward them, he abruptly said this to him, "Why and for what reason, emperor, when the Church of God is at peace, have you been induced to stir up fresh confusion and turmoil in it? Why do you indiscriminately hasten to sow again in the midst of the Lord's special and chosen people the weeds of impiety that were properly uprooted? Have you not heard what blessed Paul the apostle wrote to Timothy? 'Command them *not to teach any different doctrine nor occupy themselves with myths and endless genealogies which promote* vain *speculations rather than God's dispensation that is in faith*'; and again, '*If anyone teaches otherwise and does not apply himself to sound words and the teaching that accords with godliness, he is puffed up with conceit knowing nothing, but is stricken with a craving for speculations and disputes about words from which come envy, dissension, slander, evil suspicions, and wrangling among men who are depraved in mind and bereft of the truth, thinking that godliness is a means of gain.* Avoid such things'; and again, '*Remind them of these things, warning them before God not to dispute about words, which does no good and is*

χρήσιμον ἐπὶ καταστροφῇ τῶν ἀκουόντων· ἀλλὰ καὶ τὰς βεβήλους κενοφωνίας περιΐστασο, εἰδὼς ὅτι γεννῶσι μάχας.'

5 "Συνέπεται δὲ τούτοις καὶ ὁ θεοφόρος Ἰγνάτιος, '*Προφυλάσσω ὑμᾶς,* λέγων, *ἀπὸ τῶν θηρίων τῶν ἀνθρωπομόρφων* αἱρετικῶν, *οὓς οὐ μόνον οὐ δεῖ ἡμᾶς παραδέχεσθαι, ἀλλ' εἰ δυνατὸν μηδὲ συναντᾶν.*' Τούτων τοιγαροῦν οὕτω διωρισμένων καὶ τῆς πρὸς τοὺς δυσσεβεῖς αἱρετικοὺς ὁμιλίας ἡμᾶς ἀπαγόντων, τίς λοιπὸν πεῖσαι ἡμᾶς δυνήσεται ἐλθεῖν εἰς λόγους μετὰ τῶν ἠθετηκότων κανόνας καὶ στάθμας τῆς ἀρχαίας πίστεως καὶ τὰς θείας γραφὰς ἀφόβως εἰς πολλῶν ἀποπλάνησιν ῥερᾳδιουργηκότων; *Ὃν γὰρ τρόπον Ἰαννῆς καὶ Ἰαμβρῆς ἀντέστησαν* τῷ θεράποντι τοῦ Θεοῦ *Μωϋσεῖ, οὕτω καὶ οὗτοι ἀνθίστανται τῇ ἀληθείᾳ,* δελεαζόμενοι τῇ τε παρὰ σφίσι προκαθεδρίᾳ καὶ τῇ πλείστους ἀπολλυούσῃ αἰσχροκερδίᾳ, *ἀλλ' οὐ προκόψουσιν ἐπὶ* πολὺ ὡς ὁ λόγος φησίν· *ἡ γὰρ ἄνοια αὐτῶν ἔκδηλος ἔσται πᾶσιν, ὡς καὶ ἐκείνων ἐγένετο.* Ἀλλ' οὖν γε καὶ τοῦτο ἔξω τοῦ πρέποντος πεποιήμεθα—τὸ περὶ τῆς ἐκείνων φημὶ ἀξυνεσίας—κἂν ποσῶς γοῦν ἐπὶ σοῦ τήμερον ἀπολογήσασθαι· *τὸ γὰρ τοῦ τυχόντος ἐναντία ταῖς τῶν πολλῶν δόξαις ἀποφαινομένου φροντίζειν εὔηθες* ᾗ φησιν καὶ ἡ τῶν ἔξω παροιμία."

6 Τὸν δὲ τούτων ὑπακούσαντα τῶν λόγων καὶ δῆθεν μεγάλως δυσχεράναντα φάναι, "Καὶ περιττὸς ἐγώ σοι δοκῶ, κύρι Θεόδωρε; Μικροῦ καὶ πείθεις με λόγον σοι εἰπεῖν περιττὸν ἀληθῶς, ἵνα μηδαμῶς ὑποστρέψαι δυνηθῇς εἰς τὸ κατὰ σὲ μοναστήριον," ἤτοι τὴν ὑπερόριον ἀπόφασιν ἢ καὶ τὸν ὁπωσοῦν μόρον διὰ τῶν τοιούτων πλαγίως ὑποσημ-

the ruination of the hearers; also *shun profane and idle talking* knowing that it generates quarrels.'

"The divinely inspired Ignatios was also in agreement 5
with those words, saying, '*I am protecting you from those wild beasts in human form,* the heretics, *whom we not only must not receive but, if possible, not even meet.*' So, since this is what they declare and they guide us away from conversation with impious heretics, who else then could persuade us to enter into discussions with men who have set aside the canons and rules of the ancient faith and without fear have tampered with the holy scriptures in order to mislead many people? For *in the manner that Jannes and Jambres opposed Moses* the servant of God, *so these men also oppose the truth,* in order to entice people with the promise of authority alongside them and of the sordid gain that ruins so many; *but they will not get* far, as the passage says, *for their folly will be plain to all, as it was also in the case of those* two. In fact I too have done more than I should—concerning their stupidity, I mean—in making any defense today in your presence. *For to pay any attention when an ordinary person* is setting forth *views which are contrary to the received opinions* of many people *is foolish,* as the pagan saying has it."

When Leo heard those statements, he became extremely 6
annoyed and said, "Do I seem superfluous to you, *Kyr* Theodore? You almost persuade me to make a truly superfluous pronouncement to you: that under no circumstances may you return to your monastery," alluding by these cryptic words either to a sentence of banishment or even death of

νάμενος προβλημάτων. "Ἀλλ' οὐ πείσεις με," φησίν, "ἀπερισκέπτως δρᾶσαι τό σοι καταθύμιον, οὐδέ γε ἐπὶ ἐμοῦ μαρτυρήσεις εἰς τοῦτο ηὐτρεπισμένος· ἀνεξικάκως δὲ μακροθυμήσω καὶ καταφρονούμενος ὑφ' ὑμῶν, μόνον εἰ διαλεχθῆναι μὴ παραιτήσησθε μετὰ τῶν ἐνδιαβαλλόντων ὑμῶν τὸ κατὰ τὴν κοινὴν πίστιν φρόνημα· εἰ δὲ τοῦτο οὐ βούλεσθε, πρόδηλοί ἐστε τὴν ἑαυτῶν καθομολογοῦντες ἧτταν, ὅπερ ἀναγκάσει ὑμᾶς τοῖς ἐκείνων ἀκολουθῆσαι καὶ μὴ βουλομένους θελήμασιν."

7 Τοῦ δὲ συλλόγου παντὸς τῶν ἐπισκόπων σὺν τῷ θεοειδεῖ ποιμένι συμφώνως παραιτουμένων τὴν πρὸς τοὺς κατεγνωσμένους συνομιλίαν καὶ τὰ τοῦ μακαρίου Παύλου λεγόντων, "Ἡμῖν *δὲ εἰς ἐλάχιστόν ἐστιν ἵνα ὑπὸ* τῶν δηλουμένων προσώπων *ἀνακριθῶμεν, ἢ ὑπὸ ἀνθρωπίνης ἡμέρας,* τῶν μέν, ὡς οὐκ ἐχόντων ἱερατικὸν ἀξίωμα τὸ παράπαν, τοῦ δέ, ὅτι περ *οὐδὲ ἑαυτοὺς ἀνακρίνομεν.*" Τῆς εἰλικρινοῦς ἡμῶν εἵνεκα πίστεως τὸ πρόσωπον αἰνιξαμένων καὶ τοῦ ἄνακτος τῶν λεγομένων μὴ συνιόντος τὴν δύναμιν, πάλιν ὁ μέγας Θεόδωρος ἀναλαβὼν *τὴν τοῦ Πνεύματος μάχαιραν,* ἐμβριθέστερον ἀποκρίνεται, τὴν αὐθάδειαν τοῦ ἑαυτὸν εἰς κριτοῦ τάξιν καθιστῶντος ἐντρέψαι βουλόμενος, καί φησιν, "Βασιλεῦ, πρόσχες τοῖς παρὰ τοῦ θεσπεσίου Παύλου δι' ἡμῶν σοι λεγομένοις περὶ ἐκκλησιαστικῆς εὐταξίας, καὶ μαθὼν ὡς οὐκ ἔξεστιν βασιλέα ἑαυτὸν κριτήν τε καὶ δικαστὴν ἐν τοῖς τοιούτοις παρεισφέρειν, στοίχησον καὶ αὐτός, εἴπερ εὐσεβεῖν συνέγνωκας, τοῖς ἀποστολικοῖς κανόσι, λέγει γὰρ οὕτως· '*Ἔθετο ὁ Θεὸς ἐν τῇ Ἐκκλησίᾳ πρῶτον ἀποστόλους, δεύτερον προφήτας, τρίτον*

some sort. "But," he said, "you are not going to persuade me to carry out your desire thoughtlessly, nor will you suffer martyrdom in my presence although you are prepared for this; even though I am being treated contemptuously by you, I will continue to be patient and tolerate you, but only if you do not refuse to converse with those who are opposed to your thinking on the common faith. But if you are unwilling to do this, you are clearly acknowledging your own defeat, which will compel you to follow their wishes even against your will."

The whole assembly of bishops, however, along with the 7
godlike shepherd Theodore, unanimously refused to converse with those they despised, quoting the words of blessed Paul, "For us *it is a very small thing that we should be judged by* the persons indicated *or by any human court,* since, on the one hand they do not hold a priestly rank at all and, on the other, *we have no reason to reproach ourselves.*" As the bishops were alluding to our pure faith, but the ruler did not understand the point of what was being said, the great Theodore again took up *the sword of the Spirit* and replied more severely. Wishing to shame the presumption of the one who was setting himself up in the role of a judge, he said, "Emperor, pay attention to what the inspired Paul is saying to you through us concerning ecclesiastical government and, when you have learned that it is not possible for an emperor to set himself up as a judge and juryman in such matters, comply with the apostolic canons yourself, if you want to be orthodox, for it says this there, '*God appointed in the Church first apostles, second prophets, third teachers.*' See, according to God's

διδασκάλους.' Ἰδοὺ οὗτοί εἰσιν οἱ τὰ περὶ πίστεως διατιθέντες καὶ ἀνερευνώμενοι κατὰ τὸ τῷ Θεῷ δοκοῦν καὶ οὐ βασιλεύς· οὐδὲ γὰρ ἀπεμνημόνευσεν ὁ ἱερὸς ἀπόστολος βασιλέα διοικεῖν τὰ τῆς Ἐκκλησίας."

8 Πρὸς ταῦτα ὁ καῖσαρ ἀπεκρίνατο, "Οὐκοῦν ἐκβάλλεις με σήμερον τῆς Ἐκκλησίας, ὦ Θεόδωρε;" Καὶ ὁ ὅσιος πρὸς αὐτόν, "Οὐκ ἐγώ," φησίν, "ἀλλ' ὁ μνημονευθεὶς νυμφοστόλος αὐτῆς καὶ θεῖος ἀπόστολος Παῦλος· εἰ δὲ ὡς τέκνον ἐθέλεις εἶναι ταύτης, τὸ κωλύσον οὐδέν, μόνον ἕπου κατὰ πάντα τῷ πνευματικῷ πατρί σου," τῇ δεξιᾷ χειρὶ τὸν ἁγιώτατον καθυποδείξας Νικηφόρον.

23

Τούτων οὖν ἕως τοσούτου γυμνασθέντων, ἀλλοιωθεὶς ὥσπερ τὰς φρένας ὁ ἀλητήριος, ἐξάξαι λόγον εὐθῆ τῇ ὑπερβολῇ τῆς μανίας οὐκέτι οἷός τε ἦν, ἐκρήξας δὲ φωνὴν χολερὰν μετὰ κραυγῆς αὐτὸς δι' ἑαυτοῦ παρὰ τὸ εἰκὸς ἐκφωνεῖ τό, "'Ἐξέλθετε ἔνθεν." Οὕτω τοιγαροῦν πρὸς τὸν πατριαρχικὸν οἶκον ὁμοθυμαδὸν οἱ τῆς ὀρθοδοξίας ἐπανελθόντες ἀλεῖπται, περιεκύκλουν τὸν μέγαν τῆς εὐσεβείας προαγωνιστὴν Θεόδωρον, τοῖς διὰ λόγων γεραίροντες ἐράνοις, ὡς ἅτε δὴ τὸν κοινὸν ἐχθρὸν ἐν τῷ Θεῷ τῷ κέρατι τῶν ὀξυτάτων αὐτοῦ ἐκκεντήσαντα λόγων καὶ ἐν τῷ ὀνόματι αὐτοῦ κατὰ τὸ μᾶλλον ἐξουδενώσαντα τοὺς ἐπανισταμένους αὐτοῖς.

decree, these are the ones who arrange and examine matters concerning the faith and not an emperor, for the holy apostle did not record that an emperor should manage the affairs of the Church."

To this the emperor replied, "So, Theodore, are you ex- 8
communicating me from the Church today?" And the saint said to him, "Not I, but her bridal escort and holy apostle who was mentioned before, Paul; but if you still want to be her child, nothing will prevent it, just follow your spiritual father in everything," indicating the most holy Nikephoros with his right hand.

23

When the dispute had reached this point, the wicked man, as if he was out of his mind, was no longer able to get a word out straight because of the excess of his fury, but, with a shriek, broke out angrily, shouting in an unseemly fashion, "Get out of here!" So, the teachers of orthodoxy returned together to the patriarchal residence and surrounded Theodore, the great champion of piety, honoring him with their words, since he had gored the common enemy with the horn of his most penetrating oratory by God's will and in his name had reduced to nothing those who were attacking them.

2 Ἀμέλει πρὸς τοῦ ὑπάρχου τῆς πόλεως τοὺς ἰδίους θᾶττον καταλαμβάνειν προστασσόμενοι τόπους οἱ μάκαρες, καὶ μηκέτι τολμᾶν αὐτόθι παρρησιάζεσθαι, ὁ ἄθραυστος τῆς ὁμολογίας οἶκος Θεόδωρος, πρὸς τοὺς λέξαντας ὑποφθάς, "Εἰ μὲν ὁ πατὴρ ἡμῶν καὶ κοινὸς τῶν ὀρθοφρόνων δεσπότης," φησίν, "οὐ προσκαλέσεται ἡμᾶς, καὶ δίχα τῆς ὑμετέρας κελεύσεως τοῦτο ποιῆσαι οὐκ ἀναδυόμεθα, εἰ δὲ μή γε, παρ' ἐμοὶ ἡ ὑμετέρα πρόσταξις οὐ φυλαχθήσεται τὸ παράπαν, ἀλλὰ καὶ ἐλεύσομαι καὶ τὰ ἀνήκοντα συμφράσω." Ὅπερ οὖν καὶ ἐποίει ὁ μακαρίτης, πάντα φόβον ἀνθρώπινον ἐξ ἑαυτοῦ ἀποσεισάμενος καὶ πρὸς τὸ παθεῖν ὅλος ηὐτρεπισμένος.

3 Εἰς γὰρ τὸ ἴδιον ὑποστρέψας μοναστήριον, καὶ τοὺς μαθητὰς παρακλήσεως λόγοις πρὸς τὸν προκείμενον θωρακίσας ἀγῶνα, καὶ διεγείρας αὐτῶν τὰ φρονήματα μέχρι θανάτου καὶ πληγῶν ἀντιποιεῖσθαι τὸ δόγμα τῆς ὀρθοδόξου πίστεως, μετά τινας ἡμέρας πάλιν ἀπῄει πρὸς τὸν ἱερώτατον πατριάρχην, παραμυθούμενος αὐτὸν (συμπεπτωκότα ἤδη τῇ θλίψει διὰ τὴν τῆς Ἐκκλησίας ἀνατροπὴν καὶ κατάλυσιν) καὶ ὅτι μέγιστον κλέος ἐντεῦθεν αὐτῷ παρὰ Θεῷ ἀποκείσεται. Καὶ τί γὰρ ἦν λεγόμενον ἢ πραττόμενον παρὰ τῷ θεσπεσίῳ Νικηφόρῳ, ὃ μὴ τῇ κρίσει τοῦ Θεοδώρου ὑπήγετο καὶ τὸ ἔμπεδον αὐτόθεν ἐλάμβανεν εἴτε ὡς τῆς συμφερούσης μοίρας ὑπάρχον, εἴτε καὶ ὡς τῆς ἄλλως ἐχούσης; Τοιούτως ἦν αὐτῷ αἰδέσιμος ὁ θεῖος πατὴρ ἡμῶν, καὶ τὰ δευτέρια μετ' αὐτὸν ἐν τῇ συνόδῳ τῶν ἐπισκόπων φέρων, σοφίᾳ τε καὶ τῇ περὶ τὸ θεῖον εὐσεβείᾳ πάντων ὑπειλημμένος.

Then, indeed, when the blessed men were ordered by officers of the eparch of the city to go home very quickly and no longer dare to speak out boldly there, Theodore, that indomitable abode of the confession of the faith, interrupted and said to those who had spoken, "If Nikephoros, our father and the common master of the orthodox, is not going to challenge us, we will not hesitate to speak out despite your order. And even if he does, in my case at least, your command will not be obeyed at all, but I will go and give him some appropriate advice." This then is what Theodore of blessed memory did, shaking off all human fear and being completely ready to suffer. 2

He returned to his own monastery and, after he had armed his disciples with words of comfort for the impending struggle and roused their spirits to defend the doctrine of the orthodox faith even to the point of beatings and death, some days later he went back again to the most holy patriarch. He consoled him (as Nikephoros had already collapsed in distress at the overthrow and dissolution of the Church) by saying that very great renown would be laid up for him with God as a result. For what did the divinely inspired Nikephoros say or do that did not rely on Theodore's judgment and receive his direct involvement, whether it was supportively or otherwise? This was how our holy father was respected by Nikephoros, holding the second position after him in the synod of bishops and being esteemed above everyone for his wisdom and piety concerning what was holy. 3

4 Καὶ γοῦν μετὰ βραχὺν χρόνον τοῦ ἀοιδίμου πατριάρχου τοῦ ἱεραρχικοῦ θρόνου κατὰ τὴν εἰκάδα τοῦ Δύστρου νύκτωρ κατενεχθέντος, καὶ εἰς τὸ οἰκεῖον ἐξορισθέντος σεμνεῖον, ὅπερ αὐτὸς ἐδείματο ἐν τοῖς τῆς Ἀσίας ὀρεινοῖς τοῦ στενοῦ μέρεσιν, ὁμοίως δὲ καὶ τῶν λοιπῶν ἱερομυστῶν τὰς αὐτὰς ἀποφάσεις κομισαμένων καὶ κατὰ διαφόρους χώρας τε καὶ πολίχνας παραπεμφθέντων, καὶ τῶν δυσωνύμων Χριστομάχων τὰς ἐκκλησίας κατασχόντων καὶ τὰς ἐν αὐταῖς ἱερὰς τῶν ἁγίων εἰκόνας—ὢ τοῦ φοβεροῦ ἀκούσματος—ἀφοβητὶ καταστρεφομένων ἢ καὶ ἀναχριόντων καὶ μελετώντων κενὰ καὶ μάταια κατὰ τῶν ὑπολοίπων τῆς ὀρθοδοξίας τροφίμων, ἐπείπερ ἧκεν ἡ τῶν Βαΐων νικηφόρος τοῦ Σωτῆρος ἡμῶν Ἑορτή, ὁ πατὴρ ἡμῶν Θεόδωρος τὴν συνήθη τῷ Χριστῷ Ἀπαντὴν μετὰ τῆς συνούσης αὐτῷ ἐκποιούμενος ὁμηγύρεως, προσέταξε τοῖς τὰς σεπτὰς εἰκόνας φέρουσιν ἀδελφοῖς ὑψοῦ τοὺς πίνακας ἀνέχειν, καὶ οὕτω γε περιοδεύειν τὸν ἔγγιστα τῆς μονῆς ἀμπελῶνα, μηδένα φόβον ἔχοντας χάριν τῆς ἐνσκηψάσης Χριστομανίας· ὅπερ παρὰ τῶν πονηρῶν γειτόνων ἐποπτευθὲν καὶ κατὰ τὸ μέσον τοῦ ἄστεως θριαμβευθὲν ἦλθεν καὶ μέχρις αὐτῆς τῆς τυραννογνώμονος ἀκοῆς. Ὁ δέ, τοῦτο μαθὼν καὶ λίαν κατὰ διάνοιαν κινηθείς, δηλοῖ τῷ ἱερῷ πατρὶ ἡμῶν δι' ἑνὸς τῶν μεγιστάνων, "Οὐκ ἠρεμεῖς, οὐ καθέζῃ μεθ' ἡσυχίας, ἀλλὰ τοῦτο κἀκεῖνο εἰς ἐμὴν δῆθεν ἐπίπληξιν περινοεῖς; Ἴσθι τοίνυν ὡς εἰ μὴ τοῦ φρονήματος λωφήσειας καὶ ὑποσταλείης τοῦ διδάσκειν ἔτι τὰ περὶ πίστεως, τάχιστά σε μόρῳ καθυποβαλών, τοῖς ἐν Ἅιδου ὁμέστιον καταστήσω."

At all events, the famous patriarch was deposed from the hierarchical throne a short time later, on the night of March 20, and banished to his own monastery which he himself had built in the hilly area on the Asian side of the straits. Similarly, the remaining prelates also received the same sentence and were consigned to different regions and towns, while the hateful enemies of Christ took possession of the churches and started—what terrible news!—fearlessly destroying or whitewashing the holy icons of the saints in them and also devising empty and futile attacks against the remaining nurslings of orthodoxy. When our Savior's triumphant Feast of Palms arrived, as our father Theodore was carrying out the customary Meeting with Christ celebration along with the company that was with him, he instructed the brethren carrying the revered icons to hold up the panels and process like that around the vineyard nearest the monastery without being afraid of the fury against Christ that had occurred. This was observed by their wicked neighbors and triumphantly reported in the middle of the city, and it even reached the ears of the tyrant, Leo. When he learned of this, he was extremely upset and made this known to our holy father through one of his courtiers, "Why won't you stay quiet? Why won't you live in spiritual tranquility instead of devising this and that, apparently to rebuke me? Well then, you should know that unless you give up your intentions and stop continuing to teach matters concerning the faith, I'll put you to death very quickly and send you to Hades." 4

5 Ταῦτα ἀκούσας ὁ ἀκλόνητος πύργος τῆς ὁμολογίας, οὐ μόνον οὐκ ἐνέδωκεν τοῦ τῆς πίστεως ζήλου, ἀλλὰ καὶ τοὺς ἀνὰ τὸ ἄστυ καθηγουμένους παραβαλόντας αὐτῷ μετὰ τὴν ἁγίαν καὶ λαμπροφόρον τοῦ Σωτῆρος ἡμῶν Χριστοῦ τριήμερον ἐκ νεκρῶν ἔγερσιν, γνώμης ἕνεκεν περὶ τῆς κατεπειγούσης αὐτοὺς συνηθείας <τοῦ> τὴν ἄφιξιν πρὸς τὸν πατριαρχικὸν οἶκον ποιήσασθαι, καὶ ὑπεδέξατο καὶ τὰ χρηστὰ καὶ Θεῷ ἐράσμια συνεβούλευσέν τε καὶ διεπράξατο, χαράξας ἐπιστολὴν πρὸς τοὺς παραβραβεῦσαι τὴν ἀλήθειαν ἐγκεχειρηκότας, ἧς ἡ ἀρχή, *Νόμοις θείοις καὶ κανονικοῖς ἑπόμενοι θεσπίσμασι τοῦ μὴ δεῖν παρὰ τὴν τοῦ οἰκείου ἐπισκόπου γνώμην πράττειν τι ἢ λέγειν τῶν ὅσα εἰς ἐκκλησιαστικὴν φέρει εὐταξίαν, πολλοῦ γε εἰπεῖν εἰς δογματικὴν ἐξέλκει συζήτησιν, τούτου χάριν τῆς ὑμετέρας ἐξουσίας καὶ ἅπαξ καὶ δὶς ἐκκαλεσαμένης πρὸς τὰ τοιαῦτα τὴν καθ' ἡμᾶς εὐτέλειαν, οὐκ ἐτόλμησεν ἔξω τι τῶν νενομισμένων πράττουσα παραγενέσθαι, ὡς ὑπὸ τὴν ἱερὰν χεῖρα Νικηφόρου τοῦ ἁγιωτάτου πατριάρχου Πνεύματι θείῳ τελοῦσα,* καὶ τὰ ἑξῆς. Ταύτην δυσὶν ἀδειλάντοις μᾶλλον τῶν συνελθόντων ἐγκεχειρικότες προσώπων, πρὸς τοὺς Χριστομαχεῖν δεδιψηκότας ἐκπέμπουσιν. Οἱ δὲ τῶν ἐγκειμένων ἀναμαθόντες τὸν νοῦν, χαλεπαίνουσιν ἔτι σφοδρότερον, καὶ ῥαπίσμασι τοὺς κεκομικότας περιβαλόντες μεθ' ὕβρεων καὶ ἀτιμιῶν, τοῦ σεκρέτου ἐξελαύνουσιν, τὰ πάνδεινα αὐτοῖς πρὸς τοῖς φθάσασιν ἐπαπειλησάμενοι.

When he heard this, that unshaken tower of confession 5
did not only not flag in his zeal for the faith but, after the holy and resplendent resurrection of Christ our Savior from the dead on the third day, when the *kathegoumenoi* from across the city visited him to seek his opinion about the customary visit to the patriarchal residence that was imminent, he received them, advised them what was useful and desirable to God and implemented this by writing a letter to those who were attempting to pervert the truth. It began like this: *Following divine laws and canonical decrees that we must not do or say anything contrary to the judgment of our own bishop on matters that have a bearing on ecclesiastic good order, much less mention those matters that lead to doctrinal disputation, for that reason, though your authority summoned my unworthy self once or twice to such occasions, I did not dare to come, doing something beyond what has been sanctioned as I am subject to the holy hand of Nikephoros the most holy patriarch in the divine Spirit,* and so on. They entrusted this letter to two of the more fearless members of the group who had assembled, and sent them off to those who were thirsting to make war against Christ. But when the latter discovered the meaning of its contents, they became even more angry; they subjected the letter carriers to beatings as well as insults and abuse and drove them out of the council chamber, making terrible threats against them in addition to the previous ill-treatment.

24

Οὗτοι *μὲν οὖν ἐπορεύοντο χαίροντες ἀπὸ προσώπου τοῦ συνεδρίου, ὅτι κατηξιώθησαν ὑπὲρ τοῦ ὀνόματος* τοῦ Χριστοῦ *ἀτιμασθῆναι.* Ὁ δέ γε πατὴρ ἡμῶν Θεόδωρος οὐ διέλειπεν ἔκτοτε ἀλλεπαλλήλους χαράττων ἐπιστολὰς καὶ διεγείρων πρὸς ἀνδρείαν τοὺς ἐγγὺς καὶ τοὺς πόρρωθεν, ἐμφανῆ ἑαυτὸν τῷ λυσσῶντι τὴν αἵρεσιν ἐντεῦθεν μᾶλλον καταστῆσαι βουλόμενος, καὶ ὡς οὐ ποιεῖται λόγον τῶν αὐτοῦ ἀπειλῶν, οὔτε μὴν δέδιεν τὸν ὑπὲρ εὐσεβείας θάνατον. Εἰς ὃ καὶ μανεὶς περισσοτέρως, ὁ κακογνώμων Λέων ἐξορίαν καὶ αὐτὸν καταδικάζει. Δεξάμενος τοίνυν ὁ ἱερὸς πατὴρ ἡμῶν καὶ τῆς ὀρθοδοξίας ἀνεπαίσχυντος εἰσηγητὴς τὴν περιπόθητον αὐτῷ καὶ ἐκ πολλοῦ ἐφετὴν ἀπόφασιν, προσκαλεσάμενος τὸ πλῆθος τῶν μαθητῶν, καθίστησιν ἐν αὐτοῖς δύο καὶ ἑβδομήκοντα ἀρχηγούς, ὑφ᾽ οὓς καταμερισθῆναι τὴν ἀδελφότητα αὐθαιρέτῳ γνώμῃ προτρεψάμενος, δεδωκώς τε αὐτοῖς ἐντολὴν ὥστε μετὰ τὴν ἔξοδον αὐτοῦ μὴ ἐναπομεῖναι αὐτόθι τινὰ τῶν *θελόντων* τὴν ἀληθῆ *ζωὴν* καὶ *ἀγαπώντων* τὰς *ἀγαθὰς ἡμέρας ἰδεῖν,* καθὼς ψάλλει ὁ ἅγιος Δαυΐδ, αὐτὸς πρὸς τοῦ ἀποσταλέντος βασιλικοῦ παραληφθείς, τῷ ἐγκειμένῳ φρουρίῳ κατὰ τὴν Ἀπολλωνιάδα λίμνην καλουμένῳ Μέτωπα γεγηθὼς περιορίζεται.

2 Ἀλλὰ καὶ ἐνταῦθα δέσμιος Χριστοῦ φρουρούμενος, τῆς ὁμοίας οὐκ ἀφίστατο θεοφιλοῦς πράξεως, ἀλλ᾽ αὖθις δι᾽ οἰκείων συλλαβῶν τοὺς ἁπανταχοῦ γῆς εὐσεβεῖν προαιρουμένους εἰς τοῦτο αὐτὸ ἐπεστήριζεν καὶ πρὸς τὸ ἀγαθὸν

24

Those men *then went their way from the presence of the council rejoicing that they had been deemed worthy to suffer dishonor for the name* of Christ. From then on, our father Theodore continued to write letters in quick succession and to rouse those near and far to bravery, since he wanted in this way to make himself more conspicuous to the madman who was promoting the heresy and to show that he took no account of his threats, nor indeed was afraid to die for the sake of piety. The evil-minded Leo raged even more at this and condemned Theodore to banishment too. So when our holy father and undaunted teacher of orthodoxy received the sentence that he yearned for and had for a long time desired, he summoned the whole mass of his disciples and appointed seventy-two leaders among them, urging that the brotherhood should be divided up under them voluntarily, according to their own choice; and he gave them a command that, after his departure, any of those who *wished for the* true *life* and *loved to see good days,* as holy David chants, should not remain there. Then he was taken away by the imperial official who had been dispatched and was joyfully confined in the fortress called Metopa, which is situated near Lake Apollonias.

But there too, though guarded as a prisoner of Christ, he 2
did not give up the same conduct that was pleasing to God, but again through personal letters continued to support those throughout the land who chose to live a pious life in this respect and urge them to goodness. When the savage

παρώτρυνεν. Ὅπερ πάλιν διαγνοὺς ὁ ἀνήμερος Λέων, ἕτερον βασιλικὸν πεπομφὼς Νικήταν τοὔνομα κατ' ἐπωνυμίαν τοῦ Ἀλεξίου λεγόμενον, τὰ πάντα μὲν εὐσεβῆ καὶ χριστιανικώτατον, ἠγνοημένον δὲ τῷ θηρὶ τοιοῦτόν γε ὄντα, μετατίθησι δι' αὐτοῦ τὸν ἱεροκήρυκα ἐν τῷ τῶν Ἀνατολῶν θέματι εἰς ἕτερον ὀχύρωμα τὴν προσηγορίαν Βόνηταν, διαστειλάμενος τῷ πατρὶ διὰ τῶν ἐξυπηρετουμένων αὐτοῦ τοῖς προστάγμασιν, μηδένα μηδαμῶς ὁρᾶν, μήτε μὴν ἐκδιδάσκειν διὰ γραμμάτων τὰ περὶ πίστεως. Οὗς ὁ ἀποστολικὸς ἀνὴρ καὶ τὴν φρένα καὶ τὴν πολιτείαν ἀποστολικοῖς ἀντημείβετο λόγοις, "*Εἰ δίκαιόν ἐστι*," φάσκων, "*ἐνώπιον τοῦ Θεοῦ, ὑμῶν ἀκούειν μᾶλλον ἢ τοῦ Θεοῦ, κρίνατε· οὐ δυνάμεθα γὰρ ἡμεῖς ἃ εἴδομεν καὶ ἠκούσαμεν μὴ λαλεῖν*, καθότι *πειθαρχεῖν δεῖ Θεῷ μᾶλλον ἢ ἀνθρώποις*."

3 Ταῦτα ἀκούσας ὁ ἄναξ καὶ ἐπιμεμψάμενος τὸν φιλόχριστον Νικήταν, ὡς μὴ πεποιηκότα ἐξ ἀρχῆς τὴν ἐκδίκησιν τῆς βασιλείας αὐτοῦ, ἀποστέλλει αὐτὸν ἐκ δευτέρου, βουνευρίσαι τὸν ὁσιομάρτυρα ἑκατὸν μάστιξι διωρισμένως· ὃς ἀναβαδίσας καὶ τῷ ἀθλητῇ τοῦ Χριστοῦ τὴν ψῆφον τοῦ βασιλέως ἀπογυμνώσας, προτρέπεται μᾶλλον παρὰ τοῦ ὁσίου ἀνενδοιάστως ποιῆσαι εἰς αὐτὸν τὸ τοῦ κρατοῦντος θέλημα. Ἑωρακὼς δὲ τὸν δίκαιον ἑτοίμως ἑαυτὸν σχηματίσαντα καὶ ἄνευ τῆς ἑτέρων βίας πρὸς ὑποδοχὴν τῶν μαστίγων εὐτρεπισθέντα, ἐκλάσθη πρὸς ἔλεον ὁ θεοφιλὴς καὶ τῆς νίκης ἐπώνυμος ἄρχων, μάλιστα τὰς καταμαρανθείσας ὑπὸ τῆς ἀσκήσεως τοῦ θεσπεσίου κατιδὼν γεγυμνωμένας σάρκας.

Leo again became aware of this, he sent another imperial official, called Niketas and surnamed son of Alexios, who was a totally pious and very Christian man, although this was unknown to the beast; through him Leo transferred the holy preacher to another stronghold named Boneta in the Anatolikon theme, giving the father express orders through his minions not to see anyone at all and not to teach matters of faith by means of letters. To them this man who thought and lived like the apostles replied with apostolic words, saying, "*Whether it is right in the sight of God to listen to you rather than to God, you must judge; for we cannot but speak of what we saw and heard,* in so far as *we must obey God rather than men.*"

When the ruler heard this, he blamed the devout Niketas 3
for not carrying out the vengeance of his royal majesty in the first place, and sent him out a second time explicitly to give the saintly martyr a hundred lashes with an ox tendon whip. Niketas went back and revealed the emperor's sentence to Christ's champion, and was urged even more by the saintly man to carry out the ruler's will on him without hesitation. When Niketas, the official who loved God and who was named for victory, saw that the righteous man had readily positioned himself and without any force from other people had prepared himself to receive the lashes, he broke down in pity, especially when he observed that the divinely inspired man's naked flesh had wasted away through his ascetic practice.

4 Καὶ ἐξουδενώσας κατὰ διάνοιαν τὸ τοῦ λυμεῶνος μισάγιον πρόσταγμα, ἐνέγκας δορὰν προβάτου, καὶ ταύτην τοῖς ὤμοις τοῦ πατρὸς περιθείς, εἰς αὐτὴν ποιεῖται τὰς τῶν μαστίγων ἐπιφοράς, μονώτατος μετὰ τοῦ ἀοιδίμου ἀπολειφθεὶς ἐν τῇ κέλλῃ τοῦ πατρός· καὶ τῇ βελόνῃ τὸν ἑαυτοῦ αἱμάξας βραχίονα, τὸ ἄκρον τῆς μάστιγος τῷ ἰδίῳ καταφοινίσσει αἵματι, εἶθ' οὕτως ἐξελθὼν ἐκεῖθεν πνευστιῶν, ἐκεῖνο μὲν πρὸς γῆν ἀπέρριψεν, αὐτὸς δὲ ὡς κεκοπιακὼς δῆθεν ἐπὶ τοῦ εὐτρεπισθέντος αὐτῷ καθισματίου ἐγένετο. Τοῦτο τὸ σόφισμα καταθρήσας ὁ πατὴρ ἡμῶν, ὑπερηγάσθη μὲν τήν τε πίστιν καὶ φρόνησιν τἀνδρός, οὐ μὴν δὲ τῶν τυραννικῶν ἀπειλῶν χάριν ἀπέσχετο τοῦ κατεργάζεσθαι πρὸς τὸ ἑξῆς τὸ ἔργον Κυρίου ἐνδελεχῶς θερμοτέραις ψυχῆς προθυμίαις καὶ σφριγώσῃ διανοίᾳ καὶ νῷ διεγηγερμένῳ.

5 Ἀλλὰ καὶ αὐτόθι ἐν ἑνὶ δωματίῳ περιοριζόμενος, τοὺς ἐν διαφόροις ἐπαρχιῶν τόποις καθειργμένους πατέρας καὶ ἀδελφούς, καὶ μέντοι καὶ τὰ πνευματικὰ αὐτοῦ τέκνα, διὰ τῆς ἐνούσης αὐτῷ θεοπαρόχου ἐπεστήριζε διδασκαλίας, παρακαλῶν, νουθετῶν, παραμυθούμενος ἔτι ἐμμένειν τῇ ὁμολογίᾳ τοῦ Χριστοῦ καὶ μὴ ἐκκακεῖν ἐν ταῖς ἐν χερσὶν ὑπὲρ ἀληθείας θλίψεσιν, ἀλλὰ καὶ καραδοκεῖν τὸ λύτρον ἐκ τοῦ Θεοῦ, *ὅτι οὐκ εἰς τέλος ἐπιλησθήσεται ὁ* κατὰ Θεὸν *πτωχός,* καὶ *ἡ ὑπομονὴ τῶν πενήτων οὐκ ἀπολεῖται* εἰς τέλος, καθότι οὐ λελήθασιν τὸν Θεὸν οἱ τὰ δέοντα πράττοντες, οὐδὲ ἀνεπικούρητοι ὑπ' αὐτοῦ ἐαθήσονται· πολλοὺς δὲ καὶ τῇ χρονίᾳ ὑπερορίᾳ λειποταξίου γραφὴν ἀπενεγκαμένους διὰ συλλαβῶν ἀποτρίψασθαι τὸν τοιοῦτον ὄνειδον

Purposely disregarding the destroyer's order that hated 4
what was holy, and since he had been left all alone with the renowned father in his cell, Niketas brought a sheep's fleece and, putting this around the father's shoulders, laid the blows of the lashes onto it. Then he bloodied his own arm with a needle and reddened the tip of the whip with his own blood. He came out from the cell panting, threw the whip on the ground and, as though he was really exhausted, collapsed onto the little seat that had been prepared for him. When our father saw that clever stratagem, he was delighted at the man's faith and presence of mind, yet he did not stop continually accomplishing the Lord's work after this because of the tyrant's threats and did so with more fervent spiritual eagerness, as well as intellectual vigor and mental determination.

There too, though confined in one small room, he would 5
support the fathers and brothers who were imprisoned in different provinces, and of course his spiritual children as well, through the teaching provided by God within him. He exhorted, admonished, and encouraged them still to abide by their profession of Christ and not to lose heart during the ongoing afflictions on behalf of the truth, but to watch for the deliverance that comes from God, *because in the end the* godly *beggar will not be forgotten* and in the end *the patient endurance of the poor will not be lost,* in that those who do their duty do not escape God's notice and he will not leave them without assistance. By means of his letters he convinced many who acquired a charge of desertion during their lengthy banishment to erase such a reproach from their

τῆς σφετέρας ψυχῆς πεποίηκεν, δι' ἐξαγορεύσεως αὐτοὺς καὶ μετανοίας τῆς προσηκούσης δεξάμενος νοερῶς καὶ τῷ χορῷ τῶν διὰ Κύριον συντεταχὼς δεδιωγμένων. Γεγράφηκε δὲ καὶ πρὸς τοὺς τέσσαρας πατριάρχας, ἅμα μὲν τὸ τῆς αἱρέσεως ἀναδιδάσκων βίαιόν τε καὶ φορτικόν, ἅμα δὲ καὶ ἀξιῶν πρὸς ἐπικουρίαν τὴν ἐνδεχομένην τῶν μεταποιουμένων τῆς ὁδοῦ σφᾶς αὐτοὺς ἐπιδοῦναι.

25

Ἐπεὶ δὲ καὶ τοὺς ἀφικνουμένους ὡς αὐτὸν μετὰ χαρᾶς ὁ μέγας πατὴρ ἡμῶν ὑπεδέχετο, ἤρα γὰρ καὶ ἐβούλετο πάντας ὠφελεῖν καὶ πρὸς βίον ἐπανάγειν θεόδεκτον, συνέβη καί τι τοιοῦτον γενέσθαι. Κληρικός τις τῶν ἐπισήμων ἀπὸ τῆς τῶν Θρᾳκησίων χώρας ὁρμώμενος, πόλεως γε μὴν τυγχάνων Μασταύρας ἀνῆλθεν ἐπὶ τὰ πλησίον μέρη τῆς περιεχούσης *τὸν ἥλιον τοῦ Εὐαγγελίου* παροικίας, τοὺς συγγενεῖς ἑαυτοῦ καθὼς εἰώθει ὀψόμενος. Μαθὼν δὲ ὅτι ὁ θεῖος πατὴρ ἡμῶν Θεόδωρος ὁ Στουδιώτης αὐτόθι τὴν ὑπερορίαν κατεψηφίσθη, ὡς ἔχων ἔκπαλαι τῆς αὐτοῦ ἁγιωσύνης ἔναυλον τὴν ἀκοήν, ἐπιζητεῖ τοῦτον προσκυνῆσαι. Ὡς δὲ τῆς ἐφέσεως οὐ διήμαρτεν, ἐρωτηθεὶς ὑπὸ τοῦ ἁγίου εἰ τὴν ὀρθόδοξον ἀσπάζοιτο πίστιν καὶ τοῦτο τῇ συγκαταθέσει διομολογησάμενος, ἀκροατὴς γίγνεται καί τινων ἐντελεστέρων λόγων περὶ τῆς καθαρᾶς καὶ

souls; he accepted them spiritually through confession and the appropriate repentance and included them in the band of those who had been persecuted for the Lord's sake. He also wrote to the four patriarchs, explaining the violent and oppressive nature of the heresy and at the same time asking that they might consider devoting themselves to the possible assistance of those seeking after the true way.

25

When our great father was joyfully receiving his visitors, for he loved them and wanted to be of spiritual benefit to all and lead them to a life that was acceptable to God, something like this occurred: A notable member of the clergy, who came from the land of the Thrakesians, and, specifically, from the city of Mastaura, went up to the area near the region that embraced the *sun of the Gospel,* in order to see his own relatives, as he usually did. But when he learned that our holy father Theodore the Stoudite had been condemned to banishment there, and since he had long ago heard about his holiness, he sought him out in order to pay his respects. He did not fail in his aim and, when he was asked by the holy man if he firmly adhered to the orthodox faith and he agreed to this with conviction, he also heard a more complete exposition concerning the pure and faultless faith of those

ἀμωμήτου τῶν προσκυνούντων Χριστὸν ἐν τῇ σεπτῇ εἰκόνι τῆς παναγίας σαρκὸς αὐτοῦ πίστεως· καὶ οὕτω τρυγήσας τὴν τῶν εὐχῶν αὐτοῦ εὐλογίαν, ἐπανῆλθεν εἰς τὰ ἴδια.

2 Καὶ δὴ τοῖς συγκληρικοῖς ἑαυτοῦ συναυλιζόμενος, θαρρεῖ ἑνὶ τῶν μᾶλλον αὐτῷ προσκειμένων τὰ τῆς ὀπτασίας, ὅτι τε ἑωράκει τὸν περίφημον πατέρα τῶν πατέρων Θεόδωρον, καὶ αὐτήκοος αὐτοῦ γεγένηται διεξιόντος τὰ περὶ τῆς ἀληθοῦς πίστεως δόγματα· οἳ καὶ συνθέμενοι πρὸς ἑαυτοὺς μηκέτι συλλειτουργῆσαι τῷ ἰδίῳ ἐπισκόπῳ, ἀποτέμνουσιν ἑαυτοὺς τῆς καθολικῆς κοινωνίας. Ὡς δὲ τὴν αἰτίαν ὀψὲ γοῦν μεμαθήκει ὁ ἀνίερος τῆς τῶν κληρικῶν ἀπορρήξεως, εὐθέως καὶ ἀμελλητὶ πρὸς τὸν στρατηγὸν ἀναδραμών, καταμηνύει αὐτῷ τὰ προειρήμενα ἅπαντα. Ἦν δὲ οὗτος Ὁραβὲ ἀνὴρ τῷ ὄντι ἀλιτήμων καὶ πλήρης ἡμερῶν πονηρῶν, ὅστις καὶ διὰ τὸ δυσφημεῖν ἀθέῳ γλώττῃ εἰς τὰς ἱερὰς εἰκόνας τὴν στρατηγικὴν ἐκληρώσατο εὐδαιμονίαν.

3 Οὗτος ἀκούσας παρὰ τοῦ ἐπισκόπου τὰ περὶ τῆς διδαχῆς τοῦ μακαρίου πατρὸς ἡμῶν, πρῶτα μὲν γράφει τῷ στρατηγῷ τῶν Ἀνατολικῶν ὡς οὐκ ἔξεστι πατουμένους τοὺς τοῦ βασιλέως παρορᾶν νόμους, οὔτε μὴν τοὺς εἰς αὐτοὺς προσκρούοντας νηποινεὶ τὸν βίον παραθέειν· ἔπειτα δὲ καὶ αὐτῷ τῷ μέδοντι δι᾽ ἀναφορᾶς τά τε κατὰ τὸν ἐπίσκοπον καὶ τοὺς κληρικοὺς ἀναδιδάσκει. Ὡς δὲ τὸ γράμμα ἐδέξατο ὁ τῆς Ἑῴας στρατοπεδάρχης καὶ διεπύθετο τὰ φθάσαντα, φοβηθεὶς τὴν ἀγανάκτησιν τοῦ κρατοῦντος, ἀποστέλλει ἕνα τῶν τῆς τάξεως αὐτοῦ κακῶσαι

who worshipped Christ in the sacred icon of his all-holy flesh. And so, after reaping the blessing of Theodore's prayers, he returned home.

While meeting with his fellow clergy, he confided details 2
of his encounter to one of those who was close to him, saying that he had seen the most renowned father of fathers, Theodore, and had personally listened to him as he was describing the doctrines of the true faith. The clergy agreed with each other that they would no longer concelebrate with their own bishop, and they severed themselves from the universal communion. When, however, that unholy bishop eventually learned the cause for his clergy's severance of communion, he immediately rushed to the military governor and without hesitation informed him of all that had previously been said. This was Horabe, a really wicked man who had led a long and evil life; he had even succeeded in his military career by reviling the holy icons with his godless tongue.

When this Horabe heard from the bishop the details of 3
our blessed father's teaching, he first wrote the military governor of the Anatolikon theme that he should not disregard people who trampled on the emperor's laws, and indeed that those who offended against them should not lead their life with impunity; then in a report he explained to the ruler himself the situation regarding the bishop and the clergy. When the supreme military governor of the East received the letter and was informed of what had happened, fearing the ruler's displeasure, he sent a member of his cohort to

τὸν ἱερὸν Θεόδωρον ἐν πεντήκοντα βουνεύροις· ὅστις γενόμενος κατὰ τὸν τόπον, προφανῆ ποιεῖται τῷ ὁσίῳ τὴν καττυθεῖσαν κατ' αὐτοῦ σκαιωρίαν. Ὁ δὲ πατὴρ ἡμῶν δοξάσας τὸν Θεὸν καὶ ἐπὶ τῇ προφάσει ταύτῃ, προθύμως ἀποδύεται τὰ τῆς σαρκὸς ἐπικαλύμματα· καὶ προσχὼν τῷ ἀνδρί, "Τὸ κελευσθέν σοι," φησίν, "ὦ τέκνον, ποίησον εἰς ἐμέ." Ὁ δὲ φόβῳ συσχεθεὶς ἐξαπίνης τῇ θεωρίᾳ τοῦ αὐτοπροαιρέτου ἀθλητοῦ, καὶ αἰδῶ τὴν πρέπουσαν Χριστιανοῖς εἰς τὸν δοῦλον τοῦ Θεοῦ ἐπιδειξάμενος, ῥίπτει ἑαυτὸν ἐπὶ στόμα πρὸς τοὺς πόδας τοῦ ὁσίου, δεόμενος τῆς παρ' αὐτοῦ εὐλογίας τυχεῖν, ἧς καὶ ἀξιολόγως μετασχών, πρὸς τὸν ἀποστείλαντα αὐτὸν ἐπανέζευξεν.

4 Καὶ ἔτι τούτου λαλοῦντος καὶ τὸν λόγον τῆς ἀποστολῆς ποιουμένου, ἕτερος πονηρίας ἄγγελος ἐκ τοῦ βασιλέως πρὸς τὸν αὐτὸν στρατηγὸν παραγίνεται, Ἀναστάσιος ὄνομα, τοῦ γένους τῶν Μαρτινακίων λεγόμενος· ὃς ἀπηνὴς λίαν ὑπάρχων καὶ τῆς βασιλικῆς δυσσεβείας ὁμόζηλος, οὐχ ἁπλῶς τοῖς ὀνείδεσι τὸν τῆς Ἑῴας ὑπέβαλεν, ὡς τὰ τοῦ βασιλέως μὴ φρονοῦντα μηδὲ τοῖς αὐτοῦ ὑπείκοντα θεσπίσμασιν, ἐκείνου δὲ καὶ πεπομφέναι ἀντερίσαντος καὶ τετυφέναι τὸν ἀπεναντίας τοῦ Καίσαρος διαπραττόμενον Θεόδωρον, αὐτὸς ἀναστὰς πρὸς τὸν δίκαιον εὐθυδρόμησεν, καὶ τοῦτον ἀφιματώσας καὶ μὴ εὑρηκὼς τὸ οἱονοῦν σπάραγμα εἰς αὐτόν, ἀνακαγχάσας μέγα καὶ πλατύ, "Ποῦ," φησί, "τὰ πρὸ βραχέως στίγματα τῶν βουνεύρων;"

5 Ἀμέλει ἐπενεγκὼν τῷ ἁγίῳ ἑκατὸν καταφορὰς δριμυτάτας καθὼς ἦν αὐτῷ προστεταγμένον, ἀποκλείει αὐτὸν ἔν τινι δωματίῳ μεθ' ἑτέρου ἑνὸς μαθητοῦ αὐτοῦ, νέου μὲν

thrash holy Theodore with fifty lashes of an ox tendon whip; and when this man reached the place, he revealed to the saintly man the evil plot that had been stitched up against him. But after our father had glorified God for this opportunity, he eagerly stripped off his clothes and, looking intently at the man, said, "Do what you were ordered to do to me, my son." But the man, suddenly gripped by fear at the sight of the champion acting of his own free will in this way, showed the proper respect of Christians for the servant of God and prostrated himself at the saint's feet, begging for his blessing. After duly receiving it, he returned to the official who had sent him.

While the man was still speaking and giving an account of 4
his mission, another messenger of evil, called Anastasios and said to be of the Martinakios family, came from the emperor to the same military governor. Since he was a very cruel man who shared the emperor's zeal for impiety, he did not simply reproach the supreme military governor of the East for not sharing the emperor's opinions and not complying with his decrees, but, when the other protested that he had sent someone and beaten Theodore because he was acting in opposition to Caesar, Anastasios got up and went directly to the righteous Theodore. He stripped him bare and, when he did not find any kind of laceration on him, he laughed loudly and uproariously, and said, "Where are the marks of your recent lashes?"

Anastasios then indeed inflicted a hundred very harsh 5
strokes on the holy man, as he had been ordered, and he shut him away in a small room with another man, one of his

ὄντος τὴν ἡλικίαν, τελείου δὲ τῷ φρονήματι καὶ τῇ πίστει. Νικόλαος δ' ἦν οὗτος ὁ πολύτλας ἀριστεὺς ἀναφανεὶς καὶ αὐτὸς τῆς εὐσεβείας, ὅστις ἐξ ἐκείνου καὶ μέχρις ἡμῶν τῶν ταπεινῶν ἐν τοῖς τῆς ὁμολογίας διαπρέψας ποικίλοις παθήμασι, τέλειος ἄνθρωπος Θεοῦ ἐν τῇ καθ' ἡμᾶς κεχρημάτικε γενεᾷ. Τοῦτον τοιγαροῦν σὺν τῷ ἀθλητῇ καθείρξας Θεοδώρῳ, καὶ τὴν θύραν τοῦ κελλίου ἐπιμελῶς ἀναφράξας, μίαν τε φωταγωγὸν παρεάσας ἐν αὐτῷ, δι' αὐτῆς προσέταξεν χορηγεῖσθαι τοῖς ὁσίοις τὰ ταλαίπωρα τῆς ψυχῆς ἐφόδια διὰ χειρὸς τῶν κατασταθέντων αὐτοῖς φυλάκων.

6 Ταῦτα ὁ ἀσεβὴς εἰς τοὺς ἁγίους διαπραξάμενος, σπουδαίως πρὸς τὸν στρατηγὸν μετὰ δύο μαθητῶν τοῦ θεοφόρου ὑπέστρεψεν, φιλοπονήρως ἰσχυριζόμενος πρὸς αὐτὸν μὴ τετυφέναι τὸν ὅσιον. Ὁ δὲ φόβῳ συσχεθεὶς τοῦ μὴ διαβληθῆναι ὑπ' αὐτοῦ πρὸς τὸν ἄνακτα, ἐνέγκας τὸν φιλόχριστον ἐκεῖνον Θεοφάνην κατὰ πρόσωπον τοῦ Μαρτινάκι, μαστίζει αὐτὸν ἐν διπλῇ ποσότητι ὧν προστέταχε δοῦναι τῷ ἱερῷ πατρὶ βουνεύρων· ἐφ' οἷς ἐπιτερφθεὶς ὁ ἀλαζὼν ἐκεῖνος, ἐπιβὰς τοῖς δημοσίοις ἵπποις, πρὸς τὸν ἀποστείλαντα αὐτὸν ὠκυτάτως ἀνέλυσεν.

7 Ἀλλ' οἵας καὶ ὅσας ἀνάγκας τε καὶ κακώσεις διὰ τῆς τοιαύτης ὑπέμειναν οἱ ἀεισέβαστοι πατέρες φρουρᾶς, οὐδέ ἐστι ῥᾴδιον τῷ λόγῳ διαλαβεῖν· ἔν τε γὰρ τῇ τοῦ χειμῶνος ὥρᾳ τῷ κρύει καταπηγνύμενοι, τὴν εἰς ἄκρον ἀποβολὴν τοῦ θερμοῦ ὑπὸ τῆς βίας ὑπομένειν εἶχον τῆς ἐκ τοῦ πυρὸς ἀπούσης ἐνθέρμου παρηγορίας· πάλιν δὲ τῇ ἀντικειμένῃ τῷ ψύχει ὥρᾳ ὑπὸ τῆς ἄγαν τοῦ φλογμοῦ πυρακτούμενοι

disciples who was young in age but mature in his beliefs and faith. This was Nicholas, who was himself also shown to be a long suffering prince of piety and who, from then until the time of my humble self, distinguished himself in his various sufferings for the faith, and has been called in our generation a perfect man of God. So then, after Anastasios had shut this man in with the champion Theodore and had carefully blocked up the door of the cell, he left a single window in it and ordered that the meager provisions of life should be supplied through this to the saintly men by the hands of the guards who were appointed for them.

After settling those matters regarding the holy men, the 6
impious Anastasios quickly returned to the military governor with two of the inspired one's disciples, maliciously contending that he had not beaten the saintly man at all. The supreme military governor, who was gripped by fear that this Martinakios would slander him to the emperor, brought the Christ-loving Theophanes before him and flogged him with twice as many lashes with the ox tendon whip as he had originally ordered him to give the holy father. Delighted at this, that arrogant man mounted imperial post horses and went off very swiftly to the man who had sent him.

But it is not easy to encompass in words the nature and 7
amount of distress and ill-treatment the ever-revered fathers endured through such imprisonment, for during the wintertime, frozen with the icy cold, they were forced to endure extreme lack of warmth, since there was no warming comfort from a fire. Again, in the season opposite to winter, burned by the fiery boiling heat, they thought they were

ζέσεως, οὐδὲν ἧττον καμιναίας φλογὸς ὑποφέρειν ἐδόκουν κατάκρισιν· ἀλλὰ γὰρ καὶ αἱ τὴν σύστασιν ἐκ τοῦ χοὸς ἔχουσαι ψύλλαι οὐ μετρίαν αὐτοῖς παρεῖχον τὴν ἐπίδοσιν τῆς βασάνου, τῆς ἐκ τῶν ἐσθημάτων ὑπαλλαγῆς ἀπορουμένης τοῖς ὁμολογηταῖς τοῦ Χριστοῦ.

26

Πρός γε μὴν τοῖς εἰρημένοις καὶ ἕτερον πειρασμὸν αὐτοῖς ἐπισυνῆψεν ὁ τοῖς πόνοις τῶν ἁγίων ἀεὶ τιτρωσκόμενος ἀγκυλομήτης ὄφις· τοὺς γὰρ κατὰ καιρὸν ἄρχοντας ἐκβακχεύσας πρὸς τὰ τῷ βασιλεῖ θυμήρη φιλοτίμως συντίθεσθαι, ὑποβάλλει αὐτοῖς ὥστε καὶ αὐτὴν τὴν οἰκτρὰν καὶ ἡμερησίαν τῶν δύο τροφὴν εἰς ἑνὸς συστεῖλαι. Ἐν αἷς ἡμέραις εἰπεῖν λέγεται τὸν μέγαν Θεόδωρον πρὸς τὸν συνδέσμιον αὐτοῦ καὶ συναθλητὴν Νικόλαον, "Ὡς ὁρῶ, τέκνον, ἀποκτεῖναι ἡμᾶς βούλονται οἱ ἄνθρωποι οὗτοι τῇ ἀπανθρωπίᾳ, ᾗ νῦν ἐχρήσαντο πρὸς ἡμᾶς· δεῦρο οὖν *ἐπιρρίψωμεν ἐπὶ Κύριον* πᾶσαν *τὴν μέριμναν* ἡμῶν, καὶ ἐγὼ μὲν ἀρκεσθήσομαι τῇ θείᾳ κοινωνίᾳ ἕως ὅτου Χριστὸς παρέχει ἰσχὺν καὶ πνοὴν ζωῆς τῷδε τῷ σαρκίῳ, σὺ δὲ τὸ παρ' αὐτῶν βρωμάτιον δεχόμενος, ἔσθιε, εἴ πως περισῴζοιο τοῦ παρεδρεύοντος ἡμῖν διὰ τῆς ἐνδείας θανάτου, καὶ ἀπαγγελεῖς τῷ τε οἰκονόμῳ καὶ τοῖς ἐν Κυρίῳ ἀδελφοῖς ἡμῶν τὴν ἐμὴν ἐκ τοῦ σώματος ἔξοδον." Καὶ συνέβη ἂν τοῦτό γε τῷ

enduring no less a sentence than the fiery furnace. Also, fleas that originated from the soil considerably increased their torture, since Christ's confessors lacked a change of clothing.

26

In addition to the trials that have been mentioned, the serpent with his crooked counsels, who is always wounded by the hardships of holy men, added yet another trial for them. For after he had excited the officials at the time to assent eagerly to the emperor's whims, he suggested to them that they should restrict the pitiful daily nourishment of the two men to that of one. During those days the great Theodore is reported to have said to Nicholas, his fellow prisoner and fellow champion, "As I see it, my son, these men wish to kill us by the inhumanity that they have now employed toward us. Come then, *let us cast* all our *anxiety on the Lord,* and I will be satisfied with the Holy Communion for as long as Christ provides this flesh of mine with strength and the breath of life. But you should accept the small amount of food from them and eat it in the hope that you may somehow be preserved from the death by hunger which awaits us, and can report my departure from the body to the steward and our brothers in the Lord." This would indeed have

καρτερικῷ πύκτῃ τοῦ Χριστοῦ, εἰ μὴ Θεοῦ προμηθείᾳ *τοῦ ἐμπιπλῶντος πᾶν ζῷον εὐδοκίας* τῇ διανοίξει τῆς προνοητικῆς χειρὸς αὐτοῦ, ἡγεμονικώτερός τις σατράπης δι' ἐκείνης ὁδεύων καὶ τὰ κατ' αὐτοὺς πυθόμενος, ἀνέστειλε τὸ διαβολικὸν τοῦτο ἔργον, καὶ τὴν αὐτάρκη δίδοσθαι τοῖς διὰ Χριστὸν κατακλείστοις μετὰ σφοδρᾶς προσέταξε τῆς ἐμβριμήσεώς τε καὶ ἐπιτιμίας.

2 Οὕτως οὖν ἐν ὅλοις τρισὶν ἔτεσι σωματικῶς φρουρουμένου τοῦ περιπολοῦντος νοερῶς τὰ κατ' οὐρανὸν θεάματα πανευφήμου πατρὸς Θεοδώρου ἅμα τῷ φοιτητῇ καὶ καθ' ἡμᾶς πατρὶ Νικολάῳ, καὶ ταλαιπωροῦντος διαφόρως, (εἶχεν γὰρ λοιπὸν μετὰ τῶν εἰρημένων δυσπετημάτων καὶ τὸν στόμαχον ἰσχυρῶς ἀνορεκτοῦντα), οὐκ οἶδ' ὅπως εἰς χεῖρας ἦλθε τοῦ ἰταμοῦ ἄνακτος ἐπιστολὴ κατηχητικὴ τοῦ διδασκάλου τῆς οἰκουμένης Θεοδώρου, γενικωτέρως ἔχουσα πρὸς τοὺς διὰ Κύριον δεδιωγμένους ἢ καὶ ἄλλως πως καθειργμένους τυγχάνοντας διὰ τὴν εἰς Χριστὸν εὐσέβειαν τά τε τῆς ἀνδραγαθίας ἐπαλείμματα, καὶ τοὺς τῆς δυσφήμου τῶν εἰκονοκαυστῶν θρησκείας ψόγους καὶ δόλους. Ἣν καὶ διαναγνοὺς ὁ κοίρανος, ἀφόρητος ἦν τῇ τοῦ περικαρδίου αἵματος ἀναζέσει· καὶ δὴ αὐτίκα γράμματα στειλάμενος σὺν τῇ ῥηθείσῃ ἐπιστολῇ τῷ τῆς Ἑῴας στρατηγῷ, κελεύει, εἰ μὲν οἷόν τε, αὐτὸν ἐκεῖνον σκυλέντα, ἐν ἑκατὸν βουνεύροις καταικίσασθαι τὸν ἀθλητὴν τῆς εὐσεβείας, εἰ δὲ οὐκ ἀπαντήσοι τοῦτο, τὸν γοῦν Κόμητα τῆς Κόρτης ἐξάπαντος τοῦτό γε ποιήσοντα ἐξαποστεῖλαι.

happened to Christ's mighty combatant if, by the forethought of God *who fills every living thing with his favor* by opening his provident hand, some more authoritative satrap, who found out about them while he was traveling through there, had not put an end to that diabolical action and, with vehement indignation and a rebuke, ordered that sufficient food be given to those imprisoned for the sake of Christ.

Thus for the three whole years that Theodore, the all-blessed father, was physically imprisoned but spiritually wandering through the wonders in heaven along with Nicholas, his disciple and our father, he also suffered in a different way, for along with the misfortunes already mentioned, his stomach suffered a severe loss of appetite. Then a catechetical letter from Theodore, the world's teacher, somehow came into the hands of the reckless ruler; it was addressed to those who were being persecuted for the Lord's sake or were confined in some other way on account of their piety toward Christ, and contained general encouragements to bravery and an indication of the flaws and deceits in the blasphemous worship of the icon burners. When the tyrant read this, he could not bear it and his blood began to boil; he immediately sent word, along with the aforesaid catechetical letter, to the military governor of the East, ordering him to go in person, if he could, to thrash the champion of piety with one hundred lashes with the ox tendon whip, or, if he did not undertake this himself, then to dispatch the Count of the Tent to carry this out. 2

3 Δεξάμενος οὖν ὁ τῆς Ἀνατολῆς στρατοπεδάρχης τὴν σάκραν (Καρτερὸς δ' ἦν οὗτος), ἠπειγμένως πρὸς τὸν πανόσιον ἀφίκετο· καὶ ἐξαγαγὼν ἀμφοτέρους τῆς φυλακῆς, ὑποδείκνυσι τῷ σεβασμίῳ πατρὶ τά τε τοῦ βασιλέως γράμματα, καὶ τὴν σὺν αὐτοῖς ἀποσταλεῖσαν αὐτοῦ ἐπιστολήν, καί φησι πρὸς αὐτόν, "Ἐπιγινώσκεις ταύτην;" Τοῦ δὲ διομολογησαμένου ἑαυτοῦ εἶναι καὶ οὐκ ἄλλου τὴν τοιαύτην ἔκδοσιν, κελεύει προηγουμένως τὸν μακαρίτην γυμνωθῆναι Νικόλαον, καὶ τοῦτον διαρκῶς κακώσας ταῖς μάστιξιν, ἐπὶ τὸν μέγαν ἔρχεται Θεόδωρον. Ὃν δὴ καὶ ἑκατὸν καταφοραῖς βουνεύρων ἀπανθρώπως ἄγαν καὶ ὠμῶς καταξάνας, πάλιν πρὸς τὸν νέον μέτεισιν ἀθλητὴν Νικόλαον, καταναγκάζων αὐτὸν ἀπείπασθαι τήν τε τῶν ἱερῶν εἰκόνων προσκύνησιν καὶ τὴν πρὸς τὸν οἰκεῖον πατέρα τε καὶ διδάσκαλον ἰσχυρογνωμοσύνην. Ὡς δ' ἀπειθοῦντα καὶ εὐσταθῶς ἀνθιστάμενον τοῖς ὑπ' αὐτοῦ ἑώρα προτεινομένοις, ταῖς ῥέκαις αὐτὸν ἀποχρώντως αἱμάξας, τῷ κρύει καταπήγνυσθαι γεγυμνωμένον παρείασεν, τρίτῃ γὰρ καὶ εἰκάδι τοῦ Περιτίου μηνὸς ἡ πρᾶξις αὕτη τῶν ἀοιδίμων συνέβαινεν. Ἀμέλει κατακλείσας αὐτοὺς πάλιν ὁ ἀνοσιουργὸς τοῦ κάτω Καίσαρος ὑπηρέτης εἰς τὸ δωμάτιον οἴκαδε ἵετο.

4 Ἐν ὅσῳ δὲ ταῦτα εἰς τοὺς γενναίους ὁμολογητὰς τοῦ Χριστοῦ Θεόδωρόν τε καὶ Νικόλαον κατὰ τὸ Ἀνατολικὸν διεπράττετο κλίμα, γυνή τις ἐν τῷ θέματι τοῦ Ὀψικίου τυγχάνουσα πνεύμασι Πυθωνικοῖς κεκρατημένη, ἤρξατο κατὰ τὸ εἰωθὸς αὐτῇ ἐνεργεῖσθαι ὑπ' αὐτῶν καὶ λέγειν εἰς ὑπήκοον τῶν παρευρεθέντων πρὸς τοὺς ἐν αὐτῇ δῆθεν

When the supreme military governor of the East (this was Karteros) received the imperial letter, he came hurriedly to the all-saintly Theodore. After bringing both men out of the prison, he showed the revered father the emperor's letter and Theodore's own letter which had been sent along with it, and said to him, "Do you recognize this?" When Theodore acknowledged that this composition was his own and no one else's, he first ordered that Nicholas of blessed memory should be stripped. After he had flogged him sufficiently, he turned to the great Theodore. He lacerated him very inhumanly and savagely with one hundred strokes of the ox tendon whip, then again attacked Nicholas, the young champion, putting extreme pressure on him to renounce the veneration of the holy icons and his obstinate adherence to his own father and teacher. But when he saw that Nicholas would not comply and was valiantly resisting his demands, after making him sufficiently bloody with the thongs, he left him naked to freeze in the icy cold, for that punishment of these renowned men took place on February 23. When the profane servant of the inferior Caesar had shut them up again in the small room, he went off home. 3

At the time these punishments were being inflicted in the Anatolikon region on Christ's noble confessors, Theodore and Nicholas, a woman in the Opsikion theme, who was possessed by Pythian spirits, began to be moved by them in her usual way and, in the hearing of those who were present, 4

ἐννεοττεύσαντας δαίμονας, "Ὁ καλολέων μου καὶ νῦν ἀπέστειλεν δεσμὴν μαστίγων πρὸς τὸν Θεόδωρον, ἵνα τὰς σάρκας αὐτοῦ ἐν αὐταῖς κατακόψῃ, ἀλλὰ σπεύσατε καὶ ἴδετε τὸ γενησόμενον, καὶ ταχέως φέρετέ μοι ἀπόκρισιν. Μὴ τολμήσητε δὲ ἔνδον τῆς κέλλης γενέσθαι, ἵνα μὴ κατακαύσῃ ὑμᾶς ὁ φλογόστομος ἐκεῖνος καὶ πυρόστομος, ἀλλ' ἔξωθεν παρεδρεύοντες, τὸ μέλλον γενήσεσθαι καταμάθετε." Καὶ ὡς μετὰ δύο ἢ καὶ τριῶν ὡρῶν διάστημα πάλιν ἤρξατο ἐν ἑαυτῇ βατταρίζειν καὶ λέγειν, "Τί ἐστιν, οὐδὲν γέγονεν ὧν ἐβουλόμεθα; ἐγὼ ᾔδειν τοῦτο, ὅτι ἡ χλωροπικὴ παρασταθήσεται καὶ αὖθις ἐν τοῖς ὤμοις αὐτοῦ, καὶ οὐκ ἐάσει αὐτὸν ταῖς ὀδύναις τῶν πληγῶν κατεργασθῆναι."

5 Ἐκ δὴ τοῦ τοιούτου σφοδροτάτου δαρμοῦ τεθνᾶναι μικροῦ λέγεται τὸν μέγαν ἀριστέα τῆς Χριστοῦ ὁμολογίας Θεόδωρον· φλεγμάναντες γὰρ οἱ μώλωπες καὶ φοβερωτάτας πληγὰς ἀποκυήσαντες, τά τε τῆς σαρκὸς κατασαπέντα λακίσματα, οὐχ ὑπελείφθη ἐν αὐτῷ σχεδὸν πνεῦμα ἀνέσεως, ὑπομονῇ τὴν ἰσχὺν προστιθέμενον, ἤ τοι *νήδυμος ὕπνος* ἐπῄει κατακοιμίζων τὰ ἐκ τῆς φλεγμονῆς προσγιγνόμενα αὐτῷ ἄχη ἢ ἐπιθυμία δεινὴ τοῦ δέξασθαί τι τῶν ἐδωδίμων. Ὅθεν δὴ χυλάριον ἐπιτηδεύσας ὁ πανάριστος ὑπηρέτης καὶ συναθλητὴς αὐτοῦ καὶ συνέκδημος ὑπάρχων Νικόλαος, προσφέρεσθαι αὐτὸν ἐποίει, ἓν μόγις βαυκάλιον καθ' ἑκάστην. Ἀλλὰ γὰρ καὶ τῆς ἐξ ἰατρῶν ἀπούσης ἐπικουρίας, ἐπετράπη παρὰ τοῦ πατρὸς ὁ ἐν πνεύματι υἱὸς καὶ ἄλλος Σίλας ἢ Τιμόθεος πεφηνώς, μαχαιρίῳ

to speak to the demons that were nesting in her: "My beautiful lion just sent a bundle of whips to Theodore to shred his flesh with them, so hurry and see what will happen and bring me an answer quickly. But don't you dare go inside the cell so that flame-breathing and fiery-mouthed man doesn't burn you up; wait outside and find out what's going to happen." After an interval of about two or three hours she began to mutter to herself again and say, "What's the matter? Has nothing that we wanted happened? I know, that pale-looking thing will be placed on his shoulders again and will stop him from succumbing to the pain of the lashes."

It is said that Theodore, the great prince of confession 5
for Christ's sake, almost died as a result of such a very severe beating; for after the welts and the putrid lacerations of his flesh had become inflamed, they produced terrible wounds and there was scarcely an easy breath left in him to give strength to his endurance; and neither would a *deep sleep* come over him, dulling the pain caused by the inflammation, nor a strong yearning to eat something. Nicholas, being the best of all servants, his fellow champion and fellow exile, would thus make him take a little gruel, scarcely one small cup each day. Also, since there was no care from doctors and as he was manifestly a spiritual son and another Silas or Timothy, Nicholas was entrusted by the father to use a small

περιστατικῶς τὰς νενεκρωμένας αὐτοῦ τῆς δορᾶς ἀποκρεμάσεις χειρουργῆσαι, εἴ πως κατὰ μικρὸν ὁ λοιπὸς τοῦ σώματος ὄγκος εἰς ὁμαλισμὸν ὑγείας τῷ χρόνῳ ἐπαναδράμοι.

27

Ἐν γοῦν τῇ τοιαύτῃ τῶν σωματικῶν ὀδυνῶν διατελῶν ἀνάγκῃ ὁ πυρίμορφος στῦλος τῆς ὀρθοδοξίας Θεόδωρος, τὸ στάδιον ἅπαν τῆς ἱερᾶς διήνυσε Τεσσαρακοστῆς καὶ ἐπέκεινα, μόλις εἰς ὁλοκληρίας ἕξιν περὶ τὰς ὑστάτας τῆς ἁγίας Πεντηκοστῆς ἡμέρας ἀποκατασταθέντος αὐτῷ τοῦ σώματος. Ἀλλὰ μήπω τῆς τῶν τραυμάτων τούτων εὖ διατεθείσης συνουλώσεως, ἕτερος ἄγγελος κακεργάτης ὡς αὐτὸν τοῦ μέδοντος κατεφοίτησεν, πρὸς τὴν τῶν Σμυρναίων μεταστήσων αὐτὸν ἐπαρχίαν. Ὅς, μετὰ τῆς ἑπομένης αὐτῷ τῶν κολάκων, μᾶλλον δὲ σκυλάκων ἐπιστὰς συμμορίας, τὴν ἀναπεφραγμένην τοῦ δωματίου κατέστρεψεν θύραν, καὶ τοὺς ἱεροὺς ἐξαγαγὼν πατέρας, ἐπεζήτει παρ' αὐτοῖς ἐρασιχρήματος ὤν, ἅπερ οὐκ εἶχον τοῦ μαμωνᾶ λείψανα. Ὡς δὲ τοῦ σκοποῦ διημάρτανεν, εἴσω τῆς κέλλης γεγονότας τοὺς πινσοὺς καὶ τὰς ὀπὰς ἐπιμελῶς διερευνᾶσθαι πεποίηκεν.

2 Ἐπεὶ δὲ μάτην αὐτοῖς τὰ τῆς ἐγχειρήσεως κατεπράττετο, εἰς μανίαν τραπέντες οἱ τάλανες, τοὺς ἁγίους ἔχεσθαι

knife to cut away very carefully the deadened flaps of his skin that were hanging down, in the hope that little by little the remaining swollen mass of his body might return in time to a healthy level.

27

While he was enduring such anguish from physical pain, Theodore, the fiery pillar of orthodoxy, completed the entire course of holy Lent and beyond, though his body was barely restored to a state of complete health until about the last days of holy Pentecost. But when the scars had still not fully formed over his wounds, another evildoing messenger from the ruler descended on him to move him to the province of Smyrna. This man, with a retinue of sycophantic followers, or rather acting like the commander of a pack of dogs, broke down the barricaded door of the small room and dragged out the holy fathers; in his love for money he then began to search them for remnants of riches, which they did not have. When he failed in his aim, he had a careful examination made of the masonry and openings that were inside the cell.

Since that attempt proved to be in vain, the wretches 2
flew into a rage, and suddenly started very cruelly to urge

τῆς ὁδοιπορίας ἀμειλίκτως ἄγαν καὶ αἰψηρῶς κατήπειγον, μηδ' ὅλως ἐνδεικνύμενοι εἰς αὐτοὺς σπλάγχνα οἰκτιρμῶν, μάλιστα ὁρῶντες τὸν θεοφόρον Θεόδωρον τετρυχωμένον πάνυ τῷ σώματι καὶ οὐδὲν ἀπεοικότα νεκροῦ. Οὕτως οὖν ἐκεῖθεν μικρὸν ἠνυκότες διάστημα, ὀψὲ τῆς ὥρας εἴς τι καταλύουσι χωρίον, ἐν ᾧ *τοὺς πόδας* τῶν Χριστοῦ δεσμίων εἰς τὸ τῶν κακούργων *ἀσφαλισάμενοι ξύλον,* τὸ τῆς νυκτὸς μῆκος ἐνοδύνως αὐτοὺς διελθεῖν παρεσκεύασαν. Ἕωθεν δὲ τῶν αὐτόθι ἀπάραντες, τὴν ἐπὶ τὰ πρόσω φορὰν ὡσαύτως ἐποιοῦντο, μόλις μὲν τοῦ πατρὸς ἡμῶν διὰ τὴν κάκωσιν τῶν ποδῶν βαδίζειν δεδυνημένου, ὅμως οὖν τῇ πρὸς Θεὸν πεποιθήσει ἑαυτὸν ἐκβιαζομένου καὶ τὸ τῆς φύσεως ἀσθενὲς τῇ ἐλπίδι τῶν ἀποκειμένων τοῖς δικαίοις ἐπιρρωννύοντος ἀγαθῶν· καὶ οὕτως ἐν ὀλίγαις ἡμέραις τὴν Σμυρναίων παροικίαν καταλαβόντες, τῷ ταύτης αἱρεσιάρχῃ παραδίδονται.

3 Ὅστις τῷ τῆς δυσσεβείας ἀκράτῳ τὴν ψυχὴν μεμεθυσμένος, ἐντὸς τῶν τῆς μητροπόλεως περιβόλων τοὺς ὁμολογητὰς τοῦ Χριστοῦ ἐν ἑνὶ δωματίῳ καθείργνυσιν, ἓν καὶ μόνον χώρημα τούτῳ παρεάσας πρὸς τὸ ἐκεῖθεν δέχεσθαι αὐτοὺς τὴν δι' ἄρτου καὶ ὕδατος μόνον ἡμερησίαν τροφήν, συντυχίας τε πάσης ἀνθρωπίνης ἀπηλλάχθαι αὐτοὺς μετὰ σφοδρᾶς προστάξας τῆς ἐπιτιμήσεως. Τὴν τοιαύτην οὖν κάθειρξιν τοῦ θεοφόρου κἀκεῖσε κατακριθέντος πατρὸς σὺν τῷ μαθητῇ Νικολάῳ, ὁ αἱμοβόρος καὶ φόνιος Λέων μετά τινα χρόνον αὖθις τὸν αἱμοχαρῆ ἐκεῖνον Ἀναστάσιον τὸν ἐπίκλην Μαρτινάκιν πρὸς αὐτὸν ἀποστέλλει καταξᾶναι αὐτὸν ἀφειδῶς ταῖς διὰ βουνεύρων

the holy men to begin their journey, showing no feelings of pity at all toward them, even though they saw that the body of the divinely inspired Theodore was utterly worn out and looked like a corpse. So, when they had made their way a short distance from there, they stopped late in the day in a place where, after *securing the feet* of Christ's prisoners *in the stocks* for criminals, they made them pass a painful night. They set out from there at dawn, and traveled on in just the same way, even though our father was hardly able to walk on account of the bad condition of his feet; even so, he forced himself on through his confidence in God and strengthened the weakness of his nature with his hope for the blessings that are stored up for the righteous. In a few days they thus reached the region of Smyrna and were handed over to its heresiarch.

This man, whose soul was intoxicated by the strong wine 3
of impiety, confined Christ's confessors in a small room inside the walls of the metropolis. He left just one space in this by means of which they were to receive their daily nourishment there of bread and water alone, and ordered, under threat of violent punishment, that they be removed from all human contact. After the divinely inspired father had been condemned along with Nicholas his disciple to that kind of confinement there too, sometime later the bloodthirsty and murderous Leo again sent to him that Anastasios surnamed Martinakis, who delighted in blood, to pitilessly lacerate him with blows from an ox tendon whip. Anastasios quickly

αἰκίαις. Ὅς, καὶ ταχὺ τὴν Σμύρναν ἐφθακὼς καὶ τὸ πρόσταγμα τοῦ ἀνημέρου μετὰ πολλῆς τετελεκὼς τῆς σφοδρότητος εἰς τὸν πένταθλον πατέρα ἡμῶν Θεόδωρον, πρὸς τὴν βασιλεύουσαν ἐπαλινδρόμησεν.

4 Ἐν τούτοις τοιγαροῦν ἐταζόμενος τοῖς δι' εὐσέβειαν ἀέθλοις, ὁ ἀκράδαντος τῆς ὁμολογίας καὶ ἀκλινὴς πύργος Θεόδωρος τὰ τοῦ μακαρίου Παύλου κατεπῇδεν ἑαυτῷ διδάγματα· *Εἰ συμπάσχομεν καὶ συνδοξασθῶμεν* πάντως τῷ δι' ἡμᾶς σαρκὶ πεπονθότι Χριστῷ, ἵν' ἡμᾶς τῶν παθῶν τῆς ἀτιμίας ὡς ἀγαθὸς ἐκλυτρώσηται. Ἀμέλει ὁ τὴν αὐτόθι στρατηγίαν διέπων (Βάρδας δὲ ἦν ὁ τοῦ ἄνακτος καὶ σύγγαμβρος καὶ ὁμόφρων), ἐξ ὑπογύου χρόνου τε καὶ τ<ρ>όπου τὸ σῶμα λωβηθείς, πρὸς τὴν μητρόπολιν κατέφυγεν, ἐν ᾗ καὶ κλινήρης γεγονώς, τὴν τῆς Προνοίας ἐξεδέχετο κρίσιν.

5 Εἷς δέ τις τῶν ὑπ' αὐτῷ τεταγμένων Διογένης ὄνομα, τὸ γένος εὐγενής, τὴν πίστιν ὀρθόδοξος, ἐραστὴς ὑπάρχων τῶν διὰ Χριστὸν ἐναθλούντων τῇ πίστει, περὶ πολλοῦ τίθεται τοῦ πάντως θεάσασθαι τὸν ἅγιον καὶ τῶν εὐχῶν αὐτοῦ τὰς εὐλογίας δρέψασθαι. Καὶ γοῦν τούτου συνδραμόντος τῷ θεοφιλεῖ Διογένει, καὶ τῆς δι' ὀπῆς συντυχίας θατέρου πρὸς θάτερον γιγνομένης, ἐγνώρισε τῷ θεοφόρῳ πατρὶ τὰ κατὰ τὸν στρατηγὸν ὁ καλός τε καὶ ἀγαθὸς ἀνήρ. Ὁ δὲ μέγας φησὶ πρὸς αὐτόν, "Τάδε ἐρεῖς τῷ κυρίῳ σου· 'Ὅρα σὺ τί μέλλεις ποιεῖν ὅτι πρὸς τὸ πέρας τοῦ βίου ἴσως παραγέγονας, καὶ ὁ βοηθήσων ἢ λυτρωσόμενος οὐκ ἔστιν. Διὸ ἐννοήθητι περὶ ὧν σοι πέπρακται ἐν τῇ εὐημερίᾳ τῆς ἐξουσίας σου εἰς τοὺς ὁμολογητὰς τοῦ Χριστοῦ, καὶ μάλι-

reached Smyrna, carried out that savage man's command on our father, the pentathlete Theodore, with great severity, and then returned to the capital.

While Theodore, the unshaken and unbending tower of confession, was being tested in these contests over piety, he would repeat to himself the teachings of blessed Paul: *If we suffer with him,* at all events *we shall also be glorified* with Christ, who suffered in the flesh for us that he might redeem us in his goodness from the shame of the passions. At this time the man who held the office of military governor there (Bardas, the ruler's brother-in-law and a man who held the same views as him), had been physically maimed in a sudden and unexpected way and had fled for refuge to the metropolis, where he was bedridden and waiting for the judgment of Providence. 4

One of his subordinates, a man called Diogenes, who came from a noble family, was orthodox in his faith, and loved those who, for the sake of Christ, were suffering bravely for their faith, considered it important to see the holy man at all costs and reap the blessings of his prayers. So, when Theodore met with Diogenes, beloved of God, and a conversation between the two men was taking place through the hole, that honorable and good man made the circumstances of the military governor known to the divinely inspired father. The great man said to him, "Say this to your lord: 'Beware of what you are about to do, because you have probably come to the end of your life and there is no one to help or deliver you. So, you should reflect on your treatment of Christ's confessors and especially those in my 5

στά γε εἰς τὴν κατ' ἐμὲ μονήν· ὅτι καὶ τὸν ἀοίδιμον Θαδδαῖον αὐτὸς ἀνηλεῶς βουνευρίσας, τῷ θανάτῳ παρέπεμψας· ἀλλ' ἐκεῖνος μὲν μαρτυρίῳ τὴν τελευτὴν διαπρέψας, ἐν οὐρανοῖς νῦν κατατρυφᾷ τῆς δόξης τοῦ Παντοκράτορος Θεοῦ μετὰ πάντων τῶν ἁγίων, σὺ δὲ ταῖς σειραῖς τῶν ἰδίων ἁμαρτημάτων ἐνταῦθα τέως περισφίγγῃ μερικῶς καὶ ἐν τῷ μέλλοντι τὴν καθολικὴν ἀπεκδέχῃ, κἂν ὡς οὐ θέλεις, κατάκρισιν. Καὶ εἰ τὰ πρόσκαιρα οὕτως ἐπώδυνά τε καὶ δύσοιστα, λογίσασθαι χρὴ περὶ τῆς αἰωνίου κολάσεως τῶν ἀσεβῶν καὶ τῶν παραβαινόντων τὰς ἐντολὰς τοῦ Σωτῆρος ἡμῶν Χριστοῦ, ὅτι *ὁ σκώληξ αὐτῶν οὐ τελευτήσει καὶ τὸ πῦρ αὐτῶν οὐ σβεσθήσεται*, καθὼς ὑπηγόρευσεν ὁ προφήτης.'"

6 Ταῦτα ἀκούσας ἐκεῖνος καὶ εἰς αἴσθησιν ἐλθὼν τῶν ἑαυτοῦ πρακτέων, φόβῳ τε συλληφθεὶς τῇ τοῦ θανάτου ἀγγελίᾳ, συγγνώμην ταχέως αἰτεῖ παρὰ τοῦ ὁσίου καὶ τὴν διὰ προσευχῆς ἐπιπέμψαι αὐτῷ ἐπικουρίαν, ὑποσχόμενος ἐξ ἐκείνου κατ' ἐντολὴν τοῦ μεγάλου ἅπαντα ὁμοῦ τὰ καθ' ἑαυτὸν διατίθεσθαι καὶ ποιεῖν, μόνον εἰ τῆς τοῦ θανάτου μοίρας ἔξω κατὰ τὸ παρὸν γένηται. Ὁ δὲ θεῖος πατὴρ ἡμῶν *τὸν μὴ θέλοντα τὸν θάνατον τοῦ ἁμαρτωλοῦ ὡς τὸ ἐπιστρέψαι καὶ ζῆν αὐτὸν* φιλάνθρωπον Δεσπότην καὶ Κύριον μιμούμενος, τῷ μὲν νοσοῦντι τὴν ἱερὰν τῆς Θεομήτορος πέπομφεν εἰκόνα, προσκυνῆσαι ταύτην παρακελευσάμενος, ἐπικαλέσασθαι δὲ καὶ τὰς πρεσβείας τοῦ ἀθλητοῦ καὶ ὁσιομάρτυρος τοῦ Χριστοῦ Θαδδαίου, καὶ ταύτῃ θαρρεῖν ὡς εὖ ἔσται αὐτῷ. Αὐτὸς δὲ παννύχιον ὑπὲρ αὐτοῦ πρὸς τὸν ἐπὶ πάντων Θεὸν τὰς ἐντεύξεις ποιησάμενος, τῆς

monastery in the heyday of your authority. Remember how you yourself pitilessly lashed the renowned Thaddaios with an ox tendon whip, sending him to his death. He adorned his end with martyrdom and now delights in the glory of Almighty God in heaven with all the saints, whereas you are here for a while longer, tightly bound by the cords of all your sins, and await in the future the final judgment, even though you may not want it. If things in this ephemeral world are so painful and hard to bear, you should consider the eternal punishment of the impious and those who transgress the commandments of our Savior Christ, that *their worm will not die and their fire will not be quenched,* as the prophet stated.'"

When Bardas heard this, he understood what he had 6
done and, gripped by fear at the announcement of his death, quickly asked the saintly man to forgive him and send him aid through prayer, promising from then on that he would arrange all his affairs and act in accordance with that great man's command, if only he was released from the fate of death for the present. Our godly father Theodore imitated the benevolent Master and Lord who *does not wish the death of a sinner* but for him to be converted and live, and sent a holy icon of the Mother of God to the sick man. He advised him to venerate it and also to call on the intercessions of Thaddaios, Christ's champion and saintly martyr, and have confidence in the icon that all would be well with him. Theodore himself made entreaties all night on his behalf to God, who rules over everything, and released this man from

νόσου τοῦτον ἀπήλλαξεν, καὶ τῆς κλίνης τῇ ἐπιούσῃ ἐλεύθερον ἔδειξεν ἀστείως τὰ ἀνθρώπινα διαπραττόμενον. Καὶ ἔμεινεν ἂν ἐπ' αὐτῷ ἡ χάρις ἀμετάπτωτος τῆς εὐρωστίας, εἰ μὴ ταῖς τοῦ ἀνιέρου φενακισθεὶς ὑποθήκαις, τὸ ὑπ' αὐτοῦ εὐλογηθὲν κατεχρίσατο ἔλαιον εἰς τελειοτέρας δῆθεν ὑγιείας ἀνάληψιν.

7 Ὅπερ μαθὼν ὁ σημειοφόρος καὶ τοῦ προφητικοῦ χαρίσματος ἔμπλεως Θεόδωρος, τήν τε ὑποστροφὴν ἐξεῖπεν αὐτίκα τῆς ἀρρωστίας καὶ τὸν ἐψόμενον ἐκ ταύτης τῷ ἀθλίῳ θάνατον, ὅπερ αὐτῷ καὶ συμβέβηκεν οὐ μετὰ πολλὰς τοῦ κοινωνῆσαι τῷ αἱρεσιάρχῃ ἡμέρας· τῷ ὄντι γὰρ *οὐκ ἀζήμιον χρῆμα* κατὰ τὸν μακάριον Κύριλλον *τὸ κολλᾶσθαι πονηροῖς*. Ἀλλὰ τὰ μὲν περὶ τούτου τοιοῦτον πέρας ἐδέξαντο.

28

Ὁ δέ γε πατὴρ ἡμῶν καὶ ὁμολογητὴς τοῦ Χριστοῦ Θεόδωρος εἴκοσι μῆνας φρουρηθεὶς παρὰ τῷ ψευδοδόξῳ ἐκείνῳ μητροπολίτῃ πρὸς τοῖς ἄλλοις πατράσι καὶ ὁμολογηταῖς καὶ τοὺς οἰκείους εἶχεν μαθητὰς παρισουμένους μικροῦ δεῖν τοῖς αὐτοῦ παθήμασιν, ἐν οἷς διέλαμπεν ὅ τε φερώνυμος καὶ μέγας Ναυκράτιος καὶ ὁ τῆς πρεσβυτερικῆς ἀκριβείας στῦλος Δωρόθεος, ὁ θαυμάσιος Βησαρίων καὶ ὁ καρτερικώτατος Ἰάκωβος, ὁ γενναιότατος Δομε-

his disease; the next day saw him freed from his bed and aptly dealing with mundane matters. And the grace of good health would have remained with him unchanged, if he had not been tricked by suggestions of the unholy one into anointing himself with oil blessed by the latter, supposedly to regain more complete health.

When Theodore, that miracle worker who was filled with the gift of prophecy, learned of this, he predicted the immediate recurrence of the ailment and the ensuing death of the wretched man; and this came upon him a few days after associating with the heresiarch for, according to the blessed Cyril, *to cleave to evil people* really is *something that does not go unpunished.* Anyway, the events concerning Bardas ended like this. 7

28

Our father and Christ's confessor, Theodore, who was imprisoned for twenty months by that heretical metropolitan, along with the other fathers and confessors also had his own sufferings almost equaled by those of his disciples. Among those who shone out were the well-named great Naukratios; Dorotheos the pillar of priestly scrupulousness; the admirable Besarion; the very steadfast James; the most

τιανὸς καὶ ὁ φερέπονος Τιθόεις, ὁ ἀσκητικώτατος καὶ ἀγγελόβιος Τιμόθεος καὶ ὁ θαρραλεώτατος καὶ τῆς εὐθυμίας ἐπώνυμος ὁμολογητής. Οὗτοι πάντες σὺν ἑτέροις πλείστοις μαστίγων πολλῶν καὶ πειρασμῶν διαφόρων ἀναδεξάμενοι πεῖραν, τοῦ τῆς ὁμολογίας ἐπέτυχον κλέους, μηδὲ μέχρι ῥήματος ὑφέντες τοῖς τῶν Χριστιανοκατηγόρων συμπεσεῖν θελήμασιν· *οἱ γὰρ πιστεύσαντες ἐπισκοπεῖν Θεὸν τοὺς ἑαυτῶν βίους, οὐθὲν ἀνέχονται ἐξαμαρτεῖν.*

2 Ἀμέλει ὁ *ζηλωτὴς Θεός,* ὁ *τοὺς ὑπεναντίους αὐτοῦ ἐξαίρων,* ᾗ φησιν ὁ προφήτης, ὁ *μακρόθυμος ἐν ἐλέει,* ὁ *τὸ τόξον* μὲν τῆς δικαίας *αὐτοῦ* ὀργῆς *ἐντείνων* εἰς ἐπιστροφὴν τῶν ἁμαρτανόντων, *ἑτοιμάζων* δὲ *ἐν αὐτῷ* τοῖς ἀμετανόητα πταίουσι *σκεύη θανάτου,* ὁ μὴ *τὴν ῥάβδον τῶν ἁμαρτωλῶν ἀφιεὶς* εἰς τέλος *ἐπὶ τὸν κλῆρον τῶν δικαίων,* ἐμνήσθη *τοῦ στεναγμοῦ τῶν πεπεδημένων,* καὶ *τὸν καταφαγόντα τὸν Ἰακὼβ* καὶ τοὺς σεβαστευομένους αὐτῷ *ἠρημωκότα τόπους* εἰσεπράξατο ὧν παρηνόμησεν δίκας, ἐν τόποις οἷς ἐφαύλισε τὴν θείαν τοῦ Ἐμμανουὴλ ἐνανθρώπησιν, ἐν αὐτοῖς ἀπορρῆξαι αὐτὸν τὸ ζῆν φόνῳ μαχαίρας παρασκευασάμενος, ὡς πληρωθῆναι ἐν αὐτῷ τὴν πρόρρησιν τοῦ μακαρίου προφήτου Ἀμώς, οὕτω πως ἔχουσαν· *Ἐβουλεύσω αἰσχύνην τῷ οἴκῳ* Κυρίου, *συνεπέρανας λαοὺς πολλοὺς καὶ ἐξήμαρτεν ἡ ψυχή σου,* τοιγάρτοι *πλησμονὴν ἀτιμίας* ἐκδέξῃ, ἀλλὰ *πίε καὶ σὺ καὶ διασαλεύθητι καὶ σείσθητι· ἐκύκλωσεν ἐπὶ σὲ ποτήριον δεξιᾶς Κυρίου, καὶ συνήχθη ἀτιμία ἐπὶ τὴν δόξαν σου· διότι ἀσέβεια τοῦ Λιβάνου καλύψει σὲ καὶ ταλαιπωρία θηρίων πτοήσει σε.* Ἀλλὰ καὶ Ὠσηέ· "*Ἐθύμωσέν με Ἐφραὶμ καὶ παρώργισεν, καὶ τὸ αἷμα αὐτοῦ ἐπ᾽ αὐτὸν ἐκχυθήσεται,*

noble Dometianos; the patiently laboring Tithoeis; the most ascetic Timothy, who lived like an angel; and the most courageous confessor Euthymios, who was well named for his good cheer. All of these, along with very many others, experienced many floggings and various trials and thus gained fame as a result of their confession for Christ's sake, for they did not yield and comply with the wishes of those who were accusing Christians even in so much as a word; *for those who believe that God watches over their own lives refuse to sin in anything.*

Of course, *the jealous God who destroys his enemies,* as the 2
prophet says, the one *long-suffering* in mercy, *who stretches the bow of his* righteous anger to correct sinners and *in it makes ready the vessels of death* for those who lapse without repentance, who in the end does not *let loose the rod of sinners against the inheritance of the righteous,* remembered *the groaning of those in fetters.* And, from the one who *devoured Jacob* and *laid waste the places* revered in his name, he exacted satisfaction for his wrongdoings in the places where he disparaged the divine incarnation of Emmanuel, for he caused him to die there murdered with a knife, so that in him the prophecy of the blessed prophet Amos was fulfilled, which goes something like this: *You devised shame for the house* of the Lord; *you scattered many peoples and your soul did wrong;* accordingly, you will receive *your fill of disgrace,* but *you, drain the cup, be shaken and quake; the cup in the Lord's right hand has come round to you and disgrace has been brought on your glory; for that reason the dishonor done to Lebanon will cover you and sore distress from wild beasts will terrify you.* Also, Hosea says, "*Ephraim made* me *angry and provoked* me, *and his blood will be poured out on him and*

καὶ τὸν ὀνειδισμὸν αὐτοῦ ἀνταποδώσει αὐτῷ Κύριος." Σὺν τούτοις καὶ ἡ μεγαλοφωνοτάτη σάλπιγξ τῆς προφητείας ἐρεῖ πρὸς αὐτόν· "*Ὃν τρόπον ἱμάτιον ἐν αἵματι πεφυρμένον οὐκ ἔσται καθαρόν, οὕτως οὐδὲ σὺ ἔσῃ καθαρός, διότι τὴν γῆν μου ἀπώλεσας καὶ τὸν λαόν μου ἀπέκτεινας.*"

3 Τούτου τοιγαροῦν τοῦ θηριογνώμονος καὶ ἰταμοῦ τυράννου ἐν ἑνὶ τῶν τοῦ παλατίου νύκτωρ κατασφαγέντος εὐκτηρίων, Μιχαὴλ ὁ τοῦτον πατάξας τὰ τῆς βασιλείας μεταχειρίζεται λάβωρα· ὅστις εἰ καὶ τῇ αἱρετικῇ ζύμῃ ἀναπεποιημένος ἦν ὅλος ἄνωθεν, ἀλλ' οὖν χρηστότητος τρόποις ἐσχημάτιστο ὁ ἀνήρ, ὅθεν νόμους τίθησι τοὺς κελεύοντας πάντας τοὺς ὑπὸ τοῦ Λέοντος ἐξορισθέντας καὶ ἐν φρουραῖς κατεχομένους τῶν δεσμῶν ἀπολύεσθαι.

29

Τότε δὴ μετὰ τῶν λοιπῶν Χριστοῦ ὁμολογητῶν καὶ ὁ περιβόητος τῆς ὀρθοδοξίας κῆρυξ Θεόδωρος ἐπανήκων ἀπὸ τὴν Σμύρναν πρὸς τὴν πάτριον καὶ φίλην παροικίαν, καὶ τὰς τῆς ἁγιωσύνης καὶ ὁσιότητος ἀπολάμπων μαρμαρυγάς, καὶ παρὰ πολλοῖς μὲν ἄλλοις φιλοφρόνως ἐδεξιώθη κατὰ διαφόρους κώμας καὶ τόπους, οὐχ ἥκιστα δὲ πρὸς τῶν φιλαρέτων καὶ θεοσεβῶν ἀνδρῶν ἐκείνων τῶν λεγομένων Ξηρολόφων, ἀμοιβαδὸν ἐφθακὼς τοῖς ὁμοροῦσι μέρεσι τὰ λεγόμενα Λάκκου Μιτάτα, καὶ ὑπεδέχθη ἀξίως

the Lord will pay him back for his reproach." Along with these words, the strident trumpet of prophecy will say to him, "*In the way that a garment soaked in blood will not be clean, so neither will you be clean because you destroyed my land and killed my people.*"

So, when that bestial and headstrong tyrant was slaugh- 3
tered at night in one of the palace chapels, Michael, the man who struck him down, took into his hands the *labarum* of imperial power. Even though he had initially been created entirely with heretical leaven, the man still deceptively assumed the appearance of goodness and, as a result, established laws which ordered that all those who had been banished by Leo and were being held in prisons should be released from their bonds.

29

At that time then, along with the other confessors of Christ, Theodore, the widely acclaimed proponent of orthodoxy, gleaming with rays of holiness and saintliness, returned from Smyrna to his beloved homeland. At various villages and places he was welcomed hospitably by many people, but especially by those virtuous and pious men who are called the Xerolophoi. He reached what is called Lakkou Mitata by stages, and there he was fittingly welcomed and

καὶ παρ' αὐτοῖς διέτριψεν ἡμέρας ἱκανάς, πάντων σχεδὸν τῶν τὰ πρῶτα φερόντων τῆς ὑπ' αὐτὸν ἀδελφότητος αὐτόθι συνδεδραμηκότων, ὁμοίως δὲ καὶ τοῦ πανσόφου Ἰωσὴφ καὶ στερροτάτου ὁπλίτου τῆς ἀληθείας ἀπὸ τῆς κατὰ τὸ φρούριον τὸ καλούμενον Ἐλπίζων φυλακῆς πρὸς ὑπαντὴν ἀφικομένου τοῦ ἰδίου ἀδελφοῦ. Ἔνθα δὴ καὶ θαύματα λέγεται πεποιηκέναι ὁ θεῖος πατὴρ ἡμῶν οὐκ ἄξια λήθης, περὶ ὧν σὺν Θεῷ διαλαβεῖν τῷ λόγῳ μετρίως πειράσομαι.

2 Ὁ γὰρ τὸν ἅγιον πατέρα ἡμῶν τηνικαῦτα ὑποδεξάμενος εὐλαβέστατος ἀνὴρ τοὔνομα Λέων τῇ τοῦ ὑπάτου ἀξίᾳ τετιμημένος, ὕστερον μονάσας, διὰ τὴν πρὸς τὸν ὅσιον πίστιν τὴν Θεοδώρου τε κλῆσιν προσήκατο, καὶ κατ' ἐνιαυτὸν εἰς προσκύνησιν τῆς ἱερᾶς τοῦ λειψάνου αὐτοῦ θήκης ὁσιοπρεπῶς παρεγίγνετο. Οὗτος τοίνυν ὁ ἀοίδιμος καὶ πιστὸς Θεόδωρος εἰσελθὼν κατὰ τὸ εἰθισμένον αὐτῷ εἰς ἀφοσίωσιν τῆς πρὸς τὸν στεργόμενον θεοφόρον προσκυνήσεως, καὶ τὴν εὐχὴν ὡς ἐπόθει ἀποδεδωκὼς τῷ Κυρίῳ, καὶ τὸν τάφον τῶν πατέρων περιπτυξάμενος, ἐπειδὴ συγκαθεσθεὶς τοῖς ἀδελφοῖς, λόγος παρεισέδυ περί τε τῆς βιοτῆς καὶ τῶν ἀγώνων τοῦ μεγάλου Θεοδώρου, καθάπερ ὑπὸ πυρὸς τῇ τούτου μνήμῃ τὰ ἔνδον πυρποληθείς, δῆλος ἦν τῷ τε ἐρυθήματι τῆς ὄψεως καὶ τῇ τῶν δαψιλῶν δακρύων καταγωγῇ ἡλίκης θυμηδίας ἐμπέπληστο τῇ τῆς πολιτείας τοῦ μεγάλου ἀναμνήσει. Εἰς ὃ καὶ τῶν συνεδρευόντων αὐτῷ λίαν ἀγασθέντων καὶ εἰς κατάνυξιν ἐλθόντων, ἠξίωσεν ὁ γέρων νουνεχῶς ἀκοῦσαι τῶν ὑπ' αὐτοῦ ῥηθησομένων· ἤρξατο δὲ τῆς ὑποθέσεως ἔνθεν ἑλών.

spent a number of days, since almost all the leaders of his brotherhood had rushed to gather there. Similarly, Theodore's own brother Joseph, that most wise and steadfast warrior for the truth, arrived from his imprisonment in the fortress called Elpizon to meet him. There our holy father is said to have performed some miracles that are worth remembering. With God's help, I will try to describe them adequately in my account.

A most pious man called Leo, who had welcomed our 2
holy father at that time and who had been honored with the rank of *hypatos,* later became a monk. Because of his faith in the saint, he took the name Theodore and came every year to venerate the holy tomb of Theodore's body, as appropriate for a saint. So then, this renowned and faithful Theodore arrived, as usual, to perform veneration for the dear, divinely inspired man. After he had offered a prayer to the Lord as he had longed to do, and embraced the tomb of the fathers, he sat down with the brethren, and they started discussing the great Theodore's way of life and struggles. Then, as though he was being inwardly consumed by fire at the memory, the reddening of his face and the copious stream of tears made clear how great was the delight by which he was filled when he recalled the great man's conduct. Since those who were sitting there with him were very astonished at this and were moved to compunction, the elder discreetly requested to hear what he was going to say; and this monk Theodore began his account, taking it from there.

30

"Κατ' ἐκεῖνο καιροῦ," φησίν, "καθ' ὃν ἠξίωμαι τὸν ὁμολογητὴν τοῦ Χριστοῦ καὶ κοινὸν πάντων ἡμῶν ξενίσαι πατέρα, ἤδη παραληφθεῖσαν ἡμῖν ἐπὶ τῷ υἱῷ μου Διονυσίῳ νεᾶνιν καὶ τούτῳ συστεφθεῖσαν παρὰ πόδας συνέβη κατά τινα φθόνου βολίδα ταύτην λάβρῳ περιπεσεῖν πυρετῷ. Ἀφ' οὗ δὴ συμβάντος τὰς μὲν γαμηλίους ᾠδὰς αἱ πενθήρεις ἠμείβοντο, ἡμεῖς δὲ τῷ θρήνῳ συμπεφυρμένοι, τὸν πρόωρον θάνατον τῆς κόρης οὐκ ἀπηλπίζομεν. Τοῦτο οὖν πρὸς ἡμῶν διαγνοὺς ὁ τοῦ Θεοῦ ἄνθρωπος, ἔλαιον εὐλογήσας καὶ τοῦτο πεπομφὼς ὡς ἡμᾶς ἐξ οὗπερ ηὐλίζετο χωρίου, Πτελέας προσαγορευομένου, ἐπιχρῖσαι τῆς ἀρρωστούσης τό τε μέτωπον καὶ τοὺς ταρσοὺς ἑκατέρων τῶν χειρῶν καὶ τῶν ποδῶν προστέταχεν. Καὶ τούτου γενομένου, παραχρῆμα ἡ παῖς τὸ δῶρον τῆς ἰάσεως ἐδέξατο, καὶ ἡμεῖς εἰς εὐθυμίαν ἐπανήκομεν, δοξάζοντες τὸν Θεὸν ἐπὶ τῇ ταχίστῃ τῆς νεάνιδος σωτηρίᾳ."

2 Διπλασιάζων δὲ τὴν περὶ τούτων ἐξήγησιν, ὁ εὐγενὴς ἐκεῖνος πρεσβύτης, "Ἄλλο," φησίν, "ἀκούσατε, πατέρες. Ἀνήρ τις ὀνόματι Λέων ἀπὸ κώμης Ἀχυραοῦς οὕτω καλουμένης συνῴκει γυναικὶ ἐχούσῃ πνεῦμα ἀκάθαρτον, ἥτις τοσοῦτον ὑπὸ τοῦ δαίμονος παρεφέρετο, ὥστε καὶ τὰς ἰδίας κατεσθίειν ἀνεπαισθήτως σάρκας. Ὁ οὖν ταύτης σύμβιος πίστει φερόμενος τῇ πρὸς τὸν θεράποντα τοῦ Χριστοῦ Θεόδωρον, ἐποχουμένῳ τῷ ἀοιδίμῳ ἐπὶ κάνθωνος καὶ δι' αὐτοῦ παριόντι προσελθὼν μετὰ τῆς γυναικός,

30

"At that time," he said, "when I was thought worthy to entertain Christ's confessor and the common father of us all, the young woman whom we had just then accepted as a bride for my son Dionysios and who had received the marriage crown along with him, by some stroke of envy fell victim immediately afterward to a raging fever. When that happened, the wedding songs became songs of mourning, and we joined in the lamentation, as we feared that the girl would suffer an untimely death. When the man of God learned this about us, he blessed some oil and sent it to us from the village, called Pteleai, where he was staying and instructed us to anoint the sick girl's forehead as well as the palms of her hands and the soles of her feet. Once this was done, the girl at once received the gift of healing and we became happy again, glorifying God for the young girl's very swift recovery."

In addition to his narrative about this, that noble old man 2
said, "Listen to another story, fathers. A man named Leo from a village called Achyraous was living with a woman who had an unclean spirit. She was deranged by the demon to such an extent that she would even eat her own flesh without realizing it. Inspired by his faith in Theodore, the servant of Christ, her husband, along with his wife, approached the renowned man as he was passing by, riding on a pack ass,

ἠξίου μεταδοῦναι αὐτῇ τῆς παρὰ τῶν εὐχῶν αὐτοῦ εὐλογίας. Ὁ δὲ θαυματουργὸς πατὴρ ἡμῶν τὴν ἑαυτοῦ δεξιὰν τῇ κορυφῇ ἀκροθιγῶς ἐρείσας τῆς γυναικός, ἐποίησεν ἐπ' αὐτῇ τὴν ἐπὶ τοῖς πνευματιῶσιν εὐχήν· ἅμα δὲ τοῦ ταύτην συντελέσαι, καὶ ἡ ἀπαλλαγὴ τοῦ δαίμονος τῇ πασχούσῃ ἐπηκολούθησεν, σημείου φοβεροῦ κατὰ τὴν ὥραν τῆς διώξεως αὐτοῦ εἰς φανερὸν τοῖς βλέπουσιν γεγονότος· τῇ γὰρ ἐκβολῇ τοῦ ἀκαθάρτου καὶ πονηροῦ πνεύματος συναπερρύησαν οἵ τε τῶν χειρῶν καὶ τῶν ποδῶν αὐτῆς ὄνυχες καὶ ἔπεσον εἰς τὴν γῆν· εἰς ὃ καὶ ἐκπλαγεὶς ὁ ἀνήρ, ἐδίδου δόξαν καὶ εὐχαριστίαν τῷ Θεῷ τῷ διὰ τοῦ θεράποντος αὐτοῦ τοιαῦτα παράδοξα παρ' ἐλπίδα ποιήσαντι εἰς τὴν ἑαυτοῦ σύμβιον."

3 Τούτοις ἐχόμενα καὶ ἕτερον συνῆψεν, οὕτως εἰπὼν ὁ θαυμαστὸς τὴν πίστιν Θεόδωρος· "Ποταμός τίς ἐστι τοῖς καθ' ἡμᾶς παρακείμενος τόποις Ὀνοπνίκτης λεγόμενος, ἐξ αὐτῆς, οἶμαι, τῆς προσηγορίας τὸ τῆς ἐπιγινομένης αὐτῷ πλημμύρας σημαίνων ἐπιζήμιον, ὡς μηδὲ τοὺς ἀγνῶτας ἀμοιρεῖν τὸ βλαπτικὸν τῶν ῥευμάτων. Οὗτος ἐξοιδαίνων ἐνίοτε τοῦ χρόνου καὶ τῆς ἰδίας κρηπῖδος ὑπερχεόμενος, τὸ χωρίον Πτελέας οὐ μετρίως κατελωβᾶτο· οὗ δὴ χάριν ὥραν ἀποτηρήσαντες εὔθετον ἀνηνέγκαμεν τὰ κατ' αὐτὸν τῷ σημειοφόρῳ πατρί. Ὁ δὲ λυπηθεὶς σφόδρα τῇ σκυθρωπῇ ἀγγελίᾳ, περὶ δείλην ὀψίαν τῆς αὐτῆς ἡμέρας τὸν τόπον σὺν ἡμῖν καταλαμβάνει τῆς παρεκκλίσεως τοῦ ποταμοῦ, καὶ τὰς ἑσπερίους αὐτόθι ἀποδοὺς τῷ Κυρίῳ δοξολογίας, τὸν ἐπ' αὐτὸ τοῦτο τεκτονευθέντα σταυρὸν τῷ τόπῳ καταπήγνυσιν τῶν φθοριμαίων ὑδάτων. Ὅπερ

and asked him to give her a blessing by his prayers. Our miracle-working father lightly rested his right hand on the woman's head and offered the prayer for those possessed by evil spirits for her; the moment he completed this prayer, the woman who was suffering was released from the demon. At the moment the demon was expelled, an awesome miracle took place in full view of the onlookers for, along with the ejection of the unclean and evil spirit, the nails came out of the woman's hands and feet and fell on the ground. Her husband was astounded at this and gave glory and thanks to God who through his servant had, beyond hope, performed such miracles for his wife."

Right after these accounts Theodore added yet another. 3
This is what that man of wonderful faith said: "There is a river in our region called the Onopniktes, which indicates by its very name, I think, the destructive nature of its periodic flooding, so that even people who do not know it may be alerted to the harmful nature of its floods. At the times of year when it would swell up and overflow its banks, it would cause considerable destruction to the village of Pteleai; because of this, after we had waited for the appropriate time, we reported the situation to the wonder-working father. Theodore was most upset at the disturbing report and, late in the afternoon of that same day, went with us to the place where the river had left its course. There he offered the evening praise to the Lord and firmly planted a cross that had been constructed for this very purpose at the site of the destructive waters. When it saw this sign of the cross, the

σημεῖον σταυροῦ βλέπον τό ποτε μορμύρον ποτάμιον ῥεῖθρον ἔκτοτε καὶ μέχρι τοῦ δεῦρο ὡς δοῦλος εὐήκοος τῷ Δεσποτικῷ ὑπείκει συμβόλῳ, μὴ τολμῶν ἐκχαραδρωθῆναι κατὰ τὴν ἔμπροσθεν προπέτειαν αὐτοῦ."

4 Πρὸς δὲ τοῖς τρισὶ τούτοις καὶ τὸ εἰς αὐτὸν γεγονὸς συνῆψε τῇ λέξει θαῦμα ὁ φιλαλήθης ἄνθρωπος μετὰ δακρύων φήσας οὕτως· "Διατρίβοντος ἔτι τοῦ μακαρίου πατρὸς ἡμῶν εἰς τὴν καθ' ἡμᾶς ἑστίαν τὴν ἐν Πτελέαις, ἐγένετό με," φησίν, "κατά τινα χρείαν πρὸς ἕτερον ἀπελθεῖν χωρίον, Μετεῶριν λεγόμενον· καὶ ποιήσας τὴν διακονίαν τοῦ πράγματος, ὑπέστρεφον πάλιν εἰς τὰ οἰκεῖα. Γενομένῳ δέ μοι πρὸς τὸ παρακείμενον ὄρος τῇ λεωφόρῳ, συνηντήθη πάρδαλις καταπληκτικὸν φέρουσα εἶδος. Ἣν καὶ στᾶσαν παρευθὺ ἐνώπιόν μου καὶ βουλομένην τῷ κατ' ἐμοῦ χρήσασθαι ἅλματι αἰσθόμενος, τὸν φόβον τῆς ψυχῆς ὥσπερ ἀποβαλών, λέγω πρὸς αὐτὴν μεγάλῃ τῇ φωνῇ· 'Ἄπιθι, θηρίον ἀτίθασσον, καὶ μηδαμῶς μοι προσεγγίσῃς, ἐγὼ γὰρ πρὸς τὸν θεράποντα τοῦ Χριστοῦ σπεύδω Θεόδωρον.' Ἡ δὲ καθάπερ ἀπὸ προσώπου πυρὸς τῆς τοιαύτης φωνῆς κατεπτηχυῖα, νῶτά μοι δίδωσι παραχωροῦσα τῆς πορείας τὴν τρίβον, ἐγὼ δὲ τὸ παράδοξον τῆς ὑποστολῆς τοῦ θηρὸς θεασάμενος, σύνδακρυς ὅλος γέγονα καὶ τὸν Δεσπότην Χριστὸν ἐδόξασα, τὸν ἐξ ἀνδρολέτου καὶ πονηροῦ ζῴου ῥυσάμενόν με διὰ μόνης ἐπικλήσεως τοῦ γνησίου αὐτοῦ δούλου Θεοδώρου."

once-roaring current of the river yielded to the Master's symbol, and from that time even until now, like an obedient servant, it has not dared to break out of its channel in the furious way it used to before."

In addition to these three miracles, that man who loved 4
the truth tearfully added to his tale the miracle that happened to him. This is what he said: "While our blessed father was still staying in our home at Pteleai, I happened to go to another village called Meteorin on some business and, after I had attended to the matter, started out for home again. But when I was on the main road heading toward the nearby mountain, a terrifying female leopard encountered me. When I realized that she was standing right in front of me and wanted to leap at me, I stopped fearing for my life as it were and said to her in a loud voice, 'Go away, you vicious brute, and don't come anywhere near me, because I'm hurrying to Christ's servant Theodore.' The leopard shrank back from my words as if at the sight of fire, and turned her back on me as she got out of my way. When I observed the creature's miraculous timidity, I broke down in tears and glorified Christ our Master, who had delivered me from an evil, murderous beast through the mere invocation of the name of his true servant Theodore."

31

Καὶ ταῦτα μὲν ἡμῖν ἔγνωσται πρὸς τοῦ ἱερόφρονος ἐκείνου καὶ εὐκλεοῦς Θεοδώρου, τοῦ καὶ τὴν πολιὰν καὶ τὴν πίστιν ἀληθῶς πρεσβυτικωτάτου. Ἐπειδὴ δὲ προγενεστέρως τούτων ἕτερα γεγενῆσθαι τῷ πατρὶ κηρύττεται θαύματα, ἅπερ ἐξηγήσατο ὁ θεῖος πατὴρ ἡμῶν Σωφρόνιος, δεῖν ᾠήθην ἐνταῦθα τοῦ λόγου γενόμενος κἀκεῖνα τούτοις ἐπισυνάψαι, ὡς ἂν ἄρτιος εἴη καὶ συνεχὴς ἡ περὶ τούτων ἀξιοδιήγητος ἱστορία.

2 "Κατὰ δὴ τὸν καιρὸν ἐκεῖνον," φησίν, "ὁπότε τὴν οὐράνιον καὶ ἀγγελικὴν πολιτείαν ὁ ἐν ἁγίοις πατὴρ ἡμῶν Θεόδωρος σὺν τῇ ὑπ' αὐτὸν πολυπληθεῖ συνοδίᾳ ἐν τοῖς Στουδίου ἐπεδείκνυτο, ἀνῆλθεν μιᾷ κατὰ τὸ εἰωθὸς αὐτῷ εἰς τὸ νοσοκομεῖον ἐπισκέψασθαι τοὺς ἀνακεκλιμένους ἀδελφούς. Εἷς δέ τις τῶν αὐτόθι χρονίσας ἐν τῇ ἀρρωστίᾳ καὶ τὰς ἐκ τῶν ἀλγηδόνων προσβολὰς μηκέτι φέρειν δεδυνημένος, ἠθύμει πάνυ καὶ ἀπελέγετο τὴν ἑαυτοῦ ζωήν, ὡς καὶ τοὺς συνανακειμένους εἰς οἶκτον ἄγειν καὶ ἔλεον ταῖς τῶν λόγων ἀνακλήσεσιν. Παρὰ τούτου τοίνυν ἀξιωθεὶς ὁ τὴν φροντίδα τῶν ἀσθενῶν ποιούμενος—Συμεὼν δ' οὗτος ἦν, ὁ θαυμάσιος τῆς ὑπακοῆς υἱὸς καὶ τῆς διακρίσεως λύχνος παμφαέστατος—ἐρωτῆσαι ἐξ αὐτοῦ τὸν πατέρα ὅπως εὔξηται τῷ Θεῷ καὶ ἀπολυθῇ τάχιον τοῦ δεσμοῦ, ἐν τῷ κατιέναι τὸν θεοφόρον ποιμένα ἐπικαταλαβὼν ὁ νοσοκόμος ὀπίσω αὐτοῦ, ἀπαγγέλλει αὐτῷ τὴν τοῦ ἀρρώστου δέησιν. Ὁ δὲ μέγας Θεόδωρος ταῦτα ἀκούσας,

31

These are the things of which that holy-minded and well-known Theodore, who with his gray hair and faith was truly very venerable, informed us. But seeing that other miracles are reported to have been performed by our father Theodore prior to those, ones which our holy father Sophronios related, I thought that I should add these also to the previous ones at this point in my account, so that the narrative about these miracles, which is worth telling, might be up-to-date and complete.

"At the time," Sophronios said, "when Theodore, our fa- 2
ther among the saints, was displaying his heavenly and angelic way of life along with the numerous community under him at Stoudios, he went into the infirmary one day, as was his custom, to visit the brethren lying there. One of them, who had spent a long time in ill health and could no longer bear the attacks of pain, was very despondent and despaired of his life, with the result that he even moved his fellow patients to pity and compassion by the invocations that he uttered. The man who had care of the sick—this was Symeon, the admirable son of obedience and most radiant lamp of discernment—was entrusted by this brother with asking father Theodore on his behalf to pray to God that he be released more quickly from his earthly bond. As the divinely inspired shepherd was leaving, the infirmarian caught up with him from behind and reported the sick man's request to him. When the great Theodore heard it, he asked if the

ἤρετο εἰ ἀληθῶς οὕτως εἰρήκει ὁ κάμνων ἀδελφός· τοῦ δὲ βεβαιωσαμένου τῇ συγκαταθέσει τῶν ῥημάτων, στραφεὶς πρὸς ἀνατολὰς ὁ οὐρανόφρων καὶ τὴν μορφὴν πυρακτωθεὶς ἐκ τῆς κατὰ τὴν καρδίαν συμπαθοῦς διαθέσεως, ἐπάρας τε τὰς χεῖρας εἰς ὕψος καὶ σύνδακρυς γενόμενος, προσηύξατο κατὰ διάνοιαν πρὸς τὸν ἔχοντα ἐξουσίαν ζωῆς καὶ θανάτου Κύριον, τῶν συνόντων αὐτῷ ἀδελφῶν ταῦτα βλεπόντων. Καὶ μετὰ τὴν προσευχὴν στραφεὶς λέγει τῷ Συμεῶνι, 'Ὑπόστρεφε ταχὺ πρὸς τὸν ἀδελφόν, καθότι πεποίηκεν ὁ Κύριος ἔλεος κατὰ τὴν αἴτησιν αὐτοῦ.' Ὁ δὲ εὐθέως ὑποστρέψας, εὗρεν αὐτὸν τὴν ὑστάτην ἀποδόντα πνοήν, καὶ τοὺς παρισταμένους αὐτῷ πρὸς τὴν τῶν ὀφθαλμῶν αὐτοῦ ἐπίμυσιν τὰς ἑαυτῶν χεῖρας ἐπιβαλόντας, ὡς εὑρίσκεσθαι σαφῶς ἅμα τοῦ φάναι τὸν ὅσιον τὰ τῆς ἐξόδου καὶ τὸν ἀδελφὸν ἐκδημῆσαι τοῦ σώματος."

3 Ἕτερον ἡμῖν παράδοξον ὁ ἱερὸς οὗτος πατὴρ ἡμῶν Σωφρόνιος, ὁ καὶ διάδοχος τοῦ θρόνου αὐτοῦ τε καὶ τῶν μετ' αὐτὸν ποιμηνάντων τὴν αὐτοῦ ποίμνην γενόμενος, διηγησάμενος καταλέλοιπεν. Ἔφη γάρ ποτε πορείαν ἐκποιεῖσθαι κατὰ τὸ θέμα τῶν Παφλαγόνων ἐν τοῖς καιροῖς τῆς εἰκονομαχικῆς τρικυμίας σὺν τῷ ἀποθρίξαντι αὐτὸν πατρὶ Ἀνατολίῳ—τῷ κρατίστῳ φοιτητῇ καὶ νοταρίῳ τοῦ μεγάλου γεγονότι πατρός, καὶ πληγὰς μαστίγων καὶ φυλακὰς διὰ τὴν εὐσεβῆ πίστιν ἀνδρείως ὑποίσαντι. "Καὶ δή," φησί, "τὸ ἐξ ἑωθινοῦ μέχρις ἑσπέρας διανυσάντων ἡμῶν διάστημα, κατελύσαμεν παρὰ τὰς τοῦ χόρτου διακοπὰς πλησίον θημωνίας ἀναψύξεως χάριν, ἐγένετο δὲ κατά τινα σύμβασιν τῆς Ῥωμαϊκῆς ἐξουσίας, νούμερον στρατοῦ

troubled brother had truly spoken in this way. And when the other confirmed it by assuring him of the words, the heavenly-minded one turned toward the east with his face inflamed by the compassionate disposition in his heart; lifting up his hands and starting to weep, he silently prayed to the Lord who has power over life and death, while the brothers who were with him watched this. After the prayer he turned and said to Symeon, 'Return quickly to the brother, because the Lord has acted mercifully in accordance with his request.' Symeon returned at once and found that he had taken his final breath and those standing beside him had closed his eyes with their hands; so it was clearly determined that the holy one spoke about his decease at the same time as the brother departed from his body."

This holy father of ours, Sophronios, who became a suc- 3
cessor to Theodore's position and to those who shepherded his flock after him, has bequeathed to us an account of another miracle. He said that he was once making a journey in the Paphlagonian theme during the time of the iconoclastic upheaval along with Anatolios, the father who had tonsured him—he had been a very great student and secretary of the great father, and had bravely endured floggings and imprisonments because of his pious faith. "And so," said Sophronios, "when we had completed our journey, which had lasted from dawn to dusk, we turned off the road to rest near to some piles of cut hay; but in accordance with some arrangement by the Roman authority, an army detachment had

αὐτόθι προαναπεσεῖν. Πυραὶ γοῦν παρὰ πολλῶν πρὸς ὕδατος θερμοῦ ἐξαναφθεῖσαι χρῆσιν, οὐκ οἶδ' ὅπως τοῦ χόρτου δραξάμενον τὸ πῦρ λυγρῶς τὰς προσπιπτούσας ἐπεβόσκετο χορτοθεσίας. Ταράχου δὲ πολλοῦ καὶ στάσεως ὑπὸ τῶν στρατιωτῶν ἐκ τούτου γεγονυίας, φονίῳ τε τῷ ὄμματι καὶ κινήματι τὸν τοῦτο δεδρακότα πάντων ἐπιζητούντων, θεωρήσας ὁ ὅσιος πατὴρ ἡμῶν καὶ ὁμολογητὴς τοῦ Χριστοῦ Ἀνατόλιος τὴν χαλεπωτάτην ὁρμὴν τοῦ λαοῦ, καὶ φοβηθεὶς μήπως διαχειρίσωνται τῇ ὀξείᾳ ὁρμῇ τοῦ περιζέοντος θυμοῦ τοὺς ἀμφοτέρους ὡς ὑπευθύνους τοῦ τοιούτου κακοῦ, στὰς κατὰ ἀνατολὰς καὶ τὰς χεῖρας πρὸς οὐρανὸν ἐκπετάσας, ἐβόησεν πρὸς τὸν Θεὸν λέγων, 'Κύριε Ἰησοῦ Χριστέ, Θεὲ τοῦ οὐρανοῦ καὶ τῆς γῆς, ἐὰν προσεδέξω τοὺς ἀγῶνας Θεοδώρου τοῦ κατ' ἐμὲ πατρός, ταῖς αὐτοῦ πρεσβείαις καὶ νῦν δυσωπήθητι καὶ σβέσον τὴν πυρκαϊὰν ταύτην, ἵνα μὴ θανατώσωσιν ἡμᾶς οἱ ἄνθρωποι ἀδίκως.' Ἅμα δὲ τοῦ εἰρηκέναι αὐτὸν ταῦτα, τὸ μὲν πῦρ ἐκεῖνο ὡς ὑπό τινος ῥαγδαιοτάτης ἀπετεφρώθη βροχῆς, οἱ στρατιῶται δὲ πρὸς τὸ ἥμερόν τε καὶ ἔκθαμβον μεταπλασθέντες, ἐδόξαζον τὸν Θεὸν καὶ τὸν πανόσιον πατέρα ἡμῶν ὑπερευφήμουν Θεόδωρον."

4 Παραπλήσιον δὲ τούτου καὶ ἐν τῇ Κωνσταντινουπόλει ἔφησε γεγονέναι τεράστιον ὁ αὐτὸς οὗτος ἀοίδιμος ἀνὴρ Σωφρόνιος ἐπὶ οἰκίας ἑνὸς τῶν μεγιστάνων, εἰς τὴν Ῥάβδον τὴν οἴκησιν ἔχοντος, παρ' αὐτῆς τῆς κυρίας τοῦ οἴκου ἀκούσας τὴν ὑπόθεσιν τοῦ πράγματος, οὕτω πρὸς αὐτὸν εἰρηκυίας, "Ἡμέρας," φησί, "μεσούσης, γέγονεν ἐμπρησμὸς εἰς τὸν χορτοβολῶνα ἡμῶν, πόθεν ἢ πῶς οὐκ

already set up camp in that spot. Many of them had then lit fires to heat water and, I don't know how, but the fire had taken hold of the grass and was destructively feeding on the piles of hay in its path. The soldiers had created a great uproar and commotion as a result of this, and they were all excitedly looking for the perpetrator with murderous expressions on their faces. When Anatolios, our saintly father and Christ's confessor, saw the very dangerous surge of the crowd, he was afraid that in a sudden surge of seething anger they would kill both of us as the ones responsible for such a misfortune, so he stood facing the east and, stretching out his hands toward heaven, called upon God, saying, 'Lord Jesus Christ, God of heaven and earth, if you accepted the struggles of Theodore, my father, be won over now by his intercessions and extinguish this fire so that these men may not kill us unjustly.' No sooner had he said these words than that fire was reduced to ashes as though by a violent downpour and the soldiers, who were transformed to civility and amazement, began to glorify God and praise Theodore, our all-saintly father."

This same renowned Sophronios said that a somewhat similar miracle to this had also taken place in Constantinople at the home of one of the grandees who lived in the Rhabdos quarter. He heard the story of what happened from the lady of the house herself, who related it to him as follows: "In the middle of the day," she said, "a conflagration broke out in our hayloft, how or why I do not know, and the 4

οἶδα, καὶ τοσοῦτον ἐξήφθη τῇ τῶν εὐκαταπρήστων ὑλῶν συμφλέξει τὸ πῦρ, ὡς μέλλειν συνεμπιπρᾶσθαι καὶ τὴν ἄλλην ἅπασαν κτῆσιν τῆς ὑποστάσεως ἡμῶν. Θρυλληθέντων οὖν πάντων καὶ πρὸς τὴν τῶν ὑδάτων καὶ ὑδροστατῶν ἐπικομιδὴν σὺν βοῇ καὶ ταράχῳ διασκιδναμένων, ἔγωγε περιθέουσα καὶ λίαν ὀδυρομένη, διενεθυμήθην ὡς ἐπιστολίδιον ἀποσταλὲν προσφάτως παρὰ τοῦ μεγάλου Θεοδώρου ἐφ' ἑνὶ τέθειταί μοι τῶν ἐκ βαΐων τὴν σύστασιν εἰληχότων σκευῶν. Καὶ δὴ σπεύσασα καὶ τοῦτο μετὰ χεῖρας λαβομένη, σὺν δάκρυσιν ἐξεβόησα ὑψηλοτέρᾳ φωνῇ, 'Ὅσιε Θεόδωρε, βοήθησον ἡμῖν διὰ τῶν εὐχῶν σου κατὰ τὴν ὥραν ταύτην,' καὶ σὺν τῷ λόγῳ ῥίπτω αὐτὸ ἐξ οὗπερ ἱστάμην ἀπόπτου πρὸς τὸ κάταντες ἐπάνω τῆς φλογός. Ἡ δὲ ὥσπερ καταιδεσθεῖσα τοὺς ἐν τῷ χάρτῃ γεγραμμένους λόγους τοῦ ἁγίου πατρός, παραχρῆμά τε ὑπεστάλη τοῦ ἐπαγριαίνεσθαι καθ' ἡμῶν καὶ εἰς τὸ μεῖον κατὰ βραχὺ συνηλαύνετο, ὡς εἰκαίαν γενέσθαι τήν τε τοῦ ὄχλου τῇδε κἀκεῖσε περιδρομὴν καὶ τὴν τῶν σιφώνων κατὰ τόπους παρασκευήν, δοξάζειν τε τὸν Θεὸν ἅπαντας ἐπὶ τῷ παραδόξῳ τρόπῳ τῆς κατασβέσεως τοῦ ἐμπυρισμοῦ."

5 Ἄλλο δὲ πάλιν παράδοξον ἀπὸ τῆς Σαρδονικῆς νήσου ἧκεν ἡμῖν τοῦ σημειοφόρου πατρὸς ἡμῶν ἄκουσμα· τῷ γὰρ πρώτῳ τῆς αὐτῆς χώρας φιλοχρίστῳ καὶ θεοσεβεῖ μάλα ὑπάρχοντι ἐντυχὼν τῶν ἡμετέρων πατέρων τις, παρ' αὐτοῦ τὴν ἱστορίαν ταύτην ἐγνώρισεν λέξαντος πρὸς αὐτὸν οὕτως. "Ἐγώ," φησίν, "ἐκ πολλοῦ τὰ τριῴδια τῆς ἁγίας Τεσσαρακοστῆς, ἃ πεποίηκεν ὁ θεοφόρος πατὴρ

fire that was kindled through the burning of this highly flammable material was so great that all our other property was also about to go up in flames. Everyone was chattering in confusion and scattering in different directions with shouting and uproar to bring water and fire engines, while I ran about wailing loudly. Then I remembered that I had placed a note that the great Theodore had recently sent me in one of the palm-leaf bowls. I hurried off, took it in my hands, and tearfully shouted out in a piercing voice, 'Saintly Theodore, help us at this time by your prayers.' As I spoke, I threw the note down onto the fire from the vantage point where I was standing. As if it was filled with awe at the holy father's words written on the sheet of paper, the fire immediately stopped being angry with us and quickly reduced in size, with the result that the rushing of the crowd here and there and its preparation of water pumps in various places became pointless, and they all glorified God for the miraculous way in which the conflagration had been extinguished."

Yet another miraculous report about our miracle-working 5
father has come to us from the island of Sardinia for, when one of our fathers met the ruler of that same land, a man who loved Christ and was very devout, he learned this story from him, who related it to him as follows. "A long time ago," the ruler said, "after I acquired a copy of the *triodia* of holy Lent which Theodore, our divinely inspired father and

ἡμῶν καὶ ὁμολογητὴς τοῦ Χριστοῦ Θεόδωρος, περιποιησάμενος, ἔψαλλον αὐτὰ κατ' ἐνιαυτὸν μετὰ τῆς προσηκούσης πίστεως, ὥσπερ οὖν καὶ νῦν χάριτι Χριστοῦ. Κατ' ἐκεῖνον δὲ τὸν καιρὸν ἐπεξενώθησάν μοι μοναχοὶ (τῷ σχήματι), λέγοντες εἶναι μαθηταὶ Γρηγορίου τοῦ γεγονότος ἀρχιεπισκόπου τῆς Συρακουσαίων τῶν Σικελῶν πόλεως, οἳ καὶ διατρίψαντες παρ' ἐμοὶ ἔτυχον οὐ μετρίας παραμυθίας. Ἐπεὶ δὲ ὁ καιρὸς τῆς ἁγίας Τεσσαρακοστῆς ἐνεστήκει, προπαρασκευὴν ἐποιούμην τῆς κρατούσης παρ' ἐμοὶ τάξεως ἐν τῇ πρὸς Θεὸν δοξολογίᾳ, προβαλλόμενος τὰ τριῴδια τοῦ ἁγίου πατρὸς ἡμῶν ἐν τῇ Τεσσαρακοστῇ ψαλθῆναι, καθὼς ἦν μοι ἔθος ἐκ τῶν ἔμπροσθεν χρόνων. Ἐκεῖνοι δὲ τοῦτο ἀκούσαντες, ἐταράχθησαν ὁμοῦ καὶ ἐξέστησαν ὅτι καὶ μέχρις ἡμῶν ἐπεφθάκει ἡ τοῦ ἡγιασμένου πατρὸς ἡμῶν διδασκαλία καὶ φήμη, ἤρξαντό τε μωμοσκοπεῖν τὸν ἅγιον καὶ τὰ αὐτοῦ διακερτομεῖν ποιήματα, ὡς οὐ κατὰ λόγον συντεθέντα παιδείας· ὑφ' ὧν παραφθαρεὶς ἔγωγε τὴν διάνοιαν, τὴν θολερὰν ἀνατροπὴν τῶν κατὰ τοῦ θεοφόρου λόγων ἐξέπιον.

6 "Ὅθεν καὶ τῆς ἁγίας Τεσσαρακοστῆς ὡς ἔφην ἐνστάσης, οὐκ ἠβουλόμην ψάλαι τὰ αὐτοῦ τριῴδια, καὶ τῇ εἰσοδίῳ νυκτὶ ἐφίσταταί μοι ὁ τοῦ Χριστοῦ θεράπων Θεόδωρος, μακρὸς ὢν τὴν ἡλικίαν, κατάξηρος καὶ ὠχρὸς τὴν ὄψιν, μιξοπόλιος τὴν τρίχα καὶ ἐπιφάλακρος. Ὧιτινι παρείποντο ῥαβδοῦχοί τινες ἔνδοξοι τὴν ἰδέαν, οὓς καὶ μετὰ κινήσεως δῆθεν παρακελευσάμενος, ἀποτείνουσίν με ἀργαλέως, τύπτειν τε ἰσχυρῶς ταῖς ῥάβδοις ἐνίους συντάξας, αὐτὸς ἐμβριθέστερον ἐβόα πρός με, 'Τῶν ἐμῶν

confessor of Christ, had composed, I would chant them each year with appropriate faith, as I still do even now by the grace of Christ. At that time, I was hosting some monks (at least in their appearance) who said that they were pupils of Gregory, who had become archbishop of the Sicilian city of Syracuse; and by spending some time with me, they received considerable sustenance. Since the period of holy Lent was imminent, I began to prepare the arrangement that I maintained for the praise of God, proposing that the *triodia* of our holy father should be chanted during Lent, just as had been my custom in previous years. But when the monks heard this, they at once became upset and were astonished that the teaching and fame of our sanctified father had reached even as far as us; and they began to criticize the holy man and mock his work for not being composed in the manner that was taught. My mind was disturbed by them and I swallowed the foul refutation contained in their words against the divinely inspired man.

"As a result, once holy Lent began and, as I said, I did not 6
want to chant his *triodia,* Theodore, Christ's servant, appeared to me when night fell, advanced in age, with a gaunt and pale face, grizzled hair, and partially bald. There were some lictors accompanying him who were glorious in their appearance; with a gesture he gave them a command and they painfully stretched me out. After he had instructed some of them to beat me forcefully with their rods, he himself shouted severely at me, 'You faithless man, do you

ποιημάτων καταφρονεῖς, ἄπιστε;' Καὶ πάλιν πρὸς τοὺς δορυφόρους ἔλεγεν, 'Ἐντολὴν ἔχετε ἱκανῶς χρήσασθαι αὐτῷ ἵνα παιδευθῇ μὴ παραδέχεσθαι *ὁμιλίας κακάς*, τὰς δυναμένας μάλιστα *παραφθείρειν ἤθη χρηστά*.' Ἐν τούτοις οὖν μαστιχθεὶς εἰς κόρον, ἐδόκουν γὰρ μόλις ἀναπνεῖν, εἰς ἐμαυτὸν ἦλθόν ποτε διυπνισθεὶς σὺν θορύβῳ καρδίας καὶ ἀλγηδόσι σώματος σφοδροτάταις, ἃς καὶ ὑπέδειξα τοῖς περὶ ἐμὲ σώας φυλαχθείσας καὶ ἐνσημάντρους ἐν τῷ ἐμῷ σώματι πρὸς πίστωσιν τῶν συμβάντων μοι διὰ τὴν παραδοχὴν τῆς κατὰ τοῦ δικαίου πατρὸς ἡμῶν ἀπιστίας κακῶν· παρευθύ τε τοὺς τὴν εὐωχίαν τῆς ὀργῆς ταύτης προξενήσαντάς μοι τοῦ ἐμοῦ οἴκου ἐδίωξα· καὶ ἐξ ἐκείνου λοιπὸν ἕως τοῦ παρόντος, σεβαστὰ ἡμῖν ἐστι καὶ πρόκριτα τὰ τοῦ ἁγίου πατρὸς ποιήματα, καὶ ἔχομεν αὐτὸν ὡς ἕνα τῶν ἀποστόλων Χριστοῦ καὶ θεοπάροχον διδάσκαλον τῆς καθολικῆς Ἐκκλησίας, οὐκ ἐκ ψιλῆς ἀκοῆς ταῦτα περὶ αὐτοῦ δοξάζοντες, ἀλλὰ διὰ πραγματικῆς πείρας καὶ θείας καὶ ἀψευδοῦς καθὰ εἴρηται ἀποκαλύψεως."

32

Ἔστι δὲ καὶ ἄλλα πολλὰ τὰ εἰς ἡμᾶς ἐλθόντα τοῦ σημειοφόρου πατρὸς ἡμῶν θαύματα, ἅ, περιόντος ἔτι τῷ βίῳ, οὐ μὴν ἀλλὰ καὶ πρὸς τὴν ἀμείνω ζωὴν ἐκδημήσαντος κατὰ τὴν τῶν ἰδόντων αὐτὰ καὶ πειραθέντων ὑφήγησιν,

despise my compositions?' Then he said to his bodyguards again, 'You have been ordered to deal with him sufficiently to teach him not to accept *bad company,* especially those that can *ruin good morals.*' After I had been whipped by them to their satisfaction, for I seemed to be scarcely able to breathe, I came to my senses, waking up at some point with a pounding heart and very painful welts on my body. I showed these to the people around me, since they had been preserved and imprinted on my body, to confirm the bad things that had happened to me through my acceptance of unbelief in our righteous father. I immediately chased out of my house those men who had brought that surfeit of wrath on me. Afterward, from that time until the present, the holy father's compositions have been revered and preferred by us, and we consider him as one of Christ's apostles and a teacher of the universal Church provided by God, praising these things about him not from mere hearsay but through actual experience and divine and truthful revelation, as has been related."

32

There are many other wonders by our miracle-working father that have been reported to us; these took place and were performed both while he was still alive and after he had departed to the better life, according to the description of

ἐγεγόνει τε καὶ ἐπράχθη· ἄλλος μὲν γὰρ πνευματιώντων ἔφησεν ἀποκάθαρσιν γεγενῆσθαι πρὸς αὐτοῦ, ἕτερος δὲ τῶν ἄλλως πασχόντων σωματικαῖς ἀνωμαλίαις τὴν ὁλόκληρον ῥῶσιν. Ἔστι δὲ καί τις ἐξαπίνης ἀλγήσας κομιδῇ τὸν στόμαχον, καὶ μόνον εἰς τὴν γεγραμμένην ἐπὶ τοῦ κίονος ἀπιδὼν τοῦ ἁγίου εἰκόνα, καὶ τούτου τὸ ὄνομα πρὸς βοήθειαν ἐπικαλεσάμενος, καὶ παραυτὰ τῆς πιεζούσης ὀδύνης ἀπαλλαγείς. Ἄλλος δὲ πάλιν ἐξ ἀσυμφόρου καὶ πολὺ τὸ γεῶδες ἔχοντος βρώματος οἷόν τινα δρακόντιον ἰὸν εἰσδεξάμενος καὶ ὑπ' αὐτοῦ τὰ ἔγκατα τιτρωσκόμενος, καὶ τεθνᾶναι τὸ κεφάλαιον παρὰ πολλῶν προσδοκηθείς, τὸ ἀποκανδήλισμα τῆς ὕπερθεν τοῦ ἱεροῦ αὐτοῦ τάφου αἰωρουμένης ἐκπιὼν κανδήλης, τοῦ παρ' ἐλπίδα γενηθέντος ἐν αὐτῷ δηλητηρίου δι' ἐμέτου συντόμου τὴν λύσιν ἐξηύρατο.

2 Ὁμοίως καὶ ἕτερος τοῦ αὐτοῦ σωτηρίου ἐλαίου ἐπὶ τῆς ἑαυτοῦ παλάμης ἀπογευσάμενος, νεφρίτου λίθου ὀδύνην παγχάλεπον ἐξεκρούσατο. Ἄλλος τῷ πάθει τῆς δειλίας παρὰ φύσιν κεκρατημένος καὶ δειμαίνων καθεύδειν ἐφ' οἷς ἀφώριστο τόποις, ἀλλὰ καὶ προϊέναι κατὰ τὰς νυκτερινὰς προόδους ἐπὶ τὴν παρεισπίπτουσαν οὐ θαρρῶν διακονίαν, βραχύ τι πεπωκὼς καὶ αὐτὸς ἔλαιον ἐκ τῆς ῥηθείσης κανδήλης καὶ σφραγισάμενος ἐν τύπῳ σταυροῦ τό τε περὶ τὴν καρδίαν μέρος καὶ τὸ μέτωπον, ἀδείλαντος ἔκτοτε καὶ εὐθαρσὴς συνετηρήθη.

3 Καὶ ἁπαξαπλῶς ἐπιλείψει καὶ ἡμᾶς ὁ χρόνος εἰ τὰ καθ' ἕκαστον ἐπεξιέναι βουληθείημεν τοῦ πανοσίου πατρὸς ἡμῶν θαυματουργήματα, καθότι ἐξ ἐκείνου καὶ μέχρι τοῦ

those who saw and experienced them. One said that those with evil spirits were cleansed by him, another that those suffering in other ways with bodily indispositions obtained a complete recovery. There is also someone who suddenly had an excruciating pain in his stomach but immediately recovered from the distress which had afflicted him just by looking at the image of the holy man painted on a column and invoking his name for assistance. Someone else, again, had ingested something like snake venom from some unsuitable and very earthy food and was being harmed in his bowels by it; in short, many expected him to die but, after drinking oil from the lamp suspended above Theodore's holy tomb, he found release from the noxious substance that had unexpectedly been generated in him when he suddenly vomited.

Similarly, another man got rid of the very severe pain 2
caused by a kidney stone after tasting the same saving oil on the palm of his hand. Another was subject to a condition of abnormal anxiety and was frightened to sleep in the places to which he had been assigned; he also lacked the courage to go out on nighttime excursions for an unexpected service. But after he too had drunk a small amount of oil from the aforementioned lamp and made the sign of the cross on himself in the region of his heart and on his forehead, he was kept fearless and courageous from then on.

Time will quite simply fail me if I should wish to relate 3
each miracle of our all-saintly father by itself, because from that time until now there has been no cessation of such

νῦν οὐ διαλείπουσι γίγνεσθαι τὰ τοιαῦτα εἰς τοὺς μετὰ πίστεως προσερχομένους τῇ τιμίᾳ αὐτοῦ καὶ προσκυνητῇ σορῷ θαυμάσια, ἃ καὶ ἡμεῖς βλέπομεν καὶ οἱ μεθ' ἡμᾶς γε πάντως ὄψονται, *ἀμεταμέλητα γὰρ τοῦ Θεοῦ τὰ χαρίσματα*, ὅθεν τὸν περὶ τούτου ἀφέμενοι λόγον, πρὸς τὰ ἑξῆς τοῦ βίου τὴν ὁρμὴν ποιησόμεθα.

33

Διατρίψας τοιγαροῦν ἐν Πτελέαις ὁ μακαρίτης Θεόδωρος ἐπὶ πλείστας ὅσας ἡμέρας μεθ' ὧν εἰρήκαμεν ἀδελφῶν καὶ πατέρων χάριν τῶν εἰς ἀπαντὴν αὐτοῦ συνερχομένων τῆς εὐσεβείας ἀθλητῶν καὶ συναγωνιστῶν αὐτοῦ, ἀπάρας ἐκεῖθεν ἔρχεται σὺν αὐτοῖς εἰς τὰ μέρη τῆς Προύσης. Τούτου δὲ φημισθέντος καθ' ὅλην τὴν Ὀλύμπιον παροικίαν, συνήχθησαν πρὸς αὐτὸν σχεδὸν ἅπαντες οἱ ἐν ταῖς *ἐρημίαις καὶ ὄρεσι καὶ ταῖς ὀπαῖς τῆς γῆς* τὴν ἀρετὴν ἀρχῆθεν ἐξασκεῖν ᾑρημένοι ὡς πρώτιστον ἀθλητὴν τοῦ τῆς ὁμολογίας σταδίου ἐπιποθοῦντες τοῦτον θεάσασθαι, ἅμα δὲ καὶ τῶν εὐχῶν αὐτοῦ τρυγῆσαι τὴν εὐλογίαν. Ὁ δὲ μέγας φωστὴρ ἕκαστον μὲν καὶ πάντας περὶ τῆς νοητῆς τῶν δαιμόνων πάλης καὶ τῆς διηνεκοῦς τῶν πειρασμῶν ἐπελεύσεως κατὰ τὸ ἐγχωροῦν εἰσηγούμενος, καὶ πρὸς θεῖον ἔρωτα τὰς τούτων διεγείρων ψυχάς, ἐπευχόμενος ἀπέλυεν. Αὐτὸς δὲ ἄχρι Χαλκηδόνος ἐληλυθώς, καὶ τὸν πάλαι

miracles happening to those who approach his precious and venerable tomb with faith, miracles which we ourselves see and those after us will no doubt see, *for the gifts of God are irrevocable.* So, I will leave my discourse on this topic and make a start on the rest of his life.

33

After Theodore of blessed memory had spent very many days in Pteleai with the brethren and fathers I have mentioned for the sake of the competitors for piety and his fellow contenders who gathered to meet him, he set off from there and went with them to the district of Prousa. When this became known throughout the whole region of Olympos, almost all of those who had chosen from the beginning to practice virtue in *deserts, mountains, and caves in the earth,* collected around him as the champion competitor in the arena of confession, longing to see him and, at the same time, to reap the blessing of his prayers. The great luminary instructed each and every one as far as possible about the spiritual struggle with the demons and the constant onslaught of temptations and, rousing their souls to love of God, said a prayer and dismissed them. Theodore himself went as far as Chalcedon and greeted Theoktistos, the

μάγιστρον Θεόκτιστον ὑπ' αὐτοῦ πρώην ἀποκαρθέντα καὶ τηνικαῦτα τῷ ἰδίῳ προσκαρτεροῦντα μοναστηρίῳ μετὰ τῆς τῶν ὀρθοδόξων δογμάτων ἀκριβοῦς φυλακῆς ἀσπασάμενος, ἐκεῖθεν ἀνέρχεται πρὸς τὸν ἀοίδιμον πατριάρχην Νικηφόρον.

2 Καὶ γίνεται χαρὰ πνευματικὴ τῇ ἑκατέρων συνοψίσει καὶ χύσις δακρύων κατὰ Θεόν, δοξολογούντων ἄμφω τὸν φιλάνθρωπον Κύριον ἐφ' οἷς πεποίηκε καὶ ποιεῖ, προμηθούμενος ἀεὶ τὴν τῶν ἁπάντων ὡς εὔσπλαγχνος σωτηρίαν. Συνδιαγαγὼν δὲ αὐτῷ ἡμέρας τινὰς ὁ πατὴρ ἡμῶν Θεόδωρος, αὐτόθεν ἐπὶ τὸν τῆς Νικομηδείας ἔρχεται κόλπον καὶ κατασκηνοῖ εἰς τὰ λεγόμενα Κρησκεντίου· αὖθίς τε ἐκεῖσε πάλιν μοναστῶν καὶ μιγάδων παμπόλλη συνήγετο πληθὺς τῆς αὐτοῦ χάριν εὐχῆς τε καὶ διδασκαλίας ἐνθέου. Τότε δὴ καὶ Πέτρος ἐκεῖνος ὁ πολὺς ἐν ἀσκήσει τε καὶ τῇ τῶν θαυμάτων διαλάμπων ἀστράψει, ὁ διὰ τὴν ὑπερβάλλουσαν αὐτοῦ ἀσιτίαν Ἀβούκις εἰκότως ἐπονομασθείς, ἀπὸ τῆς κατὰ τὸν Ὄλυμπον ὀρείου διαγωγῆς πρὸς τὸν ὑψηλὸν τοῦτον κατεφοίτησεν ἱερομύστην, ἀναθέσθαι αὐτῷ περὶ τῶν ἐνδιαβαλλόντων αὐτοῦ τὸν βίον καὶ γόητα ἀποκαλούντων διὰ τὰς γινομένας ὑπ' αὐτοῦ θαυματουργίας. Ὃν ὁ μέγας τῆς διακρίσεως λύχνος δεξάμενος, καὶ τὰ περὶ πίστεως καὶ τοῦ ἰδίου βίου διερωτήσας ἐμμελέστατα, καὶ μαθὼν ὡς κατ' ἄμφω τέλειός ἐστιν ἐν Κυρίῳ ὁ θεράπων τοῦ Χριστοῦ, παρηγγύησεν αὐτῷ ἠπιοφρόνως ἀπογεύεσθαι ὀλιγάκις ἄρτου τε καὶ οἴνου καὶ τῶν λοιπῶν ἐδεσμάτων τῆς μοναχικῆς μεταλήψεως (διὰ τὴν φιλεγκλήμονα τῶν ἀσθενεστέρων γνώμην), καὶ ὑποδήμασι δὲ

former *magistros,* who had previously been tonsured by him and was at that time in his own monastery devoting himself to the strict observance of orthodox doctrines; from there he went to the renowned Patriarch Nikephoros.

There was spiritual joy at the sight of each other and an outpouring of godly tears as they both glorified the benevolent Lord for the things he had done and was doing, always compassionately providing for the salvation of all. After spending some days with him, our father Theodore went from there to the gulf of Nikomedia and settled temporarily at what is called the estate of Kreskentios. There again a very large crowd of monks and laypeople gathered on account of his prayer and godly teaching. Then that Peter, who was mighty in asceticism and conspicuous for the brilliance of his miracles, and who on account of his extreme fasting was appropriately named Aboukis, also came down from his mountain life on Olympos to visit this eminent and holy expert and to tell him about those who were casting doubt on his life and stigmatizing him as a sorcerer on account of the miracles that he was performing. Theodore, the great lamp of discernment, received him and questioned him very carefully on matters of faith and his own life; when he learned that on both matters the servant of Christ was perfect in the Lord, he gently urged him to partake occasionally of bread and wine and the other foods eaten in monasteries (because of the tendency of weaker individuals to make accusations), and to wear sandals in wintertime. He sent 2

κεχρῆσθαι ἐν ταῖς χειμεριναῖς τροπαῖς· ἐκείνοις τε ἐπέστειλεν ἐπιπληκτικώτερον θᾶττον ἑαυτῶν γενέσθαι διὰ τῆς ἐπιγνώσεως τῆς ἰδίας κακογνωμοσύνης καὶ τοῦ λοιποῦ φυλάξασθαι τοῦ μὴ κακολογεῖν τὸν ἅγιον γέροντα, ἵνα μὴ διὰ τὴν πρὸς τὸν ἀσκητὴν τοῦ Χριστοῦ δυσμένειαν παροξύνειν φωραθῶσιν τὸ ἐνεργοῦν ἐν αὐτῷ Πνεῦμα τῆς ἀληθείας. Τοιοῦτος ἦν ὁ θεῖος διδάσκαλος τῆς εὐσεβείας Θεόδωρος, τοὺς πάντας κερδαίνειν ἐν Χριστῷ βουλόμενος κατὰ τὸν εἰπόντα ἅγιον· "*Τίς ἀσθενεῖ καὶ οὐκ ἀσθενῶ; τίς σκανδαλίζεται καὶ οὐκ ἐγὼ πυροῦμαι;*"

34

Ἐπεὶ δὲ τοῖς λογάσι τῶν θεοφιλεστάτων κατὰ σύνοδον συνῆπτο μητροπολιτῶν, χρῆναι ὑπειλήφασιν ἀπὸ κοινῆς ψήφου πρὸς τὸν αὐτοκράτορα πάντες ὁμοθυμαδὸν εἰσελθεῖν (ἄτερ τοῦ θεολήπτου πατριάρχου), πρὸς τὸ τὰς διαβολάς, ἅσπερ ἐποιήσαντο κατὰ τῆς ὀρθῆς ἡμῶν καὶ ἀμωμήτου πίστεως οἱ μισόχριστοι εἰκονομάχοι, ἱστὸν ἀράχνης καθάπερ διαρρῆξαι, καὶ τὴν καθολικὴν Ἐκκλησίαν τοῦ Σωτῆρος ἡμῶν Χριστοῦ ἄμεμπτον ἀποφῆναι καὶ ἄσπιλον, ὡς τῷ αἵματι τοῦ τυθέντος ὑπὲρ αὐτῆς ἀνθρωπομόρφου Ἀμνοῦ τοῦ Θεοῦ καὶ Πατρὸς ῥαντισθεῖσάν τε καὶ καθαρισθεῖσαν. Ἑνὶ γοῦν τῶν ἐν τέλει πιστοτάτῳ μεσίτῃ χρησάμενοι, εἰσίασιν ἐν τοῖς ἀνακτόροις, οἱ τῇ θείᾳ λειτουργίᾳ

orders in writing to the others to be quicker in rebuking themselves by acknowledging their own poor judgment and in future to guard against reviling the holy elder Peter so that, because of their hostility toward Christ's ascetic, they might not be found to be provoking the Spirit of truth that was at work in him. This was the sort of man Theodore, the godly teacher of piety, was, wanting in Christ to gain an advantage for all men in accordance with the holy Paul who said, "*Who is weak, and I am not weak? Who is made to fall, and I am not indignant?*"

34

When Theodore had joined the leading and most God-loving metropolitans at the synod, they accepted as the result of a common vote that they would all go in together to the emperor (without the divinely selected patriarch) in order to tear apart like a spider's web the false accusations which the Christ-hating iconoclasts had made against our correct and undefiled faith, and to declare that the universal Church of our Savior Christ was blameless and spotless, since it had been sprinkled and cleansed by the blood of the Lamb of God and Father in human form, who was sacrificed for it. Using a very trustworthy official as their intermediary, these men, who had been invested as reverend priests of

κατεστεμμένοι τοῦ Χριστοῦ ἀρητῆρες ἱεροπρεπεῖς καὶ ὄντες καὶ δεικνύμενοι τῇ τε πράξει καὶ τῷ ἀγγελικῷ σχήματι. Καὶ δὴ ἕκαστος αὐτῶν ὡς εἶχεν δυνάμεως, τὰ χαριστήρια τῷ Καίσαρι προσφθεγξάμενος, εἶτα καὶ ἀξιώσας μὴ ἀγνοῆσαι τῆς τοῦ Θεοῦ φιλανθρωπίας τὸ εἰς αὐτὸν παρὰ προσδοκίαν ἐπισκῆψαν ἔλεος, δι' οὗ τῶν χειρῶν ἐρρύσθη τοῦ πρὶν δυσμενοῦς τυράννου, ἀλλ' ἀποδοῦναι Χριστῷ ὡς ἀπαραίτητα χρέη τὰς ὑπὲρ τούτου ὀφειλάς, ἐν τῷ μάλιστα τὴν αὐτοῦ Ἐκκλησίαν εἰς τὸν ἔμπροσθεν ἐπανάγειν τῶν ἱερῶν μορφωμάτων θεοπαράδοτον κόσμον, αὐτός, ἅτε ἀγροικίας τις ὢν καὶ συβώτης τὸ ἦθος, καὶ πάσης γραφικῆς ἱστορίας ἀμέθεκτος, οὐχ ἡδέως ταῦτα ἀκούσας, εἰπεῖν προετρέψατο καὶ τὸν μέγαν Θεόδωρον τὰ αὐτῷ δοκοῦντα.

2 Τοῦ δὲ τὰ ὅμοια τοῖς ἱεράρχαις θεηγορήσαντος καὶ τῆς ἀληθείας τὴν νίκην ἐκ τοῦ περιόντος ἀριδηλότατα παραστήσαντος, φησὶ πρὸς τὴν ἱερὰν τῶν ἐπισκόπων σύνοδον, ὁ τοῖς αἴσχεσιν ὡς αὐχήμασιν ἀνοήτως κομιδῇ βρενθυόμενος, "Ἀγαθοὶ μὲν καὶ βέλτιστοι ὑμῶν οἱ λόγοι, ἀλλ' ἐπεὶ οὔπω μέχρι καὶ τήμερον ἔγωγε προσκεκύνηκα τὸ καθόλου εἰκόνα, τούτου χάριν καθὼς εὗρον τὴν Ἐκκλησίαν, οὕτω καὶ ἀφίημι αὐτήν· ὑμῖν δὲ βραβεύω ἐξουσίαν καὶ ἄδειαν ἔχεσθαι τῶν δογμάτων τῆς, ὥς φατε, ὀρθοδόξου πίστεως, ἔξωθεν μέντοι τῆς Πόλεως ὅπου βούλεται ἕκαστος ὑμῶν ἵνα διάγῃ, μὴ ὑφορώμενος ἢ καραδοκῶν τὸν οἱονδήποτε ἐπελεύσεσθαι αὐτῷ πρὸς τῆς ἡμετέρας ἀρχῆς κίνδυνον." Ταῦτ' ἀποφηνάμενος, ἐξέπεμψεν αὐτοὺς τῶν βασιλείων. Ὁ οὖν πατὴρ ἡμῶν Θεόδωρος τῆς βασιλίδος

Christ for the divine liturgy but who also showed that they really were such by their conduct and angelic habit, entered the royal apartments. Each of them, as forcefully as he could, addressed his thanks to the Caesar, then asked him not to forget the mercy of God's benevolence that had unexpectedly come upon him and through which he had been rescued from the hands of the previous hostile tyrant; instead he should repay to Christ what he owed for this as an unavoidable debt, in particular, by restoring his Church to its former divinely sanctioned adornment with the holy images. Since he was an uncouth person with the manners of a swineherd and had no grasp of any scriptural narrative, he was not pleased to hear this and also invited great Theodore to say what he thought.

When, however, Theodore had said the same things as 2
the hierarchs in a most divinely inspired fashion and had consequently most clearly demonstrated the victory of the truth, the emperor, swaggering quite stupidly in his shameful deeds as though they were matters for pride, said to the holy synod of bishops, "Your words are all well and good, but since to this day I haven't yet venerated an icon at all, that's why I'm leaving the Church as I found it. To you I'm granting authority and a free hand to maintain the doctrines of the orthodox faith, as you describe it, but outside the City, however, wherever each of you wants to live; and you may do so without suspecting or watching anxiously for any danger coming from my regime." And with this declaration, he sent them away from the palace. So, our father Theodore left the

ἀποβάς, πάλιν εἰς τὰ Κρησκεντίου πρὸς τοὺς ἰδίους μαθητὰς παραγίνεται, κἀκεῖσε λοιπὸν τὸ ἀσκητικὸν τῆς κοινοβιακῆς διαβιώσεως ἵστησι παγκράτιον, ἕως τῆς ἀνταρσίας τοῦ λαοπλάνου καὶ ἀλητηρίου Θωμᾶ.

3 Ὁπηνίκα δὲ ἡ τυραννὶς τούτου τὴν Ἀσιάτιδα κατεληΐσατο χθόνα, τηνικαῦτα δὴ κέλευσις βασιλικὴ τοὺς κατὰ τὸν θεσπέσιον πατριάρχην Νικηφόρον πρὸς τὴν Κωνσταντινούπολιν συνελαύνει, οὐ φειδοῦς ἕνεκα τῆς πρὸς αὐτοὺς τοῦτο πραξαμένου τοῦ Καίσαρος, ἀλλὰ φόβῳ τοῦ μὴ προσρυῆναί τινας αὐτῶν τῇ τοῦ Θωμᾶ συμφατρίᾳ, καθότι ἐλέγετο τὰς ἱερὰς εἰκόνας ἀποδέχεσθαί τε καὶ προσκυνεῖν. Ταύτης οὖν ἕνεκα τῆς προφάσεως καὶ ὁ μέγας πατὴρ ἡμῶν Θεόδωρος τὴν ἐνεγκαμένην καταλαμβάνει καὶ αὖθις· ὅσον δὲ οὔπω τοῦ τρισαθλίου ἐπὶ τὴν Εὐρώπην μεταθεμένου Θωμᾶ καὶ ἁλωσίμου τῷ βασιλεῖ γεγονότος, ὁ πατὴρ ἡμῶν τοῦ Βυζαντίου ἀφορμηθείς, πρὸς τὴν πελάζουσαν τῷ Ἀκρίτᾳ χερρόνησον τὴν ἐπιλεγομένην καὶ τοῦ ἁγίου Τρύφωνος ἀποπλεῖ.

4 Ἀφ᾽ ἧς ἐν μιᾷ τῶν ἐπισήμων μετὰ τῶν ἐξεχόντων μητροπολιτῶν πρὸς τὸν ἁγιώτατον ἀνελθὼν πατριάρχην, μεγαλοπρεπῶς λίαν κατὰ τὴν ἀναλογίαν τῶν ἀψευδῶν αὐτοῦ δι᾽ εὐσέβειαν ἄθλων, καὶ τὰ πρεσβεῖα τῆς τιμῆς πρὸς αὐτοῦ ἀπηνέγκατο, διεξιόντος τοῦ ἱερομύστου Νικηφόρου τὰ ἀξιόπιστα καὶ ἀληθῆ τῆς τε ἀνδρείας καὶ παρρησίας αὐτοῦ ἐπὶ πάντων πλεονεκτήματα, τά τε στίγματα τῶν μαστίγων καὶ τὰς ἐμφρουρίους κακώσεις καὶ λιμοὺς καὶ καθημερινοὺς θανάτους, οὓς ἀνέτλη παρὰ τῶν ὑπασπιστῶν τῆς εἰκονομαχικῆς λύττης ἐν τοῖς πέντε ἔτεσιν τῆς τυραννίδος

imperial city and went back again to his own disciples on the estate of Kreskentios, and there, then, he established the ascetic contest of the cenobitic way of life, until the insurrection of Thomas, that wicked deceiver of people.

At the same time as that tyrant plundered the Asiatic ter- 3
ritory, an imperial decree forced the supporters of the inspired patriarch Nikephoros into Constantinople, not that the Caesar did that out of consideration for them, but out of fear that some of them would go over to Thomas's conspiracy, because it was said that he accepted the holy icons and venerated them. For this reason, then, our great father Theodore arrived once again in the city of his birth, but as soon as the thrice-wretched Thomas had crossed over into Europe and had been captured by the emperor, our father set out from Byzantion and sailed away to the peninsula that is near Akritas and is named for Saint Tryphon.

On one of the feast days, Theodore went up from there 4
with the prominent metropolitans to the most holy patriarch and, most magnificently in proportion to his true contests for piety, he received from him his due share of honor; for in the presence of all, the holy prelate Nikephoros recounted in detail the genuine and true preeminence of Theodore's courage and boldness of speech, the scars of his floggings, his ill treatment in prison, and the starvation and daily deaths that he endured at the hands of supporters of the raging madness of iconoclasm during the implacable and cruel Leo's five years of tyranny. He assigned first place

τοῦ ἀμειλίκτου καὶ ἀπηνοῦς Λέοντος, καὶ οὐ τοῖς διὰ λόγων μόνον ἐπαίνοις τὸ πρωτεῖον αὐτῷ ἀπεδίδου, ἀλλὰ πολλῷ μᾶλλον καὶ δι' αὐτῶν τῶν πραγμάτων· ἐπ' εὐωχίαν γὰρ τραπέντες, τὴν σὺν ἑαυτῷ ἐπὶ μιᾶς στιβάδος καθίζησιν αὐτῷ μόνῳ παραχωρεῖ, φήσας πρὸς τοὺς ἱεροὺς δαιτυμόνας, "Παραχωρήσατε, ἀδελφοί, τῷ πολυάθλῳ πατρὶ ἡμῶν τὴν προεδρείαν, καθάπερ ἐμοί, κἂν ἥκιστά γε ταύτης ὀρέγεται ὁ σοφός, ἵνα συνημμένως ἄμφω καθήμενοι, τὴν τοῦ ἄρτου κλάσιν ποιησώμεθα· ᾧ γὰρ πλέον ἐφανερώθη τὰ τεκμήρια τῆς πρὸς τὸν κοινὸν Δεσπότην ἀγάπης, πλέον δήπουθεν καὶ ὀφείλεται, καθὼς καὶ ὁ Κύριος ἐν Εὐαγγελίοις ἔφησεν· *Διαφορὰ γὰρ ὥσπερ ἐστὶ τῆς τῶν ἁγίων ζωῆς οὕτω καὶ γερῶν, ἀναλόγως τοῖς ἑκάστου κατορθώμασιν ἐπιμετροῦντος Θεοῦ τὴν ἀντέκτισιν* καὶ εἰ παρὰ Θεῷ τοῦτό γε, ἀκόλουθον ἂν εἴη καὶ παρ' ἡμῖν τοῖς μετρίοις." Οὕτως εἶχε σχέσεως πρὸς τὸν ἐν ἁγίοις Θεόδωρον ὁ τὸν ἀρχιερατικὸν ταῖς νικηφόροις ἀρεταῖς κατακοσμήσας θῶκον.

5 Ἐρρέτω φθόνος ὁ κατὰ τοῦ δικαίου Θεοδώρου κατεξανιστάμενος, αἰσχυνέσθωσαν δὴ καὶ οἱ ἐνδιαβάλλοντες τὸν θεοειδῆ τῶν μοναζόντων καθηγητὴν καὶ διδάσκαλον, καὶ *χεῖρα τιθέτωσαν* τοῖς σφῶν *αὐτῶν* κατὰ τὰ λόγια χείλεσιν, ὁρῶντες τὸ ἀλληλέγγυον τῶν τιμίων τούτων καὶ περιόπτων προσώπων. Οὐδὲ γὰρ ἂν πυκνότερον ὁ τῆς ἡμετέρας ἀγέλης ποιμὴν πρὸς τὸν ἁγιώτατον ἐφοίτα Νικηφόρον, εἰ μὴ τοῦτον ᾔδει καὶ ἀπεδέχετο πεπληροφορημένως ἀξιολογώτατον ἱεροθέτην Χριστοῦ. Οὐδ' αὖ γε πάλιν ὁ μέγας τελετάρχης ὑπέρ τε μητροπολίτας καὶ ἐπισκόπους τὸν θεῖον προετίμα Θεόδωρον, εἰ μὴ τοῦ κατ' ἀρετὴν

to him, not just by his words of praise but even more so by his actual actions; for when they turned to feasting, Nikephoros allowed only Theodore to sit with him on a single couch, saying to the holy banqueters, "Brothers, yield the place of honor to our father who has competed so much, as you do with me, even though it is the last thing this wise man wants, so that sitting beside each other we may break bread together. For, of course, more is owed to the one by whom more proofs of love for our common Master were demonstrated, as the Lord also said in the Gospels. *As there is a difference in the lives of holy men, so there is also in privileges when God measures out the recompense in proportion to the achievements of each* and, if that at any rate is the case with God, it would also be fitting among us humble men." This was the relationship which that man who adorned the patriarchal seat with his victorious virtues had with Theodore, who is now among the saints.

Away with the envy which arose against the righteous 5
Theodore! Those who deride the godlike instructor and teacher of monks should also be ashamed and should *place a hand over their own* lips, as the saying goes, seeing the mutual trust of those honorable and celebrated individuals. For the shepherd of our flock would not have visited the most holy Nikephoros so frequently unless he knew him to be, and accepted in full assurance that he was, a most worthy upholder of Christ's sacred rites. Nor again in turn would the great head of mysteries, Nikephoros, have preferred the godly Theodore in honor above both metropolitans and bishops, unless he judged in his divine wisdom that Theodore,

κλέους καὶ τῆς εἰς ἄκρον Χριστοῦ ὁμολογίας ὑπερανεστηκότα τοῦτον τῶν ἄλλων καὶ τὸ φερέγγυον αὐτόθεν ἔχοντα λογισμῷ συνέκρινεν θεοσόφῳ. Εἰ μὲν οὖν ἀπιστοίη τις τῶν δι' ἐναντίας τοῖς ὧδε γεγραμμένοις ἡμῖν ὠφελείας τῶν ἀγνοούντων ἕνεκεν, ἐγκυψάτω ταῖς ἐπιστολιμαίαις τοῦ πατρὸς ἡμῶν δέλτοις καὶ πιστὸς γινέσθω, συνιεὶς ἐκ τῶν ἐκεῖσε τὴν τῶν ἡμετέρων λόγων περὶ τούτου ἀλήθειαν. Εἰ δ' ἔτι ἐνέχεται τῇ μεμψιμοίρῳ διαθέσει, σκοπείτω πάλιν ὁ τοιοῦτος, εἰ μὴ πατρομαχίαν, μᾶλλον δὲ θεομαχίαν σαφῆ, νοσῶν ἀπελέγχοιτο, ὅπερ ἐστὶν οὐκ ἀνδρὸς ἀγαθοῦ, ἀλλὰ καὶ λίαν θεοστυγοῦς καὶ παράφρονος. Καὶ ὧδε μὲν ταῦτα· λοιπὸν δὲ πρὸς τὸ πέρας τοῦ θεοφόρου ὁ λόγος προβαινέτω, εἴπερ ἄρα τέλος ζωῆς ἀλλὰ μὴ θάνατον τοῦτο κλητέον καὶ ζωῆς ἀληθεστάτης ἀρχήν. Ὁ γὰρ τὸν προαιρετικὸν θάνατον, ἤτοι τὴν τῶν παθῶν νέκρωσιν, διὰ παντὸς τοῦ βίου ἐπιτετηδευκώς, καὶ τὴν ἐν Χριστῷ κεκρυμμένην ζωὴν τῆς προαιρετικῆς ὁσίως ἐκτετιμηκώς, οὗτος νεκρὸς ὢν τῇ ἁμαρτίᾳ ἐν τῷδε τῷ φθαρτῷ καὶ πολυπόνῳ βίῳ μετὰ τῆς φυσικῆς ζωῆς, ὡς ἀπὸ θανάτου καὶ ζωῆς πρὸς τὴν μονοειδῆ καὶ ἀΐδιον μεταβαίνειν εἰκότως συλλογισθήσεται ζωήν.

6 Ὁ τοίνυν πατὴρ ἡμῶν καὶ θεῖος ὁμολογητὴς Χριστοῦ Θεόδωρος, καὶ πρὸς αὐτὰ τοῦ βίου τὰ τέλη πεφοιτηκώς, οὐ κατώκνει κατὰ πᾶσαν χώραν καὶ πόλιν τὰ τῆς σωτηρίας φάρμακα διὰ τῶν ἰδίων ἐκπέμπειν ἐπιστολῶν, συμβιβάζων καὶ ἐνάγων πρὸς τὴν ὀρθόδοξον πίστιν τοὺς πλείονας. Ἀλλὰ γὰρ καὶ τοὺς πρὸς αὐτὸν ἐρχομένους ἐκ πάσης ἀξίας

through his renowned virtue and his supreme confession of Christ, towered above the others and had obviously earned his trust. So, if one of Theodore's opponents were to disbelieve what I have written here for the benefit of those who do not know it, he should look into our father's letters and become a believer once he perceives the truth of my words about him from their contents. And if he still persists in his criticism, he should look again, if he is not to be convicted of the sickness of fighting against the fathers, or rather, clearly of fighting against God, which is the mark not of a good man, but of one who is deranged and very hateful to God. So much for that; as for the rest, let my account move on to the divinely inspired man's final days, if this really is to be called the end of life, not death, and the beginning of what is most truly life. For Theodore, who had throughout his whole life practiced a freely chosen death, that is the mortification of the passions, and had esteemed in a saintly way the life hidden in Christ over that of his own desire, since he was dead to sin during his physical existence in this corrupt life full of pain, will appropriately be considered as having passed over from death and living to the singular and eternal life.

So then, Theodore, our father and godly confessor of Christ, though he had arrived at the very end of his life, did 6
not shrink from sending out through every land and city the remedies of salvation by means of his own letters, instructing and initiating more people to the orthodox faith. He would also graciously receive those of every rank and age

καὶ ἡλικίας εὐμενῶς ὑπεδέχετο, καὶ τοῖς νάμασι τῆς μελιρρύτου αὐτοῦ γλώσσης τὰς τούτων πρὸς ἀρετὴν κατεγλύκαινεν ψυχάς. Οὐκ ἀπὸ τῆς μεγαλωνύμου δὲ πόλεως μόνον πρὸς αὐτὸν οὗτοί τε κἀκεῖνοι ἐξίεσαν—καὶ τῶν ἁγιωτάτων μητροπολιτῶν οἱ διασημότατοι, καὶ ἡγουμένων δὲ οἱ πλείους, πρὸς δὲ καὶ μοναζόντων οἱ διαφέροντες—ἀλλὰ καὶ ἀπὸ πάσης μακρὰν ἀφεστηκυίας νήσου τε καὶ πολίχνης ἔτρεχον προθυμότατα τῆς αὐτοῦ μεταλαχεῖν θέας καὶ εὐλογίας εἰς ἐφόδιον ἀρετῆς καὶ προκοπὴν εὐσεβείας. Ἦν γὰρ ὁ ὅσιος παραδείσου μὲν παντὸς αἰσθητοῦ ὡραιότερός τε καὶ θελκτικώτερος, ἐπείπερ εἶχεν ἐντός τε καὶ ἐκτὸς τοῦ παναγίου Πνεύματος ὡς εὐόδμους καρποὺς τὰς ἡδυπνόους χάριτας, δεδόξαστο δὲ κατὰ Μωσέα τὸ πρόσωπον καὶ τὰ σημεῖα ἔφερεν τῆς αὐθαιρέτου νεκρώσεως διὰ τῆς ἄγαν τοῦ ἱεροῦ προσώπου ὠχρίας· καὶ τὴν ἡλικίαν δὲ εὐμήκης ὑπῆρχεν, πάσης τε κινύρας τὰς χορδὰς συμμέτρους ἐχούσης καὶ φωνὴν ἀφιείσης ἐναρμόνιον, ἥδίω καὶ τερπνότερον τὸν διδασκαλικὸν προϊσχόμενος λόγον.

35

Ἑπτὰ τοιγαροῦν ἐπὶ ἑξήκοντα μικροῦ τετελεκὼς ἐνιαυτοὺς τῆς ἁπάσης αὐτοῦ ἐν σαρκὶ πολιτείας, δώδεκα δὲ τῆς ὑπὲρ ἀληθείας Χριστοῦ τρίτης ἑαυτοῦ ἐξορίας, ὁ ὅσιος

who came to him and would sweetly entice their souls to virtue with the streams that flowed from his honeyed tongue. Not only did all and sundry go out to him from the greatly renowned city—the most eminent of the very holy metropolitan bishops and most of the monastic superiors in addition to the important monks—but people would also rush most eagerly from every far distant island and town to share in the sight of him and in his blessing as a support for their journey to virtue and a development of their piety. For the saintly one was more beautiful and enchanting than any garden that is perceived by the senses, since he possessed, both within and without, the fragrant graces of the all-holy Spirit like sweet-smelling fruit. His face had been glorified like Moses and he bore the signs of his voluntary mortification in the extreme pallor of his holy countenance; he was tall and offered his instructive discourse more sweetly and delightfully than any harp producing a harmonious sound with its well-tuned strings.

35

And so, after he had completed almost sixty-seven years of his whole life in the flesh and twelve years of his third banishment for Christ's truth, about the beginning of the

πατὴρ ἡμῶν περὶ τὰς ἀρχὰς τοῦ Νοεμβρίου μηνὸς νόσῳ ληφθεὶς τῇ συντρόφῳ καὶ ἄνωθεν αὐτῷ συνεισπεσούσῃ ἐκ τῶν πολυθλίπτων ἐκείνων φυλακῶν τε καὶ ἐξοριῶν καὶ τῆς ἐντεῦθεν τελείας ἀνεπιμελησίας, λέγω δὴ τῆς τοῦ στομάχου, νεκρὸς ὡρᾶτο σχεδὸν καὶ πρὸ κοιμήσεως ὁ μακαρίτης τῶν ὀρέξεων εἰς ἄκρον ἀποπαυθεισῶν. Ἐξ ἧς τετραήμερος κλινήρης γεγονώς, πάλιν εὐδοκίᾳ Θεοῦ πρὸς τὸ εὔθυμον μετεβλήθη· καὶ ὢ τῆς τοῦ τρισμάκαρος μεγαλοψυχίας, ὅτι οὐδὲ ἐπ' αὐτῇ τῇ νόσῳ ἠρεμίας ἢ ἄλλης οἱασοῦν παρακλήσεως ἐβούλετο ἀπολαύειν, οὕτως ἦν εἰς τέλος μεμισηκὼς τὴν παροῦσαν ζωήν· ἐκλελοιπὼς γὰρ ἤδη τῷ γήρᾳ καὶ τοῖς σφοδροῖς καὶ ἀνενδότοις συνθλιβόμενος πόνοις, οὐδ' οὕτως *ἐδίδου ὕπνον τοῖς ὀφθαλμοῖς,* οὐδὲ *τοῖς βλεφάροις* αὐτοῦ *νυσταγμόν,* ἢ *ἀνάπαυσιν τοῖς κροτάφοις,* πρὶν ἢ τὴν σωτήριον καὶ συνήθη τοῖς ἀδελφοῖς ἐκποιήσηται διδασκαλίαν. Ἣν καὶ ἐπὶ σκίμποδος ὤν, διὰ τὸ μὴ δύνασθαι γεγωνότερον τοῖς παροῦσι προσφθέγγεσθαι ὑπαγορεύσας ἑνὶ τῶν ταχυγράφων, δι' αὐτοῦ ταύτην τῷ χορῷ τῶν μαθητῶν προσπεφώνηκεν τὸ παριστάμενον καὶ ἐπὶ θύραις τέλος αὐτοῦ ἰσχνῶς ἐν αὐτῇ ὑποσημηνάμενος· "Ἀδελφοί," λέγων, "καὶ πατέρες ἠσθένησα καὶ πάλιν εὐχαῖς ὑμῶν ἀνακέκλημαι, ἀλλ' ἕως πότε μέλλομεν ἔρχεσθαι ἐπὶ 'τὸ πάλιν'; Ἐλεύσεται δὴ πάντως ἡ ἐπιθανάτιος ἡμέρα, ὅτε οὐχ ἕξει χώραν 'τὸ πάλιν,' χωρίζουσά με ἀφ' ὑμῶν καὶ παραπέμπουσα ἐκ τῶν ἐνθένδε." Καὶ τὰ ἑξῆς τῆς κατηχήσεως.

2 Μετὰ δὲ τὴν τετάρτην ἡμέραν, τῇ ἐπιούσῃ ἥτις ἦν ἀναστάσιμος προκαθεσθεὶς ὁ πανόσιος καὶ ὑπαναγνωσθείσης τῆς αὐτῆς κατηχήσεως, τί γίνεται; Ῥώννυται τῇ προθυμίᾳ

month of November, our saintly father Theodore was stricken with the familiar illness that had afflicted him previously as a result of those very difficult imprisonments and banishments and the consequent complete lack of care, for his stomach I mean; for our father of blessed memory looked almost like a corpse even before he passed away, since he had totally lost his appetite. After being bedridden for four days, by God's favor he was again restored to a cheerful condition. How generous was the thrice-blessed one, then, because even in his illness he did not want to enjoy rest or any other comfort whatsoever and he was like that to the end, hating this present life. For when he was already dying of old age and afflicted at the same time by severe and incessant pain, even so *he did not give sleep to his eyes,* nor *slumber to his eyelids* or *rest to his temples,* until he had delivered to the brethren his usual salvific teaching. He was lying on a low bed and, because he was unable to speak loudly enough to those who were present, he dictated this to one of the shorthand writers; through him he addressed this to the band of his disciples, subtly indicating in it that his end was imminent and saying, "Brethren and fathers, I have fallen ill and, owing to your prayers, I have recovered again, but how long am I going to resort to 'again'? The day of death, when there will be no room for 'again,' will certainly come, separating me from you and conducting me from this world." And the rest of his catechesis followed.

Four days passed; then on the next day, which was a Sun- 2
day, the all-saintly one took up his seat of office and, after the same catechesis had been read aloud, what happened?

καὶ ἐφέσει τῶν θείων, (ἐπεὶ καὶ *πόνος ὑγιείαν χαρίζεται καὶ προθυμία νεκροὺς ἀνίστησι*), καὶ εἴσεισιν εἰς τὸ κυριακὸν ἁγίως λατρεύσων τῇ ἁγίᾳ καὶ ἀχράντῳ καὶ ὁμοουσίῳ Τριάδι. Καὶ δὴ τὴν ἀναίμακτον θυσίαν προσαγαγὼν τῷ Θεῷ καὶ μεταδοὺς πᾶσι τοῖς παροῦσι τοῦ ζωοποιοῦ σώματος καὶ αἵματος τοῦ Κυρίου ἡμῶν καὶ Σωτῆρος Ἰησοῦ Χριστοῦ ἰδίαις χερσίν, ἐκεῖθεν ἐπὶ τὴν τράπεζαν ἔρχεται. Ἐφ' ᾗ καὶ δεξιωσάμενός τινας τῶν παραγεγονότων πατέρων καὶ ὁμολογητῶν φιλοφρόνως, τὰ τῆς μεταστάσεως ἑαυτοῦ διὰ πάντων καὶ φθεγγόμενος καὶ ὁμιλῶν τούτους παρεπέμπετο, ἐπεὶ καὶ πᾶς ὁ χρόνος τῆς μακαρίας ζωῆς αὐτοῦ οὐδὲν ἕτερον ἦν ἢ μελέτη θανάτου καὶ *ἐπιθυμία τοῦ ἀναλῦσαι καὶ σὺν Χριστῷ εἶναι*. Ἀμέλει ἀναπεσὼν εἰς τὴν ἑαυτοῦ κλίνην καὶ τὸν οἰκονόμον προσκαλεσάμενος (ἦν δὲ οὗτος ὁ ἀοίδιμος Ναυκράτιος ὁ καὶ διάδοχος αὐτοῦ γεγονώς), "Μή τι," φησί, "τῶν κεχρεωστημένων ἡμῖν παρημέληται;" Οὕτως ἦν ἐμμέριμνος αὐτοῦ ἡ ψυχή, διηγωνισμένη τε καὶ φροντίζουσα περὶ πάντων ἐν παντὶ καὶ ἐν πᾶσιν.

3 Εἶτα μετὰ τὴν ἑξῆς—ἦν δὲ Τρίτη τῶν ἡμερῶν, καθ' ἣν ἐφεστήκει ἡ μνήμη τοῦ μεγάλου ἱερομύστου καὶ τῆς Τριάδος ὁμολογητοῦ Παύλου—ὡς φιλόθεος καὶ φιλάγιος, τὸ ἀποστολικὸν πληρῶν καὶ αὖθις, ἐκτελεῖ τὴν θείαν μυσταγωγίαν, τὴν τοῦ ἁγίου μνήμην ἀφοσιούμενος. Τῆς δὲ ἑσπέρας καταλαβούσης, πλεῖστα ὅσα προσφθεγξάμενος τοῖς περὶ αὐτὸν καθεζομένοις κἀκεῖθεν εἰς τὸ κελλίον ἑαυτοῦ εἰσελθών, καὶ τὴν συνήθη ψαλμῳδίαν καὶ τὰς εὐχὰς ἀποδεδωκὼς τῷ Κυρίῳ, ἀνέπεσεν ἐπὶ τοῦ κλινιδίου. Καὶ περὶ ὥραν τετάρτην ὑπεισῆλθεν αὐτῷ ὁ κατὰ συνήθειαν

He was strengthened by his eagerness and took charge of the divine celebration (since *labor bestows health and eagerness raises the dead*), entering the Lord's house to piously worship the holy, undefiled, and consubstantial Trinity. After he had offered the bloodless sacrifice to God and given with his own hands to all who were present a portion of the life-giving body and blood of our Lord and Savior Jesus Christ, he went from there to the refectory. There, in a kindly way, Theodore welcomed some of the fathers and confessors who were present and continued to remind them about his own departure all the time he was speaking and conversing, since the entire span of his blessed life had been nothing other than a meditation on death and *a desire to depart and be with Christ.* As soon as he lay down on his bed, he summoned the steward (this was the celebrated Naukratios, who also became his successor) and said, "We haven't neglected any of our debts, have we?" Such was the concern of his soul, which had grappled with and taken care about everything in every way and every situation.

Then, after the following day—this was on the Tuesday, 3
when the commemoration of Paul the great theologian and confessor of the Trinity occurred—as a lover of God and of the saints, and carrying out apostolic practice, Theodore again celebrated the divine liturgy, hallowing the memory of the saint. When evening came, he addressed those who were sitting around him as much as he could, and then entered his cell, rendered to the Lord his usual singing of psalms and prayers and lay down on his little bed. Around the fourth hour of the night the usual pain came over him

πόνος καὶ δὴ φωνήσας τινὰ τῶν πρὸ τῆς κέλλης αὐτοῦ καθευδόντων, ἀπαγγέλλει αὐτῷ τὸ ἄλγημα, καὶ τῇ αὐτῇ συνδρομὴ γίνεται τῶν ἀδελφῶν τὰ τοῦ πατρὸς ὀψομένων.

4 Δισημερεύσας τοίνυν μετριοπόνως, τῇ ἐπαύριον προσκαλεσάμενος ἅπαντας, τοὺς ἐξιτηρίους ποιεῖται λόγους καί φησιν· "Ἀδελφοὶ καὶ πατέρες, τὸ ποτήριον τοῦτο κοινόν ἐστιν, ὃ ἔπιον πάντες οἱ πατέρες ἡμῶν· τὸ αὐτὸ δὴ πίνοιμι κἀγὼ καὶ πορεύομαι πρὸς τοὺς πατέρας μου. Βλέπετε τὴν παραθήκην ἣν παρεθέμην ὑμῖν, τὴν πίστιν ὑμῶν φυλάξατε ἀσάλευτον καὶ τὸν βίον ἀκηλίδωτον. Πλέον γάρ τι λέγειν οὐκ ἔχω, διὰ τὸ πάντα τὰ ὀφειλόμενα καὶ προαναγγεῖλαι καὶ διδάξαι," προσθεὶς καὶ τοῦτο ὁ τῆς εἰρήνης καὶ τῆς ἀγάπης υἱός· "Τῷ δεσπότῃ ἡμῶν τῷ ἀρχιερεῖ τὸν δι᾽ αἰδοῦς καὶ τιμῆς ἀσπασμὸν ἐξ ἐμοῦ ἀπονείματε, τοῖς λοιποῖς πατράσιν, ἱεράρχαις τε καὶ ἱερεῦσιν, τοῖς Χριστοῦ ὁμολογηταῖς τοῖς διὰ Κύριον δεδιωγμένοις, ἅπασι τοῖς ἀδελφοῖς, φίλοις τε καὶ γνωρίμοις, καὶ τοῖς ἐν τῷ ὑπὲρ τῆς πίστεως ἀγῶνι συγκεκοπιακόσιν ἡμῖν μικροῖς τε καὶ μεγάλοις." Ἐρωτηθεὶς δὲ πρὸς τοῦ σεβασμίου Ναυκρατίου περὶ τῶν ἐν ἐπιτιμίοις ὄντων μοναχῶν τε καὶ κοσμικῶν, ἀπεκρίνατο ὁ ὄντως φιλοσυμπαθέστατος καὶ Χριστομίμητος ἰατρός, "Ὁ Κύριος συγχωρήσει πᾶσιν." Κατασφραγίσας τε τρίτον τοὺς ἀδελφούς, ἐπηύξατο αὐτοῖς εἰπών, "*Ὁ Κύριος τῆς εἰρήνης* ἔσται μετὰ τοῦ πνεύματος ὑμῶν," καὶ ἀσπασάμενος τοὺς παρόντας ἅπαντας, διέμεινεν οὕτως. Τῆς τοίνυν ἀκοῆς ταύτης μέχρι πολλοῦ διαδοθείσης, παρεγένετο

and, calling out to one of the monks who were sleeping in front of his cell, he told him of his suffering, and at once the brethren gathered to see their father.

After he had passed two days in moderate pain, he summoned them all on the following day and gave his parting words, saying, "Brothers and fathers, this is the common cup which all our fathers drank; may I too drink the same one as I journey to my fathers. Take care of the legacy that I have left to you; keep your faith unshaken and your life spotless; I have nothing more to say, because I have already told and taught you all that is necessary." The son of peace and love also added this, "Give my reverent and honored greetings to our master the archbishop, to the other fathers, to the hierarchs and priests, to the confessors of Christ who have been persecuted for the Lord's sake, to all my brethren, friends and acquaintances, and to those, great and small, who labored along with us in the contest for the faith." When he was asked by the revered Naukratios about those monks and laymen who were in penance, that truly compassionate physician and imitator of Christ replied, "The Lord will forgive them all." Theodore made the sign of the cross three times over the brethren, and prayed for them, saying, "May *the Lord of peace* be with your spirit," and after he had embraced all who were present, he remained in that state. When this news spread far and wide, however, a great crowd 4

πρὸς αὐτὸν πλῆθος πολύ, οὓς εὐλογῶν καὶ κατασφραγίζων, ἀσπαζόμενός τε καὶ ἠρέμα προσφθεγγόμενος ἀπέλυεν· τοῦτο δ' ἐποίει ἐπὶ δύο ἡμέρας.

5 Καὶ τῇ Κυριακῇ ἐν ᾗ ἡ μνήμη ἐξετελεῖτο τοῦ ἁγίου καὶ ἐνδόξου μάρτυρος Μηνᾶ, ἐψαλκὼς τὰ συνήθη καὶ τῶν ἁγιασμάτων μετασχών, καὶ ἐπαλειψάμενος κατὰ τὸ ἔθος τὰ μέλη αὐτοῦ, ὑψοῦ τε τὰς χεῖρας ἄρας καὶ προσευξάμενος, περὶ ὥραν ἕκτην ὡς ᾔσθετο ἑαυτὸν ἠτονηκότα προσέταξεν ἡσυχῇ κηραψίαν γενέσθαι. Καὶ οὕτω τῶν ἀδελφῶν ἀρξαμένων τῆς ψαλμῳδίας τοῦ Ἀμώμου, καὶ φθασάντων ἐν τῷ στίχῳ τῆς δευτέρας στάσεως τῷ λέγοντι, "*Εἰς τὸν αἰῶνα οὐ μὴ ἐπιλάθωμαι τῶν δικαιωμάτων σου, ὅτι ἐν αὐτοῖς ἔζησάς με,*" αὐτόθι διατριβόντων αὐτῶν, παρέδωκεν τὴν ἁγίαν αὐτοῦ ψυχήν.

6 Καὶ προσετέθη τοῖς ἐξ αἰῶνος δικαίοις ὁ παρὰ πάντα τὸν ἑαυτοῦ βίον ὑπὲρ δικαιοσύνης δεδιωγμένος, τοῖς ὁσίοις ὁ τῆς ὁσιότητος ἐραστὴς καὶ ἐργάτης, τοῖς μάρτυσιν ὁ φιλόμαρτυς καὶ συναθλητὴς καὶ πολύαθλος, τοῖς ἀποστόλοις ὁ τὸν αὐτὸν ἐκείνοις δρόμον σταδιεύσας τῆς πίστεως, τοῖς προφήταις ὁ τῷ ἴσῳ τετιμημένος παρὰ Θεῷ χαρίσματι, καὶ τὰς ἐκείνων σφραγισάμενος διὰ πραγμάτων προρρήσεις ὡς ἅτε τὴν τοῦ Ἐμμανουὴλ ἐνανθρώπησιν διὰ συμβόλων ἱερῶν πάντῃ καὶ πάντως τιμᾶσθαι βεβαιωσάμενος· πᾶσι τοῖς ἁγίοις ἀγγέλοις ὁ παντὶ σθένει τὴν ἐκείνων ἐζηλωκὼς μετὰ σαρκὸς πολιτείαν, τῷ Παντοκράτορι Θεῷ καὶ Κυρίῳ τῆς δόξης καὶ Βασιλεῖ τῶν ἁπάντων ὁ τὰς ἐπιγείους καὶ μερικὰς βασιλείας διὰ τὸν ἐκείνου φόβον ἀντ' οὐδενὸς λογισάμενος, καὶ πᾶσαν ἀνθρωπίνην

came to him; he blessed and signed them with the sign of the cross, embraced them and spoke quietly to them, and then dismissed them. And he did this for two days.

On the Sunday when the commemoration of the holy 5
and glorious martyr Menas was being celebrated, after he had chanted the usual psalms and partaken of the holy elements, Theodore anointed his limbs as was his custom, raised his hands on high and prayed. About the sixth hour of the day, when he realized that he was exhausted, he quietly commanded that candles should be lit. And so, when the brethren had begun to sing the Blameless Psalm and had reached the verse of the second section which says, "*I will never forget your ordinances, for by them you have given me life,*" as they paused there, he gave up his holy soul.

And to the righteous of the ages was given over one who 6
throughout all his life had been persecuted for the sake of righteousness; to the saints was given over the lover and practitioner of saintliness; to the martyrs their long-suffering fellow contestant and lover of martyrs; to the apostles the one who had run the same race of faith as they had; to the prophets the one who had been honored by God with equal grace and who, through his actions, had set a seal on their prophecies, since he guaranteed that Emmanuel's incarnation would be honored through holy symbols in every way and by all means; to all the holy angels the one who in the flesh had imitated their way of life with all his strength; and to God Almighty, the Lord of glory and King of all, was given over the one who on account of fear of God counted individual earthly kingdoms as nothing, who trampled on all

δόξαν ὡς πηλὸν καταπατήσας καὶ γενόμενος κατὰ τὸ δυνατὸν θεοειδὴς καὶ Χριστοείκελος. Οὗ καὶ τὸ πανίερον καὶ τληπαθὲς σκήνωμα, τῆς προρρηθείσης χερρονήσου πρὸς τὴν Πρίγκιπον τηνικάδε μετακομισθέν, αὐτόθι τὴν ἁρμόδιον ψαλμῳδίαν τε καὶ κατάθεσιν δέχεται, ἐν ὀκτὼ πρὸς δέκα ἔτεσιν τῇ αὐτῇ παραφυλαχθὲν νήσῳ, καὶ συντηρηθὲν ὑπὸ τοῦ ἐν αὐτῷ κατεσκηνωκότος Ἁγίου Πνεύματος ἀσινὲς καὶ ἀδιάλυτον, καὶ οὕτως ὡς μηδὲ τῆς δορᾶς αὐτοῦ καθάψασθαι τὴν φθοροποιὸν ἐνέργειαν, εἰ καὶ *τῆς τὸ ὀδωδέναι λαχούσης φύσεως* σύμφυλον ἦν τὸ μακάριστον.

7 Μετετέθη δὲ ἐνδόξως πρὸς τὴν ἰδίαν αὐτοῦ ποίμνην τῶν Στουδίου, ἐν ἀρχῇ τῆς καθ' ἡμᾶς ὀρθοδοξίας ἐπὶ τῆς λειτουργίας Μεθοδίου τοῦ ἁγιωτάτου πατριάρχου καὶ καθαιρέτου τῆς τῶν ἡμιχρίστων αἱρέσεως. Καὶ κατετέθη τῇ σορῷ τοῦ πανοσίου Πλάτωνος καὶ ἡγουμένου αὐτοῦ ἅμα Ἰωσὴφ τῷ ἀρχιεπισκόπῳ Θεσσαλονίκης καὶ ἰδίῳ αὐτοῦ ἀδελφῷ, τοῦ Θεοῦ καὶ Σωτῆρος ἡμῶν Ἰησοῦ Χριστοῦ οὕτως εὐδοκήσαντος, ἵνα τούτους ἔχοντες προμηθέας καὶ ἰατροὺς τῶν τε ψυχῶν καὶ σωμάτων ἡμῶν καὶ μεσίτας πρὸς τὴν ἁγίαν καὶ ἁπλῆν καὶ ἄκτιστον καὶ ὁμοούσιον Τριάδα λυτρώμεθα ἀεὶ ταῖς αὐτῶν πρεσβείαις ἀπὸ πάσης ὀργῆς θεηλάτου, βλάβης τε καὶ ἐπηρείας ὁρατῶν καὶ νοουμένων ἐχθρῶν, δοξάζοντες Πατέρα καὶ Υἱὸν καὶ Ἅγιον Πνεῦμα τὸν ἕνα Θεὸν ἡμῶν εἰς τοὺς αἰῶνας τῶν αἰώνων. Ἀμήν.

human glory as though it were mud, and, as much as he could, became godlike and Christlike. Theodore's all-holy and long-suffering body was then transported from the previously mentioned peninsula to Prinkipo, where it received appropriate psalmody and burial on the same island and where it was carefully guarded for eighteen years. It was preserved undamaged and without decomposition by the Holy Spirit dwelling in it in such a way that the process of corruption did not even touch his skin, even though this most blessed corpse was part of *the nature that is prone to stink*.

Theodore's remains were gloriously transferred to his 7
own flock of Stoudios at the beginning of our renewed orthodoxy during the ministry of Methodios, the most holy patriarch who destroyed the heresy of the semi-Christians. They were buried in the tomb of the most saintly Plato, his superior, along with Joseph, the archbishop of Thessalonike, his own brother. God and our Savior Jesus Christ had consented to this, so that we, having them to take thought for us and as physicians of both our souls and bodies and intercessors with the holy, single, uncreated, and consubstantial Trinity, might always be delivered by their entreaties from all divine wrath, harm, and the assault of visible and spiritual enemies, glorifying the Father, Son, and Holy Spirit, our one God, to the ages of the ages. Amen.

ENCYCLICAL LETTER OF NAUKRATIOS

Τοῖς διὰ Κύριον δεδιωγμένοις καὶ πανταχοῦ διεσπαρμένοις πνευματικοῖς ἀδελφοῖς καὶ πατράσι, Ναυκράτιος ἁμαρτωλὸς μοναχός.

I

Ἕως μὲν τοῦ παρόντος, ἀδελφοί μου τιμιώτατοι καὶ πατέρες, ἀνεβαλλόμην τὸ ταπεινὸν γράμμα, ἡμέραν ἐξ ἡμέρας διεξερχόμενος καὶ κατ' ἐμαυτὸν κατέχων τὸ λυπηρόν. Καὶ δὴ τοῦτο πέπραχα διὰ πολλά, ἅ, ὡς οἶμαι, οὐδὲ τὴν τιμιότητα ὑμῶν ἀγνοεῖν, καί γε πρὸ τῶν ἄλλων, μὴ φέρων ἄγγελος ὑμῖν θλιπτικῆς ἐπιφορᾶς γενέσθαι, λέγω δή, τῆς κοιμήσεως τοῦ μακαρίου καὶ ἀοιδίμου πατρὸς ἡμῶν. Ἐπεὶ δέ, ὡς ὁρῶ, οὐ μόνον τὰ ἐνταῦθα, ἀλλὰ καὶ τὰ πόρρω δεδόνηται τῷ παραδόξῳ τοῦ ἀκούσματος ὡς καὶ τοῖς πλείοσι δύσπιστον γενέσθαι, εἰ ἆρά γε μετέστη τῶν ἐνθένδε ὁ τοῦ Κυρίου θεράπων, οὐκ οἶμαι δὲ μὴ καὶ πρὸς ὑμᾶς καταλαβεῖν τὸ παρ' ἡμῶν αἰδοῖ ὑποσιωπώμενον, ἀναγκαίως ἐπὶ τὸ γράμμα ἦλθον, ἄρτι ὑμῖν ἐνεργέστερον, καὶ μὴ βουλόμενος, ἀναγγέλλων τὸ καὶ παρ' ἑτέρων προακουτισθέν, καὶ τοῦτο οὐκ ἀποτνίως οὐδ' ἀδακρυτί. Τίς γὰρ ἂν εἰ καὶ *λιθίνην* ἔχων *τὴν καρδίαν* οὐκ ἀποστάξειε

Naukratios, a sinful monk, to the spiritual brethren and fathers who are persecuted for the Lord's sake and scattered everywhere.

I

My dearest brethren and fathers, I have kept putting off my humble letter until now, going on day after day and keeping the grievous news to myself. I did this for many reasons, which I think your dear selves may fully understand, and above all because I could not bear being the messenger to you of a grievous affliction, I mean the death of our blessed and famous father. But since I see that things have been abuzz, not only here but also far away, with the astounding rumor, hard as it is for most people to believe, that the Lord's servant did indeed depart this life, I imagine that what I have been keeping hushed up out of respect has reached you too, so of necessity I have turned to this letter, now reluctantly reporting more clearly to you what has already been heard from others, and not without lamentation and tears. For who, even though he has a *heart of stone,* would

δάκρυον θερμόν, τὴν κοινὴν ζημίαν τῆς τοῦ Θεοῦ Ἐκκλησίας ἀναλογιζόμενος; Ὁποίαν δὲ *ἀδαμαντίνην ψυχὴν* κεκτημένος, εἰ καὶ μὴ παντελῶς ἔξω τῶν ὅρων γεγονώς, ὃς οὐ πληγήσεται τῷ ἀπροσδοκήτῳ τῆς ἀκοῆς, καὶ τὰ τῆς φύσεως δράσειεν;

2

Ἀλλὰ φεῦ τῆς ἐμῆς ταλαιπωρίας· εἰς οἷον τετήρημαι ὁ δύστηνος καιρόν, καὶ ὁποῖον ἀπέκειτό μου τῇ μοχθηρᾷ ζωῇ, θάνατον ἀναγγεῖλαι τοῦ μὴ ἑαυτῷ ἐζηκότος, ἀλλὰ Χριστῷ. Ναὶ ὄντως ἀληθῶς κεκοίμηται ὁ κοινὸς πατὴρ ἡμῶν, ὁ πολλὰ ὑμᾶς καὶ φιλῶν καὶ στέργων ὡς τέκνα ἀληθινά, ὡς ἐργάτας τοῦ ἀμπελῶνος Κυρίου, *ὡς υἱοὺς ὑπακοῆς,* ὡς στρατιώτας Χριστοῦ, ὡς ὁμολογητὰς ἀψευδεῖς, ὡς συγκεκοπιακότας αὐτῷ καὶ συνηθληκότας ἐν πολλοῖς καὶ ἐν πᾶσιν. Κεκοίμηται ὁ κοινὸς πατὴρ ἡμῶν, ὁ τοῦ Χριστοῦ ἀληθῶς καὶ μαθητὴς καὶ μιμητής, τὸ *σκεῦος τῆς ἐκλογῆς, τὸ στόμα τῆς Ἐκκλησίας, τὸ κλέος τῶν ἱερέων, τὸ τῆς πίστεως ἔρεισμα,* ὁ τῶν μοναζόντων κανών, ὁ Εὐαγγελικὸς ποιμήν, *ἡ ἀποστολικὴ καρδία,* τῶν ὁμολογητῶν ὁ ἐξαίρετος, ὁ προαιρετικὸς μάρτυς, ὁ τῆς ὀρθοδοξίας ἥλιος, ὁ οἰκουμενικὸς διδάσκαλος. Καί, ὢ τοῦ ἀκούσματος, κεκοίμηται ὁ κοινὸς πατὴρ ἡμῶν, *ὁ μεγαλοφωνότατος τῆς ἀληθείας κῆρυξ,* ὁ ἀένναος τῆς διδασκαλίας βρυτήρ, ὁ

not shed a fervent tear, as he reckons up the common loss to God's Church? Who, even if he has *a spirit of steel,* unless he is completely beyond the pale, will not be stricken by the unexpected news and act according to human nature?

2

But, alas for my misery! Wretched man, that I have been preserved for such a time and with such a thing stored up for my miserable life: to report the death of the one who did not live for himself but for Christ! Yes, really and truthfully our common father has fallen asleep, he who had great love and affection for you as his true children, as workers in the Lord's vineyard, *as* sons *of obedience,* as soldiers of Christ, as truthful confessors, as fellow laborers with him and fellow contenders on many and all occasions. Our common father has fallen asleep, truly the disciple and imitator of Christ, *the chosen instrument, the mouthpiece of the Church, the glory of the priests, the bulwark of the faith,* the standard for monks, the shepherd of the Gospel, *the heart of the apostles,* the chosen confessor, the voluntary martyr, the sun of orthodoxy, the teacher of the world. Oh, what a report! Our common father has fallen asleep, *the most loud-voiced herald of the truth,* the ever-flowing fountain of teaching, the infinitely ingenious

μυριόνους τῇ θεοσκόπῳ κυβερνήσει πλωτήρ, ὁ θαυμαστὸς βουληφόρος, ὁ πιστὸς οἰκονόμος τῶν τοῦ Θεοῦ μυστηρίων, ὁ τῆς ἐπουρανίου Ἱερουσαλὴμ πολίτης, *ὁ κεκαθαρμένος νοῦς, ἡ χρυσοειδὴς ψυχή,* ἡ τῆς μετανοίας θύρα, ἡ τῶν δογμάτων πηγή, ἡ εὔηχος τοῦ Πνεύματος λύρα, τὸ ἐνδιαίτημα τῆς μακαρίας καὶ ἀρχικῆς Τριάδος.

3

Καί γε αὖθις ἐρῶ, *οὐ παρακλήσεως* εἵνεκα, *(τίς γὰρ ἂν καὶ λόγος ἐξευρεθείη τοσαύτης συμφορᾶς ἰατρός;) ἀλλὰ τὴν* περιωδυνίαν *τῆς ταπεινῆς ἡμῶν καρδίας ἐκ τῆς φωνῆς ταύτης ὑμῖν διασημαίνοντες·* κεκοίμηται ὁ κοινὸς πατὴρ ἡμῶν, *ὁ ἐπίγειος ἄγγελος καὶ οὐράνιος ἄνθρωπος,* ὁ τῆς παρθενίας ναὸς καθαρώτατος, ὁ πολλοστὸς καὶ πολυειδὴς τῇ ποικιλοστρόφῳ σοφίᾳ τοῦ πνεύματος, ὁ ἐπιτετευγμένος στοχαστής, ὁ γνήσιος Χριστοῦ ὑπηρέτης, ὁ καλλιβλέφαρος ὀφθαλμὸς τοῦ Χριστοῦ σώματος, *ὁ τῆς ὑπομονῆς ἀθλητὴς καὶ τῆς εἰκονομαχικῆς αἱρέσεως νικητής, τὸ τῆς δικαιοσύνης ὅπλον,* ἡ τῆς ἐλεημοσύνης κρήνη, ὁ ἀκριβὴς τοῦ Κυρίου νομοφύλαξ, τὸ θησαυροφυλάκιον τῶν ἀρετῶν, ὁ τὸν λόγον ἡδὺς καὶ τὴν προσηγορίαν εὐπρόσιτος.

navigator whose steering was watched over by God, the marvelous counselor, the faithful steward of God's mysteries, the citizen of the heavenly Jerusalem, *the purified mind, the golden soul,* the door of repentance, the fount of dogma, the melodious lyre of the Spirit, the dwelling place of the blessed and sovereign Trinity.

3

I will say it again, *not for solace (for what words could be found to heal so great a calamity?) but indicating to you* the great pain in my humble *heart as a result of this statement.* Our common father has fallen asleep, *the earthly angel and heavenly man,* the most pure temple of virginity, the one who was so very resourceful and versatile in the manifold wisdom of the spirit, the successful diviner of truth, the true servant of Christ, the beautifully lidded eye of Christ's body, *the champion of patient endurance and victor over the iconoclast heresy, the weapon of righteousness,* the fountain of mercy, the strict guardian of the Lord's law, the treasury of virtues, one whose words were sweet and whose manner of speech was accessible.

4

Καὶ τίς ἱκανὸς λογογραφεῖν ὁπόσας αὐτῷ καὶ ἡλίκας προσηγορίας παρέσχεν ἡ θεία χάρις, ταῖς ἐνεργείαις τοῦ *τοῖς πᾶσι πάντα* ἀποστολικῇ διαθέσει γενομένου; Ὦ, ὢ ἀειπόθητοι, τί τὸ περὶ ἡμᾶς τοὺς ταπεινοὺς τοῦτο μυστήριον καὶ τίς ἡ τοῦ Θεοῦ σοφία ἡ ἄρρητος; *Νῦν ἐδεόμην τῶν Ἱερεμίου θρήνων, καὶ εἰ δή τις ἄλλος τῶν μακαρίων ἀνδρῶν συμφορᾶς μέγεθος ἀπωδύρατο. Πέπτωκεν ἀνήρ, τῷ ὄντι στῦλος καὶ ἑδραίωμα τῆς Ἐκκλησίας, μᾶλλον δέ, αὐτὸς μὲν πρὸς τὴν μακαρίαν ζωὴν ἀρθείς, ἀφ᾽ ἡμῶν οἴχεται·* δέος δὲ μή, *τῷ ἐρείσματι τούτῳ ὑπεξαιρεθέντι,* τινὲς *συγκαταπέσωσι* καὶ *τὰ* τούτων *σαθρὰ* διελεγχθῶσιν. *Κέκλεισται στόμα* μελετῶν ἐν νόμῳ Κυρίου ἡμέρας καὶ νυκτός, *παρρησίας τε αὖ δικαίας καὶ λόγους χάριτος ἐπ᾽ οἰκοδομῇ* πίστεως *βρύον.*

5

Οἴχεται φρενὸς βουλεύματα τῆς ὄντως ἐν Θεῷ κινουμένης. Μέμυκεν ὀφθαλμὸς βλέπων ὀρθὰ καὶ διακρίνων τὸ κρεῖττον ἀπὸ τοῦ χείρονος κάλλιστα. Πέπαυται χείλη φυλάσσοντα γνῶσιν καὶ νόμον θεῖον ἐκζητούμενα ὡς ἀγγέλου Κυρίου Παντοκράτορος. Δέδεται γλῶσσα χρυσορρήμων, θείων δογμάτων ἐξηχητής. Εἷρκται χεὶρ ὡραιογράφος,

4

Who could possibly describe how great and how wonderful were the manners of speech which divine grace bestowed on him, when he was someone who, in his apostolic disposition, became *all things to all men*? O, O you ones who are always longed for, what is this mystery concerning my humble self, and what is the ineffable wisdom of God? *At this time, I would need the lamentations of Jeremiah, as indeed would whoever else among the blessed men who mourned such a magnitude of calamity. A man has fallen who really was a pillar and bulwark of the Church, or rather, has been raised to the blessed life and has left us;* and there is a fear that, with this support removed, some *may also fall* and their *rottenness* be proven. *A mouth has been closed,* which would meditate on the law of the Lord day and night *and would flow with righteous freedom of speech and words of grace to build up the* faith.

5

The counsels of a mind that was truly moved by God have departed. The eye has closed that saw what was right and distinguished so well the better from the worse. The lips have ceased to move that, like those of an angel of the Lord Almighty, upheld knowledge and sought out divine law. The tongue has been stilled that, with golden speech, expounded divine doctrines. The hand has been restrained that, with

ἐπιστολαῖς τὸν κόσμον καταπλουτήσασα καὶ πολλοὺς εἰς *ἐπίγνωσιν ἀληθείας* ἐπαναστρέψασα. Ἔστησαν *πόδες ὡραῖοι* παννύχοις στάσεσι διηρκηκότες, καὶ πολλοῖς *εὐαγγελισάμενοι εἰρήνην καὶ τὰ ἀγαθά.* Ἠρέμησε νοῦς διορατικώτατος, τὰ τοῦ Πνεύματος βάθη διερευνήσας, καὶ τὰ πόρρωθεν προβλέψας καὶ προϊδὼν ἄριστα. Κέκρυπται ὑπὸ γῆν σῶμα ἀσκητικοῖς πόνοις ἐγγυμνασθὲν καὶ πολλαῖς ἐξορίαις καὶ φυλακαῖς, πληγαῖς τε καὶ ἀπαγωγαῖς ἐξαρκέσαν.

6

Τοιοῦτος γάρ, ὦ μακαριώτατοι, ὁ ἡμέτερος πατήρ· ταὐτὸν δὲ εἰπεῖν, πολλῶν πατὴρ καὶ διδάσκαλος, ὁ δεύτερος Ἀβραάμ, οὗ ἡ παρὰ Θεοῦ εὐλογία ἐξαίρετος καὶ οὗ τὸ σπέρμα ὑπὲρ ἀριθμόν, ὁ τοῦ Προδρόμου μιμητής, ὁ τοῦ Ἠλιοῦ ζηλωτής, ὁ τῆς χάριτος Φινεές, ὁ νέος Σαμουήλ, ὁ *ἐκλελοχισμένος ἀπὸ μυριάδων,* οὗ τὴν ἀρετὴν ᾄδουσι πολλαὶ πόλεις, χῶραί τε καὶ νῆσοι, καὶ οὗ τὸν βίον καὶ τοὺς ἀγῶνας εἰκότως θρυλλεῖ τὰ πέρατα. Τίς γὰρ οὕτως ἢ ἀρετὴν ἠγάπησεν ἢ κακίαν ἐμίσησεν; Τίς οὕτως ἐπεπόθησε Θεὸν καὶ ἠγαπήθη ὑπ᾽ αὐτοῦ; Τίς ζηλῶν ἐζήλωκε τῷ Κυρίῳ, μὴ προκρίνας τι τῆς αὐτοῦ ἀγάπης μέχρι θανάτου; Τίς ἰχνηλάτησε τοὺς τῶν ἁγίων βίους καὶ ἀκορέστως τούτοις συνημιλλήθη; Τίς οὕτως *ἐνέκρωσεν,* ἀποστολικῶς

beautiful writing, enriched the world with letters and returned many to *knowledge of the truth.* The *beautiful feet* have halted that endured standing in nocturnal vigils and *preaching* to many *the good news of peace and blessings.* The most discerning mind is now at rest that investigated the depths of the Spirit, that looked far ahead and foresaw things most excellently. The body has been concealed beneath the earth that was trained in ascetic hardships and was strong enough for so many banishments and imprisonments, for beatings and arrests.

6

For such a man, most blessed ones, was our father. To repeat myself, he was a father and teacher of many, a second Abraham whose blessing from God was special and whose offspring beyond number, the imitator of the Forerunner, the emulator of Elijah, the Phinehas of grace, the new Samuel, the *one picked out from ten thousand,* whose virtue many cities, lands, and islands celebrate and whose life and contests the ends of the world repeat over and over again with good reason. For who loved virtue or hated wickedness as he did? Who yearned after God as he did and was loved by him? Who in his zeal was jealous for the Lord, and did not prefer anything above his love until death? Who sought out the lives of the saints and vied insatiably with them? Who, to speak like the apostle, *put to death his earthly members,*

εἰπεῖν, *τὰ μέλη τὰ ἐπὶ τῆς γῆς* καὶ καθῆρεν ἑαυτόν, καὶ ναὸν Θεοῦ ζῶντος ἀπειργάσατο; Τίς ἐστρατήγησε καὶ παρετάξατο πρὸς τοὺς ὑπεναντίους, καὶ προσβαλὼν εὐστόχως κατέβαλε νενικηκὼς ἄριστα; *Τίς ὀξύτερον ἐκείνου προϊδέσθαι τὸ μέλλον, τίς <ἐν> οὕτω σταθερῷ καὶ παγίῳ τῆς ψυχῆς ἤθει, ἀστραπῆς τάχιον τοῖς πράγμασιν ἐπελθεῖν ἱκανός;* Καὶ ποῦ μοι καιρὸς τὰ πλείονα λέγειν, ἃ πᾶσι πρόδηλα, κἂν ἡμεῖς μὴ λέγωμεν διὰ τὸ τῆς ἐπιστολῆς ὑπερτενὲς παρατρέχοντες;

7

Οἴμοι, οἴμοι, ἀδελφοί μου τιμιώτατοι, *πολλοῖς ἤδη προειλημμένοι πάθεσι* καὶ θλίψεσιν, *ὑπ᾽ οὐδενός γε μὴν οὕτως εἰς αὐτὰ τὰ καίρια* τῆς ψυχῆς τρωθέντες, *νῦν ἀπήνθηκεν* ἡμῖν *κόσμος ὁ κάλλιστος, Ἐκκλησία δὲ* στυγνάζει *καὶ σκυθρωπάζουσι* δῆμοι, ὅτι ἐξέλιπε μαχητής, καὶ ἀπέπτη στοχαστὴς καὶ *θαυμαστὸς σύμβουλος.* Ἐντεῦθεν ἐπιζητεῖ *τὸ ἱερὸν συνέδριον τὸν κορυφαῖον,* οἱ ὁμολογηταὶ τὸν σύναθλον, οἱ ἐν τῷ ἀγῶνι τὸν ἀλείπτην, οἱ νοσοῦντες τὸν ἰατρόν, οἱ θλιβόμενοι τὴν παραμυθίαν, οἱ ἐν συμφοραῖς τὴν παράκλησιν, οἱ ὀρφανοὶ *τὸν πατέρα,* αἱ χῆραι *τὸν προστάτην,* οἱ πένητες *τὸν τροφέα,* οἱ ἀδικούμενοι τὸν ὑπερασπιστὴν καὶ ἀντιλήπτορα, οἱ *πάντες ἐκ τῶν οἰκείων ὀνομάτων ἀνακαλούμενοι ἐπὶ οἰκείῳ πάθει, οἰκεῖον ἑαυτῷ καὶ προσήκοντα ἕκαστος τὸν θρῆνον* ποιοῦνται.

purified himself, and made himself a temple of the living God as he did? Who commanded an army, drew up his forces against the enemy, and, attacking cleverly, overthrew them in a mighty victory? *Who was more clear-sighted than he in foreseeing the future? Who was as capable as he was of facing trouble more quickly than lightning with a steadfast and firm spiritual attitude?* And where is the opportunity for me to say more, things that are evident to everyone, unless I say them cursorily because of the excessive length of my letter?

7

Alas, alas, my dearest brethren, *already preoccupied by many sufferings* and afflictions, *yet by none so* spiritually wounded *at this time. This most beautiful world has lost its bloom* for us, *the Church* looks sad and people *are gloomy,* because a warrior has passed away, and a diviner of truth and *marvelous counselor* has taken flight. Consequently, *the holy council* is seeking *its leader,* the confessors their competitor, the contestants their trainer, the sick their doctor, the afflicted their consolation, the troubled their comfort, the orphans *their father,* the widows *their protector,* the poor *their nurturer,* the wronged their champion and helper; and *everyone, recalling their own suffering on their own account,* makes *his own lamentation appropriate to himself.*

8

Τούτου τοῦ μακαρίου, τοῦ πλείοσι τούτων καὶ ἀναριθμήτοις χαρίσμασι καὶ ἀρεταῖς κατεστεμμένου καὶ ἄνωθεν φερωνύμως ἐσχηκότος τὴν κλῆσιν ἡμεῖς οἱ ταπεινοί, οἱ μετὰ πάντων καὶ πρὸ πάντων τὰ νῦν ἀπορφανισθέντες καὶ διαζευχθέντες σωματικῶς, κατελείφθημεν μεμονωμένοι. Γεγόναμεν ὡς τὸ ἀπ' ἀρχῆς, πενθοῦντες καὶ σκυθρωπάζοντες πορευόμεθα, γεγόναμεν ὄνειδος τοῖς ἐναντίοις, ἐπίχαρμα τοῖς κακοδόξοις. Ἤνοικται καθ' ἡμῶν εἰκονομάχων στόμα, *προσελογίσθημεν μετὰ τῶν καταβαινόντων εἰς λάκκον* ψαλμικῶς εἰπεῖν, *γεγόναμεν ὡς στρουθίον μονάζον ἐπὶ δώματος, παρὰ βραχὺ παρῴκησε τῷ Ἅιδῃ ἡ ψυχὴ* ἡμῶν. Ἐξηπορήμεθα, ἀπειπάμεθα ἑαυτῶν, γεγόναμεν τῷ κόσμῳ διήγημα σκυθρωπόν, καί, *ὢ τῆς δεινῆς ὄντως καὶ σκυθρωπῆς ἐρημίας, πῶς ἀκριβῶς ὡμοιώθημεν πελεκᾶνι ἐρημικῷ;* Ἐκείνου τοῦ ἀοιδίμου ἡ μετάστασις ὀδύνης πεπλήρωκεν ἡμῶν τὴν ταπεινὴν καρδίαν, δακρύων ἡμῶν τοὺς ἐσκοτισμένους ἐνέπλησεν ὀφθαλμούς, στεναγμῶν ἐπλήρωσε καρδιακῶν, βρασμῶν καὶ ἀναβρασμῶν καὶ ἐκβρασμῶν τὰ τῆς ψυχῆς αἰσθητήρια. Τὴν παροῦσαν ζωὴν μισητὴν πεποίηκεν, τὸν θάνατον ἐπιθυμητόν. Τὸ ψυχικὸν ἔαρ εἰς χειμῶνα μετέστρεψεν, τὰ τοῖς πολλοῖς περισπούδαστα ἡμῖν ἀπόπτυστα. Καὶ τὰ μὲν καθ' ἡμᾶς, ὢ σεβασμιώτατοι, οὕτω πολυστένακτα καὶ πολυώδυνα, ἄφιλά τε καὶ ἀνέορτα, μηδεμίαν παρηγορίαν ἔχοντα, πανταχοῦ τοῦ

8

We humble ones who, along with everyone and more than everyone, are now orphaned and physically separated from this blessed man who was adorned by these numerous and countless spiritual gifts and virtues and possessed in his name a calling from above, have been left behind and forsaken. We have become as we were at the beginning; we conduct our lives in lamentation and look gloomy; we have become an object of reproach for our adversaries, a source of ridicule for those with false beliefs. The mouths of the iconoclasts have opened against us; *we have been reckoned among those who go down to the pit,* to speak like the Psalmist; *we have become like a lonely bird on the housetop;* our lives *almost dwell in Hades.* We are at a total loss; we are in despair; we have become a gloomy tale for the world. *Oh, what truly dreadful and gloomy desolation! How did we become just like a desert pelican?* The death of that celebrated man has filled our humble hearts with pain; it has filled our darkened eyes with tears, it has filled the spiritual senses of our souls with heartfelt groaning, with turmoil, tumult and turbulence. It has made the present life hateful and death desirable. It has changed the soul's springtime into winter; what is greatly desired by most people is detestable to us. And so, most reverend men, our lives are filled with much groaning and much pain; they are friendless and joyless, lacking even one

ταπεινοῦ λογισμοῦ διαθέοντος καὶ μηδαμοῦ στάσιν εὑρίσκοντος, ἢ μόνον εἰς Θεὸν καὶ εἰς τὴν τοῦ ἱεροῦ τάφου παρεδρευτικὴν ἀπόβλεψιν.

9

Ὁποῖα δὲ τὰ καθ' ὑμᾶς οὐκ ἀγνοῶν ἐπερωτῶ, πυνθάνομαι δ' οὖν ὅμως, ὦ ποθεινότατοι. Καί γε τὰ ὅμοια πάντως φήσοιτε, *εἴ γάρ*, ὥς φησιν, *πάσχει ἓν μέλος συμπάσχει πάντα τὰ μέλη*. Ὅτι δὲ ὑμεῖς μέλη καὶ τῶν τιμιωτάτων, παντί που δῆλον, ὅθεν εἰκότως ἡ συνάλγησις. Τίς γὰρ ὑμῶν ἔτι παραγενομένων προσυπαντήσειε φαιδρῷ τῷ προσώπῳ καὶ ὑπτίαις χερσὶν ὑποδέξεται, καὶ περιπλακεὶς κατασπάσεται ὑμῶν τὰ τίμια πρόσωπα; Τίς ἐπερωτήσει τὰ δέοντα καὶ ψυχωφελῆ; Τίς λυπουμένους χαροποιήσειε τῇ ἐμμελεῖ νουθεσίᾳ; Τίς ἀπεγνωκότας παρακαλέσειεν; Τίς ἀθυμοῦντας ἐκ λογισμῶν καὶ κατεμπριζομένους ἀναψύξειεν; Τίς ἐπαλείψειε πρὸς τοὺς ἀγῶνας; Τίς τονώσειε πρὸς τὸν τῆς *εὐσεβείας δρόμον;* Τίς διεγείροι πρὸς εὐανδρίαν; Τίς στομώσειε πρὸς ἔνστασιν ἀληθείας; Τίς ἰατρεύσειε νενοσηκότας; Τίς πόρρω οὖσι διὰ γράμματος προσφθέγξεται τὰ ὀφείλοντα; Τίς οὕτως ἀγαπήσειε καὶ τὴν τιμίαν ψυχὴν ὑπὲρ ἑκάστου θήσειε Χριστομιμήτως, ὡς ὁ θεοδώρητος ἐκεῖνος ποιμὴν καὶ διδάσκαλος;

consolation, while our humble minds race in every direction and find no stability anywhere, except in gazing constantly on God and the holy tomb.

9

I might ask what your lives are like, though I know full well. Were I to inquire, however, you whom I so long for, you would doubtless say the same things, for *if,* as it says, *one limb suffers, all the limbs suffer together.* That you are also limbs and of the dearest kind is no doubt clear to everyone, and hence a sharing of grief is appropriate. For when you were still coming here, who would go to meet you with a cheerful face; and who would receive you with open arms and, after an embrace, would kiss your dear faces? Who would ask what you needed and what was beneficial to your souls? Who would make those who were grieving joyful with suitable advice? Who would comfort those in despair? Who would revive those who were depressed and consumed by their thoughts? Who would encourage you for the contests? Who would invigorate you for *piety's racecourse?* Who would stir up your courage? Who would steel you to face hostility to the truth? Who will now heal those who are sick? Who will recommend the appropriate conduct in a letter to those who are far away? Who, like that God-given shepherd and teacher, would have such love and would lay down his dear soul for each one in imitation of Christ?

10

Καὶ τί δεῖ τὰ πολλὰ τοῦ μακαρίου καὶ ἀξιαγάστου ἐκτραγῳδεῖν, *ἐφ' οἷς καὶ μάλιστα τὴν ζημίαν ἡμῖν ἀφόρητον ὑπάρχειν λογίζεσθε; Οὐδ' ἂν ἐπιστολῆς μέτρον ὑποδέξαιτο, καὶ ἄλλως,* οὐκ εὔκαιρον ἀριστευμάτων *πλήθη τῷ* γράμ*ματι προσάγειν οὕτως ἡμῶν τῆς* ταπεινῆς *ψυχῆς συμπεπτωκυίας τῇ λύπῃ. Τί γὰρ τῶν ἐκείνου τοιοῦτον, οἷον ἢ τῆς μνήμης ἡμῶν ἐκπεσεῖν, ἢ σιωπᾶσθαι ἄξιον νομισθῆναι;* Ἀλλ' οἴμοι τῷ ταπεινῷ, ἔνδοθεν ὑφ' ἡδονῆς τῶν λεχθέντων κινούμενος, λέληθα ἐμαυτὸν ἐμφιλοχωρῶν τῷ πάθει, καὶ ὑπομιμνήσκων ὑμᾶς τὰ τοῦ μακαρίου πρὸς ἡμᾶς πρακτικεύματα, παρηγορεῖσθαι δοκῶν, τοὐναντίον ἐπικνήθω ὑμῶν τὸ τῆς ψυχῆς τραῦμα, καὶ ἀνάπτω τὴν τῆς καρδίας φλόγα, καὶ αὔξω τὸ πάθος, καὶ δακρύων ὑμῶν τάχα τοὺς ἀδελφικοὺς ὀφθαλμοὺς ἀποπληρῶ.

11

Ἀλλά μοι δεῦρο, ὦ πατέρων ἄριστοι καὶ ἀδελφῶν γνησιώτατοι, μὴ μέχρι τούτων τὸν λογισμὸν στήσωμεν, μηδὲ καταμαλακισθῶμεν καὶ καταπέσωμεν τῷ πάθει, ἵνα μὴ κατηγορήσῃ καὶ ἡμῶν ὁ μέγας ἀπόστολος. Ἀλλὰ ἀναδράμωμεν ἐπὶ τὴν ἀρχαιογονίαν καὶ ἴδωμεν ἀπὸ τοῦ προπάτορος ἡμῶν μέχρι τοῦ δεῦρο, καί γε πρὸ τῶν ἄλλων τοὺς Θεῷ

10

Why need I declaim the blessed and marvelous man's many attributes, *on account of which I am forced to consider his loss especially unbearable? They are infinitely more than what a regular letter could encompass; besides,* it is not a fitting time *to add to* my letter *great numbers* of his brave deeds *when* my humble *soul is so downcast with grief. For which of his attributes is to be thought worthy either to be erased from my memory or to be passed over in silence?* But, alas for my humble self, stirred within by the pleasure of my words, I was carried away in dwelling on my feelings and reminding you also of the blessed one's practical actions concerning us, thinking that I was consoling you. Quite the opposite, I am irritating the wound in your souls, fanning the flame in your hearts, increasing your suffering, and perhaps filling your brotherly eyes with tears.

11

But come, O best of fathers and most genuine of brethren, let us not bring our reckoning to a halt at this point or become soft and collapse under our suffering, so that the great apostle may not accuse us as well. But let us return to our origins and consider especially those from our forefather until now who pleased God by their lives and good

εὐηρεστηκότας διὰ βίου καὶ πολιτείας ἀρίστης, λέγω δή, τοὺς πρὸ Νόμου πατέρας, πατριάρχας, Ἀβραάμ, Ἰσαάκ, Ἰακώβ, τοὺς πρὸ αὐτῶν καὶ μετ' αὐτούς· τοὺς ἐν Νόμῳ, Μωσέα καὶ Ἀαρών· τοὺς μετέπειτα, κριτὰς καὶ προφήτας· τοὺς ἐν χάριτι, ἀποστόλους, μάρτυρας, ὁμολογητάς, ἱεράρχας, ὁσίους, μέχρι τοῦ μνημονευομένου· *καὶ ὡς ἕκαστον τούτων τῇ ἰδίᾳ γενεᾷ ἐπιτρέψας* ὁ Θεὸς *ὑπηρετήσασθαι, τοῖς καθήκουσι χρόνοις πρὸς ἑαυτὸν πάλιν ἀνεκαλέσατο.*

12

Καὶ μὴ λυπείτω ὑμᾶς ἡ τοῦ ἀειμνήστου μετάστασις, εὐφραινέτω δὲ μᾶλλον ὅτι τῶν προμνημονευθέντων συναρίθμιος καὶ συμμέτοχος γέγονεν, ὡς τὰ ἴσα καὶ ἀγωνισάμενος καὶ πολιτευσάμενος ἀριδήλως, ὅτι οὐδὲ ἀπολέλοιπεν ἡμᾶς εἴπερ θέλομεν, ἀλλὰ μεθ' ἡμῶν ἐστιν, εἴ γε, ὡς αὐτὸς ἔφη, τὰς ἐντολὰς αὐτοῦ τηρήσωμεν, ὑπερτέρως ἄρτι ἰσχύων καὶ πρεσβεύειν καὶ βοηθεῖν, καὶ τοσοῦτον, ὅσον ἐν ὑποδείγματος ὅρῳ, πρότερον *δι' ἐσόπτρου* καὶ δι' *αἰνίγματος,* νῦν δὲ *πρόσωπον πρὸς πρόσωπον,* καθαρωτέρως καὶ λαμπροτέρως τῷ Θεῷ λατρεύων καὶ λειτουργῶν, καὶ ὅτι ὀλίγον προενήρξατο τῆς πρὸς Θεὸν ὁδοῦ, προοδοποιῶν ἡμῖν ταύτην, εὐτρεπίζων ἡμῖν κἀκεῖθεν ἀναπαύσεως κατάλυμα, εἴπερ εὐαρέστως Κυρίῳ βιοτεύσωμεν, καὶ

conduct, I mean the fathers who lived before the Law of Moses: the patriarchs Abraham, Isaac, and Jacob, those before them and after them; those at the time of the Law: Moses and Aaron; those after it: the judges and prophets; those during the period of grace: apostles, martyrs, confessors, bishops and saintly men up to the one we now remember. And let us then consider *how* God *commanded each* of them *to minister to his own generation and summoned them back to himself at their appointed times.*

12

Do not, then, let the death of the one who is held in everlasting remembrance grieve you, but rather be glad because he is counted among those mentioned above and has become their fellow, since he too very clearly contended in equal measure and conducted himself like them. Be glad also because he has not forsaken us, if we wish it, but is with us, if, as he said, we observe his commands. Indeed, he is now better able to intercede and help us for, in terms of an analogy, to the extent that he was formerly serving God and ministering *in a mirror dimly* now he does so more purely and more clearly *face to face.* And be glad, too, because he has started on the way to God a little earlier, preparing this for us in advance and making ready a place for us to rest there, if we live our lives in a way that is well pleasing to the Lord and

ὡς αὐτὸς ἡμῖν ἐμαθήτευσεν ἔργῳ καὶ λόγῳ. Ταῦτα παρηγορείτωσαν ὑμῶν τὴν μακαρίαν ψυχήν. Ἐν τούτοις ἀνιστορῶν ὁ καθαρώτατος ὑμῶν νοῦς Σαββατιζέτω καὶ οἱονεὶ καταπαυέτω, τὰς τοῦ τρισολβίου πατρὸς ἐντολὰς καὶ νουθεσίας καὶ μάλα ἡμέρας καὶ νυκτὸς ἀναμιμνησκόμενος, καὶ προσεχῶς ἐν ταύταις ἐνασχολούμενος καὶ μελετῶν· οὕτω γὰρ καὶ Θεῷ εὐαρεστήσομεν, ᾧ προσκεκολλήμεθα, καὶ τὸν προκείμενον ἀγῶνα ὁσίως ἐκτελέσομεν, καὶ δοξασθήσεται δι' ἡμῶν καὶ ἀντιδοξάσειεν ἡμᾶς ἐντεῦθεν καὶ ἐν τῷ μέλλοντι ἑτοιμάζων ἡμῖν βασιλείαν οὐρανῶν.

13

Καὶ ταῦτα μὲν διῆλθον, εἰ καὶ ὑπὲρ ἐπιστολὴν παρά τινων λογισθείη, πρὸς δὲ τὰ ὀφείλοντα, οὐδὲ μέρος ἐπιστολῆς, ὅτι μηδὲ βίβλος ὅλη χωρήσειε τὰ συγγραφῆς ἄξια, ἀλλ' ὅσον ἐν ἐπιτομῇ, ὁμοῦ μὲν τὰ κατὰ τὸν μακάριον ἐκεῖνον ἀνδραγαθήματα διεξιὼν καὶ τῆς ταπεινῆς ἡμῶν καὶ κατωδύνου ψυχῆς φιλιστορήματα, ὁμοῦ δὲ καὶ τῇ ἀδελφικῇ ὑμῶν ἀγάπῃ προσφθεγκτήρια καὶ οἱονεὶ παρηγορητήρια. Ἐπιζητοίητε δέ, εὖ οἶδα, πῶς τε ἡ τοῦ μακαρίου κοίμησις γέγονεν, τίς τε ἡ νόσος, καὶ ποσαήμερος ἡ κατάκλισις· τίνες δ' αὖ οἱ ἐξιτήριοι λόγοι καὶ προπόμπιοι· τίς τε ἡ *Διαθήκη* καὶ ἡ *Διάταξις*· καὶ αὖ πάλιν τίνες οἱ συν-

as he instructed us by his actions and words. Let these thoughts console your blessed souls. As your most pure minds inquire into these things, let them observe a Sabbath and, as it were, be at rest, recalling day and night our thrice-fortunate father's commands and admonitions, and attentively occupying themselves in meditation on these. In that way we will be well pleasing to God, to whom we cleave, and in a saintly way we will accomplish the contest that is set before us; God will thus be glorified through us and in return thereafter may he glorify us, also making the kingdom of heaven ready for us in the future.

13

I have gone through these matters here, even though some might think them beyond a letter, let alone part of a letter, because not even a whole book could contain what deserves to be written down, recounting as a sort of précis, on the one hand, the brave deeds of that blessed man's life and my humble and anguished soul's devoted research and, on the other, greetings of brotherly love for you and consolations, as it were. But you would wish to know, I am sure, how the blessed man died, what was his disease, and for how many days he was bedridden; moreover, what were his parting words and what those during his funeral procession; what was his *Testament* and what his *Rule;* and again, who were

δεδραμηκότες ἐν τῇ ἐσχατιᾷ ταύτῃ, ἤτοι ἐν τῇ κηδείᾳ, καὶ ὅσα ἕτερα. Καὶ τίς ἱκανὸς διὰ γράμματος ἀπαγγέλλειν ὑμῖν, καὶ ὁποία ψυχὴ ἔξω τοῦ πάθους ὑπάρχουσα ἰσχύσει λογογραφῆσαι κἂν τὸ σμικρότατον; Ὡς ἐν κεφαλαίῳ δὲ ἐροῦμεν, ὡς κἀντεῦθέν τινα παραμυθίαν εὑρέσθαι ὑμᾶς.

14

Ἡ μὲν νόσος, ἡ ἀρχαία καὶ συνήθης, λέγω δὴ τοῦ στομάχου, ἥτις ἐκ τῶν πολυχρονίων φυλακῶν καὶ ἐξοριῶν καὶ τῆς ἐντεῦθεν τελείας ἀνεπιμελησίας αὐξηθεῖσα καὶ εἰς πόνους δυσιάτους ἐλάσασα, εἰς τελείαν ἀνορεξίαν κατέληξε, καὶ τοσοῦτον ὡς σχεδὸν νεκρὸν ὁρᾶσθαι κείμενον καὶ πρὸ κοιμήσεως τὸν μακάριον. Ἐξ ἧς τετραήμερον ἐπὶ τῆς κλίνης καταπεσὼν ἐν ἀρχῇ τοῦ Νοεμβρίου μηνός, πάλιν εὐδοκίᾳ Κυρίου ἀνερρώσθη. Ἀλλ᾽ ὢ τῆς τοῦ τρισμάκαρος μεγαλοψυχίας καὶ γενναιότητος· ὅτι οὐδὲ ἐν αὐτῇ τῇ νόσῳ ἠρεμίας, ἤ τινος παρακλήσεως ἐβούλετο ἀπολαύειν, οὕτως <ἦν> εἰς τέλος μεμισηκὼς τὴν παροῦσαν ζωήν. Ἐκλελοιπὼς γὰρ ἤδη τῇ μακροημερεύσει, καὶ κατατετρυχωμένος τῷ γήρᾳ, ἄλλως τε καὶ τοῖς σφοδροῖς πόνοις ἐκείνοις βαλλόμενος, κατὰ τὸ Δαυϊτικόν, οὐκ ἐδίδου *ὕπνον τοῖς ὀφθαλμοῖς,* οὐδὲ *τοῖς βλεφάροις νυσταγμόν, ἀλλ᾽* οὐδὲ *τοῖς κροτάφοις ἀνάπαυσιν, ἕως οὗ εὗρε τόπον τῷ Κυρίῳ.* Καὶ δὴ ἐφεῦρεν. Καὶ τίς οὗτος; Ἡ ἄληκτος καὶ οἱονεὶ ἀπαράβατος κατὰ τὸ εἰωθὸς παρ᾽ αὐτοῦ ἐξηχουμένη ἑκάστοτε

those who gathered at that final occasion, that is at his funeral, and so many other things. What person would be capable of making such a report to you in writing, and what soul will be able to write down even the smallest part of this without suffering? But I will tell you in summary, so that you find some comfort from that.

14

His old and chronic sickness, that of the stomach I mean, which had been aggravated by his imprisonments and banishments over many years, and his resulting complete lack of access to care, led to incurable pains and ended in a total loss of appetite, to such an extent that it made the blessed man look almost like a corpse even before his death. As a result of this, he lay on his bed for four days at the beginning of November and by the Lord's good pleasure regained his strength again. But oh, the thrice-blessed one's greatness of soul and nobility, since, even in this illness, he did not want to enjoy peace or any comfort, thus hating this present life to the end. For though already failing because of his long life, worn out by old age, and above all afflicted by those violent pains, as David says, he did not give *sleep to his eyes* or *drowsiness to his eyelids* or *rest to his temples until he had found a place for the Lord.* And find it he did. What was it? The unceasing and, as it were, infallible salvific teaching that was customarily proclaimed by him on each occasion.

σωτήριος διδασκαλία, ἣν καὶ κλινήρης ὢν διὰ τὸ μὴ δύνασθαι γεγωνότερον τοῖς ἀδελφοῖς παρ' αὐτοῦ ἐκκλησιαζομένοις προσφθέγξασθαι, ὑπηγόρευσεν ἑνὶ τῶν γραφέων δι' ἑτέρου φωνῆς αὐτὸς προσφθεγγόμενος. Ἣν καὶ ὑποθώμεθα τῷ γράμματι, ὅπως γνοίη πᾶς τις τῶν εὖ φρονούντων κἀντεῦθεν, ὡς μηδὲ τὴν μακαρίαν αὐτοῦ κοίμησιν ἠγνοηκέναι, εἰ καὶ συμβολικῶς ταύτην προέφησεν. Ἔχει γὰρ ὧδε.

15

"Ἀδελφοὶ καὶ πατέρες, ἠσθένησα καὶ πάλιν εὐχαῖς ὑμῶν ἀνακέκλημαι. Ἀλλ' ἕως πότε μέλλομεν ἔρχεσθαι ἐπὶ 'τὸ πάλιν'; Ἐλεύσεται δὴ πάντως ἡ ἐπιθανάτιος ἡμέρα, ὅτε οὐχ ἕξει χώραν 'τὸ πάλιν,' χωρίζουσά με ἀφ' ὑμῶν καὶ παραπέμπουσα ἐκ τῶν ἐνθένδε. Οὐ μὴν διὰ τοῦτο λογιστέον ὀρφανίαν, ἀψευδὴς γὰρ ὁ εἰπών· '*Οὐκ ἀφήσω ὑμᾶς ὀρφανούς*,' καὶ '*Ἰδοὺ ἐγὼ μεθ' ὑμῶν εἰμι πάσας τὰς ἡμέρας, ἕως τῆς συντελείας τοῦ αἰῶνος*·' ἄλλως τε ὅτι καὶ ὀψόμεθα ἀλλήλους ἐν τῇ ἡμέρᾳ ἐκείνῃ, ἀλλ' εἴη εἰπεῖν ἐν χαρᾷ ἀνεκλαλήτῳ καὶ ζωῇ ἀτελευτήτῳ. Ὃ δὲ πέπονθα ἐν τῇ ἀσθενείᾳ ἴστε· πῶς ὑπὸ ῥίγους συσχεθείς, ἀνυπόστατον κλόνον ὑπέστην· εἶτα πῶς θᾶττον ἐβλήθην ὑπὸ διακαοῦς πυρετοῦ ὅλην ἡμέραν. Ἐνεθυμήθην οὖν εἰς ἐμαυτὸν πάσχων, ὅτι μήποτε καὶ ἐν τῇ μελλούσῃ κρίσει ἀπὸ τῆς τῶν Ταρτάρων

Since he was bedridden, he dictated it to one of the scribes because of his inability to deliver it loudly enough to the brethren assembled by him in the church, delivering it himself through the voice of another. This I have also included in my letter so that everyone of good understanding may know from it that Theodore was well aware of his blessed death, even though he predicted it figuratively. It is as follows.

15

"Brethren and fathers, I have fallen ill and, owing to your prayers, I have recovered again. But how much longer am I going to resort to 'again'? The day of my death will certainly come when there will be no room for 'again,' separating me from you and conducting me from this world. Nevertheless, because of that you must not consider that you are orphans; for he does not lie who said, '*I will not leave you orphans*' and '*Look, I am with you always, to the close of the age.*' Besides, we shall see each other on that day but, may one be allowed to say, in unutterable joy and everlasting life. You know what I have suffered in my illness: how, gripped by chills, I endured irresistible shivering; then, how I was quickly smitten by a burning fever for a whole day. In my suffering I thought to myself that perhaps in the coming judgment it was possible to fall from the punishment of

τιμωρίας ἔστι μεταπίπτειν εἰς τὴν Γέενναν τοῦ πυρός, καὶ δυοῖν τυχὸν τιμωρίαιν ἢ καὶ πλειόνων ὑπεύθυνος ἂν εἴη ὁ ταλαίπωρος ἄνθρωπος. Πλὴν εἴτε μιᾶς, εἴτε δυοῖν, τεκμαίρεσθαί ἐστιν ἐκ τῶν ἐνταῦθα ἀλγεινῶν τὴν ἀνυπόστατον ἐπὶ τοῖς ἁμαρτωλοῖς ὀργὴν τοῦ Θεοῦ, καὶ φόβῳ πολλῷ καὶ τρόμῳ συνέχεσθαι ἐντεῦθεν, εἰς τὸ μὴ ἐμπεσεῖν εἰς τὰς ἀνυποίστους κολάσεις ἐκείνας.

16

"Τοιγαροῦν ὁ παρὼν διωγμός, οἷς μὲν ὕλη ἀρετῆς εὑρέθη *ἐν ᾧ ἐξέλαμψαν ὡς φωστῆρες ἐν κόσμῳ, λόγον ζωῆς ἐπέχοντες, εἰς καύχημα ἐμοὶ* (εἰ θέμις εἰπεῖν) *εἰς ἡμέραν Χριστοῦ*· τί οὐ καλὸν ἐργασάμενοι, εἰς οἵαν δὲ βελτίωσιν οὐ προελθόντες; Ὅτι καὶ ἑαυτοὺς καὶ ἔσωσαν καὶ σῴζουσιν, ἐγγυμνασθέντες τοῖς πειρασμοῖς, πυρωθέντες ταῖς θλίψεσι χρυσοειδῶς, ἄλλους τε προσιέμενοι, καὶ σωτῆρες πολλῶν ὀφθέντες ὁμοταγῶν τε καὶ ἑτεροταγῶν, μεθ' ὧν εἴη μοι μερίς, καὶ εἴ τινι φίλον ἐμοὶ συντάττεσθαι· οἷς δέ, καὶ τούτοις ὀλιγοστοῖς, ὕλη κακίας, τῇ αὐθαιρέτῳ ζωῇ καὶ οἱονεὶ ἀπονοσφίσει τῆς ὑποταγῆς ἐνεργήσασι *τὰς ἑαυτῶν αἰσχύνας*. Ὅθεν γραφικῶς εὔκαιρον εἰπεῖν· *Ἐσκότασε τὸ εἶδος τοῦ προσώπου αὐτῶν, ὡσεὶ ἀσβόλη*· πρὸς οὓς καὶ βοήσομαι· '*Υἱοὶ ἄνομοι*, ἐγκατελίπετε *τὸν Κύριον*·' ἠλλάξατε

Tartarus into the Gehenna of fire and perhaps a wretched man could be liable to incur two punishments or even more. Yet, whether it is one or two, from the experience of pain here on earth one can get an idea of God's irresistible wrath toward sinners and so be restrained, by great fear and trembling, from falling into those unbearable punishments.

16

"The present persecution, for example, was found by some to be an occasion for virtue when they shone *as lights in the world, holding fast the word of life so that in the day of Christ I might be proud* (if I may say so). What did they practice that was not good? How did they not improve? Because they saved and are still saving themselves, trained by temptations, tested by afflictions like gold in a fire, attracting others and being seen as the saviors of many from the same or a different walk of life, may I, and anyone else who is associated with me as a friend, be with them. But the persecution was found by others, and there were very few of them, to be an occasion for evil as they carried out *their own acts of shame* by leading an independent life and, as it were, renouncing obedience. For that reason it is a good time to say, in words of scripture: *He darkened the form of their faces as though with soot.* To them I will also cry aloud, '*Lawless sons, you abandoned the Lord*'; you changed the rules of monastic

τὰ νόμιμα τῆς μοναδικῆς διαβιώσεως· *τροχιὰς ὀρθὰς οὐκ ἔχετε*, ἀλλ' ὡς χωλοὶ ἐκτρέπεσθε ὧδε κἀκεῖσε φερόμενοι· ἀποδιΐστασθε τῶν συνοδιῶν ὑμῶν, φιλογυνιάζετε, οἱ μὲν μεμονωμένοι τυγχάνοντες, οἱ δὲ δούλους ὠνούμενοι, ἔνιοι ἐμπορικὴν ζωὴν διαμείβοντες διὰ τὴν φιλάργυρον γνώμην.

17

"Οὐ φοβεῖ ὑμᾶς οὔτε ἀρὰ προφητική, οὔτε ἀποστολικὴ ἀπειλή, οὔτε τῆς ἐμῆς ταπεινώσεως ἡ παραίνεσις. Ὡς δὲ μεμάθηκα ὅτι καί τις τῶν τοιούτων καὶ κόρη συμφιλιάσας, πρὸς αὐτὴν τὴν ἁρπαγὴν καὶ τὴν ἀθέτησιν τοῦ Θεοῦ τοὺς πόδας ηὐτρέπισεν. Τί λέγεις, ὦ ἄθλιε καὶ ταλαίπωρε; Ποσάκις ἔψαλλες· '*Ποῦ πορευθῶ ἀπὸ τοῦ πνεύματός σου καὶ ἀπὸ τοῦ προσώπου σου ποῦ φύγω;*' Φιλιάζειν ὅλως ἤχθης μετὰ τοῦ ὄφεως τοῦ ἠπατηκότος τὴν Εὔαν καὶ συνεκβαλόντος ἐκ τοῦ παραδείσου Ἀδὰμ τὸν προπάτορα ἡμῶν; Ἐνθυμῇ ὅλως ἀρνήσασθαι ᾧ ἡρμόσθης Χριστῷ διὰ τοῦ παρθενικοῦ ἐπαγγέλματος, καὶ συναφθῆναι τῇ ἁμαρτίᾳ, δι' ἧς *θάνατος εἰς τὸν κόσμον εἰσῆλθεν;* Οὐκ ἀκούεις τῆς Γραφῆς βοώσης περὶ τῶν οὕτω πραττόντων· '*Ὁ σκώληξ αὐτῶν οὐ τελευτήσει, καὶ τὸ πῦρ αὐτῶν οὐ σβεσθήσεται*'; Οὐκ ἐπαΐεις τοῦ ἀποστόλου λέγοντος· '*Πόρνους καὶ μοιχοὺς κρινεῖ ὁ Θεός*'; Καὶ αὖθις· '*Εἴ τις τὸν ναὸν τοῦ Θεοῦ*

life; you have no *straight tracks,* but like lame men you turn aside, carried this way and that; you withdraw from your communities; you like women; some live by themselves, others buy slaves, and there are some who are engaged in a life of commerce because of their love of money.

17

"Neither a prophetic curse, nor an apostolic threat frightens you, nor an exhortation from my humble self. I have learned that one such man befriended a young girl and took steps toward actually raping her and rejecting God. What do you say, you wretched and miserable man? How often did you chant, '*Where am I to go from your Spirit and where am I to flee from your presence?*' Have you been completely led into befriending her by the serpent that deceived Eve and was cast out along with our forefather Adam from paradise? Are you concerned that you have completely denied Christ to whom you were betrothed through your vow of celibacy and have been caught up in the sin through which *death came into the world*? Do you not hear Scripture exclaiming about people who act in this way, '*Their worm shall not die and their fire shall not be quenched*'? Do you not listen to the apostle when he says, '*God will judge the immoral and adulterous,*' and again, '*If anyone destroys God's temple, God will destroy him*'?

φθείρει, φθερεῖ τοῦτον ὁ Θεός'; Τί εὑρήσεις ἐν τῷ συντελέσαι τὴν ἀνομίαν; Οὐχὶ σκότος καὶ μάχαιραν τέμνουσάν σου τὴν καρδίαν; Οὐχὶ ἀπογνώσεως βόθρον; Οὐκ αὐτὸν τὸν ἠπατηκότα σε Σατανᾶν, τὴν ἀγχόνην σε κατεπείγοντα ἀσπάσασθαι, καθάπερ τὸν Ἰούδαν ποτέ; Ἀνάνηψον ὁ ἐσκοτισμένος· φύγε τὴν παγίδα τοῦ θανάτου ὁ ἐσκελισμένος, μὴ ἁλῷς εἰς *πέταυρον Ἅιδου*, ὑφ' οὗ κἀνταῦθα τοῦ Κάϊν τὴν ζωὴν ζήσοις, *τρέμων καὶ στένων* καὶ ἀποφεύγων πᾶν πρόσωπον γνώριμον, ἔν τε τῷ μέλλοντι αἰῶνι καταδικαζόμενος ἐν τῇ Γεέννῃ τοῦ πυρός.

18

"Τί οὖν ἄλλο ποιήσω ὁ τάλας, περιωρισμένος ἐν ἑνὶ τόπῳ, πρὸς ἅπαντας τοὺς προειρημένους; Τί ἕτερον ἢ τὸ στένειν καὶ διαμαρτύρεσθαι καὶ τὴν ἐρχομένην ῥομφαίαν ἀναγγέλλειν; Καὶ εἰ μὲν ἀκούσοιεν καὶ ἐπιστρέψαιεν ἀπὸ τῆς πεπλανημένης αὐτῶν ὁδοῦ καὶ φερούσης εἰς ὄλεθρον, ἑαυτοῖς ἔσονται σωτήριοι καὶ τῇ ἐμῇ ταπεινώσει· εἰ δὲ μή, μόνοι ἀντλήσουσι τὰ κακά, μόνοι πορεύσονται τῇ φλογὶ ᾗ ἐξέκαυσαν, μόνοι *τίσουσιν ὄλεθρον αἰώνιον ἀπὸ προσώπου τοῦ Κυρίου, καὶ ἀπὸ τῆς δόξης τῆς ἰσχύος αὐτοῦ, ὅταν ἔλθῃ ἐνδοξασθῆναι ἐν τοῖς ἁγίοις αὐτοῦ, καὶ θαυμασθῆναι ἐν πᾶσι τοῖς* κατὰ τὰς ἐντολὰς αὐτοῦ πιστῶς πορευθεῖσιν, αὐτοῖς

What will you gain in perpetrating this lawless act? Isn't this darkness and a sword that is cutting through your own heart? Isn't it a pit of despair? Isn't it Satan himself who deceived you, and is now urging you to embrace the noose, as Judas once did? Come to your senses, you who have been blinded; flee from the snare of death, you who have been tripped up. Do not get caught in the *trap of Hades* in which, even here on earth, you would live the life of Cain, and would be *trembling and groaning* and fleeing from every familiar face, and in the age to come be condemned to the Gehenna of fire.

18

"What else then should I do for all those whom I mentioned before, since I, poor wretch, am confined in one place? What else except groan, warn, and announce the coming sword? If they were to listen and turn back from their wayward path that is leading them to destruction, they would be the means of salvation for themselves and my humble self. If not, they will experience their misfortunes alone, they will live their lives alone in the fire which they have kindled, and alone *they will suffer the punishment of eternal destruction and exclusion from the presence of the Lord and from the glory of his might, when he comes to be glorified in his saints and be marveled at in all those* who lived their lives faithfully according to his commandments. For while he gives

μὲν ἀποδιδοὺς τὰ ἄξια γέρα, τοῖς δὲ ἐναντίοις τὰς ἡτοιμασμένας αὐτοῖς ἀτελευτήτους κολάσεις. Ὑμεῖς δέ, ἀδελφοί μου, εὖ πορεύοισθε, παρακαλῶ, ὡς ἂν *ἀφ' ὑμῶν ἐξηχούμενος ὁ λόγος* τῆς ἀρετῆς καὶ ἐπὶ τοὺς ἀτασθάλους, ἀγάγοι αὐτοὺς *εἰς ἐπίγνωσιν ἀληθείας, πάντα στέργοντες, πάντα πιστεύοντες, πάντα ὑπομένοντες*, ἵνα πάντες ἐν πᾶσιν εὐαρεστήσαντες τῷ Κυρίῳ, φύγοιμεν κολάσεως καταδίκην, καὶ τύχοιμεν βασιλείας οὐρανῶν ἐν αὐτῷ Χριστῷ τῷ Κυρίῳ ἡμῶν, ᾧ ἡ δόξα καὶ τὸ κράτος σὺν τῷ Πατρὶ καὶ τῷ Ἁγίῳ Πνεύματι νῦν καὶ ἀεὶ καὶ εἰς τοὺς αἰῶνας τῶν αἰώνων. Ἀμήν."

19

Μετὰ δὲ τὴν τετράριθμον τῶν ἡμερῶν τῇ ἑξῆς, ἀναστασίμῳ οὔσῃ, κατὰ τὸ εἰωθὸς προκαθεσθέντος τοῦ μακαρίτου καὶ ἀναγνωσθείσης τῆς αὐτῆς κατηχήσεως, τί γίνεται; Ῥώννυται τῇ προθυμίᾳ ἐπεὶ καί, ὥς φησι, *πόνος ὑγείαν χαρίζεται καὶ προθυμία νεκροὺς ἀνίστησιν*. Ἐπεὶ δὲ ἔδει καὶ μυσταγωγίαν γενέσθαι, ἣν ἑκάστοτε διὰ πολλῆς ὁ τρισμάκαρ εἶχεν ἐκεῖνος ἐπιθυμίας, εἴσεισιν εἰς τὸ ἱερὸν καθαρῶς λατρεύσων τῷ Κυρίῳ, καὶ τὴν ἀναίμακτον προσοίσων θυσίαν. Καὶ ταύτην πεπληρωκώς, καὶ μεταδοὺς τοῖς παροῦσι, καὶ πάντα ἐκτετελεκὼς ἁρμοδιώτατα, ἐκεῖθεν ἐπὶ τὴν τράπεζαν ἀνακέκλιται, ἐφ' ᾗ καὶ δεξιωσάμενός τινας τῶν

those their deserved rewards, to his adversaries he gives the unending punishments prepared for them. But you, my brethren, please do conduct your lives well, so that *accounts* of virtue, *sounding forth from you* even to the reckless, may lead them *to knowledge of the truth,* as you live content with all things, believing all things, enduring all things so that we all, having been well pleasing to the Lord in everything, may escape condemnation to eternal punishment and gain the kingdom of heaven in Christ our Lord himself, to whom be glory and power with the Father and the Holy Spirit now and always and to the ages of the ages. Amen."

19

On the fifth day, as that was a Sunday when the one of blessed memory customarily presided, after the same catechesis had been read, what happened? He gained some strength in his eagerness, since, as the saying goes, *labor bestows health and eagerness raises the dead.* And since a celebration of the divine liturgy was also scheduled, which that thrice-blessed one always greatly desired, he entered the sanctuary to worship the Lord in purity and to offer the bloodless sacrifice. After he had done this, had distributed the elements to those who were present, and had performed everything most properly, he took his seat in the refectory

παραγενομένων πατέρων καὶ ὁμολογητῶν, καὶ φιλοφρόνως ξενίσας, τὰ τῆς μεταστάσεως διὰ πάντων καὶ προσφθεγγόμενος καὶ ὁμιλῶν τούτοις, παρεπέμπετο. Καί γε τοῦτο οὐχὶ τηνικαῦτα μόνον, ὡς ἴστε, ἀλλ᾽ ὅλος ὁ χρόνος τῆς μακαρίας τοῦ ἀοιδίμου ζωῆς οὐδὲν πλέον ἦν ἢ μελέτη θανάτου καὶ *ἐπιθυμία τοῦ ἀναλῦσαι καὶ σὺν Χριστῷ εἶναι.*

20

Ἐξ ἧς μνήμης ὁπόσος αὐτῷ καὶ ἡλίκος ὁ καθεκάστην ἀγών, καὶ τὰ διὰ σπουδῆς κατορθούμενα ἰδίᾳ τε καὶ κοινῇ, τί δεῖ καὶ λέγειν, αὐτῶν τούτων μονονουχὶ τῶν ἔργων βοώντων; Νυνὶ δὲ πολλῷ πλέον, ὡς μικροῦ ἐνιαυτὸς παρίππευσεν, ὁπηνίκα τελείως πρὸς τὴν ἔξοδον παρεσκεύαστο· ὡς πολλάκις καὶ ἐπὶ συχνῷ παρεδρεύοντί μοι αὐτῷ, ὁ πάντα βουλήσει Θεοῦ καὶ δρῶν καὶ λέγων ὅμως Χριστομιμήτῳ ταπεινώσει οὐκ ἀπηξίου προσφθέγγεσθαι καὶ τῇ ἡμετέρᾳ ταπεινώσει ἐν τούτοις· "Μή τι ἐνελίπομεν ἄρα τῶν ὀφειλόντων λαληθῆναι κατὰ τὸ ἀναγκαῖον; Μή τι τῶν κεχρεωστημένων ἡμῖν παρημέληται;" Οὕτω καὶ περὶ τῶν τοιούτων ἡ μακαρία ἐκείνη καὶ πολυμέριμνος ψυχὴ ἠγωνίζετο καὶ ἐφρόντιζεν.

where he welcomed some of the fathers and confessors who had come. After he had entertained them in a hospitable fashion, and had addressed and conversed with them in detail about his departure, he sent them on their way. And that was not the only time, as you know, but rather the whole of the famous one's blessed lifetime was nothing more than a meditation on death and *a desire to depart and be with Christ.*

20

After that recollection, what else do I need to say about the extent and magnitude of his daily struggle and what he managed to do in his enthusiasm, both in private and in public, when his actions almost speak for themselves? But as it is, there is much more. As he had passed almost the whole year completely prepared for his death, and as I would frequently sit for a long time beside him, Theodore, who did and said everything by the will of God and yet with a humility that imitated Christ, would condescend to address my humble self with these words: "We didn't leave out anything that ought to have been said, did we? We haven't neglected any of our debts, have we?" Thus, that blessed and careful soul would struggle and be concerned even with such things.

21

Καὶ μετὰ τὴν ἑξῆς (ἦν δὲ Τρίτη τῶν ἡμερῶν ἐν ᾗ ἐφέστηκεν ἡ μνήμη τοῦ μεγάλου Ὁμολογητοῦ Παύλου), ὡς φιλόθεος καὶ φιλάγιος τὸ ἀποστολικὸν πληρῶν καὶ αὖθις, ἐκτελεῖ τὴν θείαν μυσταγωγίαν, τὴν τοῦ ἁγίου μνήμην ἀφοσιούμενος. Καὶ ἑσπέρας ἤδη καταλαβούσης, πλεῖστα καὶ ὁμιλήσας καὶ προσφθεγξάμενος τοῖς συγκαθεζομένοις αὐτῷ κατὰ τὸ εἰωθός, κἀκεῖθεν ἐπὶ τὸ κελλίον αὐτοῦ εἰσελθών, καὶ τὴν συνήθη ψαλμῳδίαν καὶ τὰς εὐχὰς ἐκτετελεκώς, ἀνέπεσεν ἐπὶ τοῦ κλινιδίου. Καὶ περὶ ὥραν τετάρτην ὑπεισῆλθεν αὐτῷ ὁ κατὰ συνήθειαν πόνος, καὶ δὴ φωνήσας τινὰ τῶν πρὸ τῆς κέλλης αὐτοῦ καθευδόντων ἀδελφῶν, ἀπαγγέλλει αὐτῷ τὸ ἄλγημα καὶ τῇ αὐτῇ συνδρομὴ τῶν ἀδελφῶν γέγονε. Καὶ δισημερεύσας μετριοπόνως, τῇ ἑξῆς προσκαλεῖται τοὺς παρόντας ἅπαντας καὶ τοὺς ἐξιτηρίους ποιεῖται λόγους. Τίνες δ' οὗτοι; Οὓς ἑκάστοτε οὐ διέλειπε καὶ λαλεῖν καὶ ὑπομιμνήσκειν νύκτωρ τε καὶ μεθ' ἡμέραν, τοῦτο δὲ κατ' ἐξαίρετον· "Ἀδελφοὶ καὶ πατέρες, τὸ ποτήριον τοῦτο κοινόν ἐστιν, ὃ ἔπιον πάντες οἱ πατέρες ἡμῶν. Τὸ αὐτὸ πίνοιμι κἀγὼ καὶ πορεύομαι πρὸς τοὺς πατέρας μου. Βλέπετε τὴν παραθήκην ἣν παρεθέμην ὑμῖν· τὴν πίστιν ὑμῶν φυλάξατε ἀσάλευτον καὶ τὸν βίον ἀκηλίδωτον. Πλέον γάρ τι λέγειν οὐκ ἔχω, διὰ τὸ πάντα τὰ ὀφείλοντα καὶ προαναγγεῖλαι ὑμῖν καὶ προδιδάξαι," προσθεὶς καὶ τοῦτο ὁ τῆς εἰρήνης ὄντως καὶ τῆς ἀγάπης υἱός· "Τῷ δεσπότῃ ἡμῶν, τῷ ἀρχιερεῖ, τὸν δι' αἰδοῦς καὶ τιμῆς

21

Then, after the following day (it was the Tuesday when the commemoration of Paul the great Confessor occurred), as a lover of God and of the saints, Theodore again carried out apostolic practice and celebrated the divine liturgy, hallowing the memory of the saint. Since evening had already come, after he had discussed very many topics and addressed those who were sitting with him as was his custom, he then went into his cell, performed his usual psalmody and prayers, and lay down on his little bed. Around the fourth hour of the night the usual pain came over him and, calling out to one of the brethren who were sleeping in front of his cell, he told him of his suffering and the brethren gathered. After he had spent two days after that in moderate pain, on the following day he summoned all who were present and delivered his parting words. What were they? Those that he always unfailingly said and reminded us of day and night, but this in particular: "Brothers and fathers, this is the common cup which all our fathers drank. May I too drink the same cup as I journey to my fathers. Take care of the legacy that I have entrusted to you; keep your faith unshaken and your life spotless. I have nothing more to say, because I have already told and taught you all that is necessary." The true son of peace and love added this also, "Give my reverent and honored greetings to our master the archbishop, to the

ἀσπασμὸν ἐξ ἐμοῦ ἀπονείματε, τοῖς λοιποῖς πατράσιν, ἱεράρχαις τε καὶ ἱερεῦσιν, τοῖς Χριστοῦ ὁμολογηταῖς τοῖς διὰ Κύριον δεδιωγμένοις, ἅπασι τοῖς ἀδελφοῖς, φίλοις τε καὶ γνωρίμοις, καὶ τοῖς ἐν τῷ ὑπὲρ τῆς πίστεως ἀγῶνι συγκεκοπιακόσιν ἡμῖν, μικροῖς τε καὶ μεγάλοις."

22

Ἀλλ' εὖγε τῆς μακαρίας ἐκείνης καὶ φιλαρέτου ψυχῆς, ἥτις οὐδὲ ἐπ' αὐτῆς τῆς ὥρας ἕτερόν τι ἢ ἐμελέτα, ἢ ἠγωνίζετο, ἢ μόνον τὸ τῷ Θεῷ ἀρέσαι καὶ Θεὸν δοξάσαι. Ἀμέλει ἐρωτηθεὶς παρὰ τῆς ταπεινώσεως ἡμῶν περὶ τῶν ἐν ἐπιτιμίοις ὄντων ἀδελφῶν ἢ καὶ ξένων, τί ἂν κελεύοι, ἀπεκρίθη ὁ ὄντως φιλοσυμπαθὴς καὶ Χριστομίμητος ἰατρός· "Ὁ Κύριος συγχωρήσει πᾶσιν," ἐπενεγκὼν πρὸς πίστωσιν, ὁ ὡς ἀληθῶς ἀξιόπιστος, καὶ τὴν τοῦ Θεοῦ διὰ τοῦ θεράποντος αὐτοῦ Μωϋσέως διαταγήν· καὶ ἐκ τρίτου κατασφραγίσας, ἐπηύξατο εἰπών· "*Ὁ Κύριος τῆς εἰρήνης* ἔσται μετὰ τοῦ πνεύματος ὑμῶν," καὶ ἀσπασάμενος τοὺς παρόντας ἅπαντας, διέμεινεν οὕτως. Καὶ τὴν αὐτὴν διαδίδοται ἡ ἀκοή, καὶ παραγίνεται λαοῦ πλῆθος οὐκ ὀλίγον. Καὶ οὕτω δισημερεύσας πάλιν ἕκαστον τῶν ἐρχομένων κατασφραγίζων καὶ εὐλογῶν καὶ κατασπαζόμενος καὶ ἠρέμα προσφθεγγόμενος καὶ ἐπευχόμενος ὁ τρισμακάριος, ἀπέλυεν ἐν εἰρήνῃ, ἑκάστῳ μνήμης ἄξιόν τι καὶ σωτηρίας ἐφόδιον καταλιμπάνων.

other fathers, to the bishops and priests, to the confessors of Christ who have been persecuted for the Lord's sake, to all my brethren, friends and acquaintances, and to those, great and small, who labored along with me in the struggle for the faith."

22

Fine words from that blessed soul which loved virtue and which even at that very moment was taking thought and striving for nothing except how to please and glorify God! When he was asked by my humble self what command he would give concerning the brethren and strangers who were in penance, the truly compassionate doctor and imitator of Christ replied, "The Lord will forgive them all," and, as a truly trustworthy man he cited God's regulation given through his servant Moses as confirmation. After making the sign of the cross three times, he blessed them, saying, "*The Lord of peace* be with your spirit," and, after he had embraced all those who were present, he remained in that state. That same day the news spread, and a great crowd of people arrived. So, the thrice-blessed one spent two more days marking each of those who came with the sign of the cross; blessing, kissing, quietly addressing them, and praying, he dismissed them in peace, leaving each with something memorable and a resource for their salvation.

23

Καὶ τῇ Κυριακῇ ἐν ᾗ ἡ μνήμη ἐξετελεῖτο τοῦ μεγαλομάρτυρος Μηνᾶ, ἐψαλκὼς τὰ συνήθη, εἶθ' οὕτως μετασχὼν τῶν ἁγιασμάτων καὶ κατὰ τὸ εἰωθὸς ἐπαλειψάμενος τῶν ζωοποιῶν ἐκείνων καὶ κατασφραγισάμενος, ὑψοῦ τὰς χεῖρας ἄρας καὶ προσευξάμενος, περὶ ὥραν ἕκτην αἰσθόμενος ἑαυτὸν ἠτονηκότα, προστάσσει ἠρέμα κηραψίαν γενέσθαι· κἀντεῦθεν προσβάλλομεν τὴν ψαλμῳδίαν καὶ ἐν τῷ στίχῳ, ἐν ᾧ φησιν, "*Εἰς τὸν αἰῶνα οὐ μὴ ἐπιλάθωμαι τῶν δικαιωμάτων σου, ὅτι ἐν αὐτοῖς ἔζησάς με,*" ἐνδιατριβόντων ἡμῶν, παρέδωκε τὴν μακαρίαν καὶ καθαρὰν αὐτοῦ ψυχὴν τοῖς ἁγίοις ἀγγέλοις. Οὕτω μὲν οὖν ὡς ἐν συντομίᾳ ἡ τοῦ τρισμάκαρος κοίμησις καὶ τοῦ ἀθλητικοῦ δρόμου τὸ πέρας· καὶ αὕτη ἡ τῶν πολλῶν ἀγώνων καὶ πόνων καὶ ἱδρώτων εἰς αἰῶνα αἰῶνος κατάπαυσις.

24

Ἀλλ' ὤ, πῶς ὑμῖν ἀδακρυτὶ τὰ ἑξῆς ὑπ' ὄψιν ἀγάγω, πυρπολούμενος τοῖς λογισμοῖς, καὶ οἱονεὶ ἐξεστηκὼς τῇ καρδίᾳ; Καί μοι δότε μικρὸν ἐνδιατρίψαι τῷ διηγήματι. *Ἔκειτο οὖν* ὁ τρισμάκαρ (*καλὸν γὰρ* μηδὲ τοῦτο παραδραμεῖν, *ὥσπερ τι ξένον θέαμα), αἰδέσιμος τῇ ὄψει, ἀγγελοειδὴς τῷ σχήματι, τῆς ἐνδημησάσης πρὸς Κύριον ψυχῆς ὥσπερ*

23

On the Sunday when the commemoration of the great martyr Menas was being celebrated, after he had chanted the customary psalms and then partaken of the sacraments, Theodore also anointed himself with those life-giving elements as was the custom, crossed himself, raised his hands, and prayed. About the sixth hour, when he realized that he was exhausted, he quietly commanded that candles should be lit. At that point we started the psalm singing and as we lingered at the verse, in which it says "*I will never forget your precepts, for by them you have given me life,*" he committed his blessed and pure soul to the holy angels. Such was then, in brief, the death of the thrice-blessed one and the completion of the champion's race; and that was the eternal repose from his many struggles, labors, and exertions.

24

But oh, how can I reveal what followed without tears, inflamed by my thoughts and, as it were, distraught in my heart? Allow me to spend a little time on the description. *So the* thrice-blessed *one lay there (for it would not be good* to pass over this *like some strange spectacle), venerable in his appearance and angelic in form, since his soul was at home with the Lord and*

τινὰς φωτοειδεῖς ἀκτῖνας ἐναπομαξαμένης τῷ ἱερῷ σώματι, μεθ' οὗ καὶ ἐφ' ᾧ λελάτρευκε τῇ ἁγίᾳ Τριάδι. Προστέθειται ἐξαπίνης τοῖς προλαβοῦσι πλῆθος ἕτερον, *ὁμοῦ μὲν μοναστῶν ὁμοῦ δὲ καὶ μιγάδων, πολὺ ὅτι μάλιστα* καὶ τῶν ἐξόχων, μεθ' ὧν καὶ ἱεράρχαι καὶ ἱερεῖς, ἐπιφερόμενος ἕκαστος τὰ τῆς μακαρίας ἐκείνης κηδείας καὶ ταφῆς ἁρμόδια, οἱ μὲν κηροὺς ἐξάσπρους καὶ πολυτίμους, ὁ δὲ σινδόνα πεποικιλμένην, ἕτερος καταπέτασμα περιπόρφυρον, καὶ ἄλλοι σκεύη ἀργυρᾶ καὶ χρυσάργυρα καὶ ἠλεκτροειδῆ, καὶ οἱ μὲν ἀρώματα καὶ θυμιάματα, καὶ ἄλλος ἄλλο, καὶ ἕτερος ἕτερον, ἵνα μὴ μακρηγορῶ, πάντες δ' οὖν ὅμως πίστει σπεύδοντες ἄξιόν τι μνήμης τῷ ἱερῷ λειψάνῳ προσοῖσαι καὶ τῷ τιμίῳ τάφῳ ἐπαποθέσθαι. Γέγονε δὲ καὶ χειμὼν κατὰ τὸ νυχθήμερον ἐκεῖνο σφοδρός, ὡς πάλαι ἐπὶ τοῦ μεγάλου Πέτρου Ἀλεξανδρείας. Καὶ ἦν ἰδεῖν ὑπερφυὲς τὸ γιγνόμενον. Πάντες γὰρ κατεφρόνησαν καὶ θαλάσσης καὶ ἀέρος καὶ ἐπικλύσεως ποταμῶν, καὶ πειρασμοῦ τῶν κρατούντων, καὶ εἴ τινος ἄλλου, δεύτερα πάντα ἡγησάμενοι, ἀλλὰ καὶ δοῦλοι δεσποτῶν θεραπείαν, καὶ γεηπόνοι τὴν ἐργασίαν, καὶ ἐπίτροποι τὴν ἐπιστασίαν, καὶ πλωτῆρες καὶ ἔμποροι τὴν ἐμπορίαν, καὶ ὁδῖται τὴν οἰκείαν ὁδόν, καὶ *περιεκέχυντο εἰς αὐτὸν ὡς εἰς ἱερὸν κειμήλιον* ἀποβλέποντες, *ἢ μᾶλλον οἰκειότερον εἰπεῖν, ὡς ἔμπνουν καὶ φωνεῖν δυνάμενον.*

had impressed, as it were, some luminous rays on *his holy body with which and in which he had served the holy Trinity. Suddenly* another crowd, *partly of monks and partly of laymen,* joined those who had arrived earlier. It consisted of *very many* prominent people, among whom were bishops and priests, each one bringing items appropriate for that blessed funeral and burial: some brought very expensive white candles, one brought an embroidered winding sheet, another a purple covering, others vessels of silver, silver gilt, and electrum, some brought spices and incense, and, to cut a long story short, one brought one thing and one another; but all were thus striving with faith to bring something that was a worthy memorial for the holy corpse and place it on the precious tomb. But a violent storm took place that night and the following day, as occurred long ago in the time of the great Peter of Alexandria, and then one could see an extraordinary phenomenon, for everyone disregarded the sea, the weather, and overflowing rivers, as well as temptations by the rulers and whatever else, thinking all these things of secondary importance. Also, slaves abandoned the service of their masters, farmers their work, guardians their responsibility, sailors and merchants their merchandise, and travelers their own journeys, and *flooded around* him *as though* gazing at *a holy treasure, or rather, to put it more appropriately, as though at one inspired and able to speak.*

25

Καὶ *οὕτως σὺν ψαλμῳδίαις* καὶ φωταψίαις *ταῖς καθηκούσαις*, παννυχίσι τε *καὶ ἐπικλήσεσιν* ἱεραῖς, τῇ ἑξῆς κατὰ τὸ σύνηθες λειτουργήσαντες, περὶ ὥραν πέμπτην *παρεδόθη τῷ* ἱερῷ *τάφῳ*, ἤτοι γλωσσοκόμῳ, οὐκ ἀκαματί, οὐδ' οὐ μὴν ἀπονητί, διὰ τὸ ἐπιπεπτωκέναι τὸ τοῦ λαοῦ πλῆθος ἆραί τι τῶν ἱερῶν ἐνταφίων, ἢ τοῦ τιμίου λειψάνου. Παρεδόθη δ' οὖν ὅμως, καὶ ἀπετέθη ἐν τῷ οἰκείῳ δωματίῳ, *καθ' ὃν τόπον εἰώθει ὁ* τρισμακάριος τὰς ἱερὰς γράφειν βίβλους καὶ *λειτουργεῖν Κυρίῳ.* Τοῦτο γὰρ ἦν αὐτῷ ἀποστολικῶς καὶ μετὰ διωκτικὴν κάκωσιν καὶ γῆρας ἐργόχειρον. *Καί γε προσετέθη ὁ πατὴρ τοῖς πατράσιν·* ὁ ἱερεὺς τοῖς ἱεράρχαις καὶ πρὸ τῆς χρίσεως· *ὁ ὁμολογητὴς τοῖς ὁμολογηταῖς·* τοῖς μάρτυσιν ὁ προαιρετικὸς μάρτυς· *ὁ διδάσκαλος τοῖς διδασκάλοις·* τοῖς κήρυξιν ἡ μεγάλη τῆς ἀληθείας σάλπιγξ. *Προσθείην δ' ἂν καὶ ταῦτα· ὁ ἐγκρατὴς τοῖς ἐγκρατέσιν, ὁ ἁγνὸς τοῖς φιλάγνοις, ὁ φιλόξενος τοῖς φιλοξένοις· ὁ μέτριος τοῖς μετριόφροσιν· ὁ πάντα τοῖς πᾶσιν εὖ γεγονὼς καθ' ὅσον οἷόν τε* θεοπρεπῶς, *ἵνα τοὺς πάντας ἢ τοὺς πλείονας κερδήσῃ*, ἀποστολικοῖς κατορθώμασιν ἐπερειδόμενος.

25

And so, *with the singing of psalms* and *the proper* kindling of lights, with vigils *and* holy *invocations,* and after the usual celebration of the liturgy on the following day, about the fifth hour *he was consigned to his* holy *tomb,* that is, a coffin, not without considerable effort and even difficulty because of the crowd of people surging forward to take some piece of the holy shroud or of the precious corpse. Nevertheless, he was consigned and buried in his own cell, *where* the thrice-blessed one *had been accustomed* to write his holy books and *serve the Lord;* for, like an apostle, that was his handiwork, even after the ill-treatment during his persecution and in his old age. *The father was added to the fathers,* the priest to the bishops even before his anointing, *the confessor to the confessors,* the voluntary martyr to the martyrs, *the teacher to the teachers,* and the great trumpet of truth to the preachers. *I would add this as well: the temperate one was added to the ranks of the temperate, the chaste one to lovers of chastity, the hospitable one to the hospitable, the modest one to the modestly minded,* this man who, *in everything, was good to all men as far as possible* in a way worthy of God, *so that he might gain all or most of them, being firmly supported by his apostolic achievements.*

26

Καὶ νῦν αὐτὸς μέν, ἀποστολικὸν *ἐκτετελεκὼς δρόμον*, ἔστιν οὐρανοὺς ἐμβατεύων καὶ ἀγγέλων συμπανηγυρίζων χορείαις *ἐν τόπῳ σκηνῆς θαυμαστῆς*, ἐν ἤχῳ ἑορταζόντων ἐν Κυρίῳ ἀπολαύων τῶν αἰωνίων ἀγαθῶν· κἀκεῖθεν ἡμᾶς ἐποπτεύων ἵλεως, τὰς ὑπὲρ ἡμῶν τῶν ταπεινῶν λιτὰς τῷ Κυρίῳ προσφέρει θερμότερον. Ἡμεῖς δὲ *οἱ ταπεινοί*, τῇ μὲν ἐλπίδι μεταβαλλόμενοι, φέρωμεν εὐχαρίστως τὸ λυπηρόν, τὴν ἀοίδιμον ἐκείνην φθεγγόμενοι φωνήν· "*Ὁ Κύριος ἔδωκεν, ὁ Κύριος ἀφείλατο, ὡς τῷ Κυρίῳ ἔδοξεν, οὕτως καὶ ἐγένετο.*" Εἴ τι γὰρ γέγονε, θελήματι Κυρίου γέγονε, τοῦ συμφερόντως πάντα οἰκονομοῦντος, "*τῷ δὲ βουλήματι αὐτοῦ,*" ὥς φησιν ὁ θεῖος ἀπόστολος, "*τίς ἀνθέστηκεν;*" Πλὴν ὅτι καὶ τὸ τῆς φύσεως πανθάνομεν, καὶ *ὀρφανικῶς ἀποδυρόμενοι, τὸν ὡς ἀληθῶς καὶ* φιλόθεον καὶ φιλότεκνον πατέρα διεξερχόμεθα· καί γε μάλιστα ὁρῶντες καθεκάστην, καθάπερ πτηνοὺς τοὺς ἀδελφοὺς ἡμῶν ἄλλους ἀλλαχόθεν, τοὺς μὲν ἐγγύθεν, τοὺς δὲ πόρρωθεν προστρέχοντας τῷ πατρικῷ τάφῳ, ἀμειδεῖς τῷ προσώπῳ, ἐρρικνωμένους, αὐχμηρούς, δακρυρροοῦντας, συστρεφομένους καὶ ἐκ βάθους ποτνιωμένους ὡς καὶ ἐξ αὐτῆς ὄψεως γνωρίζεσθαι πᾶσι τὸν τρόπον, ἀλλὰ μὴν καὶ ἑτέρους πλείονας τῶν πατρικῶν ἀπολελαυκότας εὐεργεσιῶν κατ' ἀμφότερα. Ὑμεῖς δέ, ὦ μακαριώτατοι, τὰ ἴσα ἢ καὶ πλείονα εἴποιτε, ὡς ἀπολειφθέντες καὶ τῆς ἐπὶ τῇ μεταστάσει τοῦ παμμάκαρος αὐτοψίας, καὶ ἀποκλαιόμενοι, καὶ ἀποδυρόμενοι. Ἀλλ' οὖν

26

Now, *having completed* the apostolic *race,* he has entered into heaven, keeping festival with companies of angels *in a place of wondrous habitation,* and enjoying the eternal blessings to the sound of those celebrating in the Lord. From there he graciously watches over us, fervently offering his supplications to the Lord on behalf of our humble selves. And may *we humble ones,* transformed by hope, bear our grief with thanksgiving, uttering those well-known words of scripture, "*The Lord gave, the Lord has taken away; as the Lord decided, so it has come to pass.*" For if something has happened, it has happened by the will of the Lord, who manages all things for our benefit, as the holy apostle says, "*Who can resist his will?*" Though I naturally suffer *as I mourn like an orphan,* I am describing in detail *our truly* devout father who loved his children, especially since each day I see our brethren, rushing as though on wings, from different places, some from nearby, others from far away, to our father's tomb with somber expressions, worn out, unkempt, streaming with tears, subdued and pleading desperately, so that anyone can tell the state they are in, just from the sight of them; yet I see others too in greater numbers enjoying our father's benefactions in both spheres. You, most blessed ones, would say the same or even more, since you were deprived of seeing the death of the all-blessed one with your own eyes and are weeping and lamenting. But be consoled and cheered by

διὰ τῶν ἀκουσθέντων καὶ ἐλπιζομένων καὶ παρηγορήθητε καὶ ἀναψύξατε, καὶ πρὸς τὸ ἑξῆς ἔχεσθε τοῦ καλοῦ ὑμῶν δρόμου ἀνολιγώρως, εὐχόμενοι καὶ ὑπὲρ τῆς ταπεινώσεως ἡμῶν ἀδιαλείπτως, ἐπεὶ καὶ ἡμεῖς ὑπὲρ τῆς τιμιότητος ὑμῶν, εἰ καὶ τολμηρῶς, πᾶσαν ὑμῶν τὴν ἁγίαν συνοδίαν μετὰ καὶ τῶν λοιπῶν ἀδελφικῶς προσαγορεύομεν δι᾽ ὑμῶν. Οἱ σὺν ἡμῖν πλεῖστα προσαγορεύουσι τὴν ἁγιωσύνην ὑμῶν.

what you have heard and are hoping for, and in future may you not waver in maintaining your good course, and also praying unceasingly for my humble self as I also do for your dear selves, though presumptuously. I send brotherly greetings to all your holy community and everyone else through you; those with me send very many greetings to your holinesses.

TRANSLATION AND BURIAL OF THE REMAINS OF THEODORE OF STOUDIOS AND JOSEPH OF THESSALONIKE

Εἰς τὴν ἀνακομιδὴν καὶ κατάθεσιν τῶν λειψάνων τοῦ ὁσίου πατρὸς ἡμῶν καὶ ὁμολογητοῦ Θεοδώρου· ἐν ταὐτῷ δὲ καὶ μνήμη πρὸς τὸ τέλος τοῦ λόγου περὶ τῆς καταθέσεως τῶν εὑρεθέντων λειψάνων τοῦ ὁσίου πατρὸς ἡμῶν Ἰωσὴφ ἀρχιεπισκόπου γενομένου Θεσσαλονίκης.

1

Εἰκότως ἄν τις ἡμῖν ἐγκαλέσειεν, εἴ γε σιωπῇ τὴν τοῦ θείου πατρὸς καὶ ὁμολογητοῦ παραδράμοιμεν ἀνακομιδὴν καὶ τὴν τοῦ ἱεροῦ λειψάνου κατάθεσιν· εἰ γὰρ αὐτὸς οὕτω ζήλου καὶ παρρησίας εἶχεν ὡς καὶ κινδύνους καὶ ὑπερορίας καὶ πάντα ἑλέσθαι παθεῖν, πόσῳ μᾶλλον ἡμᾶς ζῆλον ἔχειν εἰκὸς λέγειν τε τὰ ἐκείνου καὶ διηγεῖσθαι καὶ ψυχαῖς φιλοθέοις χαρίζεσθαι; Τί γὰρ καὶ μεῖζον εἰς ὠφέλειαν ἔσται ἢ καὶ πρὸς ἡδονὴν χαριέστερον, ἀλλ' ἢ τηλικούτου μεμνῆσθαι ἀνδρός, καὶ ἆθλα αὐτοῦ καὶ ἀγῶνας διεξιέναι, καὶ σῶμα ἐκεῖνο τὸ πολλοῖς ἐνιδρῶσαν πόνοις, ὕμνοις σεμνύνειν καὶ εὐφημίαις γεραίρειν ταῖς κρείττοσι; Πάντως δὲ ὥσπερ ἐν τῇ ἀνακομιδῇ τούτου καὶ καταθέσει πολλή τις ἦν καὶ πολυπληθὴς ἡ πανήγυρις, οὕτω κἂν τῷ λόγῳ καὶ τῇ ἀναμνήσει τῶν γεγενημένων ἴση ἔσται καὶ ἐφάμιλλος ἡ

On the translation and burial of the remains of our saintly father and confessor Theodore; at the same time also at the end of the account a record of the burial of the remains which were discovered of our saintly father Joseph who was archbishop of Thessalonike.

1

Someone would probably find fault with me if I were to pass over in silence the return of our holy father and confessor and the burial of his holy remains. For if he possessed such zeal and boldness of speech as to choose to suffer dangers, banishments, and everything else, how much more reasonable is it that I should be zealous enough to describe what happened to him and do a favor to souls that love God? For what will be of greater benefit or provide more gracious pleasure than to recall such a great man, recount his contests and struggles, and honor with hymns and celebrate with the greatest acclamations that body which labored in many hardships? And, in the same way that there was a large and crowded festival at this man's return and burial, so too, no doubt, in my discourse and recollection of what took place, there will be just as much joy on the part of both

εὐφροσύνη μοναστῶν ὁμοῦ καὶ μιγάδων συνηδομένων καὶ γλώσσῃ εὐφήμῳ ᾀδόντων τὰ χαριστήρια.

2 Οὐκοῦν μοι διὰ ταῦτα καὶ τῆς διηγήσεως ἐχέσθω ὁ λόγος καὶ μνήμην τῶν παρόντων ποιείσθω, ὡς ἂν καὶ χρόνον τῆς ἱερᾶς μάθοιμεν ἀνακομιδῆς καὶ ὅπως ἄρα καὶ παρὰ τίνων ὁ πολύολβος οὗτος θησαυρὸς τῷ ἰδίῳ ἐναπετέθη φροντιστηρίῳ, πλοῦτος ἄσυλος τοῖς χρῄζουσιν ἀποκείμενος. Καὶ ἐχρῆν δήπου τὸν λόγον τούτων εὐθὺς ἅψασθαι ὧν καὶ μνησθῆναι προέθετο· ἀλλ' ἵνα μὴ δόξῃ τοῖς τελευταίοις μόνον κεχρημένος, τῶν δ' ἄλλων οὐδενὸς μεμνημένος δι' ὧν ὁ πολὺς ἐκεῖνος βίος καὶ τὰ παλαίσματα, ὀλίγα πρῶτον τούτων ἀναλαβὼν καὶ οἷς ἂν μάλιστα λεγομένοις οἱ ἀκούοντες συνησθεῖεν, οὕτω χρήσεται τοῖς παροῦσιν, ὡς ἂν καὶ καθ' εἱρμὸν ἔσται βαίνων ὁ λόγος, καὶ ἑαυτῷ δόξῃ πληρέστατος.

2

Ὁ θεῖος τοιγαροῦν οὗτος καὶ μέγας Θεόδωρος—ἵν' ἐντεῦθεν ἄρξωμαι—ὁ τὴν κλῆσιν λαχὼν τῇ πολιτείᾳ κατάλληλον, τὸ θεοδώρητον ὄντως χρῆμα καὶ πολυέραστον, γονέων μὲν ἔφυ ἐπισήμων καὶ διαφανῶν καὶ τὰς πρώτας ἐχόντων παρὰ βασιλέων τιμάς, πατρίδα δὲ τὴν εὐδαίμονα ταύτην ἔσχε Κωνσταντινούπολιν. Οὗτος παιδείαν ἐκ νέου τήν τε ἡμετέραν καὶ τὴν θύραθεν καθ' ὅσον ἐχρῆν

monks and lay people, rejoicing and reverently singing their thanksgivings.

So, for those reasons my account should keep closely to 2
the narrative and create a recollection from those who were present, so that we may learn when his holy return occurred and how and by whom that very rich treasure was laid to rest in his own monastery, an inviolable source of wealth stored up for those in need. I suppose my account should perhaps have immediately concerned itself with those things that it set itself to recall, but, so that it may not seem only to be concerning itself with the final events and recalling none of the others which that great life and its struggles involved, my account will first refer to a few of these, especially the ones that, when mentioned, will bring joy to those who hear it, and in the same measure will be useful to those who were there, so that, as my account proceeds sequentially, it may in itself seem very complete.

2

So then, that holy and great Theodore—that I may begin from here—who possessed a name which corresponded to his conduct, for that really was something God-given and very desirable, was born of notable and illustrious parents who held high offices from emperors; and he had this fortunate city of Constantine as his home. From childhood Theodore combined Christian and secular education as far as

συναγηοχώς, καὶ ἀρετὴν πρὸ τῶν ἄλλων ὥσπερ τινὰ κρηπῖδα τοῦ βίου βαλών, πλοῦτον μὲν καὶ δόξαν καὶ πάντα ὅσα τῆς κάτω περιφορᾶς θᾶττον καταλιμπάνει, βίον δ' ἀναλαμβάνει τὸν μοναδικὸν καὶ ἡσύχιον, ἄφθαρτα φθαρτῶν ἀνταμείβων καὶ τῶν ἀστάτων τὰ μένοντα ἀλλαττόμενος.

2 Ἐπεὶ δὲ ὁ τηνικαῦτα καιρὸς πολλὴν ἐδίδου τοῖς εἰκονομάχοις τὴν παρρησίαν, ἅτε τοῦ πονηροῦ δόγματος μικροῦ κατὰ πάντων λυττήσαντος, αὐτὸς ταῦθ' ὁρῶν οὐκ ἐν τῇ Βυζαντίδι, (ὅτι μηδ' ἐξὸν τούτῳ), ἐκτὸς δ' ἐκείνης καὶ πόρρωθεν μετὰ γεννητόρων καὶ συγγενῶν ἄλλων, οἳ πάντες τούτῳ συνείποντο, τὸ τῆς ἀσκήσεως πήγνυσι καταγώγιον· Σακκουδίων ἐκαλεῖτο τὸ τῆς ἀρετῆς αὐτοῖς φροντιστήριον, ἐν ᾧ καὶ κάλλιστα διαπρέψας καὶ πεῖραν τῆς ἀρετῆς δεδωκώς, ποιμὴν ἐκείνων καθίσταται μετὰ ταῦτα· εἶθ' ἅμα καὶ πρὸς ἱερωσύνην ἀνάγεται, Πλάτωνος τοῦ πρὸς μητρὸς αὐτῷ θείου πρὸς ἀμφότερα πείσαντος, μᾶλλον δὲ πειθοῖ βίαν συμμίξαντος. Οὗ ἆθλα εὐθὺς καὶ παλαίσματα, καὶ πρὸς βασιλεῖς ἀγωνίσματα, ὅτι μὴ τῷ ὀρθῷ λόγῳ συνέβαινον, εἶθ' ὑπερορίαι καὶ καθείρξεις, καὶ πρὸ τούτων, οἴμοι, πληγαὶ καὶ τοῦ σώματος αἰκίαι καὶ μάστιγες· τί γὰρ ἄν τις εἴποι χρονίαν παράτασιν τῶν δεινῶν καὶ σπάνιν τῶν ἀναγκαίων καὶ στέρησιν, οἷς πᾶσιν ὁ γενναῖος ἐνεκαρτέρει;

was necessary and set virtue before all else as a foundation for his life. Quickly abandoning wealth and honor and everything of the lower sphere, he took up the monastic life of tranquility, exchanging what is corruptible for the incorruptible and adopting what is abiding in place of the ephemeral.

This was a time when great freedom was being allowed to 2
those who fought against icons and, since the evil doctrine raged against almost everyone, when Theodore saw this, he set up a place to live the ascetic life with his parents and other relatives, all of whom accompanied him, not in the city of Byzantion (because for him that was impossible), but far away and outside it. Their school of virtue was called Sakkoudion, and that was where, after he had greatly distinguished himself and given proof of his virtue, he was later appointed their shepherd; at the same time he was also elevated to the priesthood, in both cases persuaded by Plato, his maternal uncle, or rather through a mixture of force and persuasion. At once Theodore's contests and struggles and his conflicts with emperors who did not comply with the right dogma began; then banishments and imprisonments; and beyond those things, alas, beatings, physical ill-treatment, and whippings. For how could anyone describe the long duration of his sufferings and the scarcity and deprivation of necessities, all of which the noble man endured?

3

Ἐπεὶ δ' οἱ τύραννοι ἐκποδῶν, ἐνδίκως ὑποστάντες τὴν δίκην, καὶ αὐτὸς ἀφίεται τῆς ὑπερορίας, τοῖς φοιτηταῖς αὖθις συνὼν καὶ πρὸς ἀρετὴν ἐπαλείφων καὶ πείθων φέρειν τὰ ἐπίπονα ἀπτοήτως. Ἀμέλει καὶ τὴν ἀνδρείαν αὐτοῦ καὶ τὴν σύνεσιν οἱ ἐπὶ τῶν σκήπτρων καταστάντες ἀγάμενοι, ἐπεὶ καὶ φιλόθεοι οὗτοι καὶ φιλάρετοι, λιπαροῦσι τὸν ὅσιον μὴ μακρὰν καὶ πόρρω τῆς βασιλίδος, ἀλλ' ἐντὸς καὶ παρ' αὐτοῖς ἀναστρέφεσθαι, ὡς ἂν ἐξῇ τούτοις καὶ συχνότερον τοῦτον ὁρᾶν καὶ ὠφελείας τῆς τοῦδε παραπολαύειν.

2 Ὡς καὶ τοῖς κρατοῦσι πεισθείς, τῆς θείας μάλιστα προνοίας τοῦτο οἰκονομούσης, τὸν τοῦ μεγάλου Προδρόμου οἶκον παραλαμβάνει, ναὸν κάλλει διαφέροντα καὶ μεγέθει, ὃν Στούδιος μὲν ὁ ἀπὸ Ῥώμης ἥκων ἀνήγειρεν, εἰς μοναστήριον δὲ ἀπέταξε, κἂν ἡ τῶν εἰκονομάχων δυσσέβεια μοναστὰς πάντας ἐκεῖθεν ἀπήλασε, τῶν ἰδίων ἀπείρξασα καταγωγίων. Ἀλλ' αὐτὸς σπουδὴν ὅτι μάλιστα πλείστην εἰσενεγκών, καὶ τοῦτο μὲν οὓς ἀπὸ Σακκουδίωνος ἐπηγάγετο μοναχούς, τοῦτο δὲ καὶ οὓς ἀλλαχόθεν ἥκοντας ἢ καὶ καρῆναι προθυμουμένους τῷ τόπῳ πάντας ἐπισυνάγων, πλῆθός τε πολυάριθμον ἐκεῖσε συνέλεξε καὶ εἰς μέγα προβῆναι ἀρετῆς τοὺς συνειλεγμένους ἐποίησεν. Ἔνθεν τοι καὶ διαβόητος πᾶσι καὶ περιφανὴς ὁ τόπος ἐτύγχανε, πάντων μικροῦ τῶν ἐν τῇ βασιλίδι τούτῳ φοιτώντων καὶ μοναστὰς τοὺς ἐκεῖ τῆς καλῆς θαυμαζόντων διαγωγῆς καὶ τῆς πολλῆς ἐκείνης ἀσκήσεως.

3

When the tyrants justly suffered judgment and were removed, Theodore too was released from his banishment and once again rejoined his disciples, encouraging them in virtue and persuading them to bear hardships fearlessly. Of course, the rulers, who admired his bravery and intelligence since they too were devout and loved virtue, begged the saintly man not to live far away from the capital, but within it and beside them, so that they could see him more often and benefit from his spiritual support.

As he was persuaded by the rulers, especially since divine 2
providence was bringing this about, Theodore took possession of the house of the great Forerunner, a shrine of extraordinary beauty and size, which Stoudios, who had come from Rome, had constructed and set apart to be a monastery, even though in their impiety the iconoclasts had driven all the monks out of it, barring them from their own cells. But Theodore made every effort, brought in monks from Sakkoudion, those who came from elsewhere, and even men eager to be tonsured, collecting them all together in that place. He assembled a sizable group there and ensured that those who had gathered made great progress in virtue. As a result, the place began to be very well known and spoken of by everyone, with almost everyone in the capital visiting it and both admiring the monks there for their good conduct and the great asceticism they found there.

4

Πλὴν ὁ φθόνος καὶ οἱ τὴν ἀρχὴν πάλιν πεπιστευμένοι, δύστροποι ὄντες καὶ περὶ τὸν βίον, εἰ καὶ μὴ περὶ τὴν πίστιν διάστροφοι, πολλὴν ἐπῆγον ταραχὴν τῷ ὁσίῳ, δυσμεναίνοντές τε αὐτῷ, καὶ τῆς παρρησίας καὶ τοῦ ὀρθοῦ βίου ἀπεχθανόμενοι. Ἀμέλει καὶ ὑπερορίᾳ διδόασιν ἔχοντες μὲν οὐδὲν ἐγκαλεῖν, ὅτι δὲ μόνον μὴ τοῖς αὐτῶν λόγοις συμφέροιτο· ἀλλ' οὐκ εἰς μακρὰν τούτων τὰ ἐπίχειρα κομισαμένων τῆς πονηρίας, ἀλλὰ ταχινὴν εὑραμένων τὴν καταστροφήν, πάλιν ἐν γαλήνῃ ὁ ὅσιος, καὶ πάλιν ἔνδον εἶχεν αὐτὸν ἡ περιώνυμος δι' ἐκεῖνον μονὴ τὰ φθάσαντα τῶν κατορθωμάτων τοῖς ἐφεξῆς ἀποκρύπτοντα. Εἶχε γὰρ καὶ τὸν κρατοῦντα πολλὴν αὐτῷ καὶ τὴν αἰδῶ καὶ τὴν τιμὴν ἀπονέμοντα, καὶ τούτου τὴν πολιτείαν ἀποσεμνύνοντα.

5

Ἐπεὶ δὲ καὶ τὴν κακίαν πολυτροπώτατος Ἀρμένιος κατὰ τὰ ἄρρητα τοῦ Θεοῦ κρίματα, οἷά τις Αἰγυπτιακὴ πληγὴ ἢ λαῖλαψ ἀγρία καὶ θύελλα, τῇ ἀρχῇ Ῥωμαίων εἰσέφρησεν, ἅρπαγμα τὴν βασιλείαν ποιησάμενος, τότε καὶ οἱ μείζονες ἀγῶνες καὶ ἡ ἀνδρεία καὶ τὰ παλαίσματα τοῦ πατρὸς παρρησίᾳ τὸν τύραννον βάλλοντος καὶ τὸ ἀναιδὲς

4

But envy and those who had again been entrusted with authority, being spiteful about his way of life even though they were not confused about the faith, brought great trouble on the saintly man, bearing ill will against him and hating him for his boldness of speech and upright life. Accordingly, they consigned him to banishment, though they had no charges to make against him except that he did not agree with their opinions. However, since it was not long before these people reaped the rewards for their wickedness and met with a swift end, once again the saintly man was at peace and once again the monastery that was renowned on his account had him within it, surpassing his previous achievements with those that followed. For even the ruler accorded him great respect and honor and extolled his conduct.

5

But when, in accordance with God's ineffable judgments, an Armenian who was very crafty at wickedness burst in upon the Roman empire like some Egyptian plague or a wild tempest and whirlwind and seized the imperial power, then came our father Theodore's greater struggles, his bravery and contests, as he attacked the tyrant, speaking openly and

αὐτοῦ διελέγχοντος φρόνημα. Ἐτόλμησε γὰρ ὁ δυσώνυμος τὰ θεῖα καθελεῖν ἐκτυπώματα καὶ εἴδωλα τὰς σεπτὰς καλέσαι εἰκόνας ἃς καὶ ἐνεπίμπρα, οἴμοι, ἢ καὶ τιτάνῳ ἐπέχριε διὰ γνώμης σκαιότητα· ἐφ' ᾧ καὶ ὁ ἅγιος περιαλγὴς ἦν, πυρὶ ἀθυμίας καταπιμπράμενος καὶ πόνοις ἀρρήτοις βαλλόμενος· ὅς γε οὐδὲ κίνδυνον τὸ παθεῖν, τὸ δὲ μὴ πολλὰ παθεῖν τοῦθ' ἡγούμενος κίνδυνον. Διά τοι καὶ πλείω τῶν ἄλλων πρός τε ἀγῶνας ἡμιλλήθη καὶ πρὸς τὴν ἐν τοῖς δεινοῖς παρετάξατο καρτερίαν· οὗ καὶ τὴν ἀνδρείαν μὴ φέρων ὁ τύραννος πρῶτα μὲν τῆς Βυζαντίδος περιορίζει καὶ καθείρξει δίδωσι χαλεπωτάτῃ, εἶτα πληγὰς ἐντείνει καὶ μαστίζει σφοδρῶς, σάρκας, οἴμοι, τὰς δροσερὰς κόπτων ἀνηλεῶς καὶ αἱμάτων ῥύακας καταφέρων.

2 Ὧι γε οὐκ ἀπέχρησε διὰ μανίας ὑπερβολὴν ἅπαξ ἢ δὶς ταῖς πληγαῖς καταξάναι, ἀλλὰ καὶ πολλάκις καὶ μεθ' ὑπερβολῆς, ἀμείβων αὐτῷ καὶ τὰς φυλακὰς καὶ ἄλλοτε ἀλλαχοῦ κατακλείων, ὡς ἂν τῷ πολυειδεῖ τῶν κολάσεων ἢ ἀπαγορεύοντα δείξῃ ἢ καὶ σμικρὸν ἐνδίδοντα. Ἀλλ' οὐ μὲν οὖν ὁ γεννάδας ἢ καθυφῆκε τῆς παρρησίας ἢ τὸ φρόνημα ἔλιπεν, ἀλλ' ἔτι μᾶλλον ἠνδρίζετο, βάλλων τε καταφανῶς καὶ τοῖς λόγοις στίζων τὸν τύραννον καὶ ταῖς ὕβρεσι στηλιτεύων. Ὃς καὶ τῶν γινομένων ἕκαστα πυνθανόμενος δεινὸν ἐποιεῖτο καὶ οὐκ ἀνεκτόν, εἰ, μικροῦ πάντων αὐτῷ ἡττημένων καὶ τῷ κράτει δεδουλωμένων, αὐτὸς οὐχ ὅπως ἀήττητος μένοι, ἀλλὰ καὶ τοὺς ἄλλους πείθοι μηδὲν τῶν δεινῶν ὑποπτήσσειν, μηδὲ δόγμασι τούτου τοῖς ἀσεβέσι συμφέρεσθαι. Ἀλλ' ὁ μὲν ἀναιδὴς οὗτος καὶ ἀλαζὼν πολλὰ

refuting his shameless arrogance. For the ill-named Leo dared to destroy the holy images and call the revered icons idols; and, alas, because of the perversity of his mind he even burned them or smeared them with lime. The holy man was deeply pained by this, consumed as he was by the fire of despondency and struck by unspeakable hardships, he who thought that suffering was not the danger, but that danger lay rather in not having much suffering. Consequently, more than the others, he hurried eagerly to the contests and stood ready to endure terrible afflictions. The tyrant could not bear Theodore's bravery, so he first banished him from Byzantion and consigned him to the harshest imprisonment; then he inflicted beatings on him and violently flogged him, pitilessly lacerating his tender flesh, alas, and producing streams of blood.

Because he was so crazy, Leo was not content to lacerate 2
Theodore with beatings once or twice, but many times and excessively; he also kept changing his prisons and shutting him up in different places at different times, so that, by the variety of punishments, he might show that Theodore either was in despair or was flagging a little. But the noble man did not stop speaking freely or forsake his purpose, and instead fought still more bravely, openly attacking and stigmatizing the tyrant by his words and denouncing him with his rebukes. Leo was infuriated each time he learned what had happened and found it intolerable that, when he had defeated almost everyone and enslaved them to his power, Theodore not only remained undefeated but was also persuading others not to cower before any of his terrible actions or consent to his impious dogmas. But, after Leo, that shameless and arrogant man, had shown great disregard for

τῆς τοῦ Θεοῦ καταφρονήσας ἀνοχῆς, καὶ τῶν ἱερῶν καταπαίξας εἰκόνων, ἑβδόμῳ τῆς βασιλείας ἔτει δίκην τῶν τετολμημένων εἰσπράττεται δυσκλεῶς τὸν βίον λιπών, καὶ τῇ κατὰ τῶν σπλάγχνων πληγῇ σωφροσύνη τοῖς ἄλλοις γενόμενος.

6

Αὐτίκα δὲ καὶ ὁ πατὴρ λύεται τῆς ὑπερορίας καὶ τῆς καθείρξεως ἀφίεται· ὃς καὶ ἀνὰ τὴν ὁδὸν διϊὼν πολλὰς μὲν εἰργάζετο τὰς θεοσημείας, πολλὰ δ' ἔπραττεν ἄλλα πρὸς ὠφέλειαν τῶν συνόντων, πολλὴν δὲ παρεῖχε τοῖς φοιτηταῖς τὴν χάριν, κοινωνῶν αὐτοῖς καὶ εὐθυμίας καὶ τῆς ἄλλης ἐν πνεύματι παρακλήσεως· ὅτε καὶ τὸν ἴδιον ἀδελφόν, Ἰωσήφ φημι, τὸν τῆς Θεσσαλονίκης τὴν προεδρίαν λαχόντα, χρόνιον ἥκοντα καὶ αὐτὸν τῆς ὑπερορίας, μεθ' ὅσης ἂν εἴποις θεᾶται τῆς ἡδονῆς ὅλος ὅλῳ περιχεόμενος καὶ χείλεσι καὶ καρδίᾳ κατασπαζόμενος. Ἀλλὰ γὰρ τίς ἂν εἴποι πάλιν λόγους ἐκείνους τοῦ ἁγίου καὶ παρρησίαν ἣν καὶ μετὰ κινδύνων καὶ ἀκινδύνως πρὸς τὸν τηνικαῦτα παραλαβόντα τὰ σκῆπτρα ζήλῳ θείῳ πυρούμενος ἐπεδείξατο; Τούτῳ γὰρ καὶ εἰς ὄψιν ἔστη καὶ τὰ δέοντα προσωμίλησε καὶ τῶν πρὶν βεβασιλευκότων παρέστησε τὴν δυσσέβειαν, οἵ, φησί, διὰ τὸ εἰς τὰς θείας πεπαρῳνηκέναι εἰκόνας καὶ τὰ ἅγια βεβηλῶσαι κἀνταῦθα δίκην οὔτι

God's forbearance and had mocked the holy icons, in the seventh year of his reign he paid the penalty for his audacious actions, for he departed this life ignominiously and, through a wound in his bowels, brought about moderation in others.

6

Our father Theodore was immediately freed from banishment and released from his imprisonment. During his return journey, he performed many miracles and did many other things to help his companions; he bestowed much grace on his disciples, sharing with them his good cheer and other spiritual comfort. When his own brother, Joseph I mean, who had obtained the office of bishop of Thessalonike, also returned from a period of banishment, with what great pleasure would you say Theodore gazed on him, as they wholeheartedly embraced and greeted each other with a kiss? But who could repeat those words of holy Theodore and the boldness he displayed, whether imperiled or not, before the man who had then assumed the scepter, fired as he was by divine zeal? For he stood facing him and preached what was needed, setting forth the impiety of the previous rulers, who, he said, because of their defilement of the divine icons and their pollution of holy places, paid an

μετρίαν ἔτισαν, κακεῖ ἀπιόντες ὅλον *πίονται* τῆς τοῦ Θεοῦ ὀργῆς *τὸν τρυγίαν* ἐνδίκως ἑαυτοῖς ἐκκενούμενον.

2 Ἀλλ' εἰ καὶ πολλὰ πρὸς πειθὼ τοῦ βασιλέως ὁ δίκαιος προετείνατο, ἀλλ' οὐκ εἶχε τοῦτον κατατιθέμενον ἢ λόγους αὐτοῦ τοὺς ἡδίστους ἀποδεχόμενον. Ἦν γὰρ καὶ οὗτος τῆς ἐναντίας μοίρας καὶ δόξης, ἔξαρνος μὲν τῶν θείων εἰκόνων ἐξ ἔτι νέου τυγχάνων, οὐ μὴν διωγμὸν ἢ κάκωσιν ἐπάγων τοῖς ὀρθοδόξοις, ἀλλὰ τῆς μὲν βασιλίδος ἀπείργων, ἀλλαχοῦ δὲ μὴ κωλύων διάγειν ἢ ταῖς εἰκόσι μὴ προσάγειν τὸ σέβας. Ἀμέλει καὶ ὁ πατήρ, ἐπεὶ μὴ ἐξῆν αὐτῷ τῷ ἰδίῳ προσμένειν σεμνείῳ, ἐν ταῖς πρὸ τοῦ ἄστεος νήσοις κατασκηνοῖ κἀκεῖ συνὼν τοῖς φοιτηταῖς καὶ ὁμιλῶν τὰ συνήθη καὶ λόγοις θείοις ἐκτρέφων· οἷς καὶ χρόνον τὸ ἀπὸ τοῦδε οὐκ ἐλάχιστον συγγενόμενος, ἑβδόμῳ καὶ ἑξηκοστῷ τῆς ἐν σαρκὶ βιοτῆς ἔτει λύεται μὲν τοῦ σκήνους, ἀνατρέχει δὲ πρὸς ὃν ἐπόθει Δεσπότην, διπλοῦς κομιούμενος τοὺς στεφάνους τοῦ τε βίου καὶ τῆς ὁμολογίας, ὅτι δὴ καὶ ἐν ἀμφοτέροις μεγάλους τοὺς ἄθλους διήνυσε, μεγάλα τὰ τρόπαια ἔστησε. Τέσσαρες γὰρ οἱ τούτῳ ἐπαναστάντες τύραννοι· τοὺς τέσσαρας οὗτος κατηγωνίσατο καὶ εἷλε καὶ ἐτροπώσατο καὶ πολλῷ τῷ περιόντι κατέβαλε, καὶ αὐτὸς μὲν οὕτω καὶ ἐβίω καὶ μετέστη, καὶ οὕτω μεταστὰς εἰς μονὰς τὰς οὐρανίους μεταπεφοίτηκεν. Ἐπεὶ ἡ τοῦτον δεξαμένη νῆσος—Πρίγκιπος ἐκαλεῖτο αὕτη—σῶμα τούτου τὸ ἱερὸν περιέλαβεν, ἧν ἐκεῖ μένον τιμίως τὸ τίμιον, πολλὴν ἀναβλύζον τὴν χάριν, πολλὴν παρέχον καὶ ἄφθονον τὴν ὠφέλειαν.

extreme penalty in this life and, going to the one to come, were *drinking* all *the dregs* of God's wrath justly poured out for them.

Although the righteous Theodore put forward many points to persuade the emperor, yet he did not win his agreement or acceptance of his most pleasant arguments; for Michael was of the opposing party and belief, having been a denier of the holy icons from a young age. However, he did not inflict persecution or ill-treatment on the orthodox, for he banned them from the capital but did not prevent them from living elsewhere and offering veneration to icons. Consequently, since our father Theodore could not remain in his own monastery, he took up residence on the islands facing the city, where, living with his disciples, he gave his customary teaching and nourished them with his holy words. After being with them for some considerable time, in the sixty-seventh year of his life in the flesh he was freed from the body and hastened to the Master for whom he yearned, to obtain a pair of crowns for his life and for his confession of faith, because in both he had accomplished great contests and set up great trophies. For four tyrants attacked him, but he conquered the four of them, and destroyed, routed, and overthrew them on many occasions. This was the way he lived and died and, departing in this way, he passed on into the heavenly dwellings. Since the island that had welcomed him—it was called Prinkipos—embraced his holy body, there the honored body remained with honor, flowing with much grace and generously providing much benefit.

2

7

Τί δ' οἱ τούτου μαθηταὶ καὶ τοῦ καλοῦ διδασκάλου κάλλιστοι φοιτηταί; Οὐκ ἀπελίμπανον οὐ μὲν οὖν οὐδὲ τελευτήσαντος τοῦ πατρός, ἀλλὰ καὶ προσήδρευον καὶ συνῆσαν καὶ τῷ τάφῳ παρέμενον, ἔχοντες αὐτῶν προστατοῦντα καὶ Ναυκράτιον τὸν σοφόν, τὸν καὶ γνώμῃ τοῦ πατρὸς τὴν ἀρχὴν ἐγκεχειρισμένον. Οἳ καὶ πάντες κοινῇ πολλαῖς ἱκετείαις, πολλαῖς ταῖς δεήσεσι τὸν Θεὸν ἐλιπάρουν δοῦναι ταῖς ἐκκλησίαις γαλήνην καὶ ἀναλάμψαι ταύταις αἰθρίαν καὶ τὴν ἀρχαίαν ἀπολαβεῖν εὐπρέπειαν. Ἐπεὶ δὲ ὁ πάντα ποιῶν καὶ μετασκευάζων Θεός, ὁ *καθαιρῶν δυνάστας ἀπὸ θρόνων* καὶ *συντρίβων ἁμαρτωλοῦ καὶ πονηροῦ τοὺς βραχίονας,* ὁ *τὴν καταιγίδα εἰς αὖραν ἱστῶν* καὶ *σκιὰν θανάτου* τρέπων εἰς *τὸ πρωΐ,* αὐτὸς ἰδὼν εἶδε κακουμένους τοὺς ὁσίους αὐτοῦ καὶ ἰδὼν ἐπεσκέψατο, καὶ ἐπισκεψάμενος τὴν μὲν πονηρὰν βασιλείαν μετ' ἤχου διώλεσε, τοῖς δὲ Χριστιανοῖς τὰ πράγματα ἐπανήγαγε· τότε δὴ τότε καὶ πατέρων οἱ θίασοι καὶ ὀρθοδόξων τὰ στίφη καὶ μοναστῶν ὁμηγύρεις σπουδῇ ἅμα πάντες πρὸς τὴν βασιλίδα εἰσέθεον, Θεῷ τὰ χαριστήρια ᾄδοντες, Θεὸν ὑμνοῦντες, Θεῷ τὴν ᾠδὴν ἀνακρούοντες.

2 Οἳ καὶ τῇ εὐσεβεῖ Θεοδώρᾳ καὶ τῷ ταύτης υἱῷ τοῖς καὶ τὰ σκῆπτρα ἀναδεδεγμένοις πολλὴν τὴν εὐφημίαν ἐπῆγον, πολλὰ τῆς αὐτοκρατορικῆς ἀρχῆς ἐμακαρίζον· οὐ γὰρ ἡ μὲν τὸν ὁμόζυγον, ὁ δὲ παῖς τὸν πατέρα μεμίμηνται, ἀλλ' ἀπεναντίας ἐκείνου τάς τε ἱερὰς ἔσεβον εἰκόνας καὶ τοὺς

7

But what about Theodore's pupils and the good teacher's most good disciples? They did not leave, not even after the father had died, but sat beside him and kept him company, remaining at his tomb with the wise Naukratios in charge of them, who, by the father's decision, had been entrusted with this authority. All of them together implored God with many supplications and entreaties to grant a period of tranquility to the churches and illuminate them with a clear sky so that they could regain their former dignity. And when God, who makes and transforms everything, *who puts down the mighty from their thrones* and *breaks the arms of the sinner and evildoer,* who *checks the hurricane to a breeze* and turns *the shadow of death to the morning,* looked and saw that his saints were being ill-treated, seeing that, he was concerned for them and, being concerned, destroyed the evil regime with a resounding crash, restoring matters for the Christians. Then indeed bands of fathers, groups of orthodox, and companies of monks all rushed in haste to the capital singing hymns of thanksgiving to God, praising God, and striking up a song to God.

They also heaped great praise on the pious Theodora and 2
her son who had taken up the scepter, congratulating them on their imperial rule, for Theodora did not imitate her husband, nor her son his father, but, in contrast to him, they revered the holy icons and utterly hated the false believers.

κακοδόξους ἐσχάτως ἐμίσουν. Διά τοι καὶ ἀπελαύνονται παρ' αὐτῶν καὶ πόλεων καὶ ἐκκλησιῶν καὶ τῶν ἄλλων συλλόγων οἱ φθόροι ἐκεῖνοι καὶ λυμεῶνες, ἀντεισάγονται δὲ οἱ εὐσεβεῖς καὶ ὀρθόδοξοι, ἡνίκα καὶ ψῆφος οἰκουμενικὴ κροτηθεῖσα, Μεθοδίου, τὸν ἀρχιερατικὸν θρόνον ἐγχειρισθέντος, ταύτης κατάρχοντος, τοὺς μὲν πιστοὺς ὡς τῆς Ἐκκλησίας προβόλους ἐσέμνυνεν αὕτη καὶ ἀνεκήρυξε, τοὺς δὲ εἰκονομάχους τέλεον ἀπερράπισε καὶ κατέβαλεν.

8

Ἐπεὶ οὖν οὕτω ταῦτα γέγονε καὶ ὑπὸ βασιλεῦσι πιστοῖς καὶ ἱεράρχαις τὰ πράγματα μετενήνεκται, σπουδὴ τηνικαῦτα καὶ τῷ θείῳ γίνεται Ναυκρατίῳ, τῷ ἡμετέρῳ φημὶ ποιμένι καὶ τοῦ πατρὸς διαδόχῳ, πῶς ἄρα καὶ τῷ μοναστηρίῳ τὸν θεόληπτον εἰσαγάγοι ἐκεῖνον καὶ πῶς σῶμα τούτου τὸ ἱερὸν μετακομίσοι καὶ σεμνοπρεπῶς τῷ τάφῳ κατάθοιτο. Ὃς συνεργὸν καὶ τὸν καλὸν Ἀθανάσιον προσλαβών, οἷα καὶ αὐτὸν τῆς τοῦ Σακκουδίωνος ποίμνης ἐπιστατοῦντα—ὅτι δὴ καὶ ὑπὸ μίαν ἀρχὴν ἄμφω ἐτύγχανε τὰ μοναστήρια—προσίασι τῷ πατριάρχῃ ἑκάτεροι, ἐν ταὐτῷ καὶ τῇ Αὐγούστῃ σὺν ἅμα καὶ τῷ ταύτης υἱῷ, τὰ τῆς ἀνακομιδῆς τοῦ πατρὸς διαγγέλλοντες καὶ ὡς καιρὸς αὐτοῖς ὁ παρὼν προσήκων ὅτι μάλιστα καὶ ἐπιτήδειος περὶ τὴν ἐγχείρησιν.

As a result, they drove those corrupters and destroyers out of cities, churches, and other assemblies and in their place brought in devout and orthodox people, when an ecumenical decree, presided over by Methodios, who had been entrusted with the patriarchal throne, was ratified; and this honored the faithful and proclaimed them guardians of the Church, completely overthrowing and driving out the iconoclasts.

8

So after these things had happened and matters had been transformed by faithful rulers and bishops, then the holy Naukratios, our shepherd, I mean, and Theodore's successor, became eager to see how he might bring that divinely inspired one to the monastery and how he might translate his holy body and lay it to rest in a tomb with fitting dignity. In collaboration with the noble Athanasios who was in charge of the flock at Sakkoudion—because both monasteries were under one administration—both men approached the patriarch and at the same time the Augusta and also her son, announcing their plans for the father's return and how the present time was especially fitting and suitable for the undertaking.

2 Ἀλλὰ γὰρ ἐνταῦθά μοι πᾶς προσεχέτω τὸν νοῦν· ἥκει γὰρ ὁ λόγος πρὸς τὴν διήγησιν ἣν καὶ ἰδίαν οἶδεν ὑπόθεσιν καὶ ἣν ἐρεῖν ἀρχόμενος οὗτος κατεπηγγείλατο.

9

Ὀκτωκαίδεκα τοίνυν ἐτῶν διαγεγονότων ἀφ' οὗ ὁ πολύαθλος τοῦ βίου μετέστη καὶ ἀφ' οὗ σῶμα αὐτοῦ τῇ νήσῳ περιεστάλη, οὐκ ἦν τοῖς βουλομένοις ἐξόν (καίτοι σπεύδουσι πρὸς τὸ πρᾶγμα) ἢ μετακομίσαι τοῦτον ἐκεῖθεν ἢ τῷ ἰδίῳ μοναστηρίῳ ἐγκαταθεῖναι ἢ ἀποδοῦναι τοῖς ποθοῦσι θησαυρὸν τὸν ποθούμενον. Οὐκ οὖν καὶ ἔμενεν ἐκεῖ κατατεθειμένος ἐφ' ὅσον χρόνον καὶ ἡ εἰκονομάχος χεὶρ ἐπεκράτει καὶ ἐφ' ὅσον ἡ ἀσεβὴς ἐπεπόλαζεν αἵρεσις. Ἐπεὶ δ' ἡ τούτων ὀφρὺς πέπτωκε καὶ εἰς τέλος διόλωλεν, οὐδ' ἐπ' ὀλίγον ὁ θεῖος μελλήσας Ναυκράτιος, ὁ καὶ ἀνωτέρω μοι δηλωθείς, εὐτρεπὴς ὅλος καὶ ἐμπαράσκευος περὶ τὴν τοῦ ἱεροῦ λειψάνου καθίσταται ἀνακομιδήν· οὐ γὰρ ἐλυσιτέλει αὐτῷ καὶ ἔτι μένειν παρ' ἄλλοις τὸν οἰκεῖον πατέρα, ὃν παρ' ἑαυτῷ μένειν πολλῷ δήπου ἐνόμιζεν οἰκειότερον.

2 Ἀμέλει καὶ τῇ Αὐγούστῃ, ὡς ἔφαμεν, καὶ τῷ πατριάρχῃ σὺν τῷ συνάθλῳ προσιὼν Ἀθανασίῳ τοιάδε πρὸς ῥῆμα ἐκείνοις μετὰ πολλῆς διεξῄει τῆς κατανύξεως· "Οἶδα," φησίν, "ὅτι καὶ πρὸ τῶν ἡμετέρων λόγων καὶ πρὸ τῆς ἡμετέρας ἐντεύξεως πολλὴν ἐναποτεθεῖσθαι ὑμῖν τὴν διάθεσιν

But at this point let everyone pay attention to me; for the 2
discourse has come to the description which it knows is its proper subject and which it promised to convey at the outset.

9

So, eighteen years had now passed since the sorely tried Theodore had died and his body had been buried on the island; it had not been possible for those who wished (even though they were eager for the task) to remove him from there, inter him in his own monastery, or restore the longed-for treasure to those who longed for it. Thus, he had remained interred there for as long as the iconoclastic hand held on to power and as long as the impious heresy prevailed. But when their arrogance was crushed and utterly perished, the holy Naukratios, who was mentioned above by me, did not delay even for a short time, but was wholly ready and prepared for the return of the holy body. For it was no good to him for his own father to stay any longer with other people, when, no doubt, he thought it much more appropriate that he should be staying with him.

Consequently, as I said, along with his fellow combatant 2
Athanasios, he approached the Augusta and the patriarch, and recounted to them in detail with great compunction the following words: "I know," he said, "that, even before our words and our appeal, you have stored up much affection

καὶ στοργὴν τοῦ μεγάλου πατρὸς καὶ ὁμολογητοῦ καὶ ἡμετέρου ποιμενάρχου· καὶ πῶς γὰρ οὐκ εἰκὸς σέβειν τὸν τηλικοῦτον καὶ τιμᾶν καὶ ταῖς πρεπούσαις ἀμείβεσθαι χάρισιν; Ἡ γὰρ ἐκείνου ἀνδρεία καὶ τὰ παλαίσματα καὶ ὁ λαμπρὸς βίος καὶ οἱ ἆθλοι πείθουσι πάντας διὰ θαύματος ἄγειν καὶ πολλῆς ἀξιοῦσθαι προνοίας τὰ κατ' αὐτὸν ἕκαστα· ὅς γε μετὰ ἐξορίαν, μετὰ μάστιγας, μετὰ μυρίας ἄλλας κακώσεις οὐδὲ τῆς ἐν τῷ μοναστηρίῳ ἔτυχε ταφῆς, οὐδ' ὁσίας εὐμοίρησε τῆς πρεπούσης· <ν>ήσῳ γὰρ τῆς Πριγκίπου ἀποβιοὺς κἀκεῖ χρόνον ὀκτωκαιδέκατον ἤδη τῇ λάρνακι μένων, οὔπω καὶ νῦν διὰ τὴν τῶν εἰκονομάχων λύτταν, διὰ τὴν κατ' αὐτοῦ ἀκήρυκτον δυσμένειαν ἢ ἐνταῦθα μετεκομίσθη, ἢ τοῖς τέκνοις ὁ πατὴρ ἀπεδόθη, ἢ τοῖς προβάτοις ὁ ποιμὴν ἐγκατείλεκται. Οὐκοῦν πρόνοιαν τὸ ὑμέτερον θέσθω κράτος, ὡς ἂν θησαυρὸς τοιοῦτος παρ' ἡμῖν εἰσαχθῇ καὶ ἔνδον τοσοῦτον πλοῦτον περιληψώμεθα· οὕτω γὰρ καὶ σῶμα τὸ ἱερὸν δεόντως περιστελοῦμεν καὶ τὰ εἰκότα ἀφοσιωσόμεθα τῷ παμμάκαρι. Τί γὰρ καὶ τοσοῦτον ἔσται τῇ βασιλίδι τῶν πολέων ἢ τίς ἄλλος κόσμος αὐτῇ εὐπρεπέστερος, ἢ τοιούτῳ ἀνδρὶ καὶ κοσμηθῆναι καὶ λαμπρυνθῆναι καὶ τῇ ἀνακομιδῇ τούτου καὶ καταθέσει πανήγυριν ᾆσαι χαρμόσυνον;"

and love toward the great father and confessor, our chief shepherd; for how could one not revere such a man, and honor and repay him with fitting thanks? His bravery, his struggles, his radiant life, and his contests cause everyone to marvel and think that each of his achievements require great care. After banishment, after whippings, after countless other abuses he did not even obtain burial in his monastery, nor was he afforded a fitting funeral service. For since he died on the island of Prinkipos, he has already remained in a coffin there for eighteen years because of the fury of the iconoclasts and their implacable hostility toward him, and he has not yet even now been transferred here, neither as a father returned to his children nor as a shepherd included among his sheep. So, let your majesty take some care that a treasure such as this may be brought to us and we may embrace such great wealth within the monastery; for then we will lay out the holy body properly and fittingly carry out the holy rites for the most blessed one. For what object as great will the queen of cities possess, or what other adornment more becoming for her, than to be adorned and distinguished by such a man and to celebrate a joyful festival at the return and deposition of his remains?"

10

Ταῦτα Ναυκράτιος καὶ Ἀθανάσιος διεξιόντες τήν τε Αὐγοῦσταν καὶ τὸν πατριάρχην εἰς συνεργίαν λαμβάνουσι καὶ πολλὴν εἰσφέροντας τὴν σπουδὴν ἐφευρίσκουσιν. Εἶχε γὰρ καὶ αὐτοὺς ἔρως τιμῆσαι τὸν ἀπελθόντα καί, ἐπεὶ μὴ ζῶντι ἐξῆν, μεταστάντι ἀποτῖσαι τὰ κατὰ πρόθεσιν. Ἔνθεν τοι καὶ προτροπῇ τῶν κρατούντων τὴν νῆσον οἱ πατέρες καταλαμβάνουσιν, οὐκ αὐτοὶ μόνον ἀλλὰ καὶ πλῆθος μοναστῶν ἄλλο τῶν τε παρ' αὐτοῖς σεμνείων καὶ ἑτέρων τῶν πόρρωθεν· κοινῇ γὰρ καὶ ἰδίᾳ ἕκαστος ἡμιλλῶντο ποῖος φθάσας πρῶτος μείζω τὴν τιμὴν εἰσενέγκοι καὶ πλείω τὴν χάριν κατάθοιτο ἢ μᾶλλον αὐτὸς ἀντιλάβοιτο· οἳ καὶ τῇ θήκῃ πελάσαντες σὺν φωτὶ πολλῷ καὶ θυμιαμάτων ἐκχύσει καὶ ἡδονῇ κεράσαντες δάκρυα, τοιαῦτα ἐπῇδον ὡς εἰκὸς τῷ πατρί· "Οἶδας τὸν περὶ σὲ πόθον ἡμῶν, ὦ πατέρων ἄριστε καὶ φιλοτεκνότατε, οἶδας τὸ περιὸν τῆς στοργῆς, οἶδας τῆς ἀγάπης τὸ ἐνδιάθετον· οὐκοῦν σοι καὶ πρεσβεύοντες ἥκομεν, παρακαλοῦντες ἀφίγμεθα, δεόμενοι ἐληλύθαμεν· ἐπίνευσον ἡμῖν δυσωποῦσιν, ἐπικάμφθητι αἰτουμένοις σε, δὸς σῶμά σου τὸ ἱερὸν μετακομίσαι τῇ ποίμνῃ σου, δὸς κόνιν σου τὴν τιμίαν ἀποθέσθαι τῇ βασιλίδι, δὸς λείψανόν σου τὸ σεπτὸν σεμνοπρεπῶς καταθέσθαι, δὸς ἐπὶ τούτῳ κοινὴν τὴν χαράν, κοινὴν στήσασθαι τὴν εὐφροσύνην· ποθοῦμεν γάρ σε ἔνδον περιλαβεῖν, ποθοῦμέν σε παρ' ἑαυτοῖς κατασχεῖν καὶ εἰσδέξασθαι· ποθεῖ σε μονή σου ἡ περιώνυμος, ποθεῖ σε τέκνων σου ἡ πληθὺς

10

As Naukratios and Athanasios were going through these points, they realized that both the Augusta and the patriarch were willing to help and discovered that they were also showing great eagerness, for their love was urging them to honor the one who had departed and, since this was not possible while he was alive, to pay for the laying out of his corpse now that he was dead. And so, urged on by the rulers, the fathers went to the island, and not just them but also a crowd of monks from the monasteries near them and others from further afield; for each, jointly and individually, vied as to who would be the first to confer greater honor and lay up for himself, or rather, himself gain more grace. They drew near to the coffin with many lights and a cloud of incense, mingling tears with pleasure and chanting the following, as was appropriate for Theodore: "You know our longing for you, noblest of fathers and most loving to your sons; you know our enduring affection; you know the deep-seated nature of our love. Therefore we have come pleading to you, we have arrived with entreaties, we have come in supplication; give us your assent as we importune you, be persuaded by our petitions, give us your holy body to transport to your flock, give us your precious dust to store away in the capital, give us your sacred relic for proper burial; grant that we may stir up communal joy and communal happiness by this, for we long to embrace you inside the city, we long to take you in and hold you fast beside us. Your renowned monastery longs for you, the multitude of your children longs for you,

οὓς ὠδίνησας καὶ ἐτελεσφόρησας καὶ εἰς μέτρον πνευματικὸν ἤγαγες· ποθεῖ σε ἡ θρεψαμένη πατρὶς ἢ μᾶλλον ἡ τῶν πόλεων βασιλίς, ἐν ᾗ καὶ τὴν εἰκόνα Χριστοῦ λαμπρῶς ἀνεκήρυξας καὶ ἐν ᾗ τοὺς ταύτης ὑβριστὰς καταφανῶς ἐστηλίτευσας.

2 "Δεῦρο ἴθι πρὸς τὸν σὸν λαόν, πρὸς τὴν σὴν ποίμνην, πρὸς τὸν τῆς Ἐκκλησίας καταρτισμόν, πρὸς τὸν ὡραϊσμὸν ταύτης, πρὸς τὴν εὐπρέπειαν. Νῦν τὴν ἀρχαίαν ἐνεδύσατο στολήν, νῦν τὸν ἴδιον περιεβάλετο κόσμον, νῦν εὐφραίνεται καὶ σκιρτᾷ, καὶ τοὺς ἑαυτῆς συγκαλεῖται τροφίμους. Ὁ γὰρ χειμὼν τῆς αἱρετικῆς ζάλης παρῆλθεν, ἡ καταιγὶς καὶ ὁ κλύδων ἔσβη καὶ παρεστάλη, εἰς γαλήνην ἡ ταραχὴ ἐληλύθει, *φωνὴ* τῆς νοητῆς *ἠκούσθη τρυγόνος* κατὰ τὸν Σολομῶντα, *ἡ συκῆ ἐξήνεγκεν ὀλύνθους αὐτῆς, αἱ ἄμπελοι κυπρίζουσιν, ἔδωκαν ὀσμὴν* αὐτῶν καὶ εὐωδίας τὰ πάντα ἐπλήρωσαν, ἃ τῆς Ἐκκλησίας νύμφης καὶ τοῦ νυμφίου Χριστοῦ μηνύματα καὶ κηρύγματα καὶ τῆς κρείττονος μεταβολῆς προαγγέλματα. Τούτοις χρώμεθα τοῖς λόγοις οἱ σοὶ φοιτηταί, τούτοις σε τοῖς ῥήμασι προσκαλούμεθα, ταῦτά σοι τρόμῳ καὶ χαρᾷ προτείνομεν· ἅψασθαι σώματός σου τοῦ ἱεροῦ παρασκεύασον, χείλη ἡμῶν καὶ καρδίας τῇ προσψαύσει ἁγίασον, μέλος ἅπαν ἐπαφώμενόν σου καὶ προσεγγίζον ἀπόσμηξον, σύναψον ἡμῖν σαυτόν, ἐλθὲ σὺν ἡμῖν, ἐπίβηθι μεθ' ἡμῶν τῆς νηός, πορείαν τὴν κατὰ θάλατταν στόρεσον, γαληνιῶντα δεῖξον τὸν πλοῦν, σηκόν σου τὸν ἱερὸν κατάλαβε, κατασκήνωσον ἐν αὐτῷ, ἴδε ἐπισυνηγμένα τὰ τέκνα σου, τὰ λογικά σου ἐπίσκεψαι πρόβατα, ὁ φιλανθρωπότατος ἐν ποιμέσι καὶ κηδεμονικώτατος, δεῖξον

those whom you brought forth in pain, brought to perfection, and led to a due measure of spirituality. Your homeland, or rather the queen of cities, which reared you, longs for you; the place in which you clearly extolled the icon of Christ and in which you manifestly denounced those who insulted it.

"Come here to your people, to your flock, to the restora- 2
tion of the Church, to its adornment, to its dignity. Now it has put on its ancient robe, now it has clothed itself in its own beauty, now it is joyful, it exults and calls its nurslings together. For the storm of the heretical surge has passed, the tempest and the flood are quelled and checked, the turmoil has turned to calm, the *voice of the* spiritual *turtledove is heard,* as Solomon says, *the fig tree has put forth its figs, the vines are in blossom, they have given out* their *fragrance* and have filled everything with a sweet smell; these are the signs and proclamations of the bridal Church and Christ the bridegroom and the announcements of a change for the better. We your disciples use these words, with these phrases we call on you, these we offer you with trembling and joy. Prepare us to touch your holy body; sanctify our lips and hearts by its touch; purify every limb that draws near and touches you; unite yourself with us, come with us, board the ship with us, make smooth the journey by sea, render the voyage calm, occupy your sacred shrine, abide in it. Look upon your assembled children, look after your spiritual sheep, you, the most benevolent and solicitous among shepherds, show

αὐτοῖς ὄψιν σου τὴν ἡδίστην, ἀκούτισον αὐτοῖς τὴν ἡδυτέραν φωνήν σου, ἐπειδὴ καὶ σιγῶν οἶδας λαλεῖν, καὶ ὁρᾶν μὴ ὁρώμενος· τοῦτο γὰρ ἡμῖν καὶ γέρας ἐκ Θεοῦ τὸ τῶν ἡμετέρων αἰσθάνεσθαι καὶ λόγων καὶ λογισμῶν καὶ ἡμῖν παρέχειν τὰ αἰτούμενα."

II

Ταῦτα τῶν πατέρων καὶ εἰπόντων καὶ φθεγξαμένων καὶ θειοτέρῳ ὥσπερ λογισμῷ τὴν πληροφορίαν ὧν ἐπεχείρουν λαβόντων, ἁψάμενοι τῆς σοροῦ καὶ πλοίου ἐπιβάντες ἄσμενοι τὸν ἀπόπλουν ἐποίουν, ᾠδὰς εὐχαρίστους καὶ ἄλλους ὕμνους κατὰ θάλασσαν ᾄδοντες. Τίς γὰρ ἐξείποι τὰ τελούμενα τηνικαῦτα, τίς τὴν ἡδονήν, τίς τὴν εὐφροσύνην καὶ τὴν ἄλλην παραστήσειεν εὐθυμίαν; Ἠγαλλιάσατο τάχα τότε καὶ ἡ θάλασσα, καὶ τρίβοι θαλασσῶν καὶ κύματα ἥδιστον ἤχησαν, καὶ πάντα νηκτὰ καὶ πλωτά, τῆς νηὸς ἐπιβαινούσης, ἐσκίρτησαν· ἑώρων γὰρ τὸν καλὸν φόρτον ἐκεῖνον τῷ θαλαττίῳ φερόμενον ὕδατι καὶ πομπευόμενον καὶ λαμπαδουχούμενον καὶ πράῳ τῷ πνεύματι δορυφορούμενον. Ἐπεὶ δὲ καὶ τῷ αἰγιαλῷ οὗτοι προσώκειλαν, ἦν ἰδεῖν συντρέχον πλῆθος μοναστῶν καὶ περικυκλοῦν τὴν σορὸν καὶ ᾄσματα ᾆδον ἐπικήδεια ἅμα καὶ χαριστήρια· ὡς γὰρ εἰς κοινὴν πανήγυριν καὶ πάνδημον ἑορτὴν ἐπειγόμενοι, οὕτω συνέρρεον οὐχ οἱ πλησίον

them your most sweet face, make your very sweet voice audible to them, since you know how to speak even when silent and to see when you are not seen. For this is also our reward from God, that you understand our words and thoughts and grant to us what we seek."

II

After the fathers had spoken and said these words, they received confirmation for their undertaking as though by some more divine reasoning. They took hold of the coffin, joyfully embarked on a ship, and began the voyage, chanting songs of thanksgiving and other hymns as they sailed. For who could relate what was being accomplished at that time, who could describe the pleasure, who would express the gladness and the other happiness? Then quickly the sea also rejoiced, the paths of the sea and the waves resounded most sweetly, everything that swims and floats jumped for joy as the ship advanced, for they were watching that noble cargo being borne along by the waters of the sea, conducted in triumph, lit by torches, and escorted by the gentle breeze. When they brought the ship to the shore, a crowd of monks could be seen gathering in haste, circling around the coffin and chanting funeral hymns and at the same time songs of thanksgiving. For, as though they were hurrying to a communal festival and a public feast, not only were those from

μόνον ἀλλὰ καὶ οἱ μακρὰν καὶ οἱ πόρρωθεν, οὐ μονασταὶ μόνον ἀλλὰ καὶ κοινωνικοὶ καὶ μιγάδες καὶ οἱ τοῦ κλήρου καὶ τοῦ λαοῦ καὶ πᾶν ὡς εἰπεῖν γένος συνέτρεχον, τὰ εἰκότα ἕκαστος τῇ πανηγύρει ἀφοσιούμενος· οἳ καὶ τῇ ἐκχύσει τῶν μύρων καὶ τῷ φωτὶ τῶν λαμπάδων καὶ αὐτὸν ἐχρώννυον τὸν ἀέρα, καὶ αὐτὴν τάχα ἐδείκνυον ἡττωμένην τοῦ ἡλίου τὴν λαμπηδόνα.

12

Ὡς δὲ καὶ τὴν σορὸν βαστάζειν ἔμελλον καὶ πρὸς τὸν ναὸν ἀποφέρειν, στιχηδὸν ἑαυτοὺς διατάξαντες καὶ οἱ μὲν προπορευόμενοι, οἱ δ' ἐπιπορευόμενοι, οἱ δ' ὡς εἰκὸς καὶ συμπορευόμενοι, ταύτην σὺν τιμῇ πολλῇ ἐν τῷ κατὰ δεξίαν τοῦ ναοῦ τέως κατέθεσαν προτε<με>νίσματι, ἔνθα καὶ μαρτύρων εἴσω κατάκειται λείψανα. Τότε καὶ ἡ βασιλὶς Αὐγοῦστα καὶ ὅσον περὶ τὰ βασίλεια πολυτελῶς τὸν τοῦ ἁγίου ἐτίμων νεκρόν, οἱ μὲν αὐτοὶ ἥκοντες, οἱ δὲ παντοῖα τῶν εὐωδῶν εἰς δεξίωσιν στέλλοντες. Ὁ δέ γε πατριάρχης οἷα καὶ μείζω τὸν περὶ αὐτὸν τρέφων πόθον (Μεθόδιος οὗτος ὁ κλεινὸς ἦν) τὸν ὅλον τῆς ἐκκλησίας συμπαραλαβὼν κλῆρον αὐτὸς ἐκεῖνος ὀψόμενός τε τὸν πατέρα ἀφίκετο καὶ τὴν ταφὴν αὐτουργήσων καὶ ὑπηρετήσων ἐπιμελέστατα· ὃς καὶ τῷ ἁγίῳ λειψάνῳ περιτυχὼν χείλη καὶ ὄμματα τούτῳ προσῆπτε καὶ πρὸ τούτων καρδίαν, περι-

nearby rushing together, but also those from further afield and even those from far away, and not only solitaries but also those from communities and those who lived in the world, members of the clergy and the laity, and the whole race, so to speak, was rushing together, each one devoting himself appropriately to the festival. With an effusion of perfumes and the radiance of the lamps they colored the very air and almost eclipsed the brilliance of the sun itself.

12

When they were about to lift the coffin and carry it to the church, they arranged themselves in rows with some leading the procession, others coming behind and others also, as is proper, accompanying it; afterward, with great honor, they set the coffin down temporarily on the right in the narthex of the church in the place where martyrs' relics are lying at rest. Then the empress Augusta and all those connected with the palace richly honored the corpse of the saint, some coming in person, others sending all kinds of fragrances as an offering. The patriarch (this was the famous Methodios), as someone who nourished an even greater yearning for Theodore, brought along with him the entire clergy of the church, and arrived in person to see the father, perform the burial himself, and minister most attentively. When he came to the holy body, he fastened his lips and eyes on it, and, more than these, his heart, embracing every

πτύσσων ἅπαν μέλος καὶ εὐκταίως κατασπαζόμενος. Ἦν γὰρ ὁρᾶν τὸ ἱερὸν σῶμα ἐκεῖνο σῶον ὅλον καὶ ἄρτιον, καὶ ἀκραιφνῆ σῷζον τὴν τῶν μελῶν σύμφυσιν καὶ ὀργάνωσιν· ἐξ οὗ καί τις ἀνεφέρετο εὐωδία καὶ φῶς οἷον ἀπέλαμπεν ἄρρητον. Διά τοι καὶ εἰς τιμὴν ἐκείνου καὶ πόθου μείζονος πίστιν καὶ τὰ ἐρρικνωμένα περιδύσαντες τῶν ἀμφίων καινὰ ἄλλα καὶ ἱεροπρεπῆ ἐσθήματα περιέθεσαν, ἐπὶ δύο ὅλας ἡμέρας τοῦ συρρέοντος πλήθους μὴ συγχωροῦντος τῷ τάφῳ δοθῆναι τὸν ἅγιον, μηδ᾽ ἀπ᾽ αὐτῶν κρυβῆναι ἀποστίλβουσαν οὕτω καὶ χαρίεσσαν ὄψιν καὶ ἡδίστην.

13

Ἀλλὰ γὰρ ὁ λόγος ἀναμεινάτω καὶ ἀναβαλέσθω μικρὸν τὴν κατάθεσιν, ἕως ἂν καὶ τὰ κατὰ τὸν θεῖον ἐξείποι Ἰωσήφ, καὶ ὅπως δὴ καὶ οὗτος ἀνεκομίσθη, καὶ τῆς αὐτῆς ἔτυχε τῷ πατρὶ κατὰ τὴν αὐτὴν ἡμέραν καὶ εἰσόδου καὶ καταθέσεως. Οὗτος τοιγαροῦν ὁ ἱερὸς ἀνήρ, ὁ ἆθλον ἀρετῆς τὴν ἀρχιερωσύνην λαβών, ὁ ἀδελφὸς κατὰ πάντα τοῦ καλοῦ χρηματίσας πατρός, ὁ τῆς Θεσσαλονικέων ἐκκλησίας τὸν θρόνον κοσμήσας, πολλὰ μὲν ἀνδρείας ὡς οὐκ ἄλλος ἐπιδειξάμενος ἔργα, πολλοὺς δ᾽ ὑποστὰς ἄθλους ἐν τοῖς ὑπὲρ ἀρετῆς πόνοις, πολλὴν δ᾽ ὑπομείνας τὴν καρτερίαν ἐν τοῖς δεινοῖς, τέλος ὑπερορίαν παρὰ τῶν αἱρεσιωτῶν καὶ φυλακὴν κατακρίνεται. Ὃς καὶ χρόνον τῇ

limb and kissing them with devotion. For one could see that holy body was whole and sound, preserving intact the union and arrangement of the limbs; and from the body a sweet smell arose, and a kind of indescribable light shone out. And so, in his honor and as confirmation of their very great desire, they stripped off the shriveled parts of its clothing and wrapped it in other new garments befitting the holy man. For two whole days the crowd that was surging round did not allow the saint to be consigned to his tomb or his most sweet and graceful face, which was shining in that way, to be hidden from them.

13

But let my account pause and postpone the interment for a while, until it tells the story of the holy Joseph: how he too was translated and on the same day obtained the same ceremonial entrance and interment as Theodore. So then, this holy man, who had received the office of bishop as a prize for virtue, who was in every way the brother of our good father, who graced the throne of the church of Thessalonike, who like no other displayed many acts of courage, undertook many contests during his sufferings on behalf of virtue, and who maintained much endurance in terrible circumstances, was finally condemned to banishment and imprisonment by the heretics. After he had endured a consider-

καθείρξει διενεγκὼν οὐκ ἐλάχιστον καὶ μυρίαις παλαίσας ταῖς θλίψεσιν ἐν ἐσχατιᾷ που θνήσκει τῆς Θετταλίας, μηδὲ ταφῆς εὐπορήσας, ὡς δέον, μηδ' ὁ τούτου νεκρὸς γῆν εὑρών, ὡς εἰκός, εἰς κατάθεσιν.

2 Οὐκοῦν καὶ ἔκειτο παρερριμμένος που καὶ ἐν τόπῳ ἀλσώδει καὶ διύγρῳ συμπεφυρμένος· τοῖς τε γὰρ ἐκεῖ φυομένοις λαχάνοις καὶ τῇ ἄλλῃ τῶν ὑετῶν ῥαγδαίᾳ καταφορᾷ καὶ ὀστέα καὶ σάρκα καὶ πάντα ἐκδαπανώμενος, ἐν ὀλίγοις λειψάνοις μόλις ἔτυχε περιλελειμμένος. Οὕτω γὰρ ἔδοξε τάχα τοῖς ὑβρισταῖς ἀτημέλητον παρερρίφθαι παντάπασι καὶ μηδὲ μετὰ πότμον πρὸς αὐτὸν σπείσασθαι, μηδ' οἰκτεῖραι καὶ συμπαθῆσαι τὸν οἴκτου καὶ συμπαθείας ἄξιον· ὃς καὶ δωδέκατόν που ἔτος οὕτω νιφόμενος καὶ καταναλούμενος, μόλις ἠδυνήθησαν Ἀθανάσιος καὶ Ναυκράτιος, οἱ μνημονευθέντες, λάθρᾳ πως καὶ ἀσυμφανῶς ἐν ὀλίγοις ὀστέοις καὶ κόνει βραχείᾳ τὸν τούτου συλλέξαι νεκρὸν καὶ ἐν λάρνακι ἀποθέσθαι. Οὐ γὰρ ἐξῆν τούτοις, ἔτι τῆς αἱρετικῆς ἰσχύος ἐπικρατούσης, ἐκεῖθεν μετακομίσαι τὸν ἅγιον, ὡς ἂν μὴ καὶ φωραθέντες καὶ αὐτὰ ἃ συνέλεξαν ἀφαιρεθεῖεν λείψανα καὶ ζημιωθεῖεν τὰ καίρια.

3 Ἐπεὶ δ' ἔτυχον ἀδείας καὶ καιροῦ τοῦ προσήκοντος ἐπελάβοντο, τότε καὶ ἀνακομίζουσιν, ὡς ἐχρῆν, καὶ φιλοτίμως τοῦτον μετὰ λαμπρᾶς τῆς δορυφορίας εἰσάγουσι. Καὶ ὅρα μοι πατέρων εὐβουλίαν καὶ σύνεσιν· κατὰ γὰρ τὴν αὐτὴν ἡμέραν, κατὰ τὸν αὐτὸν καιρὸν ἀμφοτέρους τῷ μοναστηρίῳ ἐναποφέρουσιν, ὡς συμβῆναι ἑκατέρους, τὸν μὲν ἀπὸ τῆς θαλάσσης τὸν μέγαν Θεόδωρον, τὸν δ' ἀπὸ τῆς ἠπείρου καὶ δυτικῆς γῆς τὸν ἀρχιερέα Ἰωσήφ, ἐν ταὐτῷ

able time in prison and wrestled with countless afflictions, he died in some remote spot in Thessaly and he neither received a proper burial nor did his corpse find some ground, as it should have, for its interment.

So, his body lay cast aside somewhere and jumbled up in a 2
wooded and watery place. Since his bones, flesh, and everything else had been consumed by the vegetation growing there, as well as by the violent deluge from rainstorms, it barely survived in a few relics. Those insolent men probably decided that Joseph should be cast aside completely uncared for and that even after his death they would not make their peace with him or have pity and compassion for one worthy of pity and compassion. Since for about twelve years his body was snowed on and drenched by rain in this way, Athanasios and Naukratios, who were mentioned before, were hardly able to gather up his corpse, which had been reduced to a few bones and a little dust, somehow secretly and in obscurity and put it in a coffin. For with the heretical power still in control, it was not possible for them to transport the saint from there, in case they were caught in the act, the relics themselves which they had collected were taken away, and they were punished with death.

But when they had permission and found a suitable op- 3
portunity, then they took up his remains, as was right, and reverently brought him in with a splendid escort. And please observe the fathers' intelligence and sound planning, for they carried them both into the monastery on the same day and at the same time, with the result that each of them, great Theodore from the sea and Joseph the bishop from the mainland and the west, met in the same place and

συνελθεῖν καὶ ἴσης καὶ ὁμοτίμου τυχεῖν τῆς ἀνακομιδῆς καὶ τῆς καταθέσεως. Ἔδει γὰρ τοὺς πάντα σχόντας κοινὰ—καὶ βίον καὶ ἄθλησιν καὶ ὁμολογίαν καὶ ἀδελφικὴν συμφυΐαν καὶ σύμπνοιαν—καὶ τάφον κοινὸν σχεῖν καὶ ταφὴν ὁμότιμον καὶ ἰσοστάσιον. Εἰ δ' ὁ μὲν σῶος, ὁ δ' ἐλλείπων τοῖς μέρεσι κατατέθειται, ἀλλὰ τοῦτό γε τοῖς τοῦ Θεοῦ ἐναφῶμεν κρίμασιν, ὃς πολυτρόπως τὰ καθ' ἡμᾶς διεξάγων οὐδὲ τρίχα μίαν ἀπολελεῖφθαι τῆς ἡμετέρας συγχωρήσειε κεφαλῆς, ἀλλ' ὁλοκλήρους ἀποκαταστήσειε πάλιν, ἀφθάρτους, ἀγήρως, θεοειδεῖς ὅλους καὶ τὴν κρείττω ἀλλοιουμένους ἀλλοίωσιν. Οἷς ἅπασι καὶ οἱ ἡμέτεροι μεταποιηθέντες πατέρες καὶ πολλῷ πλέον κρείττονος καὶ θαυμασιωτέρας καὶ τῆς ἀποκαταστάσεως τύχοιεν καὶ τῆς τῶν σωμάτων θεοειδοῦς ἀλλοιώσεως· ἀλλὰ ταῦτα μὲν ἕξουσιν ἐν τῷ μελλοντι.

14

Νῦν δ' ὁ λόγος ἀναλαβέτω ἣν ἀνωτέρω διηγήμασιν ἔλιπεν· οὕτω γὰρ καὶ τοῖς παραλελειμμένοις ἐπιθήσει τὸ πέρας καὶ οὕτω τὰ τῆς κηδείας καὶ τῆς καταθέσεως ἀνὰ μέρος διέλθοι. Ὡς γὰρ ὁ ἱερὸς πατήρ, τὸ πολύολβον χρῆμα καὶ θεοδώρητον, τοῖς καινοῖς ἐκείνοις ἐσθήμασιν ἠμφιάσθη, καθά μοι καὶ πρὸ μικροῦ εἴρηται, καὶ πᾶν τὸ συρρεῦσαν πλῆθος παρέμενε τῷ λειψάνῳ καὶ ἐπὶ δύο ὅλας

obtained a translation and an interment that were equal and of the same honor. For it was proper that those who had everything in common—life, struggle, profession of faith, brotherly affinity, and harmony—should also have a common grave and a burial of the same honor and of equal status. If one was whole when buried, but the other lacked some of his parts, let us leave that to the judgments of God, who, in arranging our lives in many ways, would not allow even one hair of our heads to be lost, but would restore us again complete, uncorrupted, immortal, entirely godlike, and changed in a change for the better. Our fathers too, who made common cause in all these ways, would have gained a far better and more marvelous restoration and godlike change in their bodies. But they will have these in the world to come.

14

Now let my account take up again the description it earlier left off, for in that way it will attach an ending to what has been laid aside and thus may recount in sequence the funeral and the interment. For after the holy father, the precious and God-given treasure, had been wrapped in those new garments, as I mentioned a little earlier, all the assembled crowd waited in attendance beside the body for two

ἡμέρας τούτῳ προσήδρευον· καὶ οὐδεὶς ἐτύγχανε τὴν βασιλίδα οἰκῶν ὃς ἐκεῖ μὴ παρῆν ὀψόμενός τε σῶμα τὸ ἱερὸν καὶ τῆς ἀπ' αὐτοῦ μεταληψόμενος χάριτος. Ἐπεὶ οὖν οὕτω πᾶσιν εὐκταία ἡ πανήγυρις ἦν καὶ μάλιστα τοῖς ἀφικνουμένοις μοναχοῖς καὶ τοῖς τοῦ πατρὸς φοιτηταῖς κατὰ πνεῦμα συνηδομένοις, οἷς καὶ μείζων ὁ πόθος καὶ πλείων ἡ προθυμία καὶ ἡ συνέλευσις χαρίεσσα ὅτι μάλιστα, αὐτὸς ὁ θειότατος πατριάρχης, πάντων παρόντων, χερσὶν ἰδίαις τὸν ὅσιον ἀνελόμενος τῇ σορῷ κατατίθησι καὶ τὸ ἱερὸν καλύπτει σῶμα· ἐν ταὐτῷ δὲ καὶ τὰ τοῦ ἀδελφοῦ Ἰωσὴφ λείψανα τῷ αὐτῷ δίδωσι τάφῳ, ὃς πρότερον μὲν Πλάτωνα τὸν σοφὸν ἔνδον κατεῖχε—θεῖον δὲ ἀμφοτέρων ἴστε τὸν ἄνδρα τυγχάνοντα—νῦν δ' ὡς εἰκὸς καὶ τούτους συγκατασχὼν τοὺς τὰ πάντα καὶ ὁμοτίμους καὶ ὁμοτρόπους κοινὸς γέγονε τῶν τριῶν καὶ τάφος οὗτος καὶ μνῆμα καὶ χώρημα, καὶ τί ἄλλο ἢ θησαυρὸς πολύολβος καὶ ἀκένωτος.

2 Οὕτω γὰρ πάντως καὶ τοῖς πατράσι λυσιτελὲς ἐνομίσθη καὶ οὕτως ἔδοξεν ἑκατέροις, ἑνὶ καὶ τῷ αὐτῷ λίθῳ ἅμα κεκρύφθαι καὶ σὺν ἀλλήλοις κατατεθεῖσθαι, οὐ διὰ τὴν φύσιν μόνον καὶ τὴν ἐκ ταύτης οἰκείωσιν, ἀλλὰ πολλῷ πλεῖον διὰ τὴν ἀρετὴν καὶ τὴν ἀπὸ ταύτης συνάφειαν. Καὶ νῦν ἡμῖν ὁ τάφος ἀγχοῦ τῶν μαρτυρικῶν λειψάνων ἱστάμενος ἃ κατά τινα θειοτέραν ἐκεῖσε εὕρηται ἐπιφάνειαν, πολλὴν τοῖς προσιοῦσι παρέχει οὗτος τὴν χάριν, πολλὴν τοῖς πελάζουσι δίδωσι τὴν ὠφέλειαν. Ὡς γὰρ αὐτοὺς τοὺς θείους ἐνορῶντες πατέρας, οὕτω νύκτωρ καὶ μεθ' ἡμέραν πρόσιμεν τοῖς λειψάνοις, οὕτω ταῖς ἱεραῖς αὐτῶν εἰκόσιν, αἳ τῷ τάφῳ ἱστόρηνται, τοῖς ὀφθαλμοῖς ἀτενίζομεν, ψυχῆς ἅμα

whole days, and there was no one living in the capital who did not come to see the holy body and share in its grace. Since everyone was anxious for the festival, especially the monks who had come and the father's disciples, who were rejoicing in spirit and whose longing was greater, their eagerness more intense, and their gathering especially joyful, the most holy patriarch himself, in the presence of all, lifted the saintly man with his own hands, placed him in the coffin, and covered his holy body. At the same time he also committed the relics of Joseph his brother to the same tomb which previously held within it the wise Plato—you should know that he was the uncle of them both—but which now, as is appropriate, by also containing these men who were of the same honor and the same way of life in everything, has become the common tomb and memorial and receptacle for the three of them, and what else but a precious and inexhaustible treasure.

Since that arrangement was considered altogether advan- 2
tageous by the fathers, all parties thus agreed that they should be covered together by one and the same stone slab and be laid to rest with each other, not only because of their kinship and the affinity arising from it, but much more so because of their virtue and the bond stemming from that. And now the tomb, positioned near the relics of martyrs which had been discovered there through some divine manifestation, confers much grace on those who approach it and gives great benefit to those who draw near. For as though gazing upon the holy fathers themselves, we approach their relics both night and day, fixing our eyes on their holy images which are depicted at the tomb, and at the same time

καὶ σώματος κάθαρσιν κομιζόμενοι καὶ δαψιλῆ τὴν εὐεργεσίαν ἀντιλαμβάνοντες.

15

Οὐκοῦν καὶ μὴ ἐλλίποιτε, θειότατοι πατέρες καὶ ἡμέτεροι κηδεμόνες καὶ πρεσβευταί, ἐποπτεύειν ἡμᾶς καὶ ἐπιτηρεῖν καὶ Θεὸν ὑπὲρ ἡμῶν ἱλεοῦσθαι, ὡς ἂν τά τε ἄλλα καὶ συντηροίμεθα δι' ὑμῶν καὶ σῳζοίμεθα καὶ πρὸς τὰ κρείττω διεξαγοίμεθα. *Εἰ δὲ* καὶ αὐτόθι *καταλύσαιμεν*, δέχοισθε ἡμᾶς καὶ προσλαμβάνοισθε καὶ εἰς *σκηνὰς τὰς οὐρανίους* ἐγκατοικίζοιτε· σαὶ γὰρ ἐπαγγελίαι καὶ σαὶ ὑποσχέσεις, τιμιώτατε πάτερ καὶ ποιμενάρχα Θεόδωρε, ἐπικουρεῖν ἡμῖν ἀεί, βοηθεῖν, ἐπαμύνειν, ὡς ἰδίων προΐστασθαι τέκνων καὶ πληροῦν ἃ πρὸς σωτηρίαν αἰτήματα προβαλλόμεθα. Οἴδαμεν γὰρ τὸ περὶ ἡμᾶς σου κηδεμονικὸν καὶ φιλόστοργον· ἴσμεν σου τὸ πολὺ τῆς σκέπης καὶ τὴν πλουσίαν ἀντίληψιν· ἴσμεν καὶ πεποίθαμεν ὅτι πάντα γενήσῃ ἡμῖν καὶ πλοῦτος καὶ δόξα καὶ καύχημα καὶ ὁδηγὸς καὶ καθηγητὴς καὶ διδάσκαλος, καὶ πᾶν εἴ τι σκολιὸν ἐξευμαρίσεις, καὶ λεῖα τὰ τραχέα ποιήσεις, καὶ ὁδὸν τὴν πρὸς τὰ ἄνω φέρουσαν ὁμαλίσεις, καὶ Θεὸν ἡμῖν οἰκειώσεις, οὗ σὺ πρέσβις καὶ παραστάτης καὶ λάτρις καὶ διαλλακτὴς ἀγαθώτατος.

2 Καὶ γένοιτο ἡμῖν, ὦ πατέρων θαυμασιώτατε, διὰ σοῦ τὰ κρείττω ἑλέσθαι καὶ λυσιτελῆ, πάντα παραδραμοῦσιν ὅσα

acquiring cleansing of soul and body and receiving abundant advantage.

15

Therefore, most holy fathers, our guardians and intercessors, may you not fail to watch over us, look out for us, and propitiate God on our behalf, so that in all respects we may be preserved through you, granted salvation, and brought to a better state. *If we should die* here, may you receive us, take us in, and have us dwell *in the heavenly habitations.* For we will have your professions and your promises, Theodore, our most dear father and chief shepherd, to aid us always, to help, to defend, to protect us as your own children, and to fulfill the requests we make for salvation. For we know your caring and affectionate nature regarding us; we know the extent of your protection and your abundant aid; we know and are confident that you will be everything to us, riches, glory, a cause for pride, guide, leader, and teacher, everything that is crooked you will make easy, the rough places you will make smooth, you will make level the road that leads to the world above, and will reconcile us with God, whose ambassador, attendant, servant, and most kind mediator you are.

Through you, O most wonderful of fathers, may it come 2
to pass that we choose what is better and more advanta-

ὑπὸ τὴν αἴσθησιν, καὶ πάντα ὑπερβᾶσιν τὰ ὑπὸ τροπὴν καὶ ἀλλοίωσιν. Οὕτω γὰρ καὶ τῶν ἀεὶ μενόντων ἀντιληψόμεθα καὶ οὕτω *σταίημεν τῆς ἐφέσεως, τῶν ὀρεκτῶν* καταλαβόντες *τὸ ἔσχατον* καὶ Θεὸν εὑρόντες, ὃν εὑρεῖν καὶ λαβεῖν τῶν ἀγαθῶν τὸ ἀκρότατον. Τότε γὰρ καὶ τὴν ἀληθῆ πανήγυριν ἕξομεν, καὶ χαρὰν εὐφρανθησόμεθα τὴν ἀΐδιον, καὶ τῷ φωτὶ τῆς ἀρχικῆς καὶ μακαρίας Τριάδος ἐλλαμφθησόμεθα, καὶ Θεοῦ κατανόησιν ἴδωμεν ἢ λάβωμεν, δόξαν Πατρὸς καὶ Υἱοῦ καὶ Ἁγίου Πνεύματος τρανότερον ἐποπτεύοντες, καὶ τῶν *τριῶν ἀπείρων* τὴν *ἄπειρον* καὶ ἁπλῆν *συμφυΐαν* καὶ γνωρίζοντες καὶ καταλαμβάνοντες· οὐ γὰρ *ἐν ἐσόπτροις* ἔσται ἡμῖν ἡ κατάληψις, οὐδ' *ἐν σκιαῖς καὶ αἰνίγμασιν,* ἀλλ' αὐτῇ τῇ Ἀληθείᾳ, *αὐτῇ τῇ* πρώτῃ *Πηγῇ ἐντύχοιμεν γυμνῷ τῷ νῷ* τοῖς ἀθεάτοις προσβάλλοντες καὶ τοῖς ὑπὲρ γνῶσιν ἐμβατεύοντες καὶ κατάληψιν. Οὐ γὰρ ποικίλος ἔσται οὗτος τηνικαῦτα οὐδὲ πολυειδὴς καὶ εἰς πολλὰ μεριζόμενος, ἀλλ' ἁπλοῦς καὶ μονοειδὴς καὶ μόνου Θεοῦ καὶ ὅλου χωρητικός, ἡνίκα καὶ Θεὸς τῇ μεθέξει γενόμενος καὶ Θεῷ ἀμέσως ἑνούμενος τῷ κατὰ φύσιν ὁ κατὰ χάριν κατὰ τὸ μέτρον σχοίη τῆς ἀρετῆς καὶ τὴν ἀνάβασιν ἢ θέωσιν ἢ καὶ στάσιν καὶ τάξιν τοῦ κλήρου καὶ τῆς μονῆς ἃς πολλὰς οὔσας πάσας δεῖ πληρωθῆναι καὶ μερισθῆναι κατὰ τὴν ἀξίαν ἑκάστῳ καὶ τὴν τοῦ κρείττονος μετουσίαν. Ὧν μετάσχοιμεν καὶ ἡμεῖς καὶ βασιλείαν τὴν ἄνω κληρονομήσαιμεν ἐν Χριστῷ Ἰησοῦ τῷ Κυρίῳ ἡμῶν· ᾧ ἡ δόξα καὶ τὸ κράτος σὺν τῷ Πατρὶ καὶ τῷ Ἁγίῳ Πνεύματι νῦν καὶ εἰς τοὺς αἰῶνας τῶν αἰώνων. Ἀμήν.

geous, leaving aside all that is to do with the senses and passing beyond all that is subject to alteration and change. For in that way we will receive instead the things that remain forever and thus we may *put an end to our aspirations,* having gained *the ultimate goal of our desires* and finding God, whom it is the highest good to find and receive. Then we will celebrate the true festival, we will rejoice in everlasting joy and be illuminated with the light of the sovereign and blessed Trinity. And we will attain or receive a truly spiritual understanding of God, beholding more clearly the glory of the Father and the Son and the Holy Spirit by recognizing and comprehending the *infinite* and single *nature* of the *three infinite Ones.* For our comprehension will not be *by mirrors,* nor yet by *shadows and symbols,* but *we would meet* with Truth itself, *with the* first *Fount itself,* encountering invisible things *with our mind alone* and reaching things beyond knowledge and comprehension. For at that time the mind will not be complex, nor multiform and divided into many parts, but single, uniform, and receptive of God wholly and completely; when it is becoming God by participation and is being united with God without any intermediary in accordance with God's nature and according to the measure of virtue the mind had by grace, and its ascent or divinization or the status and rank of its allotment and dwelling—all of which, being many, must be filled and distributed to each according to their worthiness and their participation in divinity. May we too share in these things and inherit the kingdom of heaven in Christ Jesus our Lord, to whom be glory and might, together with the Father and the Holy Spirit, now and to the ages of ages. Amen.

Abbreviations

AASS = *Acta Sanctorum,* 71 vols. (Paris, 1863–1940)

AB = *Analecta Bollandiana* (Brussels, 1882–)

BHG = François Halkin, *Bibliotheca hagiographica Graeca,* 3rd ed. (Brussels, 1957). See also François Halkin, *Novum auctarium bibliothecae hagiographicae Graecae* (Brussels, 1984).

BMFD = John P. Thomas and Angela Constantinides Hero, eds., *Byzantine Monastic Foundation Documents,* 5 vols. (Washington, DC, 2000)

Cyril of Alexandria, *De adoratione* = Cyril of Alexandria, *De adoratione et cultu in spiritu et veritate libri XVII,* PG 68:133–1126

Ep(p). = Georgios Fatouros, ed., *Theodori Studitae Epistulae,* 2 vols. (Berlin, 1992)

Great Katecheseis = Joseph Cozza-Luzi, ed., *Sancti patris nostri Theodori Studitae Magna Catechesis,* in *Novae patrum bibliothecae,* vol. 9, part 2, and vol. 10, part 1 (Rome, 1888–1905). See also (Book 2 only) Athanasios Papadopoulos-Kerameus, ed., *Τοῦ ὁσίου Θεοδώρου Στουδίτου Μεγάλη Κατήχησις* (Saint Petersburg, 1904). French trans., Florence de Montleau, *Les grandes catéchèses (Livre I). Les Epigrammes (I–XXIX), précédées d'une étude de Julien Leroy sur le monachisme stoudite* (Bégrolles-en-Mauges, 2002).

Lesser Katecheseis = Emmanuel Auvray and Albert Tougard, eds., *Κατηχήσεις πρὸς τοὺς ἑαυτοῦ μαθητάς; Sancti patris nostri et confessoris Theodori Studitis praepositi parva catechesis* (Paris, 1891). French trans., Anne-Marie Mohr, *Petites catéchèses* (Paris, 1993).

ODB = Alexander P. Kazhdan, Alice-Mary Talbot, Anthony Cutler, Timothy E. Gregory, and Nancy P. Ševčenko, eds., *Oxford Dictionary of Byzantium,* 3 vols. (New York, 1991)

PG = Jacques-Paul Migne, *Patrologia cursus completus: Series graeca,* 161 vols. (Paris, 1857–1866)

PmbZ Online = Ralph-Johannes Lilie et al., eds., *Prosopographie der mittelbyzantinischen Zeit Online* (Berlin, 2013–); available at http://www.degruyter.com/view/db/pmbz

REB = *Revue des études byzantines* (Paris, 1946–)

RegPatr = Venance Grumel et al., eds., *Les regestes des actes du Patriarcat de Constantinople,* vol. 1, *Les actes des patriarches,* fascicles 2–3, *Les regestes de 715 à 1206,* 2nd rev. ed. by Jean Darrouzès (Paris, 1989)

Scriptor incertus = Francesca Iadevaia, ed., *Scriptor incertus: Testo critico, traduzione e note,* 2nd ed. (Messina, 1997)

Note on the Texts

Life of Theodore of Stoudios by Michael the Monk

Sigla

O = Ottobonianus graecus 358; 16th cent.; folios 1r–65r

O_1 = Vaticanus graecus 1256; 16th cent.; folios 1r–33r

P = Parisinus graecus 755; 12th cent.; folios 307v–70v with a lacuna between 2.2 μᾶλλον δέ, and 3.2 ἐν ταῖς συνάξεσι

V = Vaticanus graecus 1669; 10th cent.; folios 199r–257r

The *Life* was first published by Angelo Mai in *Novae patrum bibliotheca,* vols. 1–7 (Rome, 1852–1854), vol. 6, part 2, pp. 291–363, and on this basis in PG 99:233–328.

This new edition of the text of the *Life of Theodore of Stoudios* by Michael the Monk (*BHG* 1745) has been transcribed from folios 199r–257r of MS Vaticanus graecus 1669 (V), the oldest surviving witness, a parchment manuscript dated to the beginning of the tenth century, now available online (see https://digi.vatlib.it/view/MSS_Vat.gr.1669). For a detailed description of this codex, see Ciro Giannelli, *Codices Vaticani graeci 1485–1683* (Vatican City, 1950), 415–19. It is a pre-Metaphrastic *menologion* containing readings for the month of November: the commemoration of Theodore occurs on

November 11 (see Tatiana Matantseva, "Le *Vaticanus graecus* 1669: Ménologe prémétaphrastique de novembre," *Scriptorium* 50, no. 1 (1996): 106–14). This transcription has been collated with the text preserved by another parchment manuscript dated to the twelfth century, MS Parisinus graecus 755 (P), originally belonging to the monastery of the Holy Trinity in Chalke. For an online facsimile of P, see https://gallica.bnf.fr/ark:/12148/btv1b10509299n/f1.item; for relevant bibliography, see *Pinakes* (https://pinakes.irht.cnrs.fr/notices/cote/50338/).

We have also taken into account two more manuscripts. First is MS Vaticanus graecus 1256 (O_1), a paper manuscript dated to the sixteenth century, in which our text is in a deplorable state, with egregious errors, misspellings, redundant repetitions of syllables, words, and phrases, and extensive omissions (see online at https://digi.vatlib.it/view/MSS_Vat.gr.1256). The second is MS Ottobonianus graecus 358 (O) of the sixteenth century (see online at https://digi.vatlib.it/view/MSS_Ott.gr.358), which is in much better shape compared to O_1. Their usefulness is limited, since O is considered a copy of V, and O_1 a copy of O (Matantseva, "Eloge des archanges Michel et Gabriel par Michel le Moine (BHG 1249a)," *Jahrbuch der Österreichischen Byzantinistik* 46 (1996): 110). However, the possibility that O is not a direct copy of V is somewhat suggested by the fact that in some cases the readings of O agree with P against those of V.

In V, the title of Theodore's *Life* has an ornamental surround on three sides enclosing the title, which is in firm capitals; in contrast, the title of the next entry in the *Menologion,* on folio 257v, appears in less firm capitals and has no surround. The first folio (fol. 199) of Theodore's *Life* is written

in a different hand from the rest of the text. This suggests that it is a replacement and was written by another, later, hand; see Matantseva, "Le *Vaticanus graecus* 1669," 107n8.

The text contains frequent examples of iotacism and often shows confusion between omicron and omega. There are no subscripts, and breathings are difficult to read. There are some mistakes in accentuation. All such instances have been tacitly corrected. As the text in the manuscript has no divisions, it has been divided into chapters and paragraphs according to the subject matter.

There are five marginalia written by later hands; four of these are indicated by omission marks in the text, and one is without any mark. All these marginalia are discussed in the Notes to the Texts, and the four marked as omissions have been included in the text and translation since they contain additional information regarding Theodore and his family.

The text in P begins after a thin decorative line separating it from the previous one in the left column of folio 307v/308v (the folios are numbered in both Greek and Arabic numerals, with the Greek numbering being one figure ahead of the Arabic one). Due to a one-folio lacuna after fol. 309v/310v, the section of text between 2.2 μᾶλλον δὲ and 3.2 ἐν ταῖς συνάξεσι is lost. The order of folios is also disturbed: folios 311/312–317/318, 325/326–326/327, 336/337, 338/339, and 340/341 are out of sequence. At each disruption, notes in the lower verso margin point the reader to the folios where the text normally continues.

Manuscript P is easy to read, and there are fewer grammatical errors in it than in V. As is evident in the Notes to the Texts, we have adopted a small number of its readings against those of V and O, but usually the P text is marred

by numerous omissions of single words. As in V, the text in this manuscript is not divided into sections. Manuscripts O and O_1, both of the sixteenth century, are of no major significance and in most cases simply corroborate the readings of V.

Encyclical Letter of Naukratios

Sigla

A = Mediolanensis Ambrosianus C 2 sup.; 9th cent.; folios 165v–72v

B = Parisinus graecus 893; 13th cent.; folios 220r–32r

C = Parisinus graecus 501; 12th–13th cent.; folios 141v–49r

D= Lesbos, Monasterii Leimonos 9; 12th cent.; folios 146r–54v

E = Lesbos, Monasterii Leimonos 13; 12th cent.; folios 260r–67v

F = Florentinus, Laurentianus graecus plut. IV 4; 12th cent.; folios 87r–95v

G = Venetus Marcianus graecus Z 141; 11th cent.; folios 235r–47r

H = Atheniensis Bibliothecae Nationalis graecus 221; 12th cent.; folios 258r–67v (with a lacuna between sections 3 ἀλλὰ τὴν and 16 ὀφθέντες ὁμοταγῶν)

I = Messanensis, Sancti Salvatoris 83; 12th cent.; folios 288v–97v

J = Venetus Marcianus graecus II 41 (1122); 13th cent.; folios 244v–53r (stops at the end of section 18)

K = Sinaiticus Monasterii Sanctae Aecaterinae 401; 1086; folios 169r–77v

L = Lipsiensis Bibliothecae Universitatis cod. graecus 15; end 12th cent.; folios 211v, 284r–87v, 66r–67v, 287v–90v

M = Neapolitanus Bibliothecae Nationalis Vittorio Emmanuele III II B 20; 1026; folios 187v–202v

N = Parisinus graecus 819; 16th cent.; folios 208v–9v, 230r–35r

O = Ottobonianus graecus 172; 16th cent.; folios 170r–83v

P = Parisinus graecus 1018; 10th cent.; folios 298r–314v

Q = Bodleianus Laud. graecus 89; 11th cent.; folios 199–202v (starting at section 11 . . . πρὸ τῶν ἄλλων . . . and ending at section 23 μεγαλο<μάρτυρος>)

R = Parisinus Coislinianus. graecus 271; 11th–12th cent.; folios 109v–17r, 99r–101r, 117r–22r

S = Parisinus Suppl. graecum 1386; 1075; folios 334v–42v, 77r–80r, 342v–49r (with a lacuna between sections 5 ὁ νέος and 7 τὸν ὑπερασπιστὴν)

T = Venetus Marcianus graecus II 47 (1104); 13th cent.; folios 232r–44r

U = Parisinus Coislinianus graecus 273; 13th–14th cent.; folios 287v–96r

V = Ottobonianus graecus 251; 10th cent.; folios 92v–97v

W = Matritensis, Bibliothecae Nationalis Esp. graecus 4605; 12th cent.; folios 216v–21v (after 5 καταπλουτή the right half of the folios has been cut off resulting in a loss of more than forty percent of the text)

The *Letter of Naukratios* (*BHG* 1756) was first published by François Combefis in *Historia haeresis monothelitarum* (Paris, 1648) and on this basis in PG 99:1825–49. This new edition has been prepared on the witness of twenty-three manuscripts, including the three earliest (although not the best) surviving ones. See the list, not intended to be complete, in Olivier Delouis, "Le *Testament* de Théodore Stoudite est-il de Théodore?," *REB* 66 (2008): 173–90, at 188. Of the manuscripts collated for this edition, one belongs to the ninth century (A), two to the tenth (P, V), six to the eleventh (G,

K, M, Q, R, S), seven to the twelfth (D, E, F, H, I, L, W), five to the thirteenth (B, C, J, T, U), and two to the sixteenth (N, O).

The earliest manuscripts are: Ambrosianus C 2 sup. (= A) of the ninth century, Ottobonianus graecus 251 (= V), and Parisinus graecus 1018 (= P), both of the tenth century. See Emidio Martini and Domenico Bassi, eds., *Catalogus codicum graecorum Bibliothecae Ambrosianae,* 2 vols. (Milan, 1906; repr. in one vol., Hildesheim, 1978), no. 162; Ernest Féron and Fabiano Battaglini, eds., *Bibliothecae Apostolicae Vaticanae . . . Codices manuscripti Graeci Ottoboniani Bibliothecae Vaticanae* (Vatican City, 1893), 142–43; Henri Omont, *Inventaire sommaire des manuscrits grec de la Bibliothèque nationale,* vol. 1, *Ancien fonds grecs: Théologie* (Paris, 1886), no. 1018 (p. 203). Unfortunately, A, besides being difficult to read at times, has a lacuna, the extent of which is indicated above and in the Notes to the Texts. Fortunately, both tenth-century manuscripts have been digitized by their respective libraries and are now accessible online (V is at https://digi.vatlib.it/view/MSS_Ott.gr.251 and P at https://gallica.bnf.fr/ark:/12148/btv1b107226096/f1.image). Together with these, a considerable number of those listed in the *Pinakes* online database for the *Letter of Naukratios* are also digitized and accessible on the internet. There, forty-nine manuscripts are included (forty-four after removing double entries and erroneous listings), of which thirteen are of the sixteenth century or later and one is not dated. We also consulted the manuscripts British Library, Add. MS 15422, Parisinus graecus 894, and Parisinus Coislinianus graecus 272, but did not make use of them.

As a more careful perusal of the relevant Notes to the Texts may indicate, the majority of manuscripts are divided

into two major families within which some particular subgroups are formed, such as those consisting of manuscripts IKQVW or EFNO (common omissions). Still, we have avoided discarding a number of manuscripts because even a rather inferior manuscript, such as the Parisinus graecus 501 (C), provides a reading that makes perfect sense (2 πλωτήρ) but is missing from all other collated manuscripts. In another instance it is only the Parisinus Coislinianus graecus 271 (R) that provides a correct phrase (8 ἢ μόνον εἰς Θεὸν καὶ εἰς τὴν τοῦ ἱεροῦ τάφου παρεδρευτικὴν ἀπόβλεψιν), followed closely by E (ἢ μόνην τὴν εἰς Θεὸν και εἰς τὸν ἱερὸν τάφον παρεδρευτικὴν ἀπόβλεψιν), whereas all other manuscripts provide a reading that violates the rules of syntax. One manuscript that has been given a relatively preferential treatment is the twelfth-century Lesbos, Monasterii Leimonos 13 (E), due to providing a number of words absent from all other manuscripts that complete the meaning. Manuscript E, in addition, may have preserved a number of readings perhaps reflecting an earlier version of the text, closer to its original redaction by Naukratios, because the phrasing is very personal in tone compared to the readings of all other manuscripts: 3 ταπεινῆς μου . . . διασημαίνων E, ταπεινῆς ἡμῶν . . . διασημαίνοντες all other manuscripts; 25 παρεδώκαμεν E, παρεδόθη all other manuscripts (reading not adopted in the main text).

As one would expect, a considerable number of manuscripts show a confusion of ο and ω, as well as of ι, ει, and η to varying degrees; breathings and accents are sometimes incorrect, and there are no iota subscripts. All instances of these errors have been tacitly corrected. This text also has been divided into chapters according to the subject matter.

Translation and Burial of the Remains of Theodore of Stoudios and Joseph of Thessalonike

Sigla

P = Parisinus graecus 1456 (Colbert 2588); 11th cent.; folios 217r–29v

Van de Vorst = Charles van de Vorst, ed., "La Translation de S. Théodore Studite et de S. Joseph de Thessalonique," in *AB* 32 (1913): 50–61

The Greek text used for this work (*BHG* 1756t) is that published by Van de Vorst with very few changes, alterations, or emendations. The original text is found in folios 217r–29v of manuscript P, dated to the eleventh century. This manuscript, which has now been digitized (https://gallica.bnf.fr/ark:/12148/btv1b10723321n/f1.image), contains fragments of two Metaphrastic *menologia* for the months of November and January, in which this text is set for January 26, displacing that of Xenophon and his children, John and Arkadios, to January 30. See Bollandist Hagiographers and Henri Omont, eds., *Catalogus codicum hagiographicorum graecorum Bibliothecae nationalis Parisiensis* (Brussels and Paris, 1896), no. 1456 (pp. 128–29).

For the text published here, two very minor typographical errors have been tacitly corrected and two emendations made. The hyphens and square brackets that Van de Vorst inserted into his text have been removed. The numbering of the paragraphs into which Van de Vorst divided his text has been kept here as chapter divisions; these, where helpful, have been subdivided into paragraphs.

Notes to the Texts

Life of Theodore of Stoudios by Michael the Monk

title εὐλόγησον πάτερ *omitted* OV

1.1 πατριὰς OV: πατρίδας P

πᾶσαν OVP: ἅπασαν O_1

ἀνδρείᾳ O: ἀνδρία PV

ἐκθυμότατος OV: εὐθυμότατος P

συλλελεχὼς OV: συλλελεγχῶς P, συλλεχὼς O_1

1.2 ἐβίω OV: ἐν βίω P

συνέταξαν ὑπόμνημα, *Jordan*: συνέταξαν, ὑπόμνημα OPV

2.2 λάλον *Alexakis*: λάλων OPV

ταμίας: ταμείας OPV

βασιλικῶν φόρων OV: βασιλικῶν φροντίδων τε καὶ φόρων P

τῆς ἐν βασιλείοις αὐλῆς <διατριβῆς>: *addition based on a similar sentence from the* Life of Athanasius I of Constantinople *by Theoktistos of Stoudios*, τοῖς (τῆς PV) ἐν βασιλείοις αὐλαῖς OPV

3.1 περίπυστος *Alexakis*: περίπατος O, περίππ . . . ος V

3.4 τ' ἀγαθὸν P: ἀγαθὸν OV

ἐπιτυχίαν OV: ἐπιθυμίαν P

4.1 καταποθέντος P: καταπορθέντος OV

μηδ' ἐβούλετο *Jordan*: μὴ δὲ βούλετο OV (*with* η *over* ε V), βούλοιτο P

δαιμόνων τε OV: τε *omitted* P

4.3 συμπονήσων *Jordan*: συμπονέσων OPV

V *after* καθαίρεσιν: *sign indicating note in lower margin, and a later hand has added at the bottom of fol. 203r* εἰς τὴν τῶν θείων . . . πίστεως

4.4 ἀμείνονος *Jordan*: ἀμείνω OPV

5.2 στρεφομένων OP: τρεφομένων V

6.2 τὴν δέ γε OV: γε *omitted* P

8.3 προσφυῶς OV: *omitted* P

9.1 σοφίας τε καὶ φρονήσεως αὐτοῦ OV: σοφίας αὐτοῦ καὶ φρονήσεως P

9.2 θήλεα *Jordan*: θήλεια PV, θήλειαν O

10.3 ταῖς ἀρεταῖς ὁσημέραι OV: *omitted* P

πειθαρχοῦντα, συνεγνωκὼς *Jordan*: πειθαρχοῦντα συνεγνωκώς, OPV

10.4 πολλοῖς *Alexakis*: πολλοὺς OPV

10.5 ποιμενομένων OV: ποιμένων P

11.2 Μαδιηνέων V *(with* ι *inserted before* η*)*: Μαδηνέων O, Μαδινηέων P

11.3 κατὰ τὸν ἔνδον *Alexakis*: κατὰ τῶν ἔνδων OPV

11.4 <μάλιστα> *added by Alexakis*

12.1 ἧς τὸ ὄνομα Θεοδότη O: *omitted* PV, *although in* V, *after* ἠγάγετο, *an omission mark appears, but the note in the right-hand margin is illegible. The same phrase is also found in Vat. gr. 608 fol. 142v, and in Vat. gr. 1256 fol. 7v.*

12.2 μοιχωμένων *Jordan*: μοιχομένων OPV

12.3 προφανῶς OV: *omitted* P

ἀπωδύρετο *Jordan*: ἀπεδύρετο OPV

12.4 *the following note is found at this point in the right-hand margin of* P *and* V: ὅτι ἐξαδέλφη ἐτύγχανε τοῦ πατρὸς ἡμῶν Θεοδώρου ἡ συστεφθεῖσα τῷ Κωνσταντίνῳ. *There is no mark to indicate that it is an omission, so we may conclude that it is an explanatory note.*

12.5 *after* ἀπελθεῖν V: *sign indicating note in margin, and a later hand has added in the left-hand margin of fol. 211v the words* τὸν μέντοι . . . ἐγκελευσάμενοι

13.2 Ἠλιοῦ τοῦ Θεσβίτου P: τοῦ θεσβίτου Ἠλιοῦ *(*α *above line)* O, τοῦ θεσβίτου *(*β *above line)* Ἠλιοῦ V

προσρήματα *Alexakis*: προτερήματα OPV

13.3 ἀνόμων OV: ἀσεβῶν P

14.1 ἅμα τῷ V: ἅμα τοῦ OP

14.3 πολεμικῆς OV: *omitted* P

14.4 πολιτείας τε καὶ P: *omitted* OV

κατήρδευε O: κατέρδευε PV

15.1 κατὰ τοῦτο τοῦ OV: κατὰ τοῦ τότε P

after Στουδίου V: *omission mark indicating an addition in the left-hand margin of fol. 214v by a later hand*: πάλαι πρὸς αὐτοῦ οἰκοδομηθεῖσαν . . . τὸν ἀριθμὸν ἐάσας τούτους ἔσεσθαι

ἐάσας τούτους ἔσεσθαι V: ἐάσας τούτους ἔσθαι P, ἐάσας ἔσεσθαι O

15.2 κατοικισθῆναι *Jordan*: κατωκισθῆναι OPV

ὑπερχομένους OV: δι' ἐρχομένους P

τῆς ἐπαγγελίας κατάπαυσιν OV: ἐπαγγελίας κατάστασίν τε και κατάπαυσιν P

15.4 <τοῖς> τῆς ἐπὶ πάσῃ *Alexakis*: τοῖς ἐπὶ πᾶσι O, τῆς ἐπὶ πᾶσι PV

ὥρας *Alexakis*: ὥρας OPV

ὑπαρχόντων αὐτῷ OV: αὐτῷ *omitted* P

ἱματιοδόχου *Jordan*: ἱματοδόχου OPV

διοίσοντα *Jordan*: δι' οἶσον OPV, *perhaps* διαφέροντα?

ὄντα *Jordan*: ὢν OPV

καί τινες *Jordan*: καί τιναι OPV

16.1 <οἷόν> *added by Jordan*

νοσημάτων OV: *omitted* P

16.4 δεινότατον OV: δεινὸν P

16.5 τοῦ Κυρίου OV: τοῦ *omitted* P

ἣν αὐτὸς *Jordan*: ἦν αὐτὸς OPV

17.1 χαιρέκακος OV *(inserted as a correction above line V)*: χαιρεσίκακος PV

after χαιρέκακος P *adds* δαίμων ἐκεῖνος

μελάντατος *Jordan*: μελαντάτης OPV

σοβαρόγνωμον OPV: *perhaps* ἑτερόγνωμον?

17.3 κατεργάσηται OV: ἐργάσηται P

17.4 ᾠκονόμησεν OV: οἰκονόμησεν P

18.1 πρόμος PV: πρόμαχος O

ἐχώριζον OV: ἐχώριζεν P

18.2 οὐδενὸς λόγου OV: μηδενὸς λόγου P

καὶ καθηγεμόνι OV: καὶ *omitted* P

μυηθέντες PV: μνησθέντες O

19.1 τραυματίου *Jordan*: τραυματία OPV
δυσὶ *Alexakis*: δύο OPV
19.2 σταθηρὰ PV: σταθερὰ O
20.1 ἐξ ἔθους OV: *omitted* P
20.2 πόνῳ *Jordan*: πόνων OPV
21.1 ἐλθὼν δὲ PV: ἐλθὼν γὰρ O
ὕπουλον PV: ὕφαλον OV *(correction in margin)*
21.2 ὡς ἐβούλετο πραγμάτων OV: πραγμάτων ὡς ἐβούλετο P
τῆς . . . θεοεχθείας *Jordan*: τὴν . . . θεοεχθείας OPV
21.3 καὶ ἐξ αὐτῆς OV: κἀξ αὐτῆς P
οὕτω γ' οὖν PV: οὕτω γὰρ O
22.1 λεκανόμαντις: λεκανομάντις O, λακανόμαντις PV *(with* ε *above* α*)*
<εἰ>σηγηθεὶς *Alexakis*: σιγηθεὶς OPV
ὑποσχέσεις κοσμικοῖς *Alexakis*: ὑποσχέσεσι κοσμικαῖς OPV
22.3 ἀμφοτέρων OV: *omitted* P
22.5 ῥερᾳδιουργηκότων *Jordan*: ῥερᾳδουργηκότων OPV
22.6 πείθεις με *Jordan*: πείθεις μοι OPV
23.1 οὐκέτι οἷός τε ἦν OV: οὐχ' οἷός τε ἦν P
23.3 συμπεπτωκότα ἤδη τῇ θλίψει OV: ἤδη τῇ θλίψει συμπεπτωκότα P
ἐχούσης; *there is no question mark in the manuscript, but one seems necessary*
δευτέρια PV: δευτερεῖα O
23.4 Δύστρου OV: Μαρτίου PVO *(in the right-hand margin)*
ὑποσταλείης *Jordan*: ὑποσταλεὶς OPV
23.5 <τοῦ> *added by Alexakis*
24.1 ὀνόματος τοῦ Χριστοῦ OP: τοῦ Χριστοῦ *added by a later hand in the margin of fol. 232v* V
24.3 ἀρχῆς *Alexakis*: αὐτῆς OPV
24.4 καταφοινίσσει OV: φοινίσσει P
24.5 τέσσαρας OV: τέτταρας P
25.1 ἐπανάγειν OV: ἐπάγειν P
οὐ διήμαρτεν O *(in the margin)* P: οὐ *omitted* V
25.4 ἀφιματώσας *Jordan*: ἀμφιματώσας OPV

ἀνακαγχάσας *Jordan*: ἀνακακχάσας OPV

25.6 ἵπποις OP: ἵπποις *added by a later hand in the left-hand margin of fol. 237v* V

26.1 ἀγκυλομήτης OV (ης *above* ος): ἀγκυλόμητος PV

ἐπιρρίψωμεν . . . ἡμῶν P: ἐπιρρίψωμεν πᾶσαν τὴν μέριμνα ἡμῶν πρὸς τὸν Κύριον OV

26.2 κοίρανος PV: τύραννος O

26.3 Περιτίου OV: Φευρουαρίου P *and gloss in the left-hand margin* V

26.4 θέματι OV: θεάματι P

ἐν αὐταῖς *Jordan*: ἐν αὐτοῖς OPV

26.5 ἀποκυήσαντες *Alexakis*: ἀποκυλήσαντες OPV

ἓν μόγις OV: ἓν καὶ μόνον P

27.1 ἀποκατασταθέντος OV: κατασταθέντος P

27.4 ἀέθλοις PV: ἄθλοις O

σαρκὶ πεπονθότι Χριστῷ PV: παθόντι Χριστῶ O

τ<ρ>όπου: ρ *added Alexakis*

27.7 τήν τε ὑποστροφὴν ἐξεῖπεν αὐτίκα τῆς ἀρρωστίας OV: αὐτίκα τῆς ἀρρωστίας τήν τε ὑποστροφὴν ἐξεῖπεν P

κατὰ . . . Κύριλλον: *omitted* P

28.2 τὸ ζῆν *Jordan*: τῶ ζῆν OPV

ἀσέβεια τοῦ Λιβάνου καλύψει σε OV: καλύψει σε ἀσέβεια τοῦ Λιβάνου P

29.1 φιλοφρόνως OV: *omitted* P

30.1 α′: *added in the left-hand margin* PV

30.2 β′: *added in margin* PV

κάνθωνος OV: ὄνου P *and gloss in left-hand margin* V

30.3 γ′: *added in margin* PV

οὕτως εἰπὼν P: οὕτως εἶπεν OV

Οὗτος *Alexakis*: οὕτως OV, *omitted* P

αὐτοῦ OP: ἑαυτοῦ V

30.4 δ′: *added in margin* PV

ἅλματι OV: αἵματι P

31.1 ε′: *added in margin* PV

31.2 *after* ἐν τῷ P *adds* οὖν

31.3 στ′: *added in margin* PV

ποιμηνάντων *correction above* ποιμαινευσάντων V: ποιμαινευσάντων OPV

θημωνίας: *this accentuation is found in the manuscripts and so remains unchanged despite the comment in Liddell and Scott*

προαναπεσεῖν OV: ἀναπεσεῖν P

πυραὶ O: πυρραὶ V, πυρκαϊαὶ P *and gloss in right-hand margin* V

31.4 ζʹ: *added in margin* PV

ἀνὴρ P: *omitted* OV

συμφλέξει *Jordan*: συνφλέξει OPV

ἱστάμην: εἱστάμην OPV

31.5 ηʹ: *added in margin* PV

Σαρδονικῆς: σαρδανικῆς OPV

ἐξέπιον OP: ἐξέσιον *with correction in the left-hand margin* V

31.6 ποιημάτων O: πονημάτων PV

Ἐντολὴν ἔχετε OV: *omitted* P

καὶ ἐνσημάντρους ἐν τῷ ἐμῷ σώματι OV: ἐν τῷ ἐμῷ σώματι καὶ ἐνσημάντρους P

32.1 θʹ: *added in margin* PV

In the left-hand margin next to Ἄλλος δὲ πάλιν P *adds* ιʹ.

τοῦ ἱεροῦ αὐτοῦ τάφου OV: τοῦ τάφου αὐτοῦ P

32.2 ιαʹ, ιβʹ: *added in margin* PV

ἀφώριστο *Jordan*: ἠφόριστο OPV

32.3 μεθ’ ἡμᾶς γε OV: γε *omitted*

33.1 ὀρθοδόξων O: ὀρθῶν PV

34.2 Κρησκεντίου *Jordan*: τρισκεντίου OPV

34.3 τινας αὐτῶν *Jordan*: τινας αὐτῶ OPV

ἐπιλεγομένην καὶ: καὶ *omitted* PV

34.5 θάνατον *Alexakis*: θανάτου OPV

34.6 τοῦ βίου τὰ τέλη πεφοιτηκώς PV: τὰ τέλη τοῦ βίου ἀπεφοιτηκώς O

χώραν καὶ πόλιν OV: πόλιν καὶ χώραν P

ἡδίω *Jordan*: ἡδείων OPV

35.4 τρίτον OV: πάντας P

ἐπηύξατο αὐτοῖς OV: ἐπηύξατο αὐτοὺς P

35.7 Κυρίου καὶ P: *omitted* OV

τῶν σωμάτων P: τῶν *omitted* OV

λυτρώμεθα OV *(after correction)*: λυτρούμεθα P

βίος τοῦ ὁσίου πατρὸς ἡμῶν Θεοδώρου *added after the end of the text between horizontal decorative lines* OV

Encyclical Letter of Naukratios

title Τοῖς διὰ Κύριον δεδιωγμένοις καὶ πανταχοῦ διεσπαρμένοις πνευματικοῖς ἀδελφοῖς καὶ πατράσι, Ναυκράτιος ἁμαρτωλὸς μοναχός ABDEFGHIJKLMNPRSTUVW

Ναυκρατίου ἐπιστολῆ τοῖς διὰ Χριστὸν δεδιωγμένοις καὶ πανταχοῦ διεσπαρμένοις πνευματικοῖς ἀδελφοῖς καὶ πατρᾶσι O

Ἐπιστολὴ Ναυκρατίου μοναχοῦ εἰς τὴν κοίμησιν τοῦ ὁσίου πατρὸς ἡμῶν Θεοδώρου τοῦ Στουδίτου πεμφθεῖσα πρὸς τοὺς ὑπὲρ εὐσεβείας δεδιωγμένους ἀδελφούς C

1 ἐνεργέστερον ABCDGHIJKLMPSUVW: ἐναργέστερον EFONRT

προακουτισθὲν BCDEFGHJLMNOPRSTUV: προακουσθὲν AIKW

ἂν εἰ καὶ ABDEFGHJLMNOPRSTU: εἰ *omitted* CKVW

λιθίνην ἔχων ABCDGHIJLMPRSTUVW: λιθίνην ἔχει EFNO, *omitted* K

κοινὴν ABCDEFGHJLMNOPRSTU: *omitted* IKVW

2 Ναὶ: *omitted* E, Καὶ J

ὁ πολλὰ . . . πατὴρ ἡμῶν ABCDEFGHJLMNOPRST: *omitted* IKVW

οἰκουμενικὸς ABCDEFGHJLMNOPRSTU: οἰκονομικὸς IKVW

ἀένναος ACDEFIJKLMNORSTVW: ἀέναος BGHP

πλωτὴρ (πλοτὴρ) C: *omitted by all other manuscripts*

3 εἵνεκα: εἵνεκεν IW, εἶναι καὶ K

ἐξευρεθείη ABCDFGHJLMNOPRSTU: εὑρεθείη IKVW

lacuna in H *begins after* ἀλλὰ τὴν

ταπεινῆς ἡμῶν *all other manuscripts*: ταπεινῆς μου E

διασημαίνοντες *all other manuscripts*: διασημαίνων E

ἐπιτετευγμένος BCEFGJLPMNRTUV: ἐπιτετεγμένος AO, ἐπιτεταγμένος IKLSW, ἐπιτευγμένος D

after γνήσιος AMT *add* τοῦ

4 ὢ[2] ABCDEIKLPRSTUVW: *omitted* FGJMNO

σοφία ἡ ἄρρητος EV: ἡ *omitted* ABCDFGJKLMNOPSTUW, σοφία ἀπόρρητος R

ἀπωδύρατο ABFGLNOPRST: ἀπωδύρετο E, ἀποδύρατο CD JMU, ἀπεδύρετο IW, ἀπεδύρατο KV

5 ἐξηχητής ABCDGIJKLPSU: ἐξηγητής EFMNORV, ἐξηχητίς TW

εἶρκται DFGINOUVW: εἴρκται ABCEJKLPRST, εἴρηται M

καταπλουτήσασα ACDIJKLMSUVW: καταπλουτίσασα BE FGNOPRT

προβλέψας: βλέψας IK

6 *lacuna in* S *begins after* ὁ νέος

ταὐτὸν δὲ εἰπεῖν, πολλῶν πατὴρ ABEFGJKLMNOPRTUV: *omitted* CDIW

after πόλεις IJKV *add* καὶ

κατέβαλεν CJLRUV: κατέβαλλεν ABDEFGIKMNOPTW

ὀξύτερον ABCDGIJLMPTV: ὀξύτερων K, ὀξύτερος EFNO RU

<ἐν> *added from the original text*

οὕτω σταθερῶ CD: οὕτως σταθερῷ ABEGJLMPTUV, οὕτω σταθηρῷ FIKNOR

τάχιον ABCDFGILNOPRTVW: τάχει E, τάχειον JMU

ὑπερτενὲς ABCDFGILNOPRTUV: ὑπερτινὲς J, ὑπέρμηκες E, ὑπερτελὲς M

7 ἀδελφοί μου: μοι W, μου *omitted* A

ἀπέπτη: ἀπέστη MU

lacuna in S *ends before* τὸν ὑπερασπιστὴν

ποιοῦνται: ποιεῖται CE

8 τούτων ER: τούτοις *all other manuscripts*

οἱ ταπεινοὶ . . . διαζευχθέντες: καὶ πρὸ πάντων *omitted* I, ταπεινοὶ ἀπωρφανισμένοι μετὰ πάντων καὶ πρὸ πάντων· καὶ τὰ νῦν διαζευχθέντες R

κακοδόξοις: ὀρθοδόξοις LS

εἰκονομάχων: οἰκονομάχων AIK

ψυχὴ ἡμῶν CEIJRW: ψυχή μου K, ζωὴ ἡμῶν ABDFGLM NOPSTUV

ταπεινὴν καρδίαν: ταπεινὴν *omitted* AC

στεναγμῶν ἐπλήρωσε καρδιακῶν ABDEFGIJKLMNOPS TUV: στεναγμὸν ἐνέπλησε καρδιακὸν C, στεναγμῶν ἡμᾶς ἐνέπλησε καρδιακῶν R

ἀνέορτα EFNO: ἀνεόρταστα ABCGIJKLMPRSTUV, ἀνεόρτατα D

ἢ μόνον εἰς Θεὸν καὶ εἰς τὴν τοῦ ἱεροῦ τάφου παρεδρευτικὴν ἀπόβλεψιν R: ἢ μόνον εἰς Θεὸν καὶ εἰς τὸν ἱερὸν τάφον παρεδρευτικῇ ἀπόβλεψης U, ἢ μόνην τὴν εἰς Θεὸν καὶ εἰς τὸν ἱερὸν τάφον παρεδρευτικὴν ἀπόβλεψιν E, ἢ μόνον ἡ εἰς Θεὸν καὶ εἰς τὸν ἱερὸν τάφον παρεδρευτικὴ ἀπόβλεψις (ἀπόλαυσις C) *all other manuscripts*

9 οὐκ ἀγνοῶν: *omitted* M, οὐκ *omitted* A

διεγείροι ABEFGJNOPSTU: διεγείρει CIKL, διεγείρειε RV, ἐγείρει D

ἰατρεύσειε CEIJKRVW: ἰατρεύσει ABFGNOPSTU, ἰατρεύει D

τίς πόρρω: τίς τοῖς πόρρω IM

10 ἀξιαγάστου DEFGIKNOW: ἀξιάγαστα ABCJLMPRSTUV

ὑπάρχειν λογίζεσθε ABCDGIJKLMPSTUV: ὑπάρχει λογίζεσθαι EFNOR

οὕτως ἡμῶν: ἡμῖν IKV

τῶν λεχθέντων κινούμενος: *omitted* IKV

ὑπομιμνήσκων E: ὑπομιμνήσκειν ABCDFGIJKLMNOPRS TU, ὑπομιμνήσκει V

lacuna in A *begins after* φλόγα

ἀποπληρῶ BCDEFGIKMNOPTUVW: ἀναπληρῶ JLRS

11 μὴ μέχρι: μηδὲ μέχρι IKW

μέχρι τοῦ δεῦρο: ἄχρι τῆς δεῦρο IW

εὐηρεστηκότας BDEGJLMPRSTU: εὐαρεστηκότας CFIKNO QVW

after τοὺς ἐν BCEFGJLMNOPRSTU *add* τῇ

after ἀποστόλους IKQVW *add* καὶ

ὁ Θεὸς E: *omitted by all other manuscripts*

πάλιν ἀνεκαλέσατο: πάλιν ἀνεκαλέσατο ὁ Θεὸς T, πάλιν ὁ δεσπότης μετεκαλέσατο R

12 γέγονεν E: πέλει T, *omitted by all other manuscripts*

after ἀριδήλως BCDGIJKLMPQRSTUV *add* καὶ ἄλλως

θέλομεν T: θέλωμεν *all other manuscripts*

καὶ πρεσβεύειν καὶ βοηθεῖν: πρεσβεύειν τε καὶ βοηθεῖν FNO

δι' R: *omitted by all other manuscripts*

καὶ ὅτι E: εἰ καὶ CRT, καὶ BDFGIJKLMNOPQSUV

καὶ ὡς αὐτὸς BCDEFGJLMNOPSTU: ὡς καὶ αὐτὸς V, ὡς αὐτὸς IKQW

τὰς τοῦ E: *after* τὰς BCDFGIJKLMNOPQRSUV *add* δὲ, T *adds* δέ γε

after πατρὸς T *adds* ἡμῶν

ἀναμιμνησκόμενος . . . ἐνασχολούμενος καὶ μελετῶν· E: ἀναμιμνησκόμενοι . . . ἐνασχολούμενοι καὶ μελετῶντες *all other manuscripts*

ἑτοιμάζων ἡμῖν BCDEGIJKLMPQRSTUW: ἑτοιμάσει ἡμῖν FNO, ἑτοιμάζων V

13 διεξιὼν E: *omitted by all other manuscripts*

φιλι(η B)στορήματα BCEGLMPRSTU: φιλοστοργήματα DFNO, φιλοστορήματα IJKQVW *(?)*

καὶ οἱονεὶ παρηγορητήρια: *omitted* IKQW

ἐπιζητοίητε δὲ: δὲ *omitted* IKQW

γέγονεν E: *omitted* BCDFGIJKLMNOPQRSTVUW

after κατάκλισις IKQ *add* καὶ

ἡ διάταξις EIKLQRW: ἡ *omitted* BCDFGJMNOPSTUV

ἀπαγγέλλειν: ἀναγγέλλειν IKW

καὶ ὁποία: καὶ ποία IKQ

εὑρέσθαι ὑμᾶς BDEFGJLMNOPRS: εὑράσθαι ὑμᾶς CIKU, εὑρᾶσθαι ἡμᾶς QT, εὑρέσθαι ἡμᾶς V

14 καὶ συνήθης: *omitted* FNO

εἰς πόνους . . . ἐλάσασα: *omitted* M

δυσιάτους: δυστάτους IKQ

ὁρᾶσθαι κείμενον Q(-ος)IK: ὁρᾶσθαι BCDFGJKLMNOPRSTUV, δεικνύειν E

καταπεσὼν BCDGIJKLMPQRSTUV: πεσὼν EFNO

εὐδοκίᾳ Κυρίου BFGLNOPRST: εὐδοκίᾳ *(*τοῦ *adds* D*)* Θεοῦ DIJKMQUVW, Κυρίου *omitted* C

τρισμάκαρος: μάκαρος R

<ἦν> *added Alexakis*

γήρᾳ: γήρει IQW

πόνοις ἐκείνοις BCDGIJKLMPQRSTUVW: ἐκείνοις *omitted* EFNO

αὐτὸς: αὐτοῖς IQ

Ἦν καὶ ὑποθώμεθα . . . γράμματι BDEFGJMNOPQSTUV: ἣν καὶ ὄπισθεν τῆς βίβλου τῶν κατηχήσεων ὁ ἀναγινώσκων ζητησάτω· ἔστι γὰρ τριακοστὴ πρώτη κατήχησις C, *and after* 15 πάλιν C *skips to* 19 Μετὰ δὲ . . .

before ἔχει: *sign indicating note in margin, and a later hand has added in the lower margin of fol. 341v the following words*: ζήτει ταύτην τὴν κατήχησιν ὄπιθεν εἰς τετράδιον ι′ κεφάλαιον λα′ καὶ ἐπισυνάψας ἀνάγνωθι μετὰ τῶν λοιπῶν S, *this indication points to fol. 77r of* S

after ὧδε: *sign indicating note in margin, and a later hand has added in the upper margin of fol. 287v the following words in red ink*: ζήτει ταύτην τὴν κατήχησιν εἰς τὸ μηνολόγιον κεφάλαιον ΝΑ′ καὶ ἐπισυνάψας ἀνάγνωθι μετὰ τῶν λοιπῶν L, ζήτ(ει) ὄπιθ(εν) τ(ῆς) διαθήκ(ης) R *in margin and after* 15 ἀνακέκλημαι LR *skip to* 19 Μετὰ δὲ . . .

γνοίη BDEFGJLMNOPQRSTUV: γνοίητε IKQW

ἀρχή: *note in left-hand margin* P

Ἀλλ᾽: *omitted* IKQ

after παραπέμπουσα DEFGNO *add* με

ἄλλως τε ὅτι JLR: ὅτι *omitted all other manuscripts*

πέπονθα BDEFIJLNOQRST: πεπόνθαμεν GKMPUV

ὅλην ἡμέραν EGJLNOPSTU: ὅλην τὴν ἡμέραν BDIKMQRV

W *stops at* ἐνεθυμήθην εἰς ἐ . . .

ἐμαυτὸν: ἑαυτὸν IQ

τῶν Ταρτάρων: τοῦ ταρτάρου JLR

ὑπεύθυνος ἂν εἴη R: ἐστὶν ὑπεύθυνος EFNO, ὑπεύθυνος εἶ GIKMQPTU, ὑπεύθυνος εἴη BDJLSV *corrected from* εἶ

ἐνταῦθα BDEFGJLMNOPRSTUV: ἐντεῦθεν IKQ

16 προελθόντες BDEFGJLNOPRSTU: προσελθόντες MV, προσελθῶτες IK, προελθῶτες Q

lacuna in H *ends after* σωτῆρες πολλῶν

ὀλιγοστοῖς: ὀλίγοις IKQ

διαβιώσεως BDEFGHJLNOPRSTU: βιώσεως IKMQV

lacuna in A *ends after the first three letters of* τροχιὰς

φιλογυνιάζετε GHIJKLMQTU: φιλογυνιάζοντες ABDEFNO PRSV

17 ὡς δὲ μεμάθηκα ABDGHIJKLMPQRSTUV: δὲ *omitted* EFNO

πρὸς αὐτὴν τὴν ἁρπαγὴν καὶ τὴν ἀθέτησιν τοῦ θεοῦ DJLRS: πρὸς ἁρπαγὴν αὐτῆς καὶ τὴν ἀθέτησιν τοῦ Θεοῦ E, πρὸς αὐτῆ τη ἁρπαγῆ καὶ τῆ ἀθετήσει του θεοῦ ABFGHIKMNOPQ TUV

ηὐτρέπισεν DEIKQTU: εὐτρέπισεν ABFGHJLMNOPRSV

βοώσης: λεγούσης IKQ

ἐπαΐεις ABDEFGHKNOPTUV: ἀκούεις JLRS, ἐπακούεις IQ, ἤκουσας M

φύγε τὴν BEFGHJLMNOPRSTUV: φεῦγε τὴν AIKQ, φεῦγε τε D

after στένων FNO *add* ἔση

18 διαμαρτύρεσθαι BLRSTU: διαμαρτύρασθαι ADEFGHIJKM NOPQV

after ὄλεθρον IKQ *add* καὶ

Κυρίου: Θεοῦ FNO

ἐν τοῖς ἁγίοις αὐτοῦ, καὶ θαυμασθῆναι ABDEFGHJLMNO PRSTU: *omitted* IKQV

θαυμασθῆναι ABDEGHJLPRSTU: θαυμαστῆναι FNO, θαυμαστοθῆναι M

τὰς ἡτοιμασμένας αὐτοῖς: *omitted* D, *only* αὐτοῖς *omitted* V

ἀγάγοι FNOR: ἀγάγοιεν ABDEGHLMPSTUV, ἀγάγειεν IJ KQ

after ἐπίγνωσιν JLRST *add* τῆς

πάντα πιστεύοντες: *omitted* IKQ

κολάσεως ABDFGHIKNOPQUV: κόλασιν EJLRST

καταδίκην FNO: *omitted* ABDEGHIJKLMPQRSTUV

J *stops at the end of this section*

19 τὴν τετράριθμον τῶν ἡμερῶν: τὰς τέσσαρας ἡμέρας E

ἀναστασίμῳ . . . μακαρίτου E: ἦν γὰρ ἀναστάσιμος αὕτη, ἐφ' ᾗ κατὰ τὸ εἰωθὸς προκαθεσθεὶς ὁ μακαρίτης *all other manuscripts*

ὑγείαν BDEFGHILNOPRST: ὑγίαν ACKMQU, ὑγίειαν V

πολλῆς: πολλὴν IQ

πολλῆς . . . ἐπιθυμίας: *omitted* C

ὁ τρισμάκαρ: ὁ τρισμακάριος V, *omitted* C

προσοίσων R: προσφέρων *all other manuscripts*

παραγενομένων: παραγεναμένων IKQ

παρεπέμπετο: παραπέμπεται IQ

20 αὐτῷ: αὐτοῦ IQ

τῶν ἔργων ER: καὶ ἔργῳ *all other manuscripts*

καὶ δρῶν: καὶ ῥῶν IKQ

ἐνελίπομεν BCDEFGHLMNOPRSTUV: ἐλλείπωμεν IQ, ἐλλίπομεν KA

21 Καὶ μετὰ τὴν ἑξῆς: *omitted* IKQ, καὶ τῇ ἑξῆς E

ἦν δὲ ABCDGHIKLMPQRSTUV: ἦν γὰρ FNO, *omitted* E

ἐκτελεῖ ABCDEFGHLMNOPRSTV: ἐκτελεῖν K, ἐκπληρεῖν I, ἐκπληροῖν Q, ἐκλεῖ U

συγκαθεζομένοις αὐτῷ BCDEFGHLMNORSTUV: καθεζομένοις αὐτῷ IKQ, αὐτῷ *omitted* A

γέγονε E: *omitted by all other manuscripts*

Καὶ δισημερεύσας ABCDFGLMNOPRSTU: καὶ δυ(η H)σιμερεύσας HIKQV, δισημερεύσας οὖν ἐκτοτε E

μετριοπόνως ABCDEFGHLMNOPRSTUV: μετριοφρόνως IKQ

διέλειπεν ABCGHIKMPQSTUV: διέλιπε EFLNOR, διέλλιπε D

τὸ αὐτὸ πίνοιμι: *after* αὐτὸ *insertion sign indicating addition of* δὴ *in right-hand margin in* V; *see also Greek text of the "Life" above in* 35.4; τὸ αὐτὸ πίνω E

πατέρας μου: πατέρα μου IKQ

παραθήκην ABCDFGHNOPRTU: παρακαταθήκην EIKLMQSV

ἐξ ἐμοῦ: *omitted* IKQ

22 ἐκείνης καὶ: καὶ *omitted* IKQ

τὸ τῷ Θεῷ ABCDGHIKLPQSTU: τὸ *omitted* EFMNOV, τῷ *omitted* R

κατασφραγίσας: κατασφραγισάμενος IKQ

ἐπηύξατο BCDEFNOTU: ἐπεύξατο AGHIKLMPQRSV

διαδίδοται ἡ: δίδοται IQ, δίδοται ἡ K

δισημερεύσας ABCDEGHIKLMPRST: δισσημερεύσας FNO, δυσημερεύσας QV

πάλιν E: *omitted by all other manuscripts*

after ἐρχομένων ABDFGHLMNOPRS *add* καὶ

ἄξιόν τι E: τι *omitted by all other manuscripts*

23 μεγαλομάρτυρος EIKTV: μεγάλου μάρτυρος ABCDFGHLM NOPRSU; Q *stops at* μεγα . . . *absence of accent above* α *might support the reading* μεγαλομάρτυρος

ἑαυτὸν ἠτονηκότα ABCDEGHIKLPRSTUV: ἑαυτοῦ ἠσθενηκότος FNO, ἑαὐτὸν εἰκότα M

ἡμῶν E: *omitted by all other manuscripts*

αὐτοῦ EFNO: *omitted* ABCDGHIKLMPRSTUV

κατάπαυσις: κατάστασις IKV

24 μοι δότε: μοι δοκεῖ IK, μοι δῷ V

τῷ ἱερῷ: τῷ *omitted* IK

πολύ RU, *see* Ep. 533.35 *of Theodore of Studios*: πολλοὶ ABCDE FGHLMNOPSTV, πολλοὶ δὲ IK

τὰ . . . κηδείας καὶ ταφῆς ἁρμόδια: κηδείας καὶ ταφῆς τὰ ἐξόδια IK, κηδείας καὶ ταφῆς τὰ ἐφόδια V

ὁ δὲ ABCDEFGLNOPRTU: οἱ δὲ IKSV

ἠλεκτροειδῆ ACDEFGHNOPRSU: ἠλεκτοἐιδῆ M, εἰλεκτροειδῆ BIKLT, εἰλεκτοειδῆ V

ἄξιόν τι E: τι *omitted by all other manuscripts*

ἐπαποθέσθαι: ἐναποθέσθαι AB

γέγονε δὲ καὶ ABCGHKLMPRSTUV: καὶ *omitted* DEFINO

γιγνόμενον BDEGHLMPSTU: γινόμενον ACIKNORV, γενόμενον F

γεηπόνοι τὴν: τὴν *omitted* IK

καὶ ἔμποροι: τὴν ἔμποροι IK

τὴν οἰκείαν ABCDFKLNOPSV: τὴν ἰδίαν I, τὴν *omitted* EGHMRT

εἰς ἱερὸν: εἰς *omitted* ADIKLS

25 παρεδόθη ABCDFGHKLMNOPRSTUV: παρεδώκαμεν E

After σάλπιγξ IK *add* καὶ

ἐγκρατέσιν ABCDFGHLNOPQRSV: ἐγκρατεύουσιν IK, ἐγκρατεῦσιν MTU

26 ἀφείλατο CIKLU: ἀφείλετο ABDEFGHMNPRSTV, ἐφείλετο O

H *stops at* γέγονε θελή . . .

καὶ ἐκ βάθους ABEFGLMNOPRSTU: καὶ ἐκ θάμβους IK, *omitted* CDV

ποτνιωμένους: *omitted* DV

ἀπολελαυκότας ERT: ἀπολελαυκότων *all other manuscripts*

after ἁγιωσύνην ὑμῶν R *adds* ἐν Χριστῶ Ἰησοῦ τῶ Κυρίω ἡμῶν· ὦ ἡ δόξα καὶ τὸ κράτος, σὺν τῶ πατρὶ καὶ τῶ ἁγίω πνεύματι, νῦν καὶ ἀεὶ καὶ εἰς τοὺς αἰῶνας τῶν αἰώνων· ἀμήν.

Translation and Burial of the Remains of Theodore of Stoudios and Joseph of Thessalonike

5.2 ἀήττητος μένοι *Jordan*: μείνῃ *Van de Vorst*, μείνοι P

7.2 ψῆφος οἰκουμενικὴ *Jordan*: οἰκουμενικῇ *Van de Vorst*, οἰκουμενικῆ P

9.2 <ν>ήσῳ γὰρ *corrected by Alexakis*: εἴσω *Van de Vorst*, ἤσω P

12.1 προτε<με>νίσματι *corrected by Van de Vorst*, προτενίσματι P

12.2 ἡδίστην *corrected by Van de Vorst*: ἥδιστον P

Notes to the Translations

Life of Theodore of Stoudios by Michael the Monk

1.1 *the chief shepherd of our flock*: Theodore became first the superior of the monastery of Sakkoudion and later of the monastery of Stoudios.

1.2 *after his death*: Theodore died on November 11, 826.

reference in verse . . . in the style of a panegyric: Some early verses commemorating Theodore have survived in manuscripts containing the *Lesser Katecheseis.* As noted in the Introduction, the "extensive record in narrative form and in the style of a panegyric" may refer to an earlier, more elegantly written life by the patriarch Methodios I, upon which Michael the Monk based his own version.

1.3 *second Basil*: The "first Basil" was Basil the Great (ca. 329–379), bishop of Caesarea from 370/1, an advocate of the communal monastic life, and a composer of monastic rules.

2.1 *The city . . . that presides over cities everywhere on earth*: Constantinople.

Constantine Kopronymos: Constantine V (emperor 741–775; *PmbZ Online* no. 3703/corr.). His nickname "Kopronymos" (dung named) refers to the legend that he defecated while being baptized.

impious father: Leo III (emperor 717–741; *PmbZ Online* no. 4242), an iconoclast.

heresy raging against Christ: Iconoclasm.

He was oppressing . . . the Master's ordinances: This sentence meta-

phorically reuses the story of the hard labor of the Israelites in Egypt (see Exodus 5:6–14) and their subsequent journey toward the Promised Land. Constantine Kopronymos, an iconoclast, is likened to the pagan Pharaoh, and the iconodules are described as the "new Israel of Christ."

2.2 *His father, truly created . . . as a light*: Theodore's father was named Photeinos (*PmbZ Online* no. 6232). His name includes the Greek word φῶς, meaning "light." Here, however, the cryptic reference to the λάλον τῶν Ἀθηναίων γλῶτταν (eloquent language of the Athenians) might be hinting at a wordplay, for the word φώς in Homer, but also in Euripides, means "man."

administrator of the imperial accounts: Photeinos served as the imperial *sakellarios,* one of the highest financial officials of the imperial court. See *ODB,* vol. 3, pp. 1828–29.

2.3 *she had been "created by God" . . . by her deeds*: This is a play on her name, Theoktiste, which means "created by God." See *PmbZ Online* no. 8023/corr.

praise in both respects: Note the rare dual form τὸν ἐξ ἀμφοῖν ἔπαινον in this phrase.

Her God-given offspring: Her son, Theodore, whose name means "given by God."

compiled at that time . . . that discourse: See Stephanos Efthymiadis and J. Michael Featherstone, "Establishing a Holy Lineage: Theodore the Stoudite's Funerary Catechism for his Mother (*BHG* 2422)," in *Theatron: Rhetorische Kultur in Spätantike und Mittelalter / Rhetorical Culture in Late Antiquity and the Middle Ages*, ed. Michael Grünbart (Berlin, 2007), 13–51.

3.1 *preliminary and elementary skills of learning*: According to the later *Vita A* (PG 99:117C, on which see the Introduction), Theodore was sent to a *grammatistes* (elementary schoolmaster) at the age of seven, who would have educated him in classical Greek literature, especially poetry.

for the lessons of childhood . . . united with it: Eusebius of Caesarea, *Historia ecclesiastica*, 5.20.6.1–2; see *Eusèbe de Césarée, Histoire ecclésiastique: Texte grec*, ed. and trans. Gustave Bardy, 4 vols. (rev. ed., Paris, 1984–2006), vol. 2, p. 62.

3.2 *more than honey and honeycomb*: Psalms 18(19):11.

3.3 *the enhypostatic God and Father*: The three elements of the Trinity—the Father, Son, and Holy Spirit—are, in orthodox theology, united in God in a single *hypostasis;* see *ODB*, vol. 2, p. 966.

those who do not merely bear its name: Theodore is known as a *philosophos,* or "lover of wisdom." From the fourth century CE this meant not a practitioner of pagan philosophy but an ardent follower of the Christian life and, more specifically, a monk.

3.4 *royal path*: The "royal path" is that of spiritual and moral moderation, which the believer should follow to lead him to God. The concept was first discussed by Origen; see *Origène, Homélies sur les Nombres*, ed. and trans. Louis Doutreleau (Paris, 1996–2001), vol. 2, sections 12.4.5–7. It was further developed by John Cassian; see *Jean Cassien, Conférences*, ed. and trans. Étienne Pichery (Paris, 1955–1959, rev. eds. 2006–2009), vol. 3, sections 24.24–26; and afterward by Byzantine theologians of the fourth century CE.

4.1 *evil tyrant . . . who ruled in the same manner as Pharaoh*: Constantine V; see note to 2.1.

fire of Gehenna: The valley of Hinnom (Gehinnom) near Jerusalem, where the kings of Judah were said to have sacrificed their children by fire to Baal; see Jeremiah 19:2–6.

wood, hay, and straw: 1 Corinthians 3:12.

the younger Leo: Leo IV (775–780; *PmbZ Online* no. 4243/corr.).

a most mighty horn . . . horn of salvation: See Luke 1:69 and Psalms 74(75):11 and 131(132):17.

bore her name more for her actions: Irene (*PmbZ Online* no. 1439/corr.) was the wife of Leo IV. On the latter's death in 780, Constantine VI (*PmbZ Online* no. 3704/corr.), their son, though a minor, was nominally emperor from 780 to 797, but was dethroned and blinded by Irene, who became sole ruler from 797 to 802. Her name means "peace" in Greek, and her iconodule beliefs meant that she enjoyed Stoudite support.

4.2 *self-trained*: The Greek αὐτογύμναστος is a *hapax legomenon.*

salt of the earth: Matthew 5:13.

lights of the world . . . word of life: See Philippians 2:15–16.

4.3 *wooded retreat on Olympos*: Mount Olympos in Bithynia (modern Ulu dağ) was an important monastic center; see *ODB*, vol. 3, p. 1525, and Klaus Belke, *Bithynien und Hellespont* (Vienna, 2020), vol. 2, pp. 860–65. The location of the monastery of Sakkoudion is not precisely known; it may have been near Arnavutköy to the west of the Arganthonios ridge, on the southeastern shore of the Sea of Marmara. See Introduction and Belke, *Bithynien und Hellespont*, vol. 2, pp. 979–80.

Plato: Plato (*PmbZ Online* no. 6285) had previously been abbot of the Symboloi monastery, also in the region of Mount Olympos in western Asia Minor; see Belke, *Bithynien und Hellespont*, vol. 2, pp. 1021–22. Theodore's encomium about him is *Laudatio sancti Platonis hegumeni* (or *Oratio funebris in Platonem*), PG 99:803–50.

the seventh council: The council assembled on September 24, 787. Sometimes referred to as the Second Council of Nicaea to distinguish it from the earlier Nicaean council (325), it was the seventh and final ecumenical council to be recognized by the Byzantine Church.

4.4 *Tarasios*: Patriarch of Constantinople (784–806; *PmbZ Online* no. 7235/corr.). For his biography, see Stephanos Efthymiadis, ed. and trans., *Life of Patriarch Tarasios by Ignatios the Deacon (BHG, 1698)* (Aldershot, 1998).

who, as befits his name . . . impiety: The author assumes that his name comes from the Greek verb ταράσσω (I confound, agitate, stir up), a pun already made by Theodore himself (see *Ep.* 53, p. 156, lines 35–39), who at one time held him responsible for "scandals" in the Church, in particular the lenient treatment of simoniac and iconoclast clergy.

5.1 *his own two brothers along with their one sister*: Theodore's two brothers were Joseph, who later became archbishop of Thessalonike (*PmbZ Online* no. 3448), and Euthymios (*PmbZ Online* no. 1844). His sister's name is unknown (*PmbZ Online* no. 6232A).

5.2 *estate of Sakkoudion*: The passage that follows is loosely based on Basil of Caesarea's *Letter* 14, in which he describes the site of

his monastery at Annesi in Cappadocia; *Saint Basile, Lettres,* ed. and trans. Yves Courtonne (Paris, 1957–1961), vol. 2, sections 14.43–45.

shrine of John the Theologian: See note to 7.2 below.

6.1 *It is no longer I who live, but Christ who lives in me*: Galatians 2:20.

6.3 *who, though he was in the form of God . . . on a cross*: Philippians 2:6–8.

7.2 *a chapel dedicated to John the son of thunder*: See Mark 3:17. The John referred to is the writer of the fourth Gospel, also called Saint John the Divine. The chapel was the subject of an epigram written by Theodore (Theodore of Stoudios, *Epigram* 90), in which it is described as having four vaults; Paul Speck, ed. and trans., *Theodoros Studites: Jamben auf verschiedene Gegenstände* (Berlin, 1968), 244–45. It is also mentioned in Theodore's *Laudatio in S. Joannem apostolum et evangelistam* (*BHG* 929), PG 99:788C.

8.1 *every perfect gift*: James 1:17.

8.2 *accidie*: A state of boredom and spiritual lethargy.

all-embracing death is brought upon a monk: See John Klimax, *Scala Paradisi* 13, PG 88:860C.

8.3 *Joseph was entrusted . . . Thessalonike*: Joseph was elected archbishop of Thessalonike at the end of 806 or in 807.

Anthony and Timothy, Athanasios and Naukratios: These four monks are singled out as "founder members" of the monastery at Sakkoudion. Anthony (*PmbZ Online* no. 533, possibly identical with *PmbZ Online* no. 532) had probably been a disciple of Plato's in the Symboloi monastery. Timothy (*PmbZ Online* no. 8502, possibly identical with *PmbZ Online* no. 8503 and/or *PmbZ Online* no. 8499), had also come from the same monastery and later moved to Stoudios. Athanasios (*PmbZ Online* no. 675/corr.) was later the protopresbyter (senior priest) of Stoudios and ultimately abbot of Sakkoudion. For Naukratios (*PmbZ Online* 5230/corr.), later steward of Sakkoudion and abbot of Stoudios, see the Introduction.

mortified their limbs on earth: Colossians 3:5.

9.1 *Basil, the revealer of heaven*: The epithet οὐρανοφάντορος is also

given to Basil the Great in the *Life of Stephen the Younger* by Stephen the Deacon (*BHG* 1666) written in the early ninth century CE. See *La Vie d'Étienne le jeune par Étienne le diacre,* ed. and trans. Marie-France Auzépy (Aldershot, 1997), section 26 (Greek text p. 122, French trans. p. 216).

Basil's ascetic rules: Basil the Great's ascetic ordinances can be found in long or short versions; see *Regulae fusius tractatae* and *Regulae brevius tractatae,* PG 31:901–1305.

books of divine wisdom: A probable reference to Basil's numerous homilies and sermons.

9.2 *the rules of Basil's ascetic treatises were disregarded*: This passage is based on one in Theodore's *Laudatio sancti Platonis* (see note to 4.3), where the credit for ridding the new monastery of unrighteous practices, such as the keeping of slaves and female animals for stock breeding, is attributed to Plato. See PG 99:824C–25C.

seek to make the improper gains: Making money by commercial enterprises.

9.3 *documents of emancipation*: The *Ekloga,* a compendium of Roman law issued in 741, describes a process whereby slaves could be emancipated by a variety of written means: in church or before at least three witnesses who had then to record their witness in a public document, by a letter of their master signed by three to five witnesses, or by a written will of their master. See *Ecloga* 8.1.1 in *The Laws of the Isaurian Era: The "Ecloga" and Its Appendices,* trans. Mike Humphreys (Liverpool, 2017), 57. It is probably the second of these processes that is being alluded to here.

10.1 *the bloodless and radiant sacrifice*: The Eucharistic liturgy.

desirable treasures: Proverbs 21:20.

the consecration of the priesthood: Canonically, Theodore would have to have been at least thirty to have been made a priest, so his consecration by Tarasios probably took place in 789/90. He received all the ecclesiastical orders up to the priesthood in one day.

10.2 *did not grant his eyes . . . temples rest*: Psalms 131(132):4.

10.3 *kathegoumenos*: An abbot who has been ordained priest.

the great theologian: Gregory of Nazianzos (329/30–ca. 390).

Though it is difficult to know . . . much more difficult: Gregory of Nazianzos, *Oration* 2.10, ed. Jean Bernardi, *Grégoire de Nazianze: Discours 1–3,* Sources chrétiennes 247 (Paris, 1978), 102.

10.4 *light . . . in the house*: Matthew 5:15; see also Mark 4:21 and Luke 8:16–18.

his obvious illness: It is possible that Plato used his illness as a pretext to persuade his monks to elect Theodore or that Michael the Monk exaggerated it. Plato was to live on for another twenty years. Theodore's apparent reluctance to accept the post of abbot is a hagiographical *topos.*

10.5 *the thirty-fifth of his lifespan*: Theodore became joint abbot of Sakkoudion in 794 at a very young age. Michael the Monk omits to mention that Plato and Theodore actually governed Sakkoudion together.

11.1 *God who girds . . . makes the blind wise*: See Psalms 17:33 (18:32) and 145(146):8.

weapons of light: Romans 13:12.

mighty . . . defender: Ὑπερτίναξ (defender) is a *hapax legomenon.* The word is absent from the English edition of Liddell and Scott, but the Greek edition supplies the Latin translation *propugnator;* see Χένρι Λιντέλ, Ρόμπερτ Σκότ, *Λεξικὸ τῆς Ἑλληνικῆς Γλώσσης,* trans. Ξενοφῶν Π. Μόσχος (Athens, 2006), vol. 8/Δ′, p. 450.

11.2 *the invisible Midianites . . . the spiritual Philistines*: The Midianites and the Philistines in the Old Testament are listed as examples of those who lead astray followers of the true faith; the allusion here is probably to the supporters of iconoclasm. See Numbers 25 and 1 Samuel 7:3–4.

11.3 *the Father of lights*: James 1:17.

apotropaic cup: See *Pseudo-Gregorii Agrigentini seu Pseudo-Gregorii Nysseni commentarius in Ecclesiasten,* ed. Gerhard H. Ettlinger and Jacques Noret (Turnhout, 2007), 2.6.30.

like a heavenly healer: Here and in the following paragraph, Michael uses an extended medical metaphor in which Theodore is described as a spiritual doctor, administering suitable remedies for the individual moral deficiencies of his monks.

11.4 *he would preach*: Version B of the *Rule of the Stoudios Monastery*

ordered that one of Theodore's *katecheseis* should be read after Matins on Wednesdays, Fridays, and Sundays; see Timothy Miller, trans., "*Stoudios: Rule* of the Monastery of St. John Stoudios in Constantinople," *BMFD*, vol. 1, no. 4, chapter 16, p. 106. This custom was clearly established by Michael's day and continued Theodore's own practice.

this great pancratiast's contest: Michael uses the analogy of a competitor in the *pankration,* the brutal combination of wrestling and boxing of the pagan Olympic Games, to refer to the physical struggles and harsh treatment Theodore would suffer in the future.

12.1 *At that time Constantine . . . sole ruler*: Constantine VI deposed his mother as co-ruler in November or December 790 and ruled alone until January 792.

the fiery surges: See Cyril of Alexandria, *De adoratione* 14, PG 68:945A.

his previous lawfully married wife: Maria of Amnia in Paphlagonia (*PmbZ Online* no. 4727), the granddaughter of Saint Philaretos the Merciful, was married to Constantine VI in November 788. They had two daughters, Irene (born between 789 and 791) and Euphrosyne (born between 790 and 792). Maria was divorced and driven from court in 795. It is not clear whether she was forced—or agreed—to become a nun. The *Chronicle of Theophanes,* AM 6287, maintains that Constantine was encouraged by his mother, who aimed to take advantage of the unpopularity that would arise from the emperor's action to strengthen her own position; see Cyril Mango and Roger Scott, with Geoffrey Greatrex, trans., *The Chronicle of Theophanes Confessor: Byzantine and Near Eastern History, AD 284–813* (Oxford, 1997), 645.

like Herod in the past: Herod Antipas married Herodias, the wife of his brother, Philip, and was censured for this by John the Baptist; see Mark 6:14–29. This passage may be modeled on chapter 45 of the *Life of Patriarch Tarasios* (Efthymiades, *Life of Patriarch Tarasios,* Greek text pp. 128–29, English trans. pp. 191–92), which compares Tarasios's refusal to marry Constantine to his mistress with the action of John the Baptist.

Theodote: Theodote (*PmbZ Online* no. 7899) is usually identified as a daughter of Plato of Sakkoudion's sister Anna, and thus a cousin of Theodore's, though this is open to question. See also note to 12.4 below.

in an adulterous manner: The Greek word μοιχεία (adultery) has given its name to the so-called Moechian Controversy, which resulted from the emperor's actions.

Christ is not united to profane souls: Cyril of Alexandria, *De adoratione* 12, PG 68:817B.

12.2 *Joseph*: Joseph (*PmbZ Online* no. 3447/corr.) was abbot of the Kathara monastery in Bithynia; see Belke, *Bithynien und Hellespont,* vol. 2, pp. 653–54. He was also steward *(oikonomos)* of Hagia Sophia in Constantinople, the official in charge of managing its property. On this office see *ODB,* vol. 3, p. 1517.

So the king of Longibardia . . . so the governor of Bosporos: Michael is referring to recent similar scandals, which are partly alluded to both in one of Theodore's letters (*Ep.* 31, p. 88, lines 94–97) and in the *Life of the Patriarch Nikephoros I of Constantinople,* trans. Elizabeth A. Fisher, in *Byzantine Defenders of Images: Eight Saints' Lives in English Translation,* ed. Alice-Mary Talbot (Washington, DC, 1998), 25–142. The latter (pp. 67–68) relates how the patriarch Nikephoros heard that the ruler of the "Tauric *klimata*" planned to abandon his wife for his mistress and wrote, sometime during the period from 806 to 808, to rebuke him and threaten spiritual penalties. The Greek word *klimata* in the plural usually refers to regions of the Crimea (see *ODB,* vol. 2, p. 1135), and this individual has been identified with the toparch of Gothia, the Byzantine ruler of the regions of the Crimea not under Khazar control. In his letter, Theodore mentions that the rulers of the regions of Gothia, Longibardia, and the "Gothic *klimata*" have put aside their wives. Michael has possibly invented the personality of the toparch of Bosporos (a city in the Crimea) in an attempt to identify one of Theodore's "Gothic" rulers. The Longibardia case refers to the divorcing (ca. 795) by Grimoald, Lombard duke of Benevento, of his wife Evanthia, interestingly enough the sister of Constantine VI's wife Maria of Amnia. See *The Life of St. Philaretos the*

Merciful Written by his Grandson Niketas, ed. and trans. Lennart Rydén (Uppsala, 2002), 22, 24.

12.3 *fulfilling all righteousness*: Matthew 3:15.

12.4 *the woman . . . was their kinswoman*: A note in the right-hand margin of fol. 200r of Biblioteca Apostolica Vaticana, Ms. Vat. gr. 1669 explains: "since the one who had been crowned with Constantine happened to be a first cousin of our father Theodore."

Prousa: Modern-day Bursa, the site of famous hot springs about ten miles from the possible location of the monastery of Sakkoudion; see Belke, *Bithynien und Hellespont,* vol. 2, pp. 949–57.

12.5 *Domestic of the Schools*: A senior military officer; see *ODB,* vol. 1, pp. 647–48.

Opsikion: By the eighth century a theme (administrative district; see *ODB*, vol. 3, pp. 2034–35) stretching from the Dardanelles to the central plateau, with its capital at Nicaea. The names of the two officers, supplied by the *Chronicle of Theophanes,* AM 6288, trans. Mango and Scott, *Chronicle,* p. 647, were Bardanios, the Domestic of the Schools (*PmbZ Online* no. 771), and John, *komes* ("count"; the word στρατηγός or "military governor" has been used imprecisely) of the Opsikion (*PmbZ Online* no. 3112).

Then they banished him: A note at this point in the left-hand margin of manuscript P reads, πρώτη ἐξορία τοῦ ὁσίου πατρὸς ἡμῶν (first exile of the blessed father), and in V, πρώτη ἐξορία καὶ ἄθλησις τοῦ πατρός (first exile and contest of the father).

monastery of holy Sergios: Probably the monastery of Saints Sergios and Bakchos, near the imperial palace in Constantinople. There is disagreement in the sources about the location of Plato's imprisonment. The *Oratio funebris in Platonem,* PG 99:832B, cites the "miserable monastery of the palace called 'Echekollas'" (possibly identical with the monastery of Saints Sergios and Bakchos); the *Chronicle of Theophanes,* AM 6288, trans. Mango and Scott, *Chronicle,* p. 647, cites the "church of the archangel Michael in the palace." In any event, Plato was held in Constantinople.

13.1 *diocese of Cherson and Cimmerian Bosporos*: From the seventh cen-

tury on, Cherson and Bosporos were bishoprics of the ecclesiastical province of Zichia, which encompassed land to the east of the straits of Kerch as well as in the Crimea.

your zeal roused most of them: 2 Corinthians 9:2.

anger, the fearsome hoplite: Initially a quotation from one of Theodore's own *katecheseis* (see *Great Katecheseis,* book 2, no. 3, ed. Papadopoulos-Kerameus, p. 16, lines 13–14), but ultimately from Gregory of Nazianzos, *Oration* 43, in *Grégoire de Nazianze: Discours 42–43,* ed. Jean Bernardi (Paris, 1992), 246.

13.2 *For passionate behavior . . . to total perdition*: See Cyril of Alexandria, *De adoratione* 12, PG 68:792D.

John the Forerunner: Saint John the Baptist, who "came before" by prophesying the coming of Jesus and who chastised King Herod; see Luke 3.

Elijah the Tishbite: The prophet Elijah stood up against Ahab the wicked king of Israel; see especially 1 Kings 21.

13.3 *Theodore also wrote to the pope of old Rome*: Pope Hadrian I (772–795). Byzantines considered Constantinople to be the "new Rome." No letters to the pope from this period have survived. The author has possibly confused this exile with later ones, when Theodore did indeed write to the pope.

An arrogant king falls into evil deeds: Proverbs 13:17.

the ways of the lawless . . . stumble: Proverbs 4:19.

the Christ-loving Irene, was restored: The author here glosses over the fact that Constantine's blinding and dethronement in August 797 by the army was instigated by his mother, Irene, who now became sole ruler of the empire. A fuller, and more hostile, account can be found in the *Chronicle of Theophanes,* AM 6289, trans. Mango and Scott, *Chronicle,* pp. 648–49.

14.1 *Joseph had been stripped of his priestly rank*: It is not clear whether Joseph was subject to a synodical excommunication, as was suggested by Grumel (*RegPatr* no. 368), or simply suspended from office. Two of Theodore's *Letters* (*Epp.* 28 and 30) report that Joseph was, for five years, ἀφωρισμένος by Tarasios, a word that can be taken to mean "excommunicated" or used in the looser sense of "excluded." The *Vita A* reports "the com-

mon vote of the Church" (see PG 99:156A), perhaps indicating a synodical action, but this is later evidence.

both of them . . . pleasing to God: The author has used the rhetorical device of an imaginary speech to present a growing *rapport* between Tarasios and Theodore.

14.2 *as Theodore himself . . . recorded*: Probably a reference to Theodore's own account in the *Oratio funebris in Platonem,* PG 99:833AB, where, however, Plato is hailed as the victor in the struggle and where Tarasios is described as giving him respect, wishing to be reconciled with him and apologizing to him.

Paul made an accommodation by circumcising Timothy: See Acts 16:3. Saint Paul had his disciple Timothy circumcised in order to make his presence more acceptable to the Jews to whom they were preaching.

If I preach circumcision, why am I still persecuted?: Galatians 5:11.

14.3 *a man should be the husband of one wife*: See 1 Corinthians 7:2.

fornication and the passions of the flesh . . . union with God: Cyril of Alexandria, *De adoratione* 14, PG 68:913C.

14.4 *renowned city*: Constantinople.

15.1 *the godless Agarenes . . . province*: "Agarenes" or "Hagarenes" is a term applied to Arabs, referring to their supposed descent from Hagar, the mother of Ishmael (see Genesis 16:11). The *Chronicle of Theophanes,* AM 6290, trans. Mango and Scott, *Chronicle,* p. 650, reports that Arab forces had reached Galatia in 797, but the immediate cause of the evacuation of Sakkoudion was probably their raid in 798 (AM 6291, p. 651) as far as the imperial stud at Malagina, for which see *ODB,* vol. 2, p. 1274, and Belke, *Bithynien und Hellespont,* vol. 2, pp. 748–51.

they took over the most sacred monastery of Stoudios: The urging of Tarasios and the empress Irene is cited as the reason that Theodore became abbot of Stoudios, since it allowed Theodore to be portrayed, in a common hagiographical *topos,* as the "modest recipient" of the honor. The previous abbot of Stoudios, Sabas (*PmbZ Online* no. 6442/corr. but in need of further correction), who had been active at the Second Council of Nicaea (787), had either died by this time or abdicated. It is significant that

Michael makes no mention of him. For the early history of the monastery of Stoudios, see the Introduction.

built long before by him: The monastery was built in approximately 454 CE.

Nazirites: An Old Testament term denoting men who have taken a strict religious vow; see Numbers 6:1–21.

Constantine Kopronymos had limited its numbers to less than ten: This is a fiction, aimed to enhance Theodore's achievement of recruiting more monks. The leading role that the abbot Sabas took at the Second Council of Nicaea (in the reign of Constantine VI) is incompatible with him being the head of a "phantom monastery" of so few monks at that time. It is, however, possible that, as a consequence of Sabas's opposition to Constantine VI's second marriage in 796, Stoudios was emptied of monks for a time. Sabas himself may well have made contact with Plato and Theodore and their community in Bithynia at this period; see Olivier Delouis, *Saint-Jean-Baptiste de Stoudios à Constantinople: La contribution d'un monastère à l'histoire de l'Empire byzantin (v. 454–1204),* 2 vols. (unpublished doctoral thesis, Université Paris 1 Panthéon-Sorbonne, 2005), vol. 1, p. 135.

15.2 *imitator of the great Forerunner . . . shrine named after him*: The Stoudios monastery was dedicated to John the Baptist (the Forerunner). The writer is again making reference to John the Baptist's criticism of Herod's relations with Herodias.

because similarity is always dear to everyone: Josephus, *Against Apion* 2.23, ed. and trans. Henry St. J. Thackeray, in *The Life; Against Apion,* Loeb Classical Library 186 (Cambridge, MA, 1926), 370.

He who comes to me I will not cast out: John 6:37.

those he had tonsured himself: The issue of the reception of *xenokouritai* (monks who had been tonsured elsewhere) divided monastic opinion in Byzantium because they could be held to have broken the custom of stability by wandering from place to place. Both versions of the Stoudite *Rule* (*BMFD,* vol. 1, no. 4, chapter 24, p. 108), however, treat *xenokouritai* in the same way as lay postulants, requiring them to spend three weeks in

the guest house to experience the monastic life before—with the abbot's permission—receiving further instruction.

new Jerusalem: See Revelation 21:2.

tally of a thousand: This figure is a symbolic exaggeration. A more realistic figure for Stoudios at the beginning of the ninth century would be three hundred to four hundred monks.

the virtue of a lawgiver . . . or of disaster: Josephus, *Against Apion* 2.15, ed. and trans. Thackeray, p. 352.

the most saintly form of God's service: See Josephus, *Against Apion* 2.22, ed. and trans. Thackeray, p. 370.

15.3 *So Theodore became a lawgiver . . . stone slabs*: Theodore is here being likened to Moses, ascending Mount Sinai to meet with God and receive the Commandments on tablets of stone; see Exodus 19:16 onward.

by the finger . . . stone slabs: Exodus 31:18.

advice of his father-in-law: In the relevant passage of Exodus (18:13 and following) Moses is advised by his father-in-law, Iothor (Jethro).

commanders of a thousand, a hundred, fifty, and ten: Exodus 18:21, 18:25. The holders of monastic functions established by Theodore are compared to the leaders of the Israelites established by Moses.

epistemonarchai: Monks in charge of discipline.

paideutai: Teachers or those in charge of the children. Stoudios had a flourishing school at this time.

epiteretai: Supervisors of monks.

deutereuon: A priest who could act in the absence of the *protopresbyteros,* or "senior priest."

15.4 *detailed regulations in verses of iambic meter*: See Theodore of Stoudios, *Epigrams,* ed. and trans. Speck, *Jamben*. For a French translation of the twenty-nine *Epigrams* concerning the monastic life, see Florence de Montleau, *Les grandes catéchèses (Livre I). Les Epigrammes (I–XXIX), précédées d'une étude de Julien Leroy sur le monachisme stoudite* (Bégrolles-en-Mauges, 2002), 569–99.

proportional punishment: For Theodore's *epitimia* (punishments or

penances), see his *Poenae monasteriales* (PG 99:1733–48) and *Monachorum poenae quotidianae* (PG 99:1748–57). See also *ODB*, vol. 3, p. 1624, where the attribution of many anonymous *epitimia* to Theodore is noted.

All who believed . . . everything in common: Acts 2:44 and 4:32.

I did not eat bread without paying . . . and those with me: 2 Thessalonians 3:8, and see Acts 20:34.

writing books with his own hands: The scriptorium at Stoudios became a celebrated center for the composition and copying of manuscripts. It was associated with the development of minuscule handwriting.

16.1 *talent of wisdom*: A reference to the parable of the talents in Matthew 25:14–30. Theodore devoted his God-given gift of wisdom to writing extensively.

Lesser Katecheseis: For published editions, see *Lesser Katecheseis* in the Abbreviations. Like the *Great Katecheseis,* these homilies were collected only after Theodore's death. They became extremely popular in Byzantine monastic circles and survive in more than seventy manuscripts dating from before the sixteenth century. Michael's reference to them as "the first book" probably reflects this popularity, since they can actually be dated to 821 and 826, that is, *after* the composition of the *Great Katecheseis.*

Great Katecheseis: For published editions, see *Great Katecheseis* in the Abbreviations. The *Great Katecheseis* were probably consulted privately by the monks at Stoudios. They do not seem to have circulated widely before the end of the tenth century, and the manuscript tradition is poor. They were probably gathered together between 795 and 814 and between Theodore's periods of exile. Some 261 *katecheseis* (homilies) have survived from the *Great Katecheseis,* but, taking both collections together, it has been estimated that only about a quarter of Theodore's homilies have come down to us; they may have numbered at least 1,500.

by improvisation: There is no evidence for a major stylistic differ-

ence between the two sets of *katecheseis*. In fact, the language of the *Great Katecheseis* is nearer to the spoken language, and they were also delivered orally.

16.2 *Panegyric . . . more notable saints*: These works are identified and enumerated (with their editions) in *Ep.*, vol. 1, pp. 25*–29*.

16.3 *another metrical work . . . their famous wives*: This set of iambics based on stories from Genesis is now lost. See *Ep.*, vol. 1, p. 37* (no. 29).

in verses of clear trimeters . . . every heresy: This work is also lost. See *Ep.*, vol. 1, p. 37* (no. 30).

16.4 *five books of Letters*: It is clear that collections of Theodore's letters had already been made by the time Michael the Monk wrote.

another doctrinal treatise . . . terrible reproach: See *Theodori praepositi Studitarum Antirrhetici adversus Iconomachos,* PG 99:327–436, and *Ep.*, vol. 1, p. 29* (no. 5). English trans. by Catherine P. Roth, *St. Theodore the Studite: On the Holy Icons* (Crestwood, NY, 1981), and Thomas Cattoi, *Theodore the Studite: Writings on Iconoclasm* (New York, 2015), 45–119.

bestially named Leo: A play on the Greek word for lion (λέων).

16.5 *studying the law of the Lord all day and night*: Psalms 1:2.

17.1 *Nikephoros*: Emperor Nikephoros I (802–811), *PmbZ Online* no. 5252/corr.

faith without works . . . dead: See James 2:26.

the man who had recently performed . . . peace: Joseph of Kathara had been used as an intermediary to negotiate with the rebel Bardanes Tourkos (*PmbZ Online* no. 766), who had revolted against Nikephoros I in Asia Minor in 803.

Tarasios . . . departed to God: Patriarch Tarasios died on February 25, 806.

the patriarch Nikephoros: Nikephoros I (patriarch of Constantinople 806–815; *PmbZ Online* no. 5301/corr.). Michael omits to mention that Theodore himself was a strong candidate to succeed Tarasios and that his relationship with the patriarch Nikephoros was ambivalent. Joseph was probably restored to the priesthood in 806 at a council of some fifteen bishops; see

John Duffy and John Parker, eds., *The Synodicon Vetus: Text, Translation, and Notes* (Washington, DC, 1979), 128, and *Epp.* 24, 25, and 43.

17.2 *God's righteous judgment*: A reference to Constantine VI's overthrow and blinding in 797.

17.3 *And there rose a sharp contention . . . by the brethren*: Acts 15:39–40.

which of them deliberated better is not ours to declare: John Chrysostom, *Homiliae in Acta apostolorum* 14.1, PG 60:246. Michael, perhaps quoting from memory, has replaced one possible comparative of the word ἀγαθός (good), ἄμεινον in the original text, with another: βέλτιον (better).

buying up the time because the days are evil: Ephesians 5:16.

17.4 *I spoke in your testimonies before kings and was not put to shame*: Psalms 118(119):46.

18.1 *rightly expounding the word*: 2 Timothy 2:15.

18.2 *each of them . . . on a different island*: They were all held on the Princes' Islands, in the Sea of Marmara off Constantinople (see Belke, *Bithynien und Hellespont,* vol. 2, p. 935); Theodore on the island of Chalke, Joseph on Prote, and Plato on Oxeia. Michael does not mention the preceding council of January 809, at which all those who refused to enter into communion with Joseph of Kathara were anathematized, though this is mentioned in Theodore's *Ep.* 48, p. 130, and in the *Chronicle of Theophanes,* AM 6301, trans. Mango and Scott, *Chronicle,* p. 665.

palace of Eleutheriou: A palace built by the empress Irene with gardens made on land reclaimed from the sea by the partial filling-in of the port of Eleutheriou on the south shore of Constantinople.

for an interrogation: This episode is also mentioned in Theodore's *Ep.* 48, although the imperial speech afterward is invented by Michael the Monk.

18.3 *foolish Nikephoros . . . hands of the enemy*: Nikephoros I was killed in battle on July 26, 811. "Scythians" is a common Byzantine term for "northern barbarians"; in this case, the Bulgars.

19.1 *Hearken, O house of the king . . . against my law*: Hosea 5:1–2, 7:16–8:1.

he summoned our holy father Theodore to meet him: There is no known historical basis to this story. Theodore's prophecy is a hagiographical *topos,* making reference to 1 Kings 13:9.

Staurakios: Crowned co-emperor with Nikephoros in December 803, Staurakios (*PmbZ Online* no. 6866/corr.) was gravely wounded in the battle against the Bulgars. He was carried to Adrianople, where he was proclaimed emperor, but was soon forced to abdicate. He became a monk and died in January 812. Michael the Monk does not mention his abdication and, probably deliberately, reverses the course of events, having him die before Michael I became emperor.

brother-in-law Michael: Emperor Michael I Rangabe (811–813; *PmbZ Online* no. 4989/corr.) married Nikephoros I's daughter Prokopia. For the rank of *kouropalates,* conferred primarily on members of the imperial family, see *ODB,* vol. 2, p. 1157.

19.2 *recalled . . . from their banishment*: It has been argued on the basis of a phrase in one of Theodore's letters (*Ep.* 453, p. 642, lines 8–9) that they were allowed to return from exile in the reign of Nikephoros, after Plato had fallen gravely ill. It may be, however, that Theodore's phrase ἐπειδὴ ὑποστροφὴ τῆς ἐξορίας ἐπὶ τοῦ Νικηφόρου should, in fact, be translated not as "when the return from exile came about in the time of Nikephoros," but "from the exile to which we had been subjected by Nikephoros." The *Chronicle of Theophanes,* AM 6304, trans. Mango and Scott, *Chronicle,* p. 678, also places their return probably shortly after Michael's coronation in October 811.

pope of old Rome: Pope Leo III (795–816).

hortatory letters: Michael the Monk is the only source to link Leo III directly with the efforts to establish détente between Theodore and the patriarch Nikephoros. There were certainly exchanges between Byzantium and Rome at this period; Theodore himself wrote at least two letters to pope Leo III (*Epp.* 33 and 34). The *Chronicle of Theophanes,* AM 6304, trans. Mango and Scott, *Chronicle,* p. 678, reports that Michael I allowed the patriarch to send the delayed official report of the latter's enthronement to Rome; Venance Grumel (see *RegPatr* no. 382)

considered that the ambassadors taking the letter *also* asked the pope to intervene in the Moechian schism. But since Theodore had already been released by the time the embassy was sent, and since it would have taken some considerable time (about six months) for it to travel to and from Rome, it is not likely that there was any direct papal connection with the settlement of the disagreements between Theodore and Nikephoros.

the man who had dared to perform the adulterous marriage: Joseph of Kathara was again banned from undertaking priestly functions in 811 or 812.

20.1 *his scattered disciples had assembled there*: It is possible that the Stoudite monk Leontios (see *PmbZ Online* no. 4589; possibly identical with no. 4590), whom Theodore denounced in a letter written to Naukratios in 810 or 811 as "once a teacher, now a denier" (*Ep.* 51, p. 153, line 59), had acted as abbot of Stoudios while Theodore was in exile and that he was supported by a breakaway group of Stoudite monks.

20.2 *vineyard of the Lord of hosts . . . side shoots to rivers*: Isaiah 5:7, and see Eusebius, *Commentaria in Psalmos,* PG 23:960D.

hardships of virtue: "Virtue" here seems to stand for the whole regime of ascetic practice.

the additional name "of the Stoudite": We know nothing of these autonomous houses founded by Stoudite monks. They are probably to be distinguished from those closely associated with Stoudios that are mentioned in Theodore's *Great Katecheseis* and *Letters:* Sakkoudion, Symboloi, Saint George (see Belke, *Bithynien und Hellespont,* vol. 1, p. 572); Saint Christopher (see Belke, *Bithynien und Hellespont,* vol. 1, p. 502); Ta Tripyliana (see Belke, *Bithynien und Hellespont,* vol. 2, p. 1057); Ta Kathara (see note to 12.2, above); and Saint Tryphon on cape Akritas (see note to 34.3, below).

21.1 *a very evil boar . . . a solitary wild beast*: Psalms 79(80):14.

Leo, the military governor of the Anatolikon theme: Emperor Leo V (813–820; *PmbZ Online* no. 4244/corr.) was of Armenian descent. On the meaning and the role of the Greek term *strategos*

at this time, translated here as "military governor," see *ODB*, vol. 3, p. 1964.

valued too highly that which went beyond what was appropriate: See Cyril of Alexandria, *De adoratione* 15, PG 68:1000A.

a pretense of Macedonian steadiness: A reference to the legendary bravery of Alexander the Great's Macedonian troops against the Persians. The *Scriptor incertus de Leone Armenio,* a fragment of a history written in approximately 820 from an iconodule perspective, reports that the thematic army of the Anatolikon "was the first to flee the battle," in reference to the Byzantine defeat by the Bulgars at Versinikia, north of Adrianople in Thrace (June 22, 813); see *Scriptor incertus,* p. 31. The *Life of the Patriarch Nikephoros,* trans. Fisher, p. 71, accused Leo of organizing a "shameful retreat."

entered the palace with no opposition: Leo seized power three weeks after the defeat at Versinikia (see preceding note) and after his troops had rebelled.

I do not find the Armenians . . . deceitful: Gregory of Nazianzos, *Oration* 43.17 (Bernardi, *Discours 42–43,* 156). The marginal gloss in V represents Gregory's original text (ὕφαλον, "crafty" instead of ὕπουλον, "deceitful"). Michael is clearly prejudiced against "Armenians" in general, probably because Byzantines perceived their Church as unorthodox, and against Leo V in particular, for his iconoclastic stance.

21.2 *the names we acquire . . . evil people*: The saints' names usually assumed by monks cancel out pagan names that they might have been given at birth.

as subsequent copies resemble . . . an evil one: Michael is here presenting the iconodule argument, based on Aristotelian philosophy as understood from the early ninth century, that an icon of Christ or a saint would represent the same intrinsically good qualities as its worthy archetype.

21.3 *For an image that is in disagreement . . . mistakenly derived from it*: Here the author is emphasizing the need to portray Christ and the saints in an approved iconographic manner, as any "untrue" likeness might itself produce "untrue" copies. As he goes on to

illustrate, the names we give to things often convey their qualities.

An idol is called an "idol" as it is a form of deceit: Michael cites etymology from two Greek words εἶδος (form) and δόλου (of deceit). See Theodore of Stoudios, *Antirrheticus* 1.16 (trans. Cattoi, *Writings on Iconoclasm,* 57–58), where he discusses the etymologies of "icon" and "idol."

For an icon is called an "icon" . . . to its archetype: The author again uses the etymology of the Greek word εἰκών (likeness, image, or portrait) to emphasize its relationship to its archetype.

the image of the emperor is called "the emperor": The example of the emperor, whose image could act as a substitute for his actual presence and be honored in the same way, had been used from Basil the Great onward; see *On the Holy Spirit* 18.5, ed. and trans. Benoît Pruche, *Sur le saint-esprit,* 2nd ed. (Paris, 1968), 406. Although the image is of an identical likeness with its prototype (so that an icon can be identified with its subject), it differs from it in terms of essence. The icon was *homonymous* but not *synonymous* with its prototype, a view endorsed by the Second Council of Nicaea in 787; see Theodore of Stoudios, *Antirrheticus,* 2.16 (trans. Cattoi, *Writings on Iconoclasm,* 68), and *Ep.* 301, pp. 441–43.

22.1 *That raging and slow-witted lion*: Again, a play on the name of the emperor Leo.

fellows . . . accustomed to wicked actions: Clement of Alexandria, *Quis dives salvetur,* 42.5.19–20, ed. Otto Stählin, *Clemens Alexandrinus dritter Band* (Leipzig, 1909), 188.

instruments of his wrath fashioned for perdition: Romans 9:22.

deceivers of young men: Josephus, *Against Apion,* 2.236, ed. and trans. Thackeray, pp. 386–88.

who trained their bodies for beauty: Josephus, *Against Apion,* 2.229, ed. and trans. Thackeray, p. 384.

another Jannes . . . John: See 2 Timothy 3:8. Michael is here playing on the Greek name Ioannes (John). "Jannes" was the name given to one of the magicians of Pharaoh who were routed by Moses and Aaron in Exodus 7:10–12. But it is also the name

given to an amphibious creature in a Greek account of an Assyrian creation myth (see following note). The author is referring to John the Grammarian (*PmbZ Online* no. 3199/corr.), who was chosen by Leo V in 814 to lead a group of churchmen in collecting a *florilegium* of texts supporting the iconoclast position. Immediately before the council of 815, which reestablished iconoclasm, he engaged in debate with a number of iconodule figures, including Theodore of Stoudios. John subsequently became abbot of the monastery of Saints Sergios and Bakchos in Constantinople and iconoclast patriarch of Constantinople (837–843).

The Labyrinth: A work known to the ninth-century scholar-patriarch Photios (858–867, 877–886; see *ODB*, vol. 3, pp. 1669–70) and mentioned in his *Bibliotheca*, a survey of pagan and Christian authors (see *ODB*, vol. 1, p. 288); see Photios, *Bibliotheca*, ed. and French trans. René Henry, *Bibliothèque* (Paris, 1959–1977), vol. 1, pp. 34–35. Photios knew that the work had been attributed to Josephus (about which he rightly had doubts), but Michael the Monk, who was familiar with at least two works by that author, may have believed it was indeed by him. Modern scholarship has established that the work known as *The Labyrinth* (because it refers to a "labyrinth of heresies") is, in fact, the *Refutatio omnium haeresium*, by Hippolytus of Rome (ca. 170–ca. 235 CE).

according to Assyrians . . . spontaneously generated: See Hippolytus, *Refutatio omnium haeresium* 5.7.6, ed. Miroslav Marcovich (Berlin, 1986), 144. In Hippolytus's text, the "Iannes" mentioned is in fact the Assyrian "Oannes," a creature part fish, part man, who, in Mesopotamian mythology, was the first man to be created and who taught mankind wisdom. It is doubtful whether Michael's Stoudite audience would have understood this recondite reference, but it is part of his attempt to blacken the reputation of John the Grammarian by linking him to a work dealing with heresies.

Lekanomantis: Lekanomantis means "the dish diviner." Lecanomancy often interpreted ripples, or the patterns of oil, in a dish

of water to predict the future and divine hidden information. See *Chronicle of Theophanes,* AM 6177, trans. Mango and Scott, *Chronicle,* p. 505n8.

unusually adept in the study of letters: John was also known as "the Grammarian," so a teacher of letters, but letters were seen and interpreted by sorcerers in their divining dishes, hence the insinuation by his detractors, like Michael, that he was "unusually" (here sinisterly) "adept" at the otherwise innocuous "study of letters."

being a very evil person . . . stirred up great trouble: See Josephus, *The Life* 27.134, ed. and trans. Henry St. J. Thackeray, in *The Life; Against Apion* (Cambridge, MA, 1926), 52.

triumphantly named tower of the orthodox faith: An allusion to the Greek word νίκη (victory or triumph), which forms part of the patriarch Nikephoros's name. Nikephoros is similarly referred to as the "tower (πύργος) of faith" in a number of iconodule sources, including a chant sung on the eve of celebration of the translation of his relics on March 13 and an anti-iconoclastic poem written at the end of the ninth century; see Ihor Ševčenko, "The Anti-Iconoclastic Poem in the *Pantocrator* Psalter," *Cahiers archéologiques* 15 (1965): 39–60, reprinted in Ihor Ševčenko, *Ideology, Letters and Culture in the Byzantine World* (London, 1982), study 13, Greek text at p. 43. One of Theodore's own letters (*Ep.* 73, p. 193, line 9) refers to Nikephoros as the "*stylos* (pillar) of the orthodox faith." This meeting between Leo and the patriarch took place in December 814. Michael the Monk has then conflated a number of meetings into one continuous account. The *Scriptor incertus,* pp. 49–53, gives a further account of these confrontations. In other saints' lives, the discussions with the emperor are extended into long dialogues in which the iconodule and iconoclast positions are debated. See, for example, *Life of the Patriarch Nikephoros,* trans. Fisher, pp. 79–100.

worldly but ungodly promises: Bribes of money or offices.

showers of tribulations: John Chrysostom uses this phrase in a number of his works; however, Michael may well be recall-

ing *Homiliae in Matthaeum* 33.7 (PG 57:396), as Theodore also quotes these homilies in his letters.

22.2 *associates of the holy patriarch*: According to *Scriptor incertus*, p. 50, the emperor then had discussions with a number of bishops and abbots, including, in Michael's account, Theodore of Stoudios.

22.3 *inventors of evils*: Romans 1:30.

our fathers . . . officiating impartially: Although the iconodule churchmen were required to discuss matters with the emperor, they were reluctant to enter into debate with his iconoclast supporters. Leo's lack of impartiality and therefore his unsuitability to act as a mediator are emphasized in the account of this discussion in the *Life of Saint Niketas of Medikion* 33–35; see Theosteriktos, *Vita Nicetae Mediciensis, AASS*, Apr. 1, Appendix, pp. xxiv–xxv; partial English translation in Paul J. Alexander, *The Patriarch Nicephorus of Constantinople: Ecclesiastical Policy and Image Worship in the Byzantine Empire* (New York, 1958, repr. 2001), 130–32.

22.4 *fire-breathing pillar of piety*: See Exodus 13:21.

the Lord's special and chosen people: See Titus 2:14.

Command them not to teach . . . that is in faith: See 1 Timothy 1:4.

If anyone teaches otherwise . . . means of gain: 1 Timothy 6:3–5.

Remind them of these things . . . idle talking: 2 Timothy 2:14, 2:16.

22.5 *Ignatios*: Ignatios, bishop of Antioch (d. ca. 140 CE).

I am protecting you . . . not even meet: See Ignatios of Antioch, *Epistula ad Smyrnaeos* 4.1; *Lettres; Martyre de Polycarpe*, ed. and trans. Pierre-Thomas Camelot, 4th ed. revised and corrected (Paris, 2007), 134–35.

in the manner that Jannes . . . case of those: 2 Timothy 3:8–9.

For to pay any attention . . . as the pagan saying has it: Aristotle, *Topica* 1.11; *Posterior Analytics; Topica*, ed. and trans. Hugh Tredennick and Edward S. Forster, Loeb Classical Library 391 (Cambridge, MA, 1960, repr. 2014), 301. Michael has subtly altered the tense of the quotation and added "of many people," to make Theodore emphasize both that Leo is *in the process* of acting foolishly and that he is acting against established views.

22.6 *Kyr Theodore*: The emperor uses the standard Greek honorific term, *kyris,* in addressing Theodore.

those who are opposed to your thinking: The Greek phrase here, τῶν ἐνδιαβαλλόντων ὑμῶν, is an allusion to the story of Balaam's ass in Numbers 22:22, where the verb is used to mean "stand in the way as an adversary" and thus "oppose."

22.7 *it is a very small thing . . . reproach ourselves*: See 1 Corinthians 4:3.

the sword of the Spirit: Ephesians 6:17.

God appointed . . . teachers: 1 Corinthians 12:28. This is a passage also cited by John of Damascus, making very similar points about the limitation of the powers of the emperor; see *St John of Damascus: Three Treatises on the Divine Images*, trans. Andrew Louth (Crestwood, NY, 2003), 2.12, pp. 68–69. In the *Life of the Patriarch Nikephoros,* trans. Fisher, pp. 101–3 (see esp. p. 101n319), the author gives "one speech from them all" in which the same allusion is made to "prophets, apostles and teachers" by an anonymous speaker who has been identified with Theodore.

for the holy apostle . . . affairs of the Church: The point that the Church, rather than the emperor, should legislate in matters of belief is also firmly made in other accounts of the episode. See, for example, *Life of the Patriarch Nikephoros,* trans. Fisher, p. 103.

23.2 *eparch of the city*: The eparch of Constantinople was the chief judicial official of the city and its environs, second only to the emperor. He was in charge of law and order, ceremonial and commercial activity; see *ODB,* vol. 1, p. 705.

23.3 *beatings and death*: See 2 Corinthians 11:23.

23.4 *the famous patriarch was deposed*: Michael the Monk gives the precise date of March 20 (815) with little other detail. The *Life of the Patriarch Nikephoros,* trans. Fisher, pp. 116–18, contains a description of Nikephoros's final address in Hagia Sophia; the *Scriptor incertus,* pp. 54–55, has a scarcely credible account of the sick patriarch being left by the bearers of his litter in the forum of the Milion in the hope that he might be killed by passing soldiers. In the event, since it was the middle of the night, no one came, and Nikephoros was subsequently taken

to the port below the Akropolis (Seraglio Point) and conveyed by ship across the Bosporos to Chrysopolis on the Asiatic shore.

March: Michael here employs the old "Macedonian" name (Δύστρος) for the period approximately covering March in the Julian calendar. See Venance Grumel, *La chronologie* (Paris, 1958), 168–69. The word μαρτίου (of March) is added in a later marginal note on fol. 230r of Ms. Vat. gr. 1669.

his own monastery . . . Asian side of the straits: The identity of this house, the monastery of Agathos near Chrysopolis (modern Üsküdar), is provided in the *Life of the Patriarch Nikephoros,* trans. Fisher, p. 118. Its precise location is unknown; see Belke, *Bithynien und Hellespont,* vol. 1, p. 376.

customary Meeting with Christ celebration: A procession of monks holding palm branches and candles, commemorating the entry of Christ into Jerusalem on Palm Sunday; see *The Lenten Triodion,* trans. Mother Mary and Kallistos Ware, 2nd ed. (London, 1999), 58.

around the vineyard: A similar ceremony of processing icons around the vineyard, this time on Easter Day, is recorded in a version of the Stoudite *Rule;* see *BMFD,* vol. 1, no. 4, chapter 2, p. 101A.

23.5 *the kathegoumenoi*: Monastic superiors; see note to 10.3, above.

customary visit to the patriarchal residence: The new iconoclast patriarch Theodotos Melissenos (*PmbZ Online* no. 7954) had been enthroned on April 1, 815 (Easter Day). This "customary visit" would probably have been to congratulate him on his appointment.

a letter . . . pervert the truth: There follows an accurate citation of the beginning of Theodore's *Ep.* 71 (p. 189, lines 3–10), sent in April 815 to the members of an iconoclast ecclesiastical council held in Hagia Sophia.

24.1 *then went their way . . . for the name*: Acts 5:41.

seventy-two leaders: See Luke 10:1, 10:17.

wished for . . . good days: Psalms 33(34):13.

the fortress called Metopa . . . Lake Apollonias: This fortress, on the south shore of Lake Apollonias (modern Lake Uluabat, or

Apolyont; see Belke, *Bithynien und Hellespont,* vol. 2, p. 779), is also mentioned in the *Life of Saint Nicholas of Stoudios,* PG 105:884A, as the place where Nicholas, the future abbot of Stoudios, was imprisoned with Theodore. See 25.5.

24.2 *called Niketas and surnamed son of Alexios*: Niketas, son of Alexios (*PmbZ Online* no. 5467), is mentioned in a number of Theodore's letters: *Epp.* 106, 139 (addressed to him in 816 and where his title of *mandator*—for which see *ODB,* vol. 2, p. 1281—is given), 146, 148, and 150.

stronghold named Boneta in the Anatolikon theme: This place, again mentioned in the *Life of Saint Nicholas of Stoudios,* PG 105:884A, has been identified with the Byzantine fortress on Maymun Daği above the town of Çardak near Lake Acı Göl; see Klaus Belke and Norbert Mersich, *Phrygien und Pisidien* (Vienna, 1990), 213–14. The fifteen-day journey from Metopa is also described in Theodore's letter (*Ep.* 146) to his disciple Naukratios.

Whether it is right . . . rather than men: Acts 4:19–20 and 5:29.

24.3 *sent him out a second time*: The episode of the beating by Niketas is corroborated in Theodore's letter to Naukratios (*Ep.* 150), written in the summer of 816.

24.5 *because in the end . . . not be lost*: Psalms 9:19(18).

He also wrote to the four patriarchs: These letters, dating from 817/8, are *Epp.* 271 and 272 to Pope Paschal I, *Ep.* 275 to the patriarch Christopher of Alexandria, and *Ep.* 276 to the patriarch Thomas of Jerusalem. A marginal note to *Ep.* 275 records that a copy of this letter was also sent to the patriarch of Antioch; see *Epp.* vol. 1, p. 319*.

25.1 *land of the Thrakesians*: The theme of Thrakesion on the western coast of Asia Minor.

Mastaura: This is probably a reference to the city in the lower Maeander valley, in the ecclesiastical province of Asia (see Belke, *Phrygien und Hellespont,* vol. 2, p. 760), rather than that of the same name in Lycia; see Hansgerd Hellenkemper and Friedrich Hild, *Lykien und Pamphylien* (Vienna, 2004), vol. 2, pp. 716–18.

sun of the Gospel: The phrase "sun of the Gospel" is used by Theo-

dore in his *Ep.* 385, p. 534, line 26, to describe John the Theologian, who, in orthodox tradition, returned from his exile on Patmos to die at Ephesus (in the province of Asia).

25.2 *rushed to the military governor*: If, as is thought, the capital of the Thrakesion theme was at Chonai (modern Honaz), then the churchman concerned here, who clearly had easy access to the military governor, may have been the bishop of that town.

Horabe: The military governor of Thrakesion (*PmbZ Online* no. 5660). It is possible that his name is a corruption of "ὁ Ραβέ . . ." with the end of a surname omitted.

25.3 *supreme military governor of the East*: The Greek term *stratopedarches* (στρατοπεδάρχης) is a more archaic version of "military governor" *(strategos)*. Michael is again referring, though more elegantly, to the military governor of the Anatolikon theme.

he sent a member of his cohort to thrash holy Theodore: This individual is named as Theophanes in 25.6, below. This account may be a "doublet," as the details are so similar to those given in the story of Niketas in 24.

25.4 *called Anastasios and said to be of the Martinakios family*: For Anastasios Martinaki(os), see *PmbZ Online* no. 316.

25.5 *a hundred very harsh strokes*: Again, we seem to have a repetition of an earlier story. Georgios Fatouros, *Epp.* vol. 1, p. 335*n636, suggests that there was only one beating of Theodore during this period in the winter of 817/8.

Nicholas: Nicholas, the future abbot of Stoudios (*PmbZ Online* no. 5576/corr.), was imprisoned with Theodore in Metopa and then Boneta from 815 to 821. For his hagiography, see *Life of Saint Nicholas of Stoudios*.

25.6 *Christ-loving Theophanes*: See note to 25.3, above.

25.7 *fiery furnace*: See Daniel 3.

26.1 *the serpent with his crooked counsels*: The devil.

let us cast all our anxiety on the Lord: See Psalms 54:23 (55:22).

who fills every living thing with his favor: Psalms 144(145):16.

some more authoritative satrap: Michael here uses the elegantly archaic word "satrap" to indicate a high official. In the *Vita A* (PG 99:197C), the same man is described as τῶν περιφανῶν τις καὶ τὰ πρῶτα βασιλεῖ δυναμένων (one of the notable men of

the first rank of power in the Empire), leading to the suggestion by Thomas Pratsch, *Theodoros Studites (759–826): Zwischen Dogma und Pragma* (Frankfurt-am-Main, 1998), 257n245, that he might have been a *protospatharios,* for which rank see *ODB,* vol. 3, p. 1748.

26.2 *a catechetical letter from Theodore, the world's teacher*: This is probably *Ep.* 381, written in early 819. The designation of Theodore as "the world's teacher" (ὁ διδάσκαλος τῆς οἰκουμένης) is also found in the *Encyclical Letter of Naukratios* 2, below, and in Theosteriktos, *Life of Saint Niketas of Medikion* 35 (*AASS,* Apr. 1, Appendix, p. xxv). It was an honorific description, not in any sense a title.

Count of the Tent: The *komes tes kortes* was an official with judicial and police duties on the staff of the military governor; see *ODB,* vol. 2, p. 1139. Fatouros, *Epp.* vol. 1, p. 374* and *Ep.* 382, p. 526, note to line 13, mistakenly identifies him as Karteros/Krateros (see below).

26.3 *Karteros*: Karteros or Krateros (*PmbZ Online* no. 4158) was at this time (early 819) military governor of the Anatolikon theme.

that punishment . . . on February 23: Again, Michael has used the old "Macedonian Month" (Περίτιος) for the date (see note to 23.4, above), and a later hand in Ms. Vat gr. 1669, fol. 237r, has added the marginal explanation φεβρουαρίου (of February). This is also another of the rare occasions (as in 23.4) when he places a precise date on an episode, although he does not give the year. The episode of the beating is described in Theodore's *Ep.* 382, written between February and May 819, where, however, the perpetrator is given as the Count of the Tent.

26.4 *Pythian spirits*: Spirits of divination, see Acts 16:16.

My beautiful lion: Again, a play on words on the name of Leo V.

the pale-looking thing: The Greek word χλωροπικὴ, translated here as "pale-looking thing," is not found in Liddell and Scott, Lampe, or the *Thesaurus Linguae Graecae,* but the gender and the accompanying words suggest that it refers to the fleece that was placed on Theodore's shoulders before the earlier flogging, described in 24.4.

26.5 *deep sleep*: Homer, *Iliad* 2.2 and *Odyssey* 12.79.

Silas or Timothy: Two of the missionary companions of Saint Paul; see Acts 15:22–18:5.

27.1 *Pentecost*: Pentecost in the Orthodox Church celebrates the fifty days of Easter. In 819 the actual day of Pentecost, which marks the descent of the Holy Spirit upon the Apostles, fell in May.

remnants of riches: Michael the Monk here uses the term "mammon," echoing Mathew 6:24, to emphasize that monks were most unlikely to possess anything of value.

27.2 *securing the feet of Christ's prisoners in the stocks*: See Acts 16:24.

they thus reached the region of Smyrna: The removal of Theodore and Nicholas to Smyrna (modern Izmir), a journey of over 150 miles, is also alluded to in *Epp.* 406 and 407.

heresiarch: The unnamed iconoclast cleric is referred to as the metropolitan of Smyrna in 28.1, below, and is designated ἀσεβάρχης (leader of the ungodly) in Theodore's *Ep.* 415, p. 578, line 14.

27.3 *Anastasios surnamed Martinakis*: This is the same man as the Anastasios Martinakios of 25.4–6, above. Again, there is a possibility that the episodes of beating have been multiplied by Michael the Monk.

the pentathlete Theodore: An allusion to the Pentathlon, a particularly grueling series of events in the ancient Olympic Games; compare the use of the epithet "pancratiast" in 11.4.

27.4 *If we suffer . . . glorified*: See Romans 8:17.

Bardas, the ruler's brother-in-law: Bardas (*PmbZ Online* no. 789) is here described as the "brother-in-law" (σύγγαμβρος) of Leo V. In the *Life of the Patriarch Nikephoros,* trans. Fisher, p. 118n405, the Greek text reading ἀνεψιὸς (nephew or cousin) is given. At this point he was military governor of the Thrakesion theme.

27.5 *Diogenes, who came from a noble family*: This was probably his surname (see *PmbZ Online* no. 1338). Nothing more is known of him, but this mention of a Diogenes is much earlier than the late tenth-century individual cited as the first attested member of the family in *ODB*. The eleventh-century author Michael Psellos also described the family as "ancient and flourishing"; see *ODB,* vol. 1, p. 627.

Thaddaios: Thaddaios (*PmbZ Online* no. 7252/corr.) was a Stoudite monk of humble origins, possibly of Bulgarian extraction. He was the addressee of two of Theodore's Letters (*Epp.* 126 and 183, and see *Epp.* vol. 1, p. 340*n334) and is mentioned in many more. Theodore also mentions him in his *Lesser Katecheseis* (nos. 29, 43, and 133). The *Synaxarion of Constantinople* 353/354.51–355/356.54 contains a short *Life of Thaddaios* (*BHG* 2415e); Hippolyte Delehaye, ed., *Synaxarium ecclesiae Constantinopolitanae e codice Sirmondiano nunc Berolinensi: Propylaeum ad Acta sanctorum Novembris* (Brussels, 1902). During Second Iconoclasm, Thaddaios headed a group of ten Stoudite monks but was beaten and died shortly afterward of his wounds, either on November 22 or December 29, 816.

their worm will not die and their fire will not be quenched: Isaiah 66:24.

27.6 *does not wish the death of a sinner*: Ezekiel 33:11.

tricked by suggestions . . . complete health: The unnamed "unholy one" is the metropolitan of Smyrna.

27.7 *to cleave to evil people . . . unpunished*: See Cyril of Alexandria, *De adoratione* 15, PG 68:1000B.

28.1 *imprisoned for twenty months*: If we take this indication of time at face value, Theodore remained in the custody of the metropolitan of Smyrna until January or February 821.

Naukratios . . . named for his good cheer: Michael here singles out Stoudite monks, clearly close associates of Theodore, who were considered to have suffered greatly for their faith during Second Iconoclasm and were memorialized in his own day. Each is given a complimentary characteristic. For Naukratios, see the Introduction. *Naukrator* is the Greek term for the master of a ship, an allusion to Naukratios's later position as abbot of Stoudios. For Timothy see note to 8.3, above. The priest Dorotheos (*PmbZ Online* no. 1406) is the addressee of a number of Theodore's letters (*Epp.* 124, 188, 239, and 531) and is mentioned in numerous others. He is also mentioned in *Lesser Katecheseis* 133. Besarion (*PmbZ* Online no. 1011) is the addressee of three of Theodore's letters (*Epp.* 128, 235, and 252).

James (Iakobos, see *PmbZ Online* no. 2632) is the addressee of two letters (*Epp.* 189 and 328) and is mentioned in *Epp.* 186, 190, 195, 199, and 441, as well as in *Lesser Katecheseis* 115 and 133. Dometianos (*PmbZ Online* no. 1355) is the addressee of one letter (*Ep.* 180) and is mentioned in *Epp.* 41, 109, and 178; he is also mentioned in *Lesser Katecheseis* 2 and 38. Tithoeis (*PmbZ Online* no. 8506) is the addressee of three letters (*Epp.* 178, 179, and 365) and is mentioned in *Epp.* 106, 109, 116, 130, 133, 223, and 225. Euthymios (*PmbZ Online* no. 1848) is the addressee of Theodore's letters *Epp.* 181, 246, and 343 and is mentioned in *Ep.* 41; the Greek verb *euthymeo* means "to be cheerful."

for those who believe . . . sin in anything: Josephus, *Against Apion* 2.160, ed. and trans. Thackeray, p. 356.

28.2 *the jealous God who destroys his enemies . . . long-suffering*: Nahum 1:2–3.

who stretches the bow . . . laid waste the places: See Psalms 7 (especially 7:12 onward), 124(125):3, and 78(79):11.

he exacted satisfaction . . . murdered with a knife: Leo V was murdered on Christmas Day, 820, at the altar of the chapel of Saint Stephen in the area of the Great Palace known as Daphne by a group of conspirators disguised as priests.

the prophecy of the blessed prophet Amos . . . terrify you: Not in fact a quotation from Amos, but Habakkuk 2:10, 2:16–17.

Ephraim made me angry . . . for his reproach: Hosea 12:15 (12:14), slightly adjusted to fit the context.

In the way that a garment . . . killed my people: Isaiah 14:19–20.

28.3 *Michael, the man who struck him down*: Only indirectly, for the assassination was actually carried out by men who then released Michael (*PmbZ Online* no. 4990/corr.), a high-ranking army officer, from imprisonment. He was crowned as Michael II (820–829) by the patriarch Theodotos later the same day. Theodore's reaction to this event, as witnessed in his *Epp.* 417 and 424, was to downplay the possible charge of sacrilege that could have been brought against the conspirators and to express his joy at the course of events.

labarum of imperial power: The *labarum* was originally a Christian

standard, which was either cross shaped or depicted various monograms of the name of Christ, see *ODB,* vol. 2, p. 1167. It was associated with the first Christian emperor, Constantine I.

all those who had been banished . . . released from their bonds: Theodore was released from imprisonment in Smyrna in January or February 821.

29.1 *Xerolophoi*: It is unclear who the Xerolophoi (*PmbZ Online* no. 8594) were. It is possible they were a group of iconodule monks who had taken refuge in Asia Minor, but who came originally from a monastery in the region of Xerolophos/Xerolophon, one of the hills of Constantinople; see Belke, *Bithynia und Hellespont,* vol. 2, p. 1073.

Lakkou Mitata: A *mitaton* (see *ODB,* vol. 2, p. 1385) was a recognized "lodging place" or "inn," while the term *Lakkou* possibly indicates that there was a group of these lodgings near a "pond" or "pit" *(lakkos)*. See Belke, *Bithynien und Hellespont,* vol. 2, p. 721.

fortress called Elpizon: The location of this fortress is unknown. See Belke, *Bithynien und Hellespont,* vol. 1, p. 551.

29.2 *Leo*: Leo/Theodore (*PmbZ Online* no. 4421) may be the Leo (*PmbZ Online* no. 4441/corr.) who commissioned the *Life of Saint Nicholas by Michael* (*BHG* 1348) that was written in the first half of the ninth century but modeled on an earlier work by the patriarch Methodios; see chapter 2, English trans. John Quinn and Bryson Sewell, "The Life of Saint Nicholas the Wonderworker," St. Nicholas Center, accessed December 10, 2020, http://www.stnicholascenter.org/pages/michael-the-archimandrite. If so, and if "Archimandrite Michael," the author of that *Life,* can be identified with Michael the Monk, he would then have been personally acquainted with Leo/Theodore, making the detailed account of these miracle stories a personal recollection. On this see Dirk Krausmüller, "Patriarch Methodios, the Author of the Lost First Life of Theodore of Stoudios," *Symbolae Osloenses: Norwegian Journal of Greek and Latin Studies* 81, no. 1 (2006): 144–50, http://dx.doi.org/10.1080/00397670701495161.

hypatos: The Greek term for consul, but an honorific title by this time; see *ODB,* vol. 2, pp. 963–64.

came every year . . . tomb of the fathers: The tomb containing the relics of Theodore, his brother Joseph, and their uncle Plato was constructed after the return of their relics to Stoudios in 844 (see 35.4, below, and the *Translation and Burial*), which indicates that the narration of the miracle stories is taking place in Stoudios.

elder: The unnamed elder would have been a senior Stoudite monk, possibly the abbot. Given the detail in these stories, Michael could conceivably be referring to himself.

30.1 *At that time*: At this point numbering of the miracles begins in the margins of manuscripts P and V; there are eleven in total, continuing to 32.2, below.

Dionysios: See *PmbZ Online* no. 1347.

Pteleai: Modern Pamukçu to the south of modern Balıkesir; see Belke, *Bithynien und Hellespont,* vol. 2, pp. 958–59.

30.2 *Achyraous*: South of Balıkesir on the river Makestos (Simav Çayı); see *ODB,* vol. 1, p. 15, and Belke, *Bithynien und Hellepont,* vol. 1, pp. 364–66.

30.3 *Onopniktes*: Literally, "The Ass Drowner"; see Belke, *Bithynien und Hellespont,* vol. 2, pp. 865–66.

evening praise to the Lord: Portions, if not the whole, of Vespers.

30.4 *Meteorin*: Location unknown, but see Belke, *Bithynien und Hellespont,* vol. 2, p. 779.

31.1 *Sophronios*: Sophronios (*PmbZ Online* no. 6848) was abbot of Stoudios from 849 to 853, after Nicholas of Stoudios, and may well have been personally known to Michael the Monk.

31.2 *Symeon*: See *PmbZ Online* no. 7198/corr. Theodore composed an iambic poem to instruct and encourage the Stoudite infirmarian; see Theodore of Stoudios, *Epigrams,* ed. and trans. Speck, *Jamben,* no. 17, pp. 148–49, French trans. de Montleau, *Les grandes catéchèses,* p. 587.

31.3 *Paphlagonian theme*: The region east of the Sangarios River along the south coast of the Black Sea.

Anatolios: Anatolios (*PmbZ Online* no. 348/corr.) is the addressee of three of Theodore's letters (*Epp.* 81, 164, and 311) and is men-

tioned in two more (*Epp.* 384 and 411). He had briefly been won over to iconoclasm in 818/9, a matter that Michael either did not know of or chose to conceal.

31.4 *one of the grandees who lived in the Rhabdos quarter*: The unnamed couple (see *PmbZ Online* nos. 11517 and 11517A) lived in an area of southwestern Constantinople that took its name from the "Rod *(rhabdos)* of Aaron" that was deposited by the emperor Constantine in the church of Saint Aimilianos there.

a note . . . Theodore had recently sent me: Many of Theodore's letters were addressed to high-ranking women. This one probably contained a very short message, as in another example of an *epistolion* (short letter or note), *Ep.* 266, p. 394, which is only some six printed lines long.

sheet of paper: The Greek word used here, *χάρτης,* could refer to paper made of rags or vegetable matter. A *chartopoios* (papermaker) at Stoudios is mentioned in one of Theodore's *katecheseis;* see de Montleau, *Les grandes catéchèses,* no. 35, p. 306, with further discussion by Julien Leroy on pp. 110–11.

31.5 *ruler of that same land*: The unnamed *protos* of Sardinia (*PmbZ Online* no. 11639/corr.) cannot be identified. Little is known about Byzantine Sardinia in this period (see *ODB,* vol. 3, pp. 1842–43), but Thomas, the metropolitan of Sardinia (*PmbZ Online* no. 8445), was represented at the Second Council of Nicaea in 787 by a deacon from the church of Catania (Sicily) and, in the tenth-century compilation of the *Book of Ceremonies,* the protocol for addressing the ruler of Sardinia *(archon)* is given. It is possible that the *protos* was the "*archon* of Carales" (modern Cagliari), a regional official or military commander known from seals of the first half of the ninth century.

triodia of holy Lent which Theodore . . . had composed: The *Triodion* was a liturgical hymnbook containing the variable parts of services in the Lenten and Easter periods (see *ODB,* vol. 3, pp. 2118–19). Theodore composed a number of hymns *(triodia)* for these periods, which soon became popular in the Byzantine Church and have survived to the present day; see *Epp.* vol. 1, p. 34*(e).

some monks: See *PmbZ Online* no. 10561.

Gregory . . . of Syracuse: Gregory Asbestas (*PmbZ Online* nos. 2480 and 22348, and see *ODB*, vol. 1, pp. 202–3), a protégé of the patriarch Methodios I (*PmbZ Online* no. 4977/corr.), was archbishop of Syracuse between 844 and approximately 852/3, and again from 858 to 867. The implied criticism of Theodore by Gregory's followers in this episode may well reflect hostility that existed in Michael the Monk's time between partisans of the rival ninth-century patriarch Ignatios (*PmbZ Online* no. 2666/corr. and 22712), among whom were the Stoudite monks, and those of the patriarch Photios (*PmbZ Online* no. 6253/corr. and 26667), among whom was Gregory Asbestas.

31.6 *lictors*: This translates the Greek word ῥαβδοῦχοι (literally, "rod-bearers"), the Byzantine equivalent of the Roman lictors, the bodyguards of important figures such as magistrates.

bad company . . . good morals: 1 Corinthians 15:33.

32.3 *for the gifts of God are irrevocable*: Romans 11:29.

33.1 *deserts, mountains, and caves in the earth*: Hebrews 11:38.

Theoktistos, the former magistros: Theoktistos (*PmbZ Online* no. 8046) was a high-ranking court official and is mentioned in the *Chronicle of Theophanes,* AM 6295, trans. Mango and Scott, *Chronicle,* p. 655, as one of those who supported the emperor Nikephoros's bid for the throne in 802. He was subsequently given the title of *patrikios* and appointed to the judicial position of *quaestor* (see *ODB,* vol. 3, p. 1765). By 808, he had risen to the rank of *magistros,* as he is addressed as such by Theodore in *Ep.* 24; see also *Chronicle of Theophanes,* AM 6303, trans. Mango and Scott, *Chronicle,* p. 674. He had presumably been tonsured by Theodore at some point between 808 and Theodore's exile in 815 and had subsequently founded his own monastery in or near Chalcedon.

33.2 *estate of Kreskentios*: This property, situated on the Gulf of Nikomedia (Gulf of İzmit; İzmit Körfezi), was not a monastery but a country estate. See Belke, *Bithynien und Hellespont,* vol. 2, p. 694.

Peter . . . appropriately named Aboukis: Peter of Atroa (773–837; see *PmbZ Online* no. 6022/corr.) was clearly famous for his asceti-

cism in Theodore's own time. His epithet "Aboukis" (without a mouthful) is probably derived from the Greek word *boukin,* meaning "a mouthful."

those who were casting doubt . . . miracles that he was performing: In chapter 37 of the *Life of Saint Peter of Atroa,* the jealousy of "certain bishops and abbots," their attribution of Peter's miracles to "Beelzebub," and his visit to Theodore are all described; see *La vie merveilleuse de Saint Pierre d'Atroa (†837)*, ed. and French trans. Vitalien Laurent (Brussels, 1956).

acknowledging their own poor judgment: The *Life of Saint Peter of Atroa,* chapter 38 (cited above), purports to contain the text of a letter written by Theodore to rebuke Peter's detractors. While accepting that Theodore may well have written on Peter's behalf (see *Ep.* 560), it is doubtful whether the letter in question is genuine, both on linguistic grounds and because it appears to praise the miracle workings of ascetics, a matter on which Theodore was generally more reserved. Even if such a letter was written, the text in the *Life of Saint Peter of Atroa* was probably greatly elaborated by Peter's hagiographer, the monk Sabas.

wanting in Christ . . . all men: See 1 Corinthians 9:19.

Who is weak . . . not indignant: 2 Corinthians 11:29.

34.1 *the synod*: It is not clear where this gathering of clerics took place, or whether the patriarch Nikephoros himself was present. In the latter case, the meeting would have been at Chalcedon. Theodore refers to this gathering at the beginning of his *Ep.* 429, a letter written on behalf of "all the abbots" to the new emperor, Michael II. The patriarch's absence might have been for a number of reasons: the fact that he had, as the *Chronicle of Theophanes continuatus,* book 2 reports, already sent a letter (now lost) calling for the restoration of image veneration and had received a negative response (see *Chronographiae quae Theophanis continuati nomine fertur libri I–IV,* eds. and English trans. Michael Featherstone and Juan Signes-Codoñer [Berlin, 2015], p. 73); that he felt another effort by the bishops alone might nonetheless be useful, or simply that he was in failing health.

their intermediary: This was possibly the *sakellarios* Leo (see note to 29.2, above) who is the addressee of Theodore's *Ep.* 478, dating from 823, where he is mentioned as having facilitated an audience with the emperor "some three years previously." He was clearly an iconodule.

divinely sanctioned adornment: The Greek word κόσμον (adornment) also carries the sense of "proper order."

manners of a swineherd: Michael II's "rusticity and boorishness" were also commented upon in the *Chronicle of Theophanes continuatus* 2.3, ed. Featherstone and Signes-Codoñer, *Chronographiae*, p. 67.

34.2 *insurrection of Thomas*: The revolt of Thomas the Slav (see *ODB*, vol. 3, p. 2079) took place after the assassination of Leo V in the winter of 820/1.

34.3 *that tyrant plundered the Asiatic territory*: Thomas marched through Asia Minor in 821 and besieged Constantinople from late 821 to the spring of 822. Even if Thomas was an iconodule, Michael the Monk did not view him favorably, and Theodore himself described the revolt as the "assault of the Arabs," possibly a derogatory reference to Thomas's alliance with the Caliph Ma'mūn (see *Ep.* 475).

captured by the emperor: Thomas the Slav was captured and executed in October 823.

the peninsula . . . Saint Tryphon: The peninsula of Saint Tryphon was on the north coast of Cape Akritas (modern Tuzlaburu) to the south of Chalcedon; see Belke, *Bithynien und Hellespont*, vol. 2, pp. 1066–67. It is likely that Theodore and his disciples lived in the monastery of Saint Tryphon there, which had been in existence since the sixth century.

34.4 *Theodore went up from there . . . holy patriarch*: Patriarch Nikephoros remained at Chalcedon until his death.

as the Lord also said in the Gospels: Michael is comparing the great love that Theodore had for Christ with that of the woman who anointed his feet with ointment; see Luke 7:36–50, especially 7:47.

As there is a difference . . . achievements of each: Cyril of Alexandria, *De adoratione* 17, PG 68:1125C–D.

that man . . . victorious virtues: Michael here makes a pun on Nikephoros's name.

34.5 *should place a hand over their own lips*: See Wisdom 8:12.

look into our father's letters: A clear indication that collections of Theodore's *Letters* were already widely circulated by Michael's day.

34.6 *His face had been glorified like Moses*: See Exodus 34:30.

35.1 *Theodore was stricken*: This account of Theodore's death in 35.1–5 is closely based, sometimes word for word, on that in the *Encyclical Letter of Naukratios* 14–23 (see below).

he did not give sleep . . . his temples: Psalms 131(132):4.

he dictated this to one of the shorthand writers: An interesting hint at the way that the *katecheseis* were preserved. This is *Lesser Katecheseis* 31, pp. 113–18, which is partly given by Naukratios in his *Encyclical Letter* 15–19, below.

35.2 *labor bestows health and eagerness raises the dead*: Gregory of Nazianzos, *Oration* 43.37, ed. Jean Bernardi, *Discours 42–43*, 208.

a desire to depart and be with Christ: Philippians 1:23.

35.3 *commemoration of Paul*: November 6, the feast day of Paul the Confessor, bishop of Constantinople (died 350).

Around the fourth hour of the night: The Byzantine monastic day was divided into twenty-four "hours," regulated by the sun. Since the amount of sunlight is not constant throughout the year, the number and length of these hours increased or decreased month by month. The "fourth hour of the night" in November would thus have been between 8:30 and 9:40 p.m.

35.4 *Take care of the legacy . . . keep your faith*: See 1 Timothy 6:20. The "legacy" almost certainly refers to his teaching and the traditions he had established within the community. Theodore refers to this spiritual legacy in *Ep.* 247, pp. 379–80, and *Ep.* 504, p. 747, lines 12–14.

our master the archbishop: A reference to Joseph of Thessalonike, Theodore's brother.

the Lord of peace: 2 Thessalonians 3:16.

35.5 *commemoration of . . . Menas*: November 11.

the Blameless Psalm: Psalm 118 (119). The psalm takes its name from the opening line, "Blessed are the blameless. . . ." It is also

used in funeral rites; see *Εὐχολόγιον το Μέγα,* 3rd ed. (Venice, 1869), 402, for the funeral rite for laymen; for same wording used for monks, see p. 422. The quotation that follows is from verse 93. Theodore is, in fact, participating in his own funeral service.

35.6 *Theodore's all-holy . . . to Prinkipo*: It is not clear where Theodore died. While Michael states that he died on the peninsula of Saint Tryphon (see 34.3, above), the *Translation and Burial* 6.2 suggests that he died on the island of Prinkipo (Büyükada), one of the Princes' Islands; see Belke, *Bithynien und Hellespont,* vol. 2, pp. 936–38.

carefully guarded for eighteen years: It is likely that a group of Stoudites remained on Prinkipo from 826 until their return to Constantinople in 843. The *Translation and Burial* 9.2 comments that Theodore's body was protected "from the fury of the iconoclasts."

the nature that is prone to stink: Cyril of Alexandria, *De adoratione* 12, PG 68:788B.

35.7 *Theodore's remains . . . Stoudios*: The transfer and reburial took place on January 26, 844.

Methodios: Patriarch Methodios I (843–847).

destroyed the heresy of the semi-Christians: Iconoclasm ended in 843.

buried in the tomb . . . own brother: See the *Translation and Burial* 14.

Encyclical Letter of Naukratios

title *fathers . . . scattered everywhere*: The phrasing here indicates that the work must have been written before the restoration of orthodoxy in 843; see Introduction.

1 *the Lord's servant did indeed depart this life*: Theodore died on November 11, 826.

heart of stone: Ezekiel 11:19.

a spirit of steel: John Chrysostom, *Homiliae in Genesim* 36.2, PG 53:334.

2 *workers in the Lord's vineyard*: See Matthew 20:1.

as sons of obedience: See 1 Peter 1:14.

the chosen instrument: Acts 9:15.

the mouthpiece of the Church: An expression used on a number of occasions by Gregory of Nyssa in his *In canticum canticorum;* see, for example, Hermann Langerbeck, ed., *Gregorii Nysseni Opera* (Leiden, 1960–1992), vol. 6, p. 228.

the glory of the priests: This is the first line of a *sticheron* (hymn) written by Patriarch Germanos I (715–730), a celebrated defender of the icons at an earlier period, and one entered into the diptychs of the saints at the iconodule Second Council of Nicaea in 787. See *Menaion* for January, *stichera* in honor of the patriarch Athanasios at Vespers on January 18, *Μηναῖον του Ἰανουαρίου* (Athens, 1970), 274–76.

the bulwark of the faith: Gregory of Nazianzos, *Letter* 79, ed. and trans. Paul Gallay, *Lettres* (Paris, 1964–1967), vol. 1, p. 99. See also his *Oration* 25.11, ed. and trans. Justin Mossay and Guy Lafontaine, *Grégoire de Nazianze: Discours 24–26,* Sources chrétiennes 284 (Paris, 1981), 180.

the heart of the apostles: Theodore, *Ep.* 274 (to the Bishop of Monemvasia and the abbot Methodios), p. 405, line 18.

most loud-voiced herald of the truth: Acts of the Council of Ephesus (431); Eduard Schwartz, ed., *Acta conciliorum oecumenicorum* (Berlin, 1928; repr., Berlin, 1960), vol. 1, part 1.6, p. 108. The reference is originally to the apostle Paul.

ever-flowing fountain of teaching: Naukratios here uses the somewhat unusual word βρυτήρ (fountain) used by Theodore himself in his *Homilia II in nativitatem B. V. Mariae,* once thought to be by John of Damascus; see PG 96:692B.

the purified mind: Philo Judaeus, *Legum allegoriarum libri I–III* 3.100 and 3.200, ed. Leopold Cohn, *Philonis Alexandrini opera quae supersunt* (Berlin, 1896; repr., Berlin, 1962), vol. 1, pp. 135, 157.

the golden soul: A phrase used twice by Theodore himself. It is found in his *Panegyric on Theodore the Confessor* 18.34; see Stephanos Efthymiadis, "Le panégyrique de S. Théophane le Confesseur par S. Théodore Stoudite (*BHG* 1792b): Édition cri-

tique du texte intégrale," *AB* 111 (1993): 259–90. Also in his *Lesser Katecheseis* 74, p. 259, lines 37–38.

3 *not for solace . . . result of this statement*: Basil of Caesarea, *Letter* 29, ed. and trans. Roy J. Deferrari, *Saint Basil, the Letters,* 4 vols. (Cambridge, MA, 1926), 170.

the earthly angel and heavenly man: John Chrysostom, *De paenitentia* 2.5, PG 49:291.

beautifully lidded eye: This translates the unusual adjective καλλιβλέφαρος, used by Theodore himself in his *Ep.* 511, p. 759, line 19.

the champion of patient endurance . . . heresy: Theodore, *Panegyric on Theodore the Confessor* 1.10.

the weapon of righteousness: Probably here taken from Theodore, *Panegyric on Theodore the Confessor* 18.2, but earlier used by both Gregory of Nazianzos and John of Damascus.

4 *someone who . . . became all things to all men*: A comparison with Saint Paul; 1 Corinthians 9:22.

O you ones who are always longed for: Theodore himself uses the unusual word ἀειπόθητος in his *Ep.* 225, p. 359, line 128 (addressed to Naukratios himself); also in *Ep.* 420, p. 589, line 37 (addressed to the *magistros* Stephanos).

what is this mystery . . . wisdom of God: Naukratios is perhaps pondering why God has chosen him to be Theodore's successor and to write the latter's eulogy.

At this time, I would need . . . has left us: Basil of Caesarea, *Letter* 29, ed. and trans. Deferrari, *Letters,* p. 170. The "lamentations of Jeremiah" refer to the book of Lamentations, probably written to commemorate the destruction of Jerusalem by the Babylonians in 586 BCE and traditionally ascribed to the prophet Jeremiah.

some may also fall . . . be proven: See Basil of Caesarea, *Letter* 29, ed. and trans. Deferrari, *Letters,* pp. 170–72.

A mouth has been closed . . . build up the faith: Basil of Caesarea, *Letter* 29, ed. and trans. Deferrari, *Letters,* p. 172.

meditate on the law of the Lord day and night: See Psalms 1:2.

5 *The counsels of a mind . . . have departed*: Basil of Caesarea, *Letter* 29, ed. and trans. Deferrari, *Letters,* p. 172.

The lips that . . . divine law: See Acts 7:53; Galatians 3:19.

golden speech: The adjective *chrysorremon* is usually used as an alternative to *chrysostomos* (golden mouth) when describing the celebrated fourth-century Father of the Church John Chrysostom (see, for example, John of Damascus, *Oratio de iis qui in fide dormierunt* 6, PG 95:252C). Naukratios is here comparing Theodore's doctrinal teaching with Chrysostom's.

The hand . . . enriched the world with letters: For details of Theodore's own literary works, see the *Life* 14.4 and 16.1–4, where it is emphasized that they were often written in his own hand.

knowledge of the truth: 1 Timothy 2:4.

beautiful feet . . . peace and blessings: Romans 10:15.

6 *second Abraham . . . offspring beyond number*: The "Blessing of Abraham" refers to the covenant made by God with Abraham "and his seed," the benefits of which are enumerated by Moses in Deuteronomy 28:3–13. Galatians 3:16 and Romans 4:16 emphasize that all those who have faith are the "children of Abraham." Theodore is compared to Abraham because he has kept the true, orthodox faith and influenced many others to do so.

imitator of the Forerunner: John the Baptist was known in Greek as *Prodromos* (Forerunner). Theodore is seen as emulating his preaching of the true faith.

emulator of Elijah: See 3 Kings 18 (1 Kings 18) where the prophet Elijah defends the worship of the Hebrew God against that of the god Baal. This is thus a veiled reference to Theodore's defense of orthodoxy against the iconoclasts.

Phinehas of grace: See Numbers 25:1–9. Phinehas took violent action against Israelites who had begun to worship Baal; Naukratios is here perhaps emphasizing Theodore's more peaceful methods of persuasion.

new Samuel: Probably an allusion to the prophet Samuel's insistence that prophets and judges were more important than kings (see 1 Samuel 12) and that war should be made on false

believers, such as the Philistines and Amalekites. The theme of the superiority of priests to lay rulers is taken up by Michael the Monk; see the *Life* 22.7.

the one picked out from ten thousand: Song of Songs 5:10.

put to death his earthly members: Colossians 3:5.

a temple of the living God: See 1 Corinthians 6:19.

Who was more clear-sighted . . . spiritual attitude: Basil of Caesarea, *Letter* 28, ed. and trans. Deferrari, *Letters,* p. 164.

7 *already preoccupied . . . appropriate to himself*: This whole section draws heavily, and in many places directly, on Basil of Caesarea, *Letter* 28, ed. and trans. Deferrari, *Letters,* pp. 164–66.

the Church looks sad: Reminiscent of a phrase used by Theodore himself in *Ep.* 544 (to Joseph, the abbot of the Monastery of Kerameon), p. 822, line 17. This letter was written in the two months preceding Theodore's death; given Theodore's state of health, it might well have been dictated to Naukratios.

marvelous counselor: Isaiah 9:6.

8 *possessed in his name a calling from above*: A reference to Theodore's name, derived from *theodoretos* (God-given).

The mouths of the iconoclasts have opened against us: See Psalms 21:14 (22:13).

we have been reckoned . . . go down to the pit: Psalms 87:5 (88:4).

we have become like a lonely bird on the housetop: Psalms 101:8 (102:7).

almost dwell in Hades: Psalms 93(94):17.

Oh, what truly dreadful . . . like a desert pelican: Basil of Caesarea, *Letter* 29, ed. and trans. Deferrari, *Letters,* p. 172. The second sentence quotes Psalms 101:7 (102:6).

9 *if . . . one limb suffers, all the limbs suffer together*: 1 Corinthians 12:26.

piety's racecourse: See 2 Timothy 4:7.

10 *on account of which . . . passed over in silence*: See Basil of Caesarea, *Letter* 28, ed. and trans. Deferrari, *Letters,* p. 160.

11 *great apostle*: Most likely a reference to Saint Paul and his teaching on the virtues of suffering. See 2 Corinthians 1:5–6 and 2 Corinthians 4:8–12.

our forefather: Adam.

how God commanded . . . appointed times: Basil of Caesarea, *Letter* 28, ed. and trans. Deferrari, *Letters,* p. 166.

12 *if, as he said, we observe his commands*: An echo of Christ's exhortation in John 14:15.

in a mirror dimly . . . face to face: 1 Corinthians 13:12.

13 *his parting words*: A reference either to Theodore's last address to his monks, quoted at length by Naukratios in 15–18, below, or to the final words of comfort and spiritual guidance given to those who visited him on his deathbed, in 19–23, below.

Testament . . . Rule: It is significant that Naukratios gives us no further details of either of these documents. Olivier Delouis, "Le *Testament* de Théodore Stoudite est-il de Théodore?," *REB* 66 (2008): 173–90, has shown that the so-called *Testament* is, in fact, a composite document produced after Theodore's death. See also Olivier Delouis, "Le *Testament* de Théodore Stoudite: Édition critique et traduction," *REB* 67 (2009): 77–109; English trans. Timothy Miller, "*Theodore Studites: Testament* of Theodore the Studite for the Monastery of St. John Stoudios," in *BMFD,* vol. 1, pp. 67–83. The Stoudite *Hypotyposis* (Rule) was similarly composed after Theodore's death; for an English translation of two versions of it, again by Timothy Miller, see "*Stoudios: Rule* of the Monastery of St. John Stoudios in Constantinople," in *BMFD,* vol. 1, pp. 84–119.

I will tell you in summary: The account that follows (14–23) was used, often word for word, by Michael the Monk in the *Life*; see 35.1–5.

14 *sleep to his eyes . . . the Lord*: Psalms 131(132):4–5.

It is as follows: The following sections 15–19 provide the text of what came to be identified as *Lesser Katecheseis* 31, pp. 113–18. The Greek text here differs in a number of minor points from that in Auvray's edition.

15 *I will not leave you orphans*: John 14:18.

Look . . . to the close of the age: Matthew 28:20.

punishment of Tartarus . . . Gehenna of fire: The abyss of Tartarus, deeper even than the ancient Greek Hades, was deemed to be

a place of particular suffering for the wicked after death. For Gehenna, see note to the *Life* 3.4.

God's irresistible wrath toward sinners: See *Prayer of Manasseh* 5. The *Prayer of Manasseh* is chanted during the service of Great Compline in the Orthodox Church.

16 *The present persecution . . . occasion for virtue*: Theodore is here contrasting the behavior of those who preserved the monastic virtues in the face of iconoclastic persecution with that of those, whom he then goes on to berate, who have broken their vows and fallen from the highest standards of monastic life.

as lights in the world . . . might be proud: Philippians 2:15–16.

from the same or a different walk of life: Both monks and laypeople.

their own acts of shame: Jude 13.

an independent life and . . . renouncing obedience: Theodore castigates those monks who made personal decisions to accept iconoclast teachings, in some cases in defiance of their abbots or the patriarch.

He darkened the form of their faces as though with soot: Lamentations 4:8.

Lawless sons, you abandoned the Lord: Isaiah 1:4.

straight tracks: Hebrews 12:13.

some live by themselves: Theodore, a firm believer in the communal monastic life, here criticizes those who have abandoned it. See Theodore's *Ep.* 450, in which the same accusations occur with longer explanations.

17 *Where am I to go from your Spirit . . . presence*: Psalms 138(139):7.

death came into the world: Romans 5:12.

their worm shall not die . . . quenched: Isaiah 66:24.

God will judge the immoral and adulterous: In fact, from Hebrews 13:4, not by Saint Paul, who is the apostle referred to.

If anyone destroys God's temple, God will destroy him: 1 Corinthians 3:17.

trap of Hades: Proverbs 9:18.

trembling and groaning: Genesis 4:12.

18 *they will suffer . . . in all those*: 2 Thessalonians 1:9–10.

accounts of virtue, sounding forth from you: See 1 Thessalonians 1:8.

to knowledge of the truth: 1 Timothy 2:4.

content with all things . . . enduring all things: See 1 Corinthians 13:7.

19 *Sunday*: The Greek phrasing means literally, "a resurrection day"; Sunday is the day in the week when Christ's resurrection is celebrated.

customarily presided: Over the *synaxis* (liturgical assembly) of the brethren.

after the same catechesis had been read: Barely well enough to attend the service, Theodore was clearly too weak to deliver this homily himself, as was his usual custom.

labor bestows health and eagerness raises the dead: Gregory of Nazianzos, *Oration* 43.37, ed. Bernardi, *Discours 42–43*, 208.

a desire to depart and be with Christ: Philippians 1:23.

21 *commemoration of Paul the great Confessor*: November 6, the feast day of Paul the Confessor, bishop of Constantinople (died 350).

Around the fourth hour of the night: Between 8:30 and 9:40 p.m.; see note to the *Life* 35.3.

the legacy that I have entrusted to you: See 1 Timothy 6:20 and note to the *Life* 35.4.

our master the archbishop: As at *Life* 35.4 above, a reference to Joseph, archbishop of Thessalonike, Theodore's brother.

22 *brethren and strangers*: Naukratios here uses the word ξένοι (strangers), which could refer to monks from monasteries other than Stoudios or to laypeople; Michael the Monk (see *Life* 35.4) clearly understands the latter (κοσμικοί).

God's regulation given through his servant Moses: A reference to Exodus 34:6–10, where God's covenant with Moses and the Israelites emphasizes his forgiveness and mercy.

The Lord of peace: 2 Thessalonians 3:16.

23 *the commemoration of the great martyr Menas*: November 11.

About the sixth hour: Between 11 a.m. and noon.

I will never forget your precepts . . . life: Psalms 118(119):93.

24 *So the thrice-blessed one lay there . . . able to speak*: Significant passages in 24 and 25 have been copied word for word from Theodore's own *Ep.* 533, addressed to the metropolitan Peter of Nicaea, describing the death of metropolitan Michael of Synnada, which took place on May 23, 826.

a violent storm took place . . . great Peter of Alexandria: The premeta-

phrastic Greek accounts of the martyrdom of Bishop Peter I of Alexandria (d. November 25, 311; *BHG* 1502 and 1502a) mention a "great storm" that arose while the saint was imprisoned during the night before his execution. See Joseph Viteau, *Passions des saints Écaterine et Pierre d'Alexandrie, Barbara et Anysia* (Paris, 1897), 77, and Paul Devos, "Une Passion grecque inédite de S. Pierre d'Alexandrie et sa traduction par Anastase le Bibliothécaire," *AB* 83 (1965): 157–87, chapter 10.

temptations by the rulers: As iconoclast policies were still officially in place, attempts were probably made to prevent Theodore being honored so publicly.

25 *with the singing of psalms . . . achievements*: See Theodore's *Ep.* 533, p. 806, lines 39–47.

about the fifth hour: Between 10:20 and 11:10 a.m.

he was consigned and buried in his own cell: Since Naukratios does not say where he composed his *Letter,* and Michael the Monk (see the *Life* 35.6) maintains Theodore died at Cape Akritas, this detail has caused some debate. The *Translation and Burial,* however, clearly states that Theodore died on the island of Prinkipo (Büyükada), one of the Princes' Islands off Constantinople.

like an apostle, that was his handiwork: Naukratios uses the word ἐργόχειρον (handiwork), a term frequently used by Theodore in his letters and *katacheseis* to describe worthy monastic activity. He probably has in mind Saint Paul's exhortations in 1 Thessalonians 4:11 and Ephesians 4:28 and the fact that, like that apostle, Theodore's "handiwork" consisted, to a large extent, of writing letters.

26 *having completed the apostolic race*: See 2 Timothy 4:7.

in a place of wondrous habitation: Psalms 41:5 (42:4).

we humble ones: See Theodore's *Ep.* 533, p. 806, line 48.

The Lord gave, the Lord has taken away . . . come to pass: Job 1:21.

Who can resist his will?: Romans 9:19.

as I mourn like an orphan . . . our truly: See Theodore's *Ep.* 533, p. 806, line 48.

our father's benefactions in both spheres: Naukratios uses the phrase

κατ' ἀμφότερα, literally meaning "on both sides." He is referring to Theodore's achievements during his life on earth but also now in heaven as an intercessor.

Translation and Burial of the Remains of Theodore of Stoudios and Joseph of Thessalonike

title *translation*: The Greek word ἀνακομιδή has a number of meanings, but in this case refers to the ceremony during which remains were transferred from one place to another. The day of the translation often itself became a feast day and was marked by annual processions; see *ODB,* vol. 3, pp. 1779–81. The *Life of Saint Nicholas of Stoudios,* PG 105:904B, gives the date as January 26. The year was 844.

1.1 *our holy father and confessor*: Theodore of Stoudios. The "our" indicates that the writer is himself a Stoudite monk.

2.1 *who possessed a name . . . that really was something God-given*: The Greek phrase τὸ θεοδώρητον ὄντως (really was something God-given) is a play on Theodore's name, which means, literally, "God-given."

notable and illustrious parents . . . emperors: The writer, probably in the interests of brevity, does not give the names of Theodore's parents, Theoktiste and Photeinos (who served as the imperial *sakellarios*). On them and this office, see notes to the *Life* 2.2–3.

2.2 *great freedom was being allowed . . . against icons*: A reference to the reigns of the iconoclast emperors Leo III (717–741; *PmbZ Online* no. 4242) and Constantine V (741–775; *PmbZ Online* no. 3703/corr.).

Sakkoudion: For Sakkoudion, see notes to the *Life* 4.3 and 5.2.

Plato, his maternal uncle: See *PmbZ Online* no. 6285 and note to the *Life* 4.3.

contests and struggles: The period covered here is from 796 (when Plato, Theodore and Joseph were all exiled and imprisoned in various parts of the empire by Constantine VI) to 797 CE (when they were released on the orders of the new empress, Irene). See the *Life* 12–13.

3.1 *the tyrants . . . were removed*: Leo IV was murdered, and Constantine VI was dethroned and subsequently blinded on the orders of his mother, Irene. See notes to the *Life* 4.1 and 13.3.

3.2 *the rulers*: Empress Irene and Constantine VI (albeit blinded).

Stoudios, who had come from Rome: The false tradition that the fifth-century founder, Stoudios, had come from Rome is not found in the *Life* by Michael the Monk but appears in the later *Vita A* (*BHG* 1755), PG 99:145B. It also appears in a Latin description of Constantinople written by an English visitor between 1063 and 1100; see Krinje N. Cigaar, "Une description de Constantinople traduit par un pélerin anglais," *REB* 36 (1976): 211–67, at 262. For the foundation of the monastery, see the Introduction.

driven all the monks out of it: This account differs slightly from that of Michael the Monk, who maintained that Constantine V had limited its numbers to "less than ten." In both cases, this is probably an exaggeration; see note to the *Life* 15.1.

good conduct and the great asceticism: The Stoudite way of life at this period is described in greater detail in the *Life* 15.

4.1 *being spiteful . . . confused about the faith*: Probably a reference to the emperor Nikephoros I (802–811; *PmbZ Online* no. 5252/corr.) and the patriarch Nikephoros I (patriarch of Constantinople 806–815; *PmbZ Online* no. 5301/corr.) who, though not iconoclasts, agreed that Joseph of Kathara (*PmbZ Online* no. 3447/corr.), who had previously married the emperor Constantine VI to his mistress Theodote in 796 and had been dismissed from office under Irene, should be allowed to resume his priestly functions. This move was strongly objected to by the Stoudites. See the *Life* 17, where the differences with the patriarch are glossed over.

banishment: Theodore and Joseph were again exiled from 809 to 811; see the *Life* 18.

met with a swift end: The emperor Nikephoros I was killed in battle against the Bulgarians in 811; the patriarch Nikephoros was later deposed by Leo V.

the ruler accorded him great respect and honor: Michael I Rangabe

(811–813; *PmbZ Online* no. 4989/corr.) was an iconodule. This peaceful period at Stoudios is described in the *Life* 19 and 20.

5.1 *Armenian*: Emperor Leo V (813–820; *PmbZ Online* no. 4244/corr.) was of Armenian descent.

some Egyptian plague: For the ten plagues visited by God upon Egypt after Pharaoh refused to release the Israelites from captivity, see Exodus 7–11.

he even burned them or smeared them with lime: These details of Leo's iconoclast behavior are not found in the *Life* by Michael the Monk, but the whitewashing of images by the iconoclasts was already being depicted in the Khludov Psalter (ca. 843–847). Accusations that the iconoclasts burned icons are found in the proceedings of the Second Council of Nicaea (787); see the *Acts* of the Council of Nicaea II (787), ed. Erich Lamberz, *Acta conciliorum oecumenicorum: Series secunda* (Berlin, 2008–2016), vol. 3, p. 644, English trans. Daniel J. Sahas, *Icon and Logos: Sources in Eighth-Century Iconoclasm* (Toronto, 1986), 74.

banished him from Byzantion: Theodore was again banished from Constantinople in 815.

5.2 *Leo was not content . . . once or twice*: By the time this text was written, it is clear that accounts of Theodore's multiple beatings, true or not, were implicitly believed. See notes to the *Life* 24–26.

shutting him up in different places: Theodore was successively imprisoned at Metopa, Boneta, and Smyrna (see notes to the *Life* 24.2 and 27.2).

in the seventh year . . . audacious actions: Leo V was murdered on Christmas Day 820. The *Chronicle of Theophanes continuatus* 2.25, ed. Featherstone and Signes-Codoñer, *Chronographiae*, pp. 60–62, contains a vivid description of his wounds but does not specifically mention that to his bowels, probably meant here as a particularly shameful detail, as it was similar to the reported death of the heretic Arius in a latrine (see *ODB*, vol. 1, p. 172). Leo's death led to a softening of attitudes toward iconodules.

6.1 *Theodore was immediately freed from banishment*: In early 821.

Joseph . . . bishop of Thessalonike: Joseph (*PmbZ Online* no. 3448)

was appointed archbishop of Thessalonike in late 806 or early 807.

the man who had then assumed the scepter: Michael II (820–829; *PmbZ Online* no. 4990/corr.).

drinking all the dregs: Psalm 74:9 (75:8).

6.2 *islands facing the city*: The Princes' Islands.

Prinkipos: The present-day Büyükada; see also note to the *Encyclical Letter* 25. Michael the Monk maintained that Theodore died at the monastery of Saint Tryphon on Cape Akritas, south of Chalcedon (see note to the *Life* 34.3), and that his body was later taken to Prinkipo(s).

7.1 *Naukratios*: For Naukratios (*PmbZ Online* 5230/corr.), previously *oikonomos* (steward) of Sakkoudion and Theodore's successor as abbot of Stoudios, see the Introduction.

who puts down the mighty from their thrones: Luke 1:52.

breaks the arms of the sinner and evildoer: Psalm 9:36 (10:15).

checks the hurricane to a breeze: Psalm 106(107):29.

the shadow of death to the morning: Amos 5:8.

7.2 *Theodora and her son who had taken up the scepter*: Empress Theodora (842–856; *PmbZ Online* no. 7286/corr.), wife of the iconoclast emperor Theophilos (829–842; *PmbZ Online* no. 8167/corr.), served as regent for her young son Michael III (842–867; *PmbZ Online* no. 4991/corr.).

an ecumenical decree . . . was ratified: Following a synod, probably held in the Blachernai Palace in Constantinople in March 843, the Acts of the Second Council of Nicaea in 787 were confirmed. Methodios I (*PmbZ Online* no. 4977/corr.) was appointed patriarch either on March 4 or 11, 843.

8.1 *the holy Naukratios*: The adjective "holy" (θεῖος) indicates that Naukratios was dead at the time this work was composed. He died on April 18, 848.

Athanasios: Athanasios (*PmbZ Online* no. 675/corr.) was a founding member of the monastery of Sakkoudion, later the protopresbyter (senior priest) of Stoudios and ultimately abbot of Sakkoudion. See the *Life* 8.3.

both monasteries were under one administration: This explanation is perhaps an indication that, by the time this work was written,

Stoudios and Sakkoudion each had his own abbot. See Charles van de Vorst, "La translation de S. Théodore Studite et de S. Joseph de Thessalonique," *AB* 32 (1913): 28.

9.1 *eighteen years had now passed*: Theodore had died in 826; the translation of his body took place on January 26, 844 (see note to title, above).

9.2 *the Augusta and the patriarch*: Empress Theodora and the patriarch Methodios.

the following words: The author is at pains to establish the veracity of his account; Naukratios's speech is, however, a construct.

10.1 *chanting the following*: The passage that follows may well reflect the prayers that were offered up on the occasion of Theodore's translation, but they have clearly been reworked by the writer.

10.2 *voice of the spiritual turtledove . . . fragrance*: Song of Songs 2:12–13.

11.1 *the sea also rejoiced . . . jumped for joy*: See Psalms 95(96):11 and 97(98):7. The transference of Theodore's remains by ship is depicted in the *Menologion of Basil II* (Vat. gr. 1613, p. 175); see *Il menologio di Basilio II (cod. vaticano greco 1613)* (Turin, 1907), 175 and the online facsimile, https://digi.vatlib.it/view/MSS_Vat.gr.1613. Interestingly, the miniature shows a small casket, rather than a coffin with a miraculously preserved body in it as the *Translation and Burial* relates.

12.1 *on the right . . . relics are lying at rest*: In the *Life of Saint Nicholas of Stoudios,* PG 99:904B, the location of the tomb is given as "on the right toward the east [end] of the Forerunner's shrine." The tomb was thus probably located inside a chapel dedicated to the martyrs in the narthex at the east end of the main church of Stoudios.

empress Augusta: Theodora.

entire clergy of the church: The clergy of Hagia Sophia.

13.1 *died in some remote spot in Thessaly*: Joseph died on July 15, 832, in central Greece, having been again exiled after the death of Theodore by the emperor Theophilos (829–842). It is curious that the writer does not name the precise spot where Joseph died, or indeed where his bones were scattered and later, apparently, found.

13.2 *Those insolent men*: The iconoclasts.

with the heretical power still in control: The discovery of Joseph's remains must, therefore, have taken place before the first celebration of the Feast of Orthodoxy on March 12, 843, and their transportation to Constantinople after this date.

13.3 *hair of our heads to be lost*: See Luke 21:18.

14.1 *most holy patriarch*: Patriarch Methodios.

14.2 *their holy images which are depicted at the tomb*: The portraits of Plato, Theodore, and Joseph were on a vertical surface above the tomb.

15.1 *If we should die here . . . in the heavenly habitations*: Gregory of Nazianzos, *Oration* 15.30, PG 36:664.

everything that is crooked . . . you will make smooth: See Isaiah 40:4; Luke 3:5.

15.2 *put an end to our aspirations*: Gregory of Nazianzos, *Oration* 43.82, ed. Bernardi, *Discours 42–43*, 306.

the ultimate goal of our desires: Gregory of Nazianzos, *Oration* 21.1, ed. Jules Mossay and Guy Lafontaine, *Grégoire de Nazianze: Discours 20–23* (Paris, 1980), 112.

the infinite and single nature of the three infinite Ones: Gregory of Nazianzos, *Oration* 40.41, ed. Claudio Moreschini and Paul Gallay, *Grégore de Nazianze: Discours 38–41* (Paris, 1990), 294.

by mirrors: See 1 Corinthians 13:12.

shadows and symbols: Gregory of Nazianzos, *Oration* 24.19, ed. Justin Mossay and Guy Lafontaine, *Grégoire de Nazianze: Discours 24–26* (Paris, 1981), 82.

we would meet . . . with the first Fount itself: Gregory of Nazianzos, *Oration* 7.17; ed. Marie-Ange Calvet, *Grégoire de Nazianze: Discours 6–12* (Paris, 1995), 222.

with our mind alone: Gregory of Nazianzos, *Poemata moralia* 10.81, PG 37:686.

dwelling: See John 14:2.

Bibliography

Editions and Translations

Life of Theodore of Stoudios by Michael the Monk

Mai, Angelo, ed. and trans. *Vita et conversation sancti patris nostri et confessoris Theodori abbatis monasterii Studii a Michaele Monacho conscripta.* PG 99:233–328.

Encyclical Letter of Naukratios

Combefis, François, ed. and trans. *Naucratii confessoris encyclica de obitu Sancti Theodori Studitae.* PG 99:1825–49.

Popović, Radomir, ed. and trans. "Преподобни Навкратије Окружна посланица о упокојењу преподобног Теодора Студита / Ὅσιος Ναυκράτιος Encyclica de obitu s. Theodori Studitae." *Теолошки погледи / Theological Views* 1 (2017): 29–50.

Vasilik, Vladimir V., trans. "Окружное послание преподобного Навкратия о кончине преподобного Феодора Студита." *Studia Slavica et Balcanica Petropolitana* 11, no. 1 (2012): 127–40.

Translation and Burial of the Remains of Theodore of Stoudios and Joseph of Thessalonike

Van de Vorst, Charles, ed. "La translation de S. Théodore Studite et de S. Joseph de Thessalonique." *AB* 32 (1913): 50–61.

Further Reading

Alexander, Paul J. *The Patriarch Nicephorus of Constantinople: Ecclesiastical Policy and Image Worship in the Byzantine Empire.* Oxford, 1958.

Brubaker, Leslie. *Inventing Byzantine Iconoclasm.* London, 2012.

Brubaker, Leslie, and John Haldon. *Byzantium in the Iconoclast Era c. 680–850: A History.* Cambridge, 2011.

Cholij, Roman. *Theodore the Stoudite: The Ordering of Holiness.* Oxford, 2009.

Hatlie, Peter. *The Monks and Monasteries of Constantinople, ca. 350–850.* Cambridge, 2007.

Montleau, Florence de. *Théodore Stoudite: Les grandes catéchèses (Livre I). Les Epigrammes (I–XXIX), précédées d'une étude de Julien Leroy sur le monachisme stoudite.* Bégrolles-en-Mauges, 2002.

Parry, Kenneth. *Depicting the Word: Byzantine Iconophile Thought of the Eighth and Ninth Centuries.* Leiden, 1996.

Pratsch, Thomas. *Theodoros Studites (759–826): Zwischen Dogma und Pragma.* Frankfurt-am-Main, 1998.

Tollefsen, Torstein Theodor. *St. Theodore the Studite's Defence of the Icons: Theology and Philosophy in Ninth-Century Byzantium.* Oxford, 2018.

Treadgold, Warren T. *The Byzantine Revival: 780–842.* Stanford, 1988.

Index

L = *Life of Theodore of Stoudios;* E = *Encyclical Letter of Naukratios;* T = *Translation and Burial of the Remains of Theodore of Stoudios and Joseph of Thessalonike*